EFFECTS OF HEATING ON FOODSTUFFS

EFFECTS OF HEATING ON FOODSTUFFS

Edited by

R. J. PRIESTLEY

National Food Research Institute
Pretoria, South Africa

APPLIED SCIENCE PUBLISHERS LTD
LONDON

APPLIED SCIENCE PUBLISHERS LTD
RIPPLE ROAD, BARKING, ESSEX, ENGLAND

British Library Cataloguing in Publication Data

Effects of heating on foodstuffs.
1. Food, Effect of heat on
I. Priestley, R J
664   TX357

ISBN 0-85334-797-2
WITH 35 TABLES AND 57 ILLUSTRATIONS
© APPLIED SCIENCE PUBLISHERS LTD 1979

Printed in Great Britain by Galliard (Printers) Ltd, Great Yarmouth, Norfolk

Preface

According to legend, man was introduced to the phenomenon of fire by an accidental lightning flash. However, he quickly learned to control and exploit the beneficial effects of heat both as a means of providing warmth and of improving the palatability of his food. Even before this time, some food materials were probably dried using solar heat. Nowadays, there are few foodstuffs which are never subjected to some form of heat treatment. Most meats, fish, fruits, vegetables, nuts, cereals, legumes, dairy products and beverages may be prepared or preserved by some method involving the application of heat. In the last few decades the impact of processed commodities has led to a considerable decline in the fresh produce market.

Heating is the most common treatment applied to food either in the home or in industry. It is used for cooking, dehydration or concentration, pasteurisation or sterilisation, or to aid extraction, mixing or emulsification. Although man's understanding of these operations has now developed to the stage where most food processes are based on sound scientific principles, our knowledge is still far from complete. This is largely due to the inherent complexity and variability of the biological materials we know as food.

It was felt that there was a need for a text dealing primarily with changes occurring in foodstuffs as a result of heating, particularly chemical and physicochemical changes, whether they be deleterious or beneficial. Most of the information in this field is presently scattered in isolated research reports, textbooks dealing with specific commodities and processes, or in textbooks of a more general nature which, of necessity, treat the subject rather superficially. The nutritional and microbiological effects of heating have already been well documented and are not emphasised in this volume, although their importance cannot be ignored. Similarly, lipid-degradation reactions, which are given little attention here, are the subject of several excellent reviews.

The contents of this book are divided into two main sections: the first four chapters deal with basic food components and subsequent chapters are devoted to specific commodities. In this way, the structure and properties of these components and some of the fundamental changes encountered during the heating of a number of foodstuffs are considered individually, thus avoiding unnecessary duplication.

Obviously, a volume such as this is the result of a combined effort and I gratefully acknowledge the patience and co-operation of all the contributors. An inevitable consequence of multi-authorship is a variation of individual approach and style. While such variation has been kept within reasonable limits, no deliberate attempt has been made to restrict the authors to a rigid pattern of writing. I believe this would have detracted from the 'readability' of the book, which is intended as a collection of reviews to be used by researchers and processors and not primarily as a college textbook, although it is hoped that it will provide a useful source of information for students and teachers alike.

R. J. P.

Pretoria
South Africa

Contents

List of Contributors

A. AITKEN, Ph.D.

Section Head, Torry Research Station, P.O. Box 31, 135 Abbey Road, Aberdeen AB9 8DG, Scotland.

RUTH E. BALDWIN, Ph.D.

Professor of Food Science and Nutrition, University of Missouri–Columbia, College of Agriculture, Department of Food Science and Nutrition, 219 Gwynn Hall, Columbia, Missouri 65211, USA.

J. J. CONNELL, Ph.D., F.I.F.S.T.

Assistant Director, Torry Research Station, P.O. Box 31, 135 Abbey Road, Aberdeen AB9 8DG, Scotland.

O. J. COTTERILL, Ph.D.

Professor of Food Science and Nutrition, University of Missouri–Columbia, College of Agriculture, Department of Food Science and Nutrition, 219 Gwynn Hall, Columbia, Missouri 65211, USA.

C. T. GREENWOOD, Ph.D., D.Sc., C.Chem., F.R.I.C., F.I.F.S.T., F.R.S.E.

Group Research Director, Cadbury–Schweppes Ltd., 1–10 Connaught Place, London W2 2EX, England.

S. D. HOLDSWORTH, M.Sc., F.R.I.C., F.I.Chem.E., F.I.F.S.T.

Co-ordinator of Research, Campden Food Preservation Research Association, Chipping Campden, Glos. GL55 6LD, England.

D. A. LEDWARD, M.Sc., Ph.D., A.I.F.S.T.

Lecturer, Department of Applied Biochemistry and Nutrition, University of Nottingham, Sutton Bonington, Loughborough, Leics. LE12 5RD, England.

R. L. J. LYSTER, M.A., Ph.D.

Principal Scientific Officer, National Institute for Research in Dairying, Shinfield, Reading RG2 9AT, England.

D. N. MUNRO, M.A., D.Phil.

Research Executive, Cadbury–Schweppes Ltd., 1–10 Connaught Place, London W2 2EX, England.

R. J. PRIESTLEY, Ph.D., A.I.F.S.T., M.R.S.H.

National Food Research Institute, Council for Scientific and Industrial Research, P.O. Box 395, Pretoria, South Africa.

M. L. WOOLFE, M.Sc., Ph.D., A.I.F.S.T.

Lecturer, Department of Food Science and Nutrition, University of Strathclyde, 131 Albion Street, Glasgow G1 1SD, Scotland.

CHAPTER 1

Proteins

D. A. LEDWARD

University of Nottingham, Loughborough, UK

1.1 AMINO ACIDS, POLYPEPTIDES AND PRIMARY PROTEIN STRUCTURE

The essential building blocks for proteins are the amino acids of which well over a hundred have been identified and characterised. However, only about twenty-five of these are important in protein chemistry, the structures of which are shown in Table 1.1. All amino acids possess both an amino and a carboxylate group so that, depending on the pH of the system, the molecule may be positively charged, both positively and negatively charged or negatively charged. For example, the simplest amino acid, glycine, will exist as $NH_3^+-CH_2-CO_2H$ at low pH, $NH_3^+-CH_2-CO_2^-$ at neutral pH and $NH_2-CH_2-CO_2^-$ at high pH values. The actual pH values at which the equilibrium concentration of $NH_3^+-CH_2-CO_2H$ and $NH_3^+-CH_2-CO_2^-$ are the same is the pK value for the carboxylate group while the pK value of the amino group is that pH at which the concentrations of $NH_3^+-CH_2-CO_2^-$ and $NH_2-CH_2-CO_2^-$ are equal. The pK value for the carboxylate group is normally in the range 1·5–3·5 and that of the amino group in the range 9–10·5; the actual values vary according to the amino acid and also depend on the nature of the solvent and the temperature (Edsall and Wyman, 1958).

It can be seen from the formulae in Table 1.1 that the α-amino acids differ in the nature of the side-chains attached to the central carbon atom. Some possess non-polar groups (glycine, alanine, valine) while others possess polar groups (glutamic acid, aspartic acid, histidine, lysine) which may also ionise. Thus, aspartic acid has pK values of 1·995, 3·910 and 10·006 while lysine has pK values of 2·16

1

TABLE 1.1
STRUCTURES OF THE AMINO ACIDS AT pH 7

α-Amino acids of general formula $\overset{\displaystyle R}{\underset{\displaystyle \quad}{NH_3^+{-}CH{-}CO_2^-}}$

Group 1   R = *Non-polar aliphatic group*

Glycine (Gly)	Alanine (Ala)	Valine (Val)	Leucine (Leu)	Isoleucine (Ile)
H	CH₃	H₃C–CH–CH₃	(CH₃)₂CH–CH₂	H₃C–CH₂–CH–CH₃

Group 2   R = *Hydroxyl-containing group*

Serine (Ser)   Threonine (Thr)   Tyrosine (Tyr)   Diiodotyrosine   Thyroxine

Group 3   R = *Non-hydroxyl aromatic group*

Phenylalanine (Phe)   Tryptophan (Trp)

TABLE 1.1   *Contd*

Group 4   R = *Acidic group or its amide*

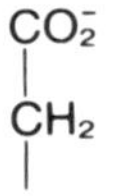

CO_2^-	$CONH_2$	CO_2^-	$CONH_2$
CH_2	CH_2	CH_2	CH_2
		CH_2	CH_2
Aspartic acid (Asp)	Asparagine (Asp–NH₂)	Glutamic acid (Glu)	Glutamine (Glu–NH₂)

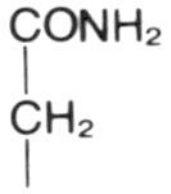

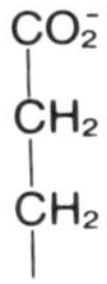

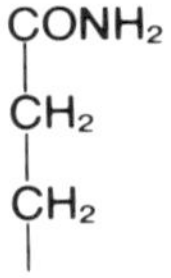

Group 5   R = *Basic amino group*

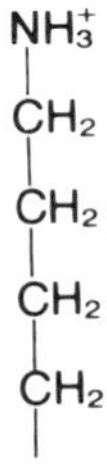

NH_3^+
CH_2
CH_2
CH_2
CH_2
Lysine
(Lys)

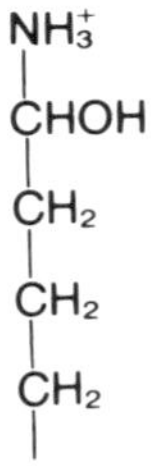

NH_3^+
$CHOH$
CH_2
CH_2
CH_2
Hydroxylysine
(Hylys)

$HN^+\!\!-\!CH$
$HC\underset{\underset{H}{N}}{}C\!-\!CH_2\!-\!\rightleftharpoons\! HC\underset{\underset{H}{N}}{}C\!-\!CH_2\!-$
$N\!\!-\!CH$

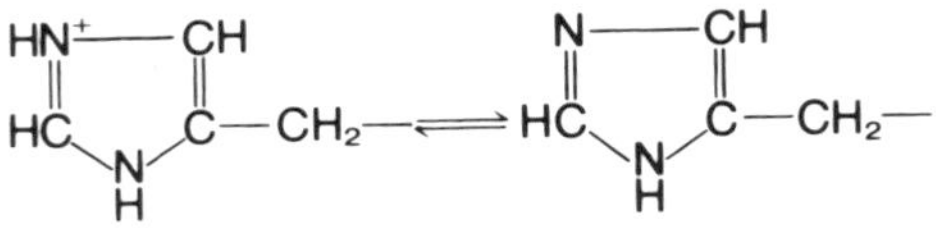

Acidic   Basic

Histidine
(His)

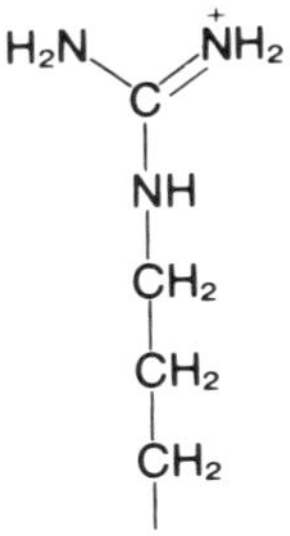

$H_2N\underset{NH}{\overset{+NH_2}{\diagdown C \diagup}}$
CH_2
CH_2
CH_2
Arginine
(Arg)

TABLE 1.1 *Contd*

Group 6   R = *sulphur-containing group*

Cysteine (CysH) Cystine(a) (CySSCy) Cystine(b) Methionine (Met)

Group 7   α-imino acids

Proline (Pro)   Hydroxyproline (Hypro)

(α-CO$_2$H), 9·18 (α-NH$_2$) and 10·79 (ϵ-NH$_2$). The imidazole group of histidine has a pK value of 6·00 and thus, at pH 7, both the acidic and basic forms will exist as shown in Table 1.1.

Two amino acids can condense together to form a dipeptide, the two residues being joined by a peptide bond, *e.g.*

$$2(\overset{+}{N}H_3-CH_2-CO_2^-) \rightarrow \overset{+}{N}H_3-CH_2-CO-NH-CH_2-CO_2^-$$

(Gly)   Glycylglycine(Gly–Gly)

This polymerisation can be continued indefinitely as all amino acids can, by peptide-bond formation, combine with all other amino acids so that an infinite number of polypeptides are theoretically possible. The presence of the peptide bond has a powerful effect in increasing the acidity of neighbouring groups such that, in polypeptides, the α-amino groups at the end of the chains have characteristic pK values below 8. It can be seen that the essential unit of the polypeptide chain is the repeating sequence

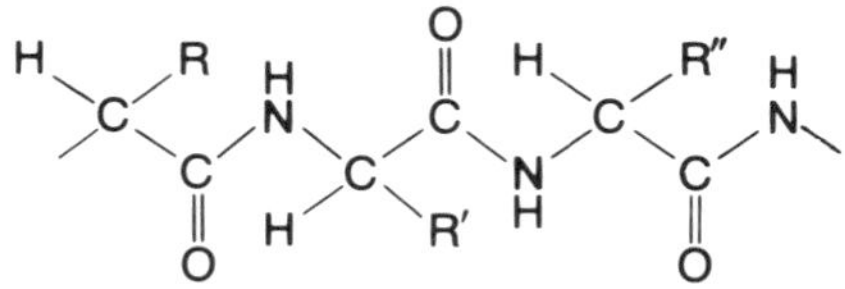

It is well established that provided an α-imino acid (proline or hydroxyproline) is not one of the residues, the C–C bonds and the C–N linkages between the CHR and NH groups are single bonds so that rotation around these bonds is comparable to that found in ordinary hydrocarbon chains. However, owing to resonance between the structures

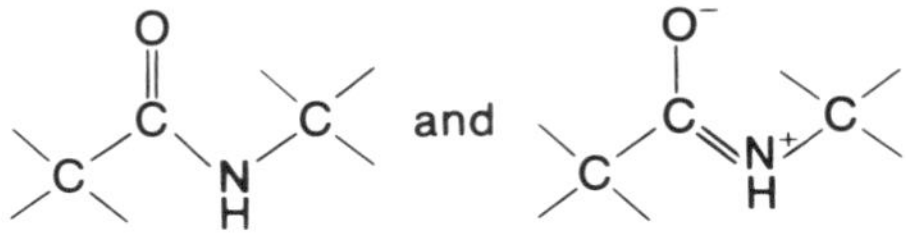

the C–N bonds between the CO and NH groups possess a large amount of double-bond character so that the atoms shown above are constrained to assume an almost coplanar configuration similar to that found in ethylene. These stable configurations may be either *cis* or *trans*,

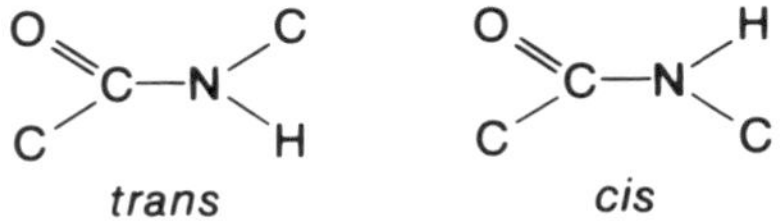

and, in general, the *trans* configuration is favoured in most peptides.

The peptide bond is relatively stable and thus a polypeptide may only be broken down to its constituent amino acids by powerful hydrolysing conditions such as hot, concentrated acid or alkali. Not all peptide bonds are equally susceptible to digestion and the susceptibility of different peptide bonds may vary with the nature of the hydrolysing agent. For example, crystalline trypsin will only break peptide bonds in which the carboxylate group of lysine or arginine participates while cyanogen bromide will only rupture peptide bonds involving methionine. Thus, selective digestion with different enzymes and chemicals, and subsequent analysis of the fragments, may be used to determine the sequence of amino acids in a polypeptide, *i.e.* its *primary structure.*

Proteins, which are to be found in all living systems, are natural polypeptides whose molecular weight may range from a few thousand to several million.

1.2 SECONDARY AND HIGHER PROTEIN STRUCTURES

If the only constraints placed on the polypeptide chain of a protein were due to the partial double-bond character of the peptide unit then, to a large extent, the protein would behave as a random coil. A random coil has no permanent configuration but alternates between an almost infinite number of spatial arrangements made possible by the free rotation around each bond. In the classical text by Flory (1953), the distribution functions for the chain displacement vectors for polymer chains of freely jointed segments are derived and demonstrate that the most probable separation of the terminal residues of the chain is given by $n^{1/2}l/\sqrt{3/2}$, where n is the number of residues and l is the length of the valence bonds. Thus, the most probable configurations for a random coil tend to be more like spheres than extended chains. However, very few native proteins have this type of configuration owing to the large number of interactions that are possible between the different amino acid residues which give rise to the *secondary*, *tertiary* and *quaternary* protein structures. The *secondary* structure of a protein is the name given to the regular folding of the chain caused by interactions between the residues of the chain. If proteins consisted solely of a single helix they would have very elongated structures and thus, in most proteins, this type of organisation is periodically interrupted to permit additional folding. This spatial conformation in three dimensions has been called the *tertiary* structure. The term *quaternary* structure has been used to describe proteins that contain more than one peptide chain to indicate the spatial relationships among the separate chains or *sub-units*.

1.2.1 Bonding
The most common types of interactions that give rise to the secondary and higher protein structures are as follows.

1.2.1.1 *Hydrogen Bonds*
The simple interpretation of a hydrogen bond is as a donation of

electric charge from an electronegative atom to a hydrogen atom. Only strongly electronegative atoms such as F, O or N will normally form hydrogen bonds although, on occasions, hydrogen bonds may form between hydrogen and C or S atoms. Hydrogen bonds, although essential in maintaining several biological structures are, compared to true covalent bonds, very weak. Thus, in ice, the O–H covalent bond, which is 0·99-Å long, requires about 110 kcal·mol^{-1} to break it while the O–H hydrogen bond, which is 1·77-Å long, only requires about 4·5 kcal·mol^{-1} to rupture it. Not all hydrogen bonds are equally strong, the strength varying with the nature of the electronegative atom and the chemical environment of the atoms involved (Pauling, 1954). As shown earlier, the peptide group has an excess of negative charge on the oxygen of the C$=$O group beyond that characteristic of simple carbonyl compounds (ketones and aldehydes) while there is excess positive charge on the N–H bond, and thus hydrogen bonds between the C$=$O group of one amino acid residue and the N–H group of another residue are relatively strong. Each peptide group can, if steric considerations allow, participate in two hydrogen bonds, *i.e.*

The different peptide units may be either in the same chain, in which case a helix is generated, or in neighbouring chains.

Although the main hydrogen bonds of interest in protein structure are those between different peptide units, several others can exist and may make significant contributions to the overall integrity of the structure. Thus, several proteins contain groups which are capable of taking part in hydrogen bonding leading to additional stabilisation of the molecule. For example, the connective-tissue protein, collagen, is more stable when the proline residues in the polypeptide chains are hydroxylated and can take part in hydrogen bonding (Ramachandran *et al.*, 1973). Also, hydrogen bonds may well exist between water and suitable groups along the polypeptide chain in such a way that the water molecules form an integral part of the structure of the protein.

As energy (heat) is required to rupture hydrogen bonds, they will break endothermally and so structures stabilised by such forces will be thermally unstable.

1.2.1.2 Disulphide Linkages and Other Non-peptide Covalent Bonds

Non-peptide covalent bonds between different amino acid residues play an important part in protein structure as they can serve to crosslink peptide chains or to join different portions of the same chain, provided of course the chain loops back on itself to bring the two reactant residues together. By far the most common such crosslink is the disulphide linkage formed between two half cystine residues to form a cystine residue (Table 1.1). The general structure of this crosslink is

The disulphide linkage is relatively stable but may be cleaved by oxidation when the cystine is converted to cysteic acid, *i.e.*

$$R\text{-}S\text{-}S\text{-}R' \rightarrow RSO_3^- + R'SO_3^-$$

or by reduction to yield cysteine residues with free SH groups, *i.e.*

$$R\text{-}S\text{-}S\text{-}R' \rightarrow RSH + R'SH$$

These SH groups are very reactive and in the presence of air will spontaneously oxidise to reform the disulphide (cystine) group.

Orthophosphate groups may also serve to crosslink protein chains by diester linkages with the hydroxyl groups of the appropriate amino acid residues. For example, two seryl residues may combine thus

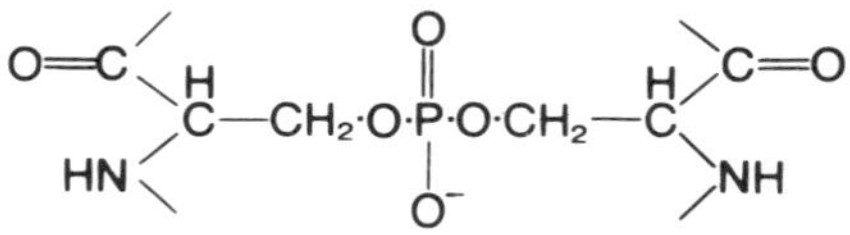

$$O=C\underset{HN}{\overset{H}{\diagdown}}\overset{\diagup}{\underset{C}{\diagdown}}-CH_2\cdot O\cdot\overset{O}{\underset{O^-}{\overset{\parallel}{P}}}\cdot O\cdot CH_2-\underset{\diagdown}{\overset{H}{C}}\overset{\diagup}{\underset{NH}{\diagdown}}C=O$$

The orthophosphate linkage may not necessarily involve two hydroxyl groups as it can form between the nitrogenous group of an amino acid residue of one chain and a hydroxyl group of another chain, *i.e.* an –N–P–O– bond may form instead of the –O–P–O– bond shown above. Also pyrophosphate instead of orthophosphate may link the chains, or chain segments, in an –O–P–O–P–O– type linkage.

Disulphide and phosphate linkages are the only types of covalent bonds normally found between polypeptide chains, although one exception is the unusual crosslinks found in the connective-tissue protein, collagen. The first of these bonds to be identified was of the *intramolecular* type in which the linkage was between two chains of the same tropocollagen molecule. Bailey *et al.* (1970) suggested that these crosslinks were mediated through the oxidative deamination of lysine residues to form aldehydes which then underwent an aldol condensation, *i.e.*

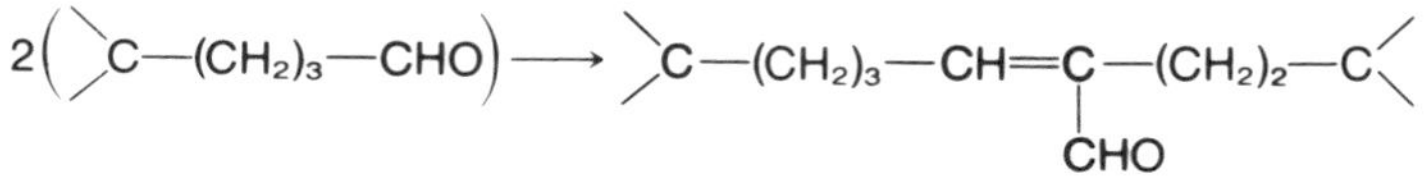

$$2\left(\overset{\diagdown}{\diagup}C-(CH_2)_3-CHO\right)\longrightarrow \overset{\diagdown}{\diagup}C-(CH_2)_3-CH=\underset{CHO}{\overset{|}{C}}-(CH_2)_2-C\overset{\diagup}{\diagdown}$$

However, collagen also possesses some *intermolecular* crosslinks, *i.e.* links between polypeptide chains in different tropocollagen molecules and the nature of these is still the subject of extensive research. Bailey *et al.* (1974) have reviewed the present knowledge of the subject and conclude that of all the proposed structures only two, *i.e.* dehydrohydroxylysinonorleucine (I) and hydroxylysino-5-keto-norleucine (II) exist *in vivo* as crosslinking components. These cross-links are formed by the condensation of aldehydes, produced by the oxidative deamination of specific lysine or hydroxylysine residues, and other reactive groups of which the ϵ-NH$_2$ groups of hydroxy-lysine are most important.

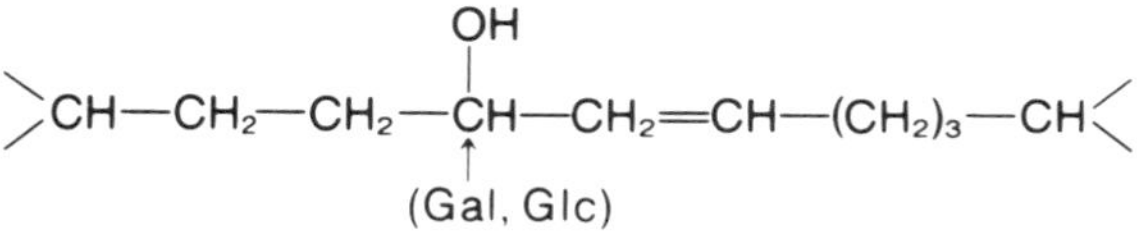

$$\overset{\diagdown}{\diagup}CH-CH_2-CH_2-\underset{\underset{(Gal, Glc)}{\uparrow}}{\overset{\overset{OH}{|}}{CH}}-CH_2=CH-(CH_2)_3-CH\overset{\diagup}{\diagdown} \tag{I}$$

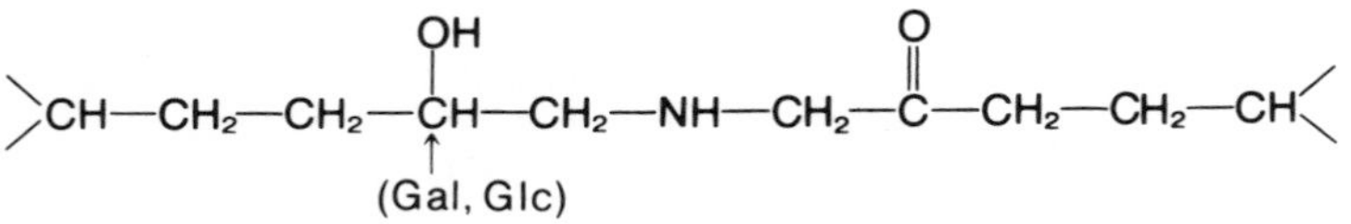

$$\text{>CH—CH}_2\text{—CH}_2\text{—CH(OH)—CH}_2\text{—NH—CH}_2\text{—C(=O)—CH}_2\text{—CH}_2\text{—CH<}$$

$$\uparrow$$
$$(\text{Gal, Glc})$$

(II)

As shown in the above structures, the crosslinking units may be bound to galactosyl (Gal) or glucosyl (Glc) units (arrowed) and, although the function of these sugar residues is uncertain, it has been suggested that they may facilitate aldimine bond formation by lowering the pK of the ϵ-NH$_2$ group (Bailey *et al.*, 1974). These crosslinks, which are labile, are only found in the tissues of immature animals since with maturity they become very stable and non-reducible. The mechanism of this maturation process has not been elucidated but it does not appear to be simple reduction of the double bonds. Recent evidence suggests that it involves addition of lysine and/or hydroxylysine residues to the double bond of the labile crosslink to yield stable derivatives that are capable of crosslinking up to three different tropocollagen molecules (Davis *et al.*, 1975). Although these lysine-derived crosslinks appear to be unique to collagen, their absence in other proteins has not been shown conclusively. Other covalent bonds between amino acid residues appear to be very rare in naturally occurring protein systems. However, processing techniques may cause other types of covalent bonds to form. One of importance in food systems is the reaction, under alkaline conditions, between lysine and cysteine to form lysinoalanine, *i.e.*

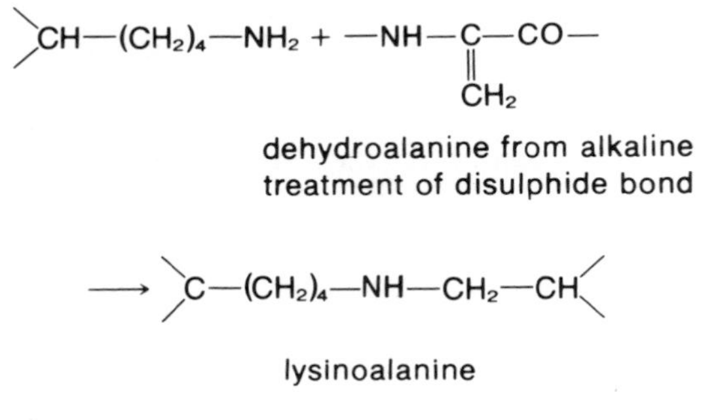

$$\text{>CH—(CH}_2\text{)}_4\text{—NH}_2 + \text{—NH—C(=CH}_2\text{)—CO—}$$

dehydroalanine from alkaline
treatment of disulphide bond

$$\longrightarrow \text{>C—(CH}_2\text{)}_4\text{—NH—CH}_2\text{—CH<}$$

lysinoalanine

This crosslink is undesirable because, in addition to rendering the amino acids nutritionally unavailable, it has been claimed that the complex itself is toxic, although this has been questioned (van Beek *et al.*, 1974).

As would be expected, all these covalent bonds are relatively stable to heat and when they do rupture they do so endothermically. Most of the bonds are at least as stable to heat as peptide bonds although the labile crosslink dehydrohydroxylysinonorleucine will cleave when heated to about 80°C (Jackson *et al.*, 1974).

1.2.1.3 Hydrophobic Interactions

When a non-polar group is transferred from the ideal gas state to water it is accompanied by a negative entropy of hydration and it has been suggested that these inert solutes promote the ordering of neighbouring water, *i.e.* the 'iceberg effect' (Frank and Evans, 1945). Thus, when a protein is dissolved in water, the non-polar side-chains of alanine, valine, leucine, isoleucine, phenylalanine, tyrosine, methionine and tryptophan will attempt to approach each other, with the exclusion of water, to minimise the negative entropy associated with the hydration process. Hydrophobic interactions can, therefore, be regarded as a partial reversal of the thermodynamically unfavourable solution process (Figs. 1.1 and 1.2).

This explanation of hydrophobic interactions is quite adequate for most situations such as the non-aqueous interior of proteins, but Franks (1975) has questioned whether it is valid in predominantly

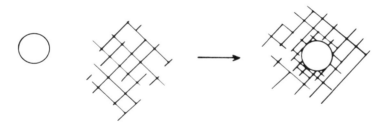

FIG. 1.1 Hydrophobic hydration.

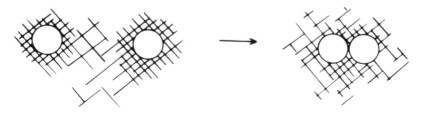

FIG. 1.2 Hydrophobic interaction.

aqueous environments such as the exterior surface of proteins dissolved in water. He suggests that in such cases the hydrophobic
groups are stabilised by longer-range interactions with the water
acting as a 'cement' (Fig. 1.3). When hydrophobic interactions are
broken, the process is weakly exothermic and, as the temperature of a
system is increased, so the strength of any hydrophobic interactions
increases.

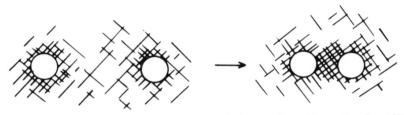

FIG. 1.3 Proposed long-range hydrophobic interaction. (From Franks, 1975.)

1.2.1.4 *Salt Linkages* (*Ionic Bonds*)

It is apparent that most polypeptides will, at all but the extremes of
pH, contain both negatively charged groups such as the carboxylate
groups of aspartic and glutamic acids and positively charged groups
such as the guanidinium group of arginine and the ϵ-amino group of
lysine. A strong salt linkage will form when groups of opposite charge
come into juxtaposition. Similarly, strong repulsive forces occur
between ionic groups possessing the same charge.

These ionic interactions are presumably only stable in the absence
of water since, in the presence of water, the ions will be strongly
hydrated. However, salt linkages that are protected from water in the
hydrophobic interior of a protein can contribute to the overall stability of the protein. Like all ionic bonds, these linkages are more or less
athermal as they rupture with little evolution or absorption of heat
and their stability is not markedly dependent on temperature. Other
types of weak interactions between residues in a polypeptide may
occur (*e.g.* London–van der Waals forces) but these are of minimal
importance and will not be discussed in this chapter.

1.2.2 Structure

In the early 1950s, Pauling and others discussed the general constraints necessary to define the secondary structures of protein chains

and, although the great importance of hydrophobic interactions was not stressed, their deliberations gave rise to models that have proved remarkably successful. The constraints imposed by the model builders of this era were: (1) the covalent interatomic distances and bond angles associated with a polypeptide chain must be maintained within narrow tolerances; (2) the atoms in the peptide must remain coplanar; (3) for maximum stability each N–H group must hydrogen bond to a C=O group and each C=O group to a N–H group. There are two general structures that fulfil these conditions:
(a) Configurations in which hydrogen bonds form between C=O and N–H groups of different residues in the same chain. In this case a helix is generated; several such helices are possible but the most common is undoubtedly the α-helix.
(b) Structures in which hydrogen bonds form between the C=O and N–H groups of adjacent, more or less parallel, chains, i.e. the β-structure or pleated sheet.
The considerations discussed so far in this chapter allow us to explain the structures of most proteins found in foodstuffs and some of the most common will now be described.

1.2.2.1 α-Helix
This helix, which is shown diagrammatically in Fig. 1.4, has 3·7 amino acid residues per coil and is stabilised primarily by hydrogen bonds between C=O and N–H groups of adjacent coils, i.e. the sequence may be written

$$C-\{NH\cdot CH(R)\cdot CO\}_3\ N$$
$$O-\ -\ -\ -\ -\ -H$$

This type of linkage, however, may not be the only stabilising bond present in the helix since, in order to explain the observation that polyglutamic acid will form an α-helix while polyaspartic acid will not, Franks (1975) has suggested that the polyglutamic helix may be partially stabilised by long-range hydrophobic interactions between the side-chains (see the earlier discussion on hydrophobic interactions), the shorter side-chains of polyaspartic acid being unable to take part in such bonding. An alternative explanation of this phenomenon is that polyglutamic acid may form additional hydrogen bonds between the side-chain carboxyl groups while, for steric reasons, polyaspartic acid cannot (Brahms and Spach, 1963).

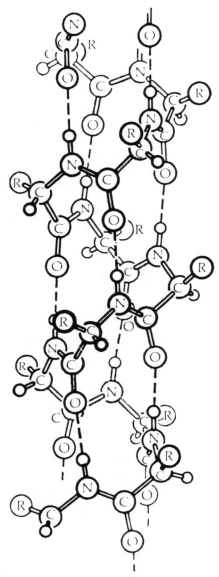

FIG. 1.4   The α-helix with 3·7 amino acid residues per coil. The NH and CO of each peptide bond are linked by hydrogen bonds. (From Pauling *et al.*, 1951.)

Although the α-helix is found extensively in nature, it is unusual for a protein to be 100% helical and the only one of which the author is aware is the muscle protein, tropomyosin. This rod-like protein consists of two adjacent α-helices joined by a disulphide bond (Cummins and Perry, 1973). As has been shown earlier, a regular helix will generate a relatively rigid cylinder and portions of the myosin of muscle and the blood protein, fibrinogen, are all of the same general type, although in these cases the helical content is less than 100%. However, not all proteins of high α-helical content are cylindrical and most globular proteins appear to contain regions of this structure. Typical values are about 15% for ribonuclease, about 30% for egg-white lysozyme (in this case the helices are distorted slightly), about 45% for ovalbumin and serum albumin, and about 75% for myoglobin and haemoglobin. Myoglobin was the first protein to have its tertiary structure fully determined (Kendrew, 1961) and a schematic representation of the molecule is shown in Fig. 1.5 where it can be seen that the helical regions are joined by eight non-helical ones. Proline residues cannot fit into an α-helix because the C(5) atom of the pyrrolidine ring (Table 1.1) occupies the position of the peptide (amide) hydrogen, which for other amino acid residues bonds with the next coil of the helix. Thus, the four proline residues of myoglobin are situated in the non-helical regions. However, there are several such regions without proline and these non-helical regions are stabilised by various types of interaction such as hydrogen bonds involving the hydroxyl group of threonine, hydrophobic interactions between aromatic residues and salt links between charged groups. The haematin group in myoglobin is partially buried in the interior of the molecule (Fig. 1.5) where it is bonded to the protein chain by a co-ordination link from an imidazole residue of histidine to the iron atom. This, however, is not the only linkage as there are several weaker attachments between the haematin group and the protein. For example, there are over 90 non-polar (hydrophobic) contacts.

1.2.2.2 β-Structure or Pleated Sheet

As well as the different helices, Pauling and Corey (1951) also postulated the existence of proteins with the β- (pleated sheet) structure. Depending on the direction of the polypeptide chains, the pleated sheets may be either parallel or antiparallel (Fig. 1.6). In multichain fibrous proteins such as silk fibroin or stretched β-keratin, the chains are antiparallel although x-ray analysis of several globular

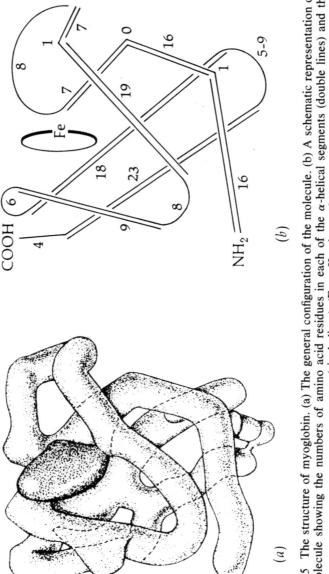

FIG. 1.5 The structure of myoglobin. (a) The general configuration of the molecule. (b) A schematic representation of the molecule showing the numbers of amino acid residues in each of the α-helical segments (double lines) and the corners (single lines). (From Kendrew, 1961.)

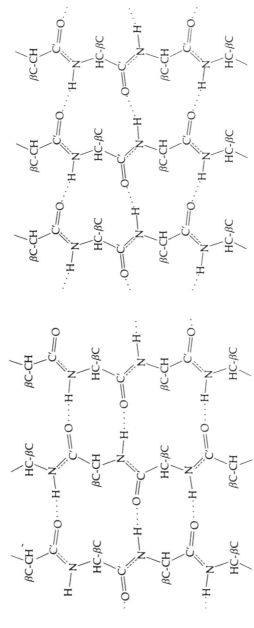

FIG.1.6 Diagrammatic representations of the pleated sheet (β-structures). The antiparallel chain structure is shown on the left, the parallel chain structure on the right. (From Pauling and Corey, 1951.)

proteins indicates that both parallel and antiparallel configurations occur.

The β-structure and α-helix are not mutually exclusive as, for example, lysozyme, which is about 30% α-helical, also contains a well-characterised region of antiparallel β-sheet.

1.2.2.3 Tropocollagen

Of prime importance in determining the secondary, tertiary and quaternary structure of the collagen triple helix is the unique sequence of the amino acid residues. Glycine, in all but the terminal regions of the individual peptide chains, occupies every third position, and the chains are composed of sequences ultimately rich and poor in imino acid residues (proline and hydroxyproline) and correspondingly rich and poor in non-polar and polar residues. Sequences of the type Gly–Pro–Pro (or Hypro) are very common in the non-polar regions, e.g.

———————limited flexibility———————→
(bonds arrowed r have limited
rotational freedom)

If the chain consisted solely of proline residues, one stable configuration for the polymer would be the *trans* form of the poly-L-proline II helix (Fig. 1.7). However, in collagen-like chains, the freedom of rotation of the rest of the chain makes this configuration unstable unless additional stabilisation occurs. This is achieved by the aggregation of three peptide chains, each chain coiling along a left-hand three-fold axis, *i.e.* the chains appear to climb in a clockwise fashion around a common axis, three residues completing one turn. The three chains are aligned, with their axes parallel, such that translation perpendicular to the axis of one chain finds a similar position in either of the neighbouring chains. If more than the bare backbone configuration is considered then, as in tropocollagen, it is necessary to deform the chains so that they are no longer parallel but wind about each other in a gentle right-handed spiral, *i.e.* go anticlockwise around one another on 'climbing' the common axis, a rotation of $-324°$ taking

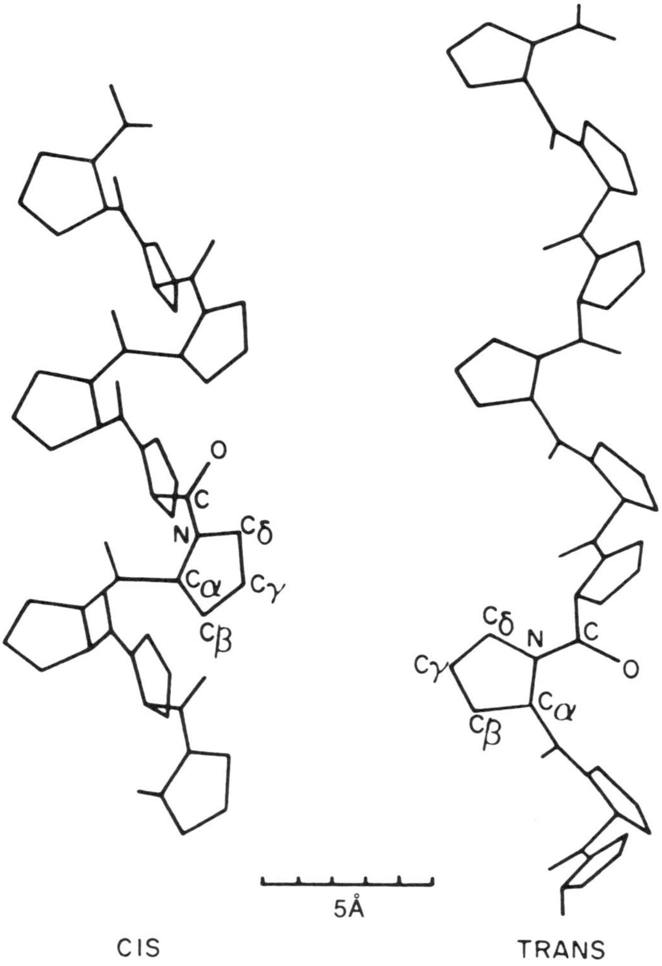

FIG. 1.7 Diagrammatic representation of the poly-L-proline II helix.

one back to the original chain (*cf.* 360°) and a rotation of − 108° taking one to a similar residue on the next chain (*cf.* 90°). Although the overall dimensions of the rod-like triple helix are well established, there is still controversy about the inter-chain bonding. Present evidence appears to favour a model proposed by Ramachandran and co-workers which was modified to its present form in 1968. In this model there are two hydrogen bonds per tripeptide, one between the N–H group of glycine in one chain and the carbonyl oxygen in position 3 in an adjacent chain, and another from a peptide hydrogen atom of one chain to the oxygen of a water molecule, with a hydrogen of the water molecule binding to a carbonyl oxygen of another chain. If hydroxyproline occupies the third position, further stabilisation of this structure can occur through hydrogen bonding involving the hydroxyl group (Ramachandran *et al.*, 1973). As discussed earlier, covalent bonds between the chains may also occur.

1.2.2.4 *Conjugated Proteins*

In foodstuffs, the structures of several proteins are modified by combination with characteristic non-amino acid substances (*prosthetic* groups) and it is worthwhile briefly identifying the main types.

(a) *Nucleoproteins*, where the prosthetic groups are nucleic acids.

(b) *Mucoproteins*, when combination is with large amounts ($> 4\%$) of carbohydrate measured as hexosamine. The carbohydrate portions of these are complex polysaccharides and in several cases are bound by ester bonds to serine residues in the protein.

(c) *Glycoproteins*, when the prosthetic group is a small amount ($< 4\%$) of carbohydrate measured as hexosamine. This group includes many of the common albumins (water-soluble proteins) and globulins (salt-soluble proteins). In ovalbumin, the carbohydrate is covalently linked to the protein by an amide bond between asparagine and C [1] of N-acetylglucosamine. It is apparent that the distinction between glyco- and mucoproteins is purely arbitrary.

(d) *Lipoproteins*, when the prosthetic group is lipid material, *e.g.* phosphatidyl, glycerides, cholesterol. Egg yolk is a rich source of these water-soluble complexes.

Other types of conjugated proteins are flavoproteins, haemoproteins and metalloproteins, where the nature of the prosthetic group is indicated by the prefix.

From the brief outline given, it can be seen that proteins can exist in foods in several forms and these variations are further complicated by the way the protein may be combined with other material. For example, in animal tissues, little collagen is present as tropocollagen as these monomers aggregate to form well-defined fibres which themselves are bound to glycoproteins, mucopolysaccharides, etc. in the tissue. Because of these interactions between proteins and other components of biological material, the ease with which proteins may be extracted and purified from different sources will vary. Thus, *fibrous* proteins found in animal tissues such as collagens and keratins tend to be relatively insoluble whereas the *globular* proteins found in muscle and egg white are easily solubilised. The chapters on the various food commodities contain examples of the different ways proteins may be present in foods and so these topics will not be dealt with here.

1.3 PROPERTIES OF PROTEINS

1.3.1 Amphoteric Behaviour

Like amino acids, proteins are *ampholytes*, *i.e.* they act as both acids and bases and, at all but the extremes of pH, possess both positively and negatively charged groups. The isoelectric point, pE, of a protein is that pH at which the *net* charge on the molecule is zero, *i.e.* it is the pH of the solution in which the protein will not migrate when an electric field is applied. Care must be taken not to confuse this with the isoionic point, pI, of a protein, as pI and pE can be very different under certain conditions. The pI is defined as the pH of a solution of the protein in which the only other ions present are hydrogen and hydroxyl ions. Thus, if we consider a protein of pI = 5, an isoionic solution will have $[H^+]$ of about $10^{-5}M$ and $[OH^-]$ of about $10^{-9}M$ and therefore, to preserve electrical neutrality in the system, the protein must carry a negative charge of about $10^{-5}M$. Therefore, it will migrate in an applied electric field. However, provided the protein is present at relatively high concentration (so that the charge can be distributed among several molecules) and pI is not far removed from neutrality then, to a first approximation, pI = pE.

Since the polar groups present in a protein have such varying pK values, it is not surprising that the titration curves of proteins are complex. Owing to the presence of the carboxylate groups of the acidic amino acids, plus of course the carboxylate group at the terminal end of the chain, most protein solutions are good buffers below about pH 5. Similarly, owing to the ϵ-amino group of lysine, the guanidinium group of arginine and the phenolic hydroxyl groups, most proteins are good buffers at pH values above 9. However, at neutral pH values, the only significant buffering is by the imidazole group of histidine and the α-amino groups at the chain ends (of which there is only one per chain) and thus, in this pH region, most proteins have limited buffering capacity. However, this buffering is of great importance in many living tissues.

1.3.2 Ion-Binding to Proteins

As ampholytes, proteins can bind both anions and cations and specific combinations with small ions are important in several foods. If a neutral salt is added to an aqueous protein solution and the anions and cations bind equally, then the *net* charge on the protein will remain unaltered (and the pE will be unaffected). But if the anion is bound more strongly than the cation, then the net charge on the protein will become more negative and, if this preferential binding occurs at pE, pE will decrease compared to the value in pure water (or a solution in which cation and anion binding is equal). Also, if anions are preferentially bound, the pH of the solution increases and Edsall and Wyman (1958) claim that this occurs because protons become bound to the increased negative charge. Similarly, if preferential cation binding occurs, there is a decrease in pH of the solution and an increase in the pE of the protein.

Several ions will form insoluble salts with proteins and this phenomenon is widely used to remove proteins from solutions, *e.g.* trichloroacetic acid (TCA) is used to separate protein nitrogen from non-protein nitrogen. As well as simple salt formation, some ions (*e.g.*, Cu^{2+} and Ni^{2+}) will combine with proteins to form co-ordination complexes with the free amino groups, peptide groups, imidazole groups, etc.

As well as small ions, it is possible to obtain interactions between proteins and charged macromolecules such as alginates and pectates. These types of complexes may have great potential in the food industry for developing new textured foods.

Because of the diversity of groups on a protein, numerous chemical reactions may occur with other compounds, many of which may be important in food systems (*e.g.*, reactions between amino groups and sugars to give brown 'Maillard' pigments) but these types of reactions are dealt with in other chapters and will not be discussed here.

1.3.3 Solubility

As would be expected for an ampholyte, protein solubility is markedly dependent on the pH and ionic composition of the solution. The dependence on pH is relatively easy to understand. Protein solubility is minimal at the isoelectric point since at this pH the *net* charge on the protein is zero and consequently, electrostatic repulsive forces are minimal while crystal-lattice forces in the solid are maximal, *i.e.* interaction between the protein molecules is maximal.

The relationship between salt concentration and solubility is more complex. *Globulins*, which are soluble in 5–10% salt solutions, are insoluble in water while *albumins* are readily soluble in both water and dilute salt solutions. However, in concentrated salt solutions, all proteins become less soluble. The increase in solubility in dilute salt solutions observed with globulins is known as '*salting-in*' and can be explained in terms of the relative affinity of the protein molecules for each other and for the solvent, *i.e.* the ions of the neutral salt will interact with the protein, thereby decreasing protein–protein interactions and consequently increasing the solubility. The decrease in solubility of proteins at high salt concentration is known as '*salting-out*', the mechanism of which is complex and not completely understood although a qualitative interpretation in terms of 'dehydration' of the protein by the added salt can be made. Thus, the large numbers of salt ions in the solution will 'hydrate' and organise water molecules around them, thus reducing the water available for the protein molecules. Since protein solubility depends on water 'clustering' around the hydrophilic groups, the 'dehydrated' proteins will precipitate.

Low salt concentrations have little effect on the pH dependence of protein solubility; minimum solubility still occurs at the pE although, if unequal binding of anions and cations occurs, pE will vary with salt concentration and this will, of course, be reflected in the pH dependence of the solubility. At high salt concentrations, the overall effect of pH on solubility becomes less marked as the ions tend to minimise the electrostatic forces between the protein molecules.

Non-polar solvents that are miscible with water, such as methanol, ethanol and acetone, all cause proteins to precipitate from aqueous solution, this effect being markedly affected by the presence of neutral salts.

In an aqueous protein solution, not all the water will be 'free' as some will be 'bound' to the protein via one or all of hydration of charged groups, hydrogen bonds and possibly in some forms of hydrophobic interaction. A great deal of research effort has been, and is being, devoted to elucidate the nature of 'bound' water in proteins but space prohibits its detailed discussion here. Suffice to say that, in most proteins, it is extremely difficult (by conventional drying techniques) to remove the last 5–10% by weight of water and that on freezing protein solutions, up to 50% of the protein weight of water appears not to freeze, even when cooled to $-180°C$ (Duckworth, 1971).

1.3.4 Swelling of Proteins

Several native proteins which are not soluble in water may, however, interact with aqueous solutions to form swollen, gel-like systems, examples being actomyosin and collagen in muscle, and are capable of immobilising even more water than soluble proteins. There are two main mechanisms whereby this swelling occurs:

(i) *Lyotropic* swelling, which tends to be irreversible and is caused by non-ionic reagents which act by altering the water structure around the protein, interrupting hydrogen bonds and/or through direct competition with internal hydrophobic interactions.

(ii) *Osmotic (Donnan)* swelling, which is reversible and caused by interactions between ions and charged sites on the protein. This may be explained thus: at all pH values other than the pE, the protein possesses *excess* negative or positive charge and, to maintain electrical neutrality in the swollen phase, small ions of opposite charge migrate from the solution to the swollen phase. These excess ions in the swollen phase give rise to an osmotic pressure which causes the swelling. Also, as the activities (concentrations) of the ions must be the same in the swollen and aqueous phases, the hydrogen ion concentration in the two phases will differ.

The swelling of insoluble proteins by these mechanisms will continue until it is restrained by the intermolecular forces between the protein molecules and an equilibrium swollen volume is achieved. Thus, both soluble and insoluble proteins can immobilise water and this ability to bind water is often called their *water-holding capacity* (WHC). Owing to the pH dependence of osmotic swelling, two-phase systems such as meat tend to have minimal WHC at their isoelectric points.

Globular proteins may themselves form gels and thus 'bind' more water than when soluble. However, this complex phenomenon only appears to occur under conditions known to radically alter their protein structure and therefore these types of systems will be dealt with after the concept of protein denaturation has been discussed.

1.3.5 Enzymic Activity

Several proteins can, with a high degree of specificity and great efficiency, direct transformations of organic compounds through defined reaction sequences. These natural catalysts of biochemical reactions are known as *enzymes* and are generally named in terms of the reactions they catalyse. A well-established practice is to add the suffix *-ase* to the name of the compound transformed (*substrate*); thus urea is attacked by urease, arginine by arginase, *etc.* Enzymes may also be classified by groups that catalyse similar reactions such as proteinases, lipases and oxidases. In addition, an older nomenclature has persisted and such names as pepsin, trypsin and rennin are widely used. In order to standardise terminology, an International Commission on Enzymes has devised a complete, but rather complex, system of nomenclature (see *Enzyme Nomenclature*, 1965) but these recommendations have not yet achieved general usage.

The accepted view to explain the mechanisms of enzymic catalysis is that the enzyme (*E*) forms an intermediate complex with the substrate (*S*) prior to the transformation to the final product (*P*), *i.e.*

$$E + S \rightleftharpoons ES \rightarrow E + P$$

The binding of *E* and *S* is very specific and only occurs at the active site(s) of the enzyme where the nature and conformation of the amino acids (plus possibly a prosthetic group) are such as to allow the substrate to bind. Covalent, ionic, hydrogen and hydrophobic bonds may all help to stabilise the enzyme–substrate complex. As substrate binding is so dependent on the conformation and nature of the groups at, and in the vicinity of, the active site, it is not surprising that the ability of an enzyme to catalyse a reaction (its *activity*) is very dependent on any factors which change the nature of the active site. Thus, the activity of an enzyme will usually vary with the pH and ionic strength of the solution. This is especially so if an ionic group is involved at the active site and the activity depends on the group being either in the ionised or non-ionised form, such as histidine in trypsin. The pH of maximum activity is known as the optimum pH. Also, if sulphydryl groups (SH) or histidine residues are involved at the active site then mild oxidation, which alters the nature of these groups, will greatly diminish the activity of the enzyme. It is possible that molecules other than the substrate may bind to the enzyme and impair its efficiency. If the inhibitor (*I*) can bind reversibly to the active site, *i.e.*

$$E + I \rightleftharpoons EI$$

then competitive inhibition occurs and the rate of reaction depends on the ratio of the inhibitor and substrate concentrations. However, if the inhibitor binds at some position other than the active site, yet still ivates the enzyme, *i.e.*

$$E + I \rightleftharpoons EI$$

and

$$ES + I \rightleftharpoons ESI$$

where both *EI* and *ESI* are inactive, then non-competitive inhibition occurs with the rate depending only on the concentration of inhibitor. The activity of an enzyme invariably increases with temperature until at some elevated temperature a conformational change occurs which destroys the active site and renders the enzyme inactive, *i.e.* denaturation occurs (see later).

1.4   EFFECT OF HEAT ON PROTEINS

Since hydrogen bonds play a major rôle in maintaining the secondary and higher structures of proteins, it is not surprising that a radical change in structure usually occurs on heating. This radical change in structure, which occurs without severance of any covalent links, is known as *denaturation* (Tanford, 1968). This definition is not absolute as the meaning of a 'major' or 'radical' change is purely arbitrary although, in most cases, this structural change can be unequivocally identified. However, minor conformational changes may occur prior to denaturation and in this chapter these will be referred to as *predenaturational transitions*. Since most of the bonds maintaining the conformation of the protein rupture during denaturation, the protein will take up a predominantly random-coil configuration. However, most thermally denatured proteins do possess regions of order which may persist from the native state or form by new interactions after the protein is unfolded (Tanford, 1968). It seems probable that these ordered regions are maintained primarily by hydrophobic interactions which, as discussed earlier, are stable to heat.

Both denaturation and predenaturational transitions are reversible. However, following denaturation, the proteins will often interact, either with themselves or other molecules, to form aggregates (precipitates, gels, etc.) and these postdenaturation reactions are virtually irreversible. If the heat supplied to the protein is excessive, then covalent bonds may rupture leading to *thermal degradation* of the molecules. The possible reactions that a protein may undergo during heating are summarised below and the rest of this chapter will be devoted to a discussion of these.

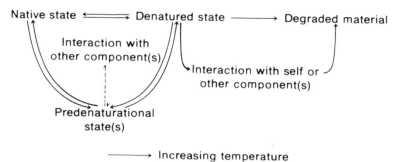

────────→ Increasing temperature

1.4.1 Predenaturational Transitions

These minor conformational changes are normally of little importance in food systems as they have a minimal effect on the properties of the material. However, if the changes allow reactions to occur that are not possible in the native state, then they may have a marked effect on the properties. For example, it has been claimed that the predenaturational change that myoglobin undergoes at temperatures below the denaturation temperature partially exposes the haematin group and allows it to react with other proteins to form the brown 'cooked-meat haemoproteins' of cooked meat (see Chapter 5).

1.4.2 Thermal Denaturation

Even if denaturation does not take place in clearly separable stages, intermediate conformations between the native and denatured states must occur. Thus, a protein must unwind in some progressive manner to the final state yielding a very large number of intermediate states. As the interactions that stabilise the native structure tend to be co-operative, these intermediate states will be relatively unstable and it is possible that all such intermediates will be transient so that, at any given time, all but a negligible fraction of the molecules are in either the native or denatured form, *i.e.* the transition is *two-state*. If this criterion holds for protein denaturation, then it is possible to determine the thermodynamic parameters associated with the transition from analysis of the equilibrium data. Thus, determination of the equilibrium concentration of the native $[N]$ and denatured $[D]$ fractions as a function of temperature enables the apparent enthalpy,

ΔH_{app} (from $\Delta H_{app} = - \mathrm{Rd} \ln K_{app}/\mathrm{d}(1/T)$) where K_{app} is the apparent equilibrium constant) and ΔCp_{app}, the apparent difference in heat capacity, at a given temperature and pressure, between the native and denatured states (from $\mathrm{d}\Delta H_{app}/\mathrm{d}T$) to be determined (Tanford, 1968). The denaturation temperature, T_D, is taken to be the temperature at which $[N] = [D]$.

Within the last decade, the development of sensitive micro-calorimeters, capable of measuring the weak heat effects associated with protein denaturation, has enabled these thermodynamic parameters to be determined directly. The calorimetric and equilibrium values of ΔH_D and ΔCp will only be equal for a two-state process whereas for a *multistate* process, *i.e.* a process with 'stable' intermediates, $\Delta H_D > \Delta H_{app}$ and thus it should be possible to differentiate between these two types of processes. However, the limited results so far obtained on different proteins tend to be contradictory. For example, Danforth et al. (1967) reported that the denaturation of ribonuclease was not two-state while Brandts and Hunt (1967) obtained data that suggested it was. Privalov et al. (1971) made a careful study on the denaturation of ribonuclease, chymo-trypsinogen and myoglobin and claimed that all three proteins dena-ture in two separate processes:

(i) A predenaturational stage that is probably connected with a labilisation of the structure involving an increase in heat capacity and no change in enthalpy; and
(ii) a two-state denaturational stage accompanied by an increase in enthalpy.

Recently, Brandts (1976) re-investigated the denaturation of ribo-nuclease and suggested that the process is not two-state although all the steps but one are associated with zero enthalpy change. Hope-fully, the controversies will soon be resolved but at present it is not possible to unequivocally assign detailed mechanisms to protein denaturations.

Whatever the mechanism of denaturation it is apparent that, because of the complex interactions that are possible between the protein and the solvent, the thermal stability of the native structure will be dependent on the nature of the environment. It is normal for proteins to have maximum thermostability at their isoelectric points although the relative stabilities on either side of the pE vary quite markedly for different proteins. For example, lysozyme, β-lactoglo-bulin and ribonuclease all remain relatively stable down to a pH of about 2 while ferrimyoglobin (metmyoglobin), which is more stable than ribonuclease at pH 7, will denature at about 30°C at pH 5. The generally accepted explanation is that proteins that are very unstable to acid have buried (uncharged) histidyl groups which become very unstable as the pH is reduced below the normal pK of the groups and thus help to 'drive' the denaturation. Similarly, buried tyrosyl residues may serve to drive protein denaturation at pH values above 10 or 11.

The thermal stability of proteins in foods will also be affected by the environment. For example, tropocollagen has a T_D of about 37°C, while in the connective tissue of muscle the organisation of the molecules in the collagen fibres increases the T_D to about 60°C (Chapter 5).

As with protein solubility, the effect of inorganic salts on thermal stability is complex. In general, it seems that dilute salt solutions tend to decrease stability while at higher concentrations some tend to increase and others continue to decrease stability (Finch and Ledward, 1973). Organic compounds usually decrease protein stability by destroying hydrogen and/or hydrophobic bonds, although the effectiveness of different components varies with the nature of the molecule (Tanford, 1968).

In view of the large structural changes that occur during denaturation, it is not surprising that several properties also change during these transitions. For example, any physical property which is dependent on molecular size and shape (viscosity, light scattering, volume sedimentation), or conformation (optical rotatory dispersion, circular dichroism, enzyme activity) will change. Other properties will alter owing to the difference in environment of specific residues in the native and denatured states. Thus, aromatic residues which are buried in the interior of the native molecule are exposed to the solvent following denaturation and will affect the ultraviolet absorption spectra. Polar residues which may not be free to ionise in the native state will, on exposure to the solvent, bind or release protons with—if the solution is unbuffered—a concomitant change in pH, as is found with metmyoglobin at acid pH.

In view of the gross conformational changes that occur on denaturation, it is not surprising that all enzymes lose their activity during this process. However, it should be noted that an enzyme–substrate complex is often more stable than the isolated enzyme. As well as these changes due to denaturation itself, the denatured state may well react further, either with itself or other molecules, to yield stable reaction products.

1.4.3   Aggregation, Precipitation and Gelation

The major emphasis in protein-denaturation studies has been on the conformational changes of isolated molecules in dilute solutions and there has been little study of the phenomenon of aggregation that often follows denaturation in moderately concentrated protein solutions. It is not clear what are the major forces causing denatured proteins to aggregate but, because of the stability of most aggregates, some covalent bonds must form. In ovalbumin (Frensdorf *et al.*, 1953), bovine serum albumin (Warner and Levy, 1958) and some vegetable proteins (Tombs, 1970), disulphide interchange between a thiol group of one molecule and a disulphide bond of another are important. Also, as aggregation appears to be pH dependent (and maximal at the pE), electrostatic forces must contribute to the stabilisation of these aggregates and, as non-polar residues tend to become exposed on denaturation, it seems probable that hydrophobic interactions also occur. At the relatively high temperatures normally involved in protein denaturation, hydrogen bonds between the different molecules are unlikely to occur although, on cooling, these types of bonds may form leading to additional stabilisation (see Chapter 5). If several different proteins are all heated in one system then co-aggregation between the different proteins—either between denatured–denatured proteins or denatured–native proteins—may well occur and could be very important in determining the properties of some heated foods. Unfortunately, these mixed protein–protein interactions have received little attention.

Protein aggregation causes turbidity and ultimately leads to the formation of either a *precipitate* (where two phases form, a solid phase very concentrated in protein with very little water and an aqueous phase containing virtually no protein) or a one-phase *gel mesh* containing both protein and water. For example, albumin heated at different temperatures shows markedly different modes of aggregation. At 70°C, the ultimate product is a gel while at 100°C a precipitate forms (Tombs, 1970). As stated earlier, denatured proteins are more or less spherical and if completely random aggregation occurred, almost spherical particles should form. Obviously the surface of a protein is not uniform with regard to the probability that surface contact will lead to adhesion and thus some orientation may be expected. But the reason why different conditions alter the mode of aggregation from a highly orientated gel to a less orientated form (precipitate) is not so apparent. Electron micrographs of gels formed from globular proteins indicate that the mesh structure is built up by aggregation of the almost spherical individual particles (Tombs, 1970). An increase in the randomness of aggregation leads to smaller effective strand lengths and precipitation, rather than gelation. Even when precipitation occurs the mode of aggregation leads to different 'shaped' precipitates (Tombs, 1970).

The formation of these different protein aggregates often has a marked effect on the physical properties of a foodstuff. Thus, if a precipitate forms then there is usually a marked decrease in water-holding capacity (WHC) while the formation of a gel may actually improve the WHC of the system.

Most globular proteins will only form gels at concentrations of 20–30% but gelatin, which is derived from insoluble collagen by procedures involving the destruction of the secondary and higher structures, will form gels at concentrations as low as 1%. In this unique system, the aggregation between the individual polypeptide chains is through hydrogen bonds which, as they only form at relatively low temperatures (30–40°C), cause the gels to be thermo-reversible. In many ways the gelation of gelatin can be regarded as the partial renaturation of collagen, the imino acid rich regions forming the hydrogen-bonded triple helix by side-to-side aggregation with similar regions on other chains to form the gel junction points. ·Between these junctions the polar regions of the chains remain relatively flexible so that an infinite, three-dimensional elastic gel network is generated (Ledward, 1968).

1.4.4 Thermal Degradation

The reactions just discussed occur spontaneously following dena-turation. However, proteins may undergo further reactions following excessive heating and Bjarnason and Carpenter (1970) made a study of some of these. On heating proteins (containing about 14·1% water) at 115°C, the only changes noted were an appreciable loss in cystine content and some loss of lysine with concomitant evolution of hydrogen sulphide and ammonia. They suggested that the mechanisms responsible for the loss of cystine could involve both disulphide and peptide-bond hydrolysis via mechanisms (I) and (II) below.

(I) $R \cdot CH_2-S-S-CH_2R' \cdot \xrightarrow{\text{H}_2\text{O}} R \cdot CH_2SH + R' \cdot CH_2SOH$

plus some breakdown of $R'CH_2SOH \rightarrow H_2S\uparrow + R'CHO$

Lysine destruction probably occurs due to Maillard reactions involving the amides of asparagine and glutamine or the carbonyl compounds formed by cystine degradation (mechanism II), *e.g.*

When heated at 145°C, more complex reactions occur and there are marked losses of all the amino acids except glutamic acid and those possessing paraffin side-chains (except isoleucine which tends to racemise to alloisoleucine). For example, the products of cystine destruction are far more complex indicating that C–C-bond rupture occurs while the imidazole group of histidine and the guanidinium group of arginine may eliminate ammonia. Also, serine and threonine may degrade by the β-elimination of water (Table 1.1) followed by a similar breakdown to that shown in mechanism (IIb) above. These authors found that, even at 145°C, there was little peptide-bond hydrolysis; N-terminal analysis of the proteins suggested that only 0·3–0·4% of the peptide bonds were broken. However, in an aqueous environment, peptide-bond hydrolysis may be more important, as Courts (1958) found that gelatin solutions held at 70°C for 24 h were completely degraded by peptide-bond hydrolysis, the rate of hydrolysis increasing as the pH was shifted away from neutrality. In this sulphur-free protein, the peptide bonds involving the amino groups of serine and threonine were most labile at both acid and alkaline pH values. Aspartic acid peptides were very susceptible to acid hydrolysis while those involving glutamic acid were very stable. Those involving glycine were intermediate in stability.

The reactions discussed above are those which may occur in relatively pure protein systems. As might be expected, when other components are present, the number of possible reactions increases, an example being Maillard browning between carbohydrate material and the ϵ-NH$_2$ groups of lysine. These types of reactions are discussed elsewhere in this volume.

REFERENCES

Bailey, A. J., Peach, C. M. & Fowler, L. J. (1970) In: *Chemistry and Molecular Biology of the Intercellular Matrix*, ed. Balazs, E. A. Vol. 1, p. 385. New York: Academic Press.

Bailey, A. J., Robins, S. P. & Balian, G. (1974) *Nature*, **251**, 105.

Bjarnason, J. and Carpenter, K. J. (1970) *Brit. J. Nutr.*, **24**, 313.

Brahms, J. & Spach, C. (1963) *Nature*, **200**, 72.

Brandts, J. F. (1976) EMBO Workshop—reported in *Nature*, **261**, 279.

Brandts, J. F. & Hunt, L. (1967) *J. Am. Chem. Soc.*, **89**, 4826.

Courts, A. (1958) *Biochem. J.*, **58**, 74.

Cummins, P. & Perry, S. J. (1973) *Biochem. J.*, **133**, 765.

Danforth, R., Krakover, H. & Sturtevant, J. M. (1967) *Rev. Sci. Instr.*, **38**, 484.

Davis, N. R., Risen, O. M. & Pringle, G. A. (1975) *Biochemistry*, **14**, 2031.

Duckworth, R. B. (1971) *J. Fd. Technol.*, **6**, 317.

Edsall, J. T. & Wyman, J. J. (1958) *Biophysical Chemistry*. Vol. 1. New York: Academic Press.

Enzyme Nomenclature 1965—Recommendation (1964) of the International Union of Biochemistry. Amsterdam: Elsevier.

Finch, A. & Ledward, D. A. (1973) *Biochim. Biophys. Acta*, **295**, 296.

Flory, P. J. (1953) *Principles of Polymer Chemistry*. New York: Cornell University Press.

Frank, H. S. & Evans, M. W. (1945) *J. Chem. Phys.*, **13**, 507.

Franks, F. (1975) Water—A Comprehensive Treatise, ed. Franks, F. Vol. 4, p. 1. New York: Plenum Press.

Frensdorf, H. K., Watson, M. T. & Kauzmann, W. (1953) J. Am. Chem. Soc., 75, 5157.

Jackson, D. S., Ayad, S. & Mechanic, G. (1974) Biochim. Biophys. Acta, 336, 100.

Kendrew, J. C. (1961) Sci. Am., 205, 96.

Ledward, D. A. (1968) Ph.D. Thesis, University of Leeds.

Pauling, L. (1954) General Chemistry, 2nd ed. San Francisco: W. H. Freeman.

Pauling, L. & Corey, R. B. (1951) Proc. Natl. Acad. Sci., 37, 729.

Pauling, L., Corey, R. B. & Branson, H. R. (1951) Proc. Natl. Acad. Sci., 37, 205.

Privalov, P. L., Khechinashvili, N. N. & Atanasov, B. P. (1971) Biopolymers, 10, 1865.

Ramachandran, G. N., Bansed, M. & Bhatnagar, R. S. (1973) Biochim. Biophys. Acta, 322, 166.

Ramachandran, G. N., Doyle, B. B. & Blout, E. R. (1968) Biopolymers, 6, 1771.

Tanford, C. (1968) Advan. Protein Chem., 23, 121.

Tombs, M. P. (1970) In: Proteins as Human Food, ed. Lawrie, R. A., p. 126. Westport, Conn.: Avi. Publ. Co.

van Beek, L., Feron, V. J. & de Groot, A. P. (1974) J. Nutr., 104, 1630.

Warner, R. C. & Levy, M. (1958) J. Am. Chem. Soc., 80, 5735.

CHAPTER 2

Carbohydrates

C. T. GREENWOOD and D. N. MUNRO

Cadbury–Schweppes Ltd., London, UK

Carbohydrates form one of the most important sources of dietary energy, and as such have a vital rôle to play in the food industry. As will be seen below, these materials are very widely distributed in nature. Carbohydrates can be composed of both small or large molecules, and in the latter case, their diverse chemical structures enable them to perform a variety of specific tasks in all forms of life, but particularly in plants.

Modern food technology utilises the numerous characteristic properties of carbohydrates, which can vary from inducing sweetness to gel formation, and often temperature dependence is all-important. This chapter outlines the structural chemistry of carbohydrates and the effect of heat on properties which are of importance to the food industry.

2.1 NOMENCLATURE

The term *carbohydrate* originally arose from the concept that all naturally occurring compounds of this type, for example, glucose ($C_6H_{12}O_6$), sucrose ($C_{12}H_{22}O_{11}$) and starch ($C_6H_{10}O_5$) possessed an empirical formula of the form $C_x(H_2O)_y$, which indicated that they were hydrates of carbon. This definition is, of course, far too rigid and there are now many classes of carbohydrates, *e.g.* deoxysugars, such as rhamnose, and sugar acids or uronic acids, which do not fit. The term applies to polyhydroxy compounds which have the ability to reduce Fehling's solution either before or after hydrolysis with mineral acid.

Carbohydrates are conveniently classified as follows:

Monosaccharides or simple sugars (*e.g.*, fructose, glucose).
Disaccharides which consist of two monosaccharide units joined together (*e.g.*, lactose, sucrose).
Trisaccharides with three or more units (*e.g.*, raffinose).
Tetrasaccharides, etc.

The term *oligosaccharide* is a generic one used to describe a series of smaller monosaccharide units joined together with an upper limit of 12–15 in number. With higher numbers, the material is termed a *polysaccharide.*

In principle, monosaccharides can have varying numbers of carbon atoms in the molecule, and in common nomenclature, this is indicated in the name by adding the suffix *-ose, i.e.* a *triose* has three carbon atoms, a *tetraose* four carbon atoms, *etc.* By using the prefix *aldehydo-* or *keto-*, a distinction is made between those sugars which have a potential aldehyde group at one end of the chain, and those which have a ketone group in the structure. For example, glucose is an *aldehydohexose* whilst fructose is a *ketohexose.*

It will be seen below that in carbohydrates, whether they are simple sugars or complex polysaccharides, the sugar units normally exist in a ring with either six atoms, the *pyranose* form, or five atoms, the *furanose* form.*

It should be noted that monosaccharides and all oligosaccharides are materials which can be crystallised for purification, and hence have a characteristic melting point, optical rotation, *etc.* In contrast, this situation does not apply to polysaccharides which always occur in admixture with other biopolymers, and their isolation is difficult to achieve without concomitant degradation and often structural modification. No polysaccharide is a uniquely defined chemical substance.

2.2 MONOSACCHARIDES

Simple sugars are generally colourless crystalline solids with a sweet taste. Sweetness depends on the detailed stereochemistry of the molecule, and in this section the general problems of ring formation

*This nomenclature arises because sugars can be regarded as derivatives of pyrans and furans.

and the conformation and configuration of monosaccharides will be discussed in relation to the hexoses, glucose and fructose. All hexoses char or caramelise very readily on heating directly, and decompose extensively on heating in alkali.

2.2.1 Glucose

Glucose can exist as a linear molecule, the aldehydo form, or the pyranose and furanose forms in which one oxygen atom is incorporated into the ring. These three forms are shown in Fig. 2.1a. Here the rings are represented in the Haworth convention in which they are regarded as being quite flat with the hydrogen atoms and hydroxyl groups at right angles to the plane of the ring. As will be seen below, the actual *conformation* of the ring is now known, and this knowledge is of great importance in understanding the properties of monosaccharides: it is becoming of more importance in the field of polysaccharides.

Glucose, like any other sugar, exhibits optical activity and can exist as one of two optical isomers, the D- or L- forms*, examples of which are shown in Fig. 2.1b. (The particular pictorial representation used for the D-form results from the classical work of Fischer who evolved the system for sugar configurations based on D-glyceraldehyde.) The various carbon atoms in the sugar ring are numbered as shown in Fig. 2.1a, with the first carbon labelled 1, C(1), the next C(2), and so on round the ring. The hydroxyl group on C(1) is most reactive and accounts for the reducing properties of sugars. In addition, it can also take up two positions relative to the plane of the sugar ring. These two *anomeric* forms are known as the α- and β-sugars. For example, for D-glucopyranose, the two anomers shown in Fig. 2.1c exist, and each sugar can be crystallised and characterised.

In aqueous solution, D-glucose exhibits an equilibrium between the various isomers of this sugar. It is said to undergo *mutarotation* to give a mixture of the aldehydo form, α- and β-D-glucopyranose, and α- and β-D-glucofuranose. The proportions of each isomer will vary with the temperature.

The ring form in (say) α-D-glucopyranose is not planar and can exist theoretically in a number of alternative *conformations*, which relate one to another by rotation about bonds in the closed ring.

*In polysaccharides both D- and L- forms of sugars are found in contrast to the proteins, which are composed entirely of L-amino acids.

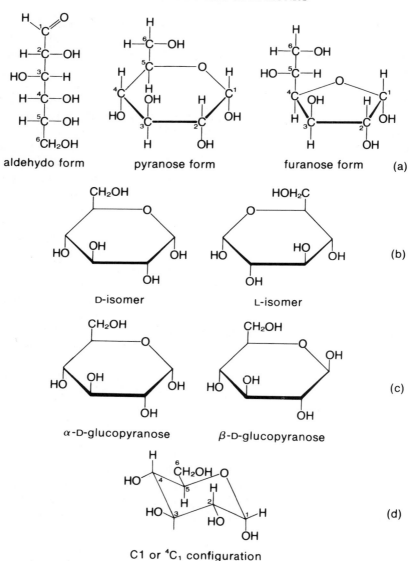

FIG. 2.1   The various structural forms of glucose. (a) The linear aldehydo form and the pyranose and furanose rings in the Haworth convention; (b) the optical isomers; (c) the anomeric forms; (d) the favoured ring conformation. In (b) and (c), some hydrogen atoms and ring carbon atoms have been omitted for clarity.

Indeed, to maintain the tetrahedral angle, the ring must be non-planar, and not flat as indicated in the Haworth formulae.

Various *chair* and *boat* conformations have been proposed, and in these the hydrogen atoms and hydroxyl groups become axial or equatorial to the ring. Recent work suggests that maximum stability, *i.e.* minimum interference between substituent axial and equatorial bonds, occurs in one of the chair conformations known as C1, or $^4C_1$, in a newer nomenclature.* This conformation is shown in Fig. 2.1d, and the internal energy is low enough to make interconnections to other conformations relatively unlikely. Qualitatively, this conclusion can be readily verified from three-dimensional scale models, and recent x-ray and spectroscopic work show that this conformation is present in the crystalline solid.

Similar conformations exist for the *furanose* form where the most likely stable form entails four ring atoms co-planar and one outside the plane. In the case of the five-numbered ring, however, the conversions of the different conformations appear to be easy.

The open chain form of glucose adopts a *planar zig-zag* conformation which is very flexible. Monosaccharides can be maintained in this conformation by reducing C(1) to the alcohol to form a sugar alcohol, *e.g.* glucose yields sorbitol.

α-D-Glucopyranose, or '*dextrose*' occurs widely in nature, and is present in honey and most fruits and berries, the amount in the latter varying with the species, maturity and state of preservation.

D-Glucose exists as a solid in three crystalline forms:

α-D-glucopyranose (anhydrous; m.p. = 146°C);
α-D-glucopyranose monohydrate (m.p. = 83°C); and
β-D-glucopyranose (anhydrous; m.p. = 150°C).

In aqueous solution and melts and glasses, D-glucose mutarotates to give a tautomeric mixture containing some 62% of the β-form. Commercially, this monosaccharide is produced from starch by enzymic degradation. An acid- or α-amylolytically- degraded starch suspension is converted completely into glucose by treatment with the enzyme *amyloglucosidase*. (This enzymic conversion is more efficient and eliminates the side reactions which occur on acid

*Here C represents the 'chair', conformation and the two numbers indicate ring atoms which appear above and below the best plane when the ring is viewed so that the numbering is clockwise from above.

degradation.) The liquid medium is then purified, evaporated, cooled, and crystallisation induced to form *α*-D-*glucopyranose monohydrate* or *dextrose hydrate*. *Anhydrous* D-*glucose* is obtained by evaporative crystallisation in a vacuum pan of the redissolved dextrose hydrate.

Dextrose finds many uses in the food industry on the basis of sweetness, osmotic pressure, body, flavour retention and enhancement ability, and moisture content. In the United States, large amounts of dextrose are used in the baking industry where not only does it function as a fermentable sugar, but it also improves the flavour, aroma, and colour of the bread crust due to Maillard-type reactions (see below). The beverage industry uses substantial quantities of dextrose to add sweetness and body, whilst these same properties are utilised in the canning industry. Dextrose is used in confectionery to control sweetness and softness, and to regulate crystallisation.

2.2.2 Fructose

D-Fructose (*β*-D-fructopyranose, or D-lævulose) occurs in vegetables, *e.g.* potatoes or onions, and is very widely distributed in fruit. Amounts of this sugar depend on the species, and its state of maturity and preservation. In honey, fructose accounts for one-half of the sugar present.

Commercially produced from glucose by an enzymic process, fructose is a white crystalline powder. It is the sweetest of all naturally-occurring sugars, being twice as sweet as glucose and 1·2–1·8 times that of sucrose. In water, pure fructose mutarotates to form a complex tautomeric mixture which includes *α*-D-fructopyranose, *β*-D-fructopyranose, *α*-D-fructofuranose, and *β*-D-fructofuranose (see Fig. 2.2). The proportions vary significantly with the temperature and pH. Furthermore, if a concentrated aqueous solution of D-fructose is heated, the sugar dehydrates and produces a series of crystalline, non-reducing, dimeric, dianhydrides.

2.2.3 Fructose–Glucose Syrups

A recent food development in the United States is to use the enzyme *glucose isomerase* to convert dextrose to fructose to form a mixture of approximately equal parts of these two sugars. This is similar to sucrose in sweetness but economically advantageous. (The mixture is

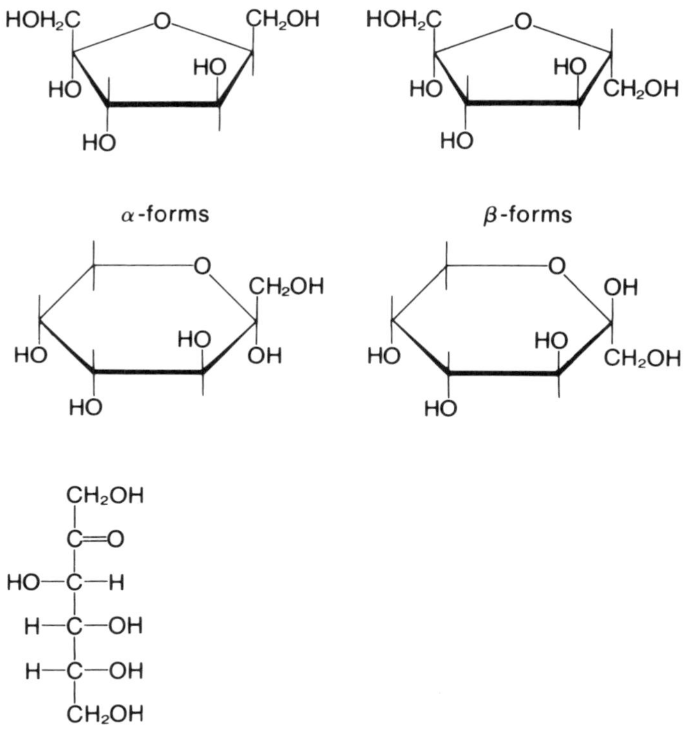

FIG. 2.2 Various structural forms of fructose.

sweeter than the normal glucose syrup.) The scheme of preparation is:

$$\text{starch} \rightarrow \text{dextrose} \xrightarrow[\text{glucose isomerase}]{} \text{D-glucose} + \text{D-fructose}$$

and the process utilises immobilised glucose isomerase on diethyl-aminoethyl-cellulose (DEAE-cellulose). Isomerisation of a purified glucose syrup is carried out to form about 42% fructose, conversion to higher levels requiring disproportionately greater amounts of enzyme per unit weight of fructose produced. The fructose–glucose syrup is refined before use with carbon and ion-exchange resins.

2.3 OLIGOSACCHARIDES

2.3.1 Introduction

Oligosaccharides are found free in all living matter. When present in relatively high concentration, their special properties and structure is of particular value to the living system, *e.g.* the presence of *sucrose* throughout all plant material, and the presence of *lactose* in mammary secretions. Many combined oligosaccharides occur in polysaccharides, *e.g. maltose*, a degradation product of starch.

2.3.2 Nomenclature

Consider joining together two glucose units to form a disaccharide. In the first instance, the units can be regarded as linking together by the elimination of water, for example, between C(1) of one sugar and C(4) of the next to form a $(1 \rightarrow 4)$ *glycosidic linkage*. However, the hydroxyl at C(1) can be either in the α- or β-configuration, and so an α-linked or β-linked disaccharide is formed as shown in Fig. 2.3, *i.e.* maltose or cellobiose. The systematic nomenclature for maltose is

$$4\text{-}O\text{-}\alpha\text{-}D\text{-glucopyranosyl-}D\text{-glucopyranose}$$

where '4' indicates substitution at C(4) of the glucose with a reducing group; 'O' indicates substitution of the oxygen at position 4; α shows the stereochemistry of the glycosidic linkage; and D is the chirality of the glucose units.

A simpler system is to use as symbols for sugar units, the first three letters of the name, *e.g.* Glu = glucose, Fru = fructose, together with 'p' for pyranose and 'f' for furanose. On this basis, maltose is 4-O-α-D-Glu p-D-Glu p.

All oligosaccharides will form crystalline compounds, and hence have characteristic melting points, solubilities and chromatographic characteristics. As with monosaccharides, mutarotation occurs in water because the anomer gives tautomeric forms. The pure compounds are odourless. Most oligosaccharides are sweet and are used for this purpose in food, although often their moisture-retention characteristics are of value.

2.3.3 Sucrose

Sucrose (β-D-fructofuranosyl-α-D-glucopyranoside, see Fig. 2.4a) occurs throughout plant material—seeds, leaves, fruits, roots, *etc.*— where it is the energy source for metabolic processes in the tissues.

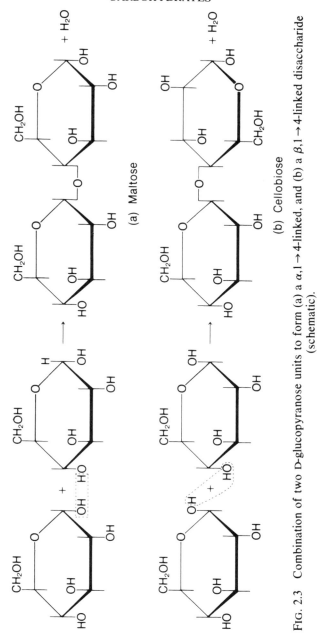

FIG. 2.3 Combination of two D-glucopyranose units to form (a) a α,1→4-linked, and (b) a β,1→4-linked disaccharide (schematic).

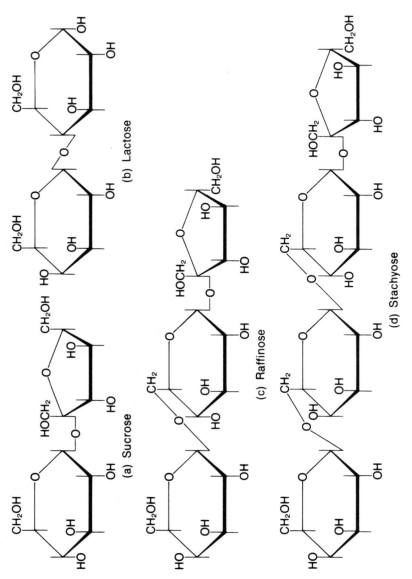

FIG. 2.4 Oligosaccharide structures.

Commercial sources are sugar cane (*Saccharum officinarum*) from which sucrose is obtained directly by evaporation and purification of the plant juice, and sugar beet (*Beta vulgaris*), from which the sucrose is extracted by hot water, and then crystallised after purification. Sucrose is used for both its sweetness and as a bulking agent, *e.g.* in confectionery.

2.3.4 Lactose

This disaccharide (4-O-β-D-galactopyranosyl-D-glucopyranose, see Fig. 2.4b) occurs to the extent of 5% in the milk of mammals. Commercially, it is obtained from whey (a by-product of cheese manufacture) by filtration and evaporative condensation followed by recrystallisation.

2.3.5 Raffinose and Stachyose

Raffinose (a triose) and stachyose (a tetraose) (see Fig. 2.4c/d) are widely distributed in plants where they occur in association with sucrose. The amount is, however, much lower, *e.g.* the concentration of raffinose in sugar beet is about 0·05%. Larger quantities of stachyose are found in lentils (*Ericum lens*) and soyabeans (*Soya max*), and are responsible for flatulence after ingestion.

2.3.6 Glucose Oligomers: 'Glucose Syrups'

'Glucose syrups' are considered in this section as they are mixtures of glucose oligomers produced by the degradation of starch by acid catalyst or by specific enzymes. Such a reaction carried out to completion, under optimum conditions, produces only glucose as described above. However, when stopped at an intermediate stage, a *glucose syrup* is formed which contains glucose and a series of glucose oligomers. These products have many uses in the food industry.

The extent of degradation is measured by the dextrose equivalent (D.E.), which may be expressed as:

$$\text{D.E.} = \frac{\text{Weight of reducing sugar expressed as dextrose}}{\text{Weight of total dry matter expressed as dextrose}} \times 100$$

This property of a hydrolysate is inadequate to describe a particular degradation product; a complete description of a material of intermediate D.E. must define the distribution of glucose oligomers within the product. Only when the D.E. = 0, *i.e.* when no degradation has occurred, as in unmodified starch, and when the D.E. = 100, *i.e.* conversion to glucose is complete, can the properties be defined unambiguously.

Glucose syrups are prepared commercially from a starch slurry, usually direct from the wet-milling plant. This slurry is first 'liquefied' by dispersing the starch granules into apparent solution and reducing the viscosity by high-temperature cooking with acid, prolonged treatment at a lower temperature with enzymes, or a combination of both methods.

In acid treatment, acidified starch suspension is heated at temperatures increasing to *ca.* 150°C. Product characteristics are controlled by regulation of the temperature and the amount of acid used during the reaction, but reaction to high D.E. values (*i.e.* hydrolysis to form sugars of low molecular weight) is not satisfactory, as recombination reactions occur reducing the ultimate yield of glucose, and secondary products are formed which produce undesirable tastes and colours in the finished syrup. High D.E. syrups may be produced, however, by treatment of a partially acid-degraded syrup with saccharifying enzymes, usually of a thermostable type. The nature of the final syrup may be modified at this stage, use of the appropriate amylase producing syrups rich in maltose, a readily-fermentable sugar.

The final purified product is either concentrated to the required solids' content for sale as a syrup, or dried to a solid. Many high D.E. syrups tend to crystallise when cooled, so they are stored and transported from factory to user at an elevated temperature.

End-product application directly governs the specific glucose-syrup properties to be used; the main types of syrup are:

Low D.E. glucose syrups (D.E. 10–35) which have a comparatively low content of small sugars and a high viscosity. Such syrups are ideal carriers for flavour, as the syrups themselves contribute little to the overall taste. They are used to provide cohesion and thickness to products where a sweet flavour is undesirable, *e.g.* a glucose syrup of D.E. ~ 34 may find use in the medium for canning vegetables.

Intermediate D.E. glucose syrups (D.E. 40–60) of two types are available. Normal syrups of D.E. ~ 42 are used extensively as modifiers of consistency and as a substitute for sucrose. In jellies and boiled sweets, the syrup acts as an effective impurity, preventing the formation of crystallites of sucrose, the cause of both opacity and undesirable texture in the product. Syrups in this D.E. range are also produced with high levels of fermentable sugars by an acid–enzyme conversion process for use in the brewing industry.

High D.E. glucose syrups (D.E. ~60) owe their most useful properties to the high levels of glucose and small sugars present. This characteristic is widely utilised in baked goods; both glucose and maltose are readily fermented by yeast to provide leavening; the water absorption of the product is increased because of the hygroscopic nature of this syrup; and attractive crust colours are developed by Maillard-type reactions. In jams, high D.E. glucose syrups provide a suitable osmotic pressure to inhibit growth of microorganisms and prevent sucrose crystallisation at a level of sweetness which does not obscure the fruit flavour.

2.4 SOME HEAT-DEPENDENT PROPERTIES OF MONO- AND OLIGOSACCHARIDES

The polyhydroxyl character of all sugars leads to extensive inter- and intra-hydrogen bonding. As a consequence of this phenomenon in the crystalline state, melting points are often high, whilst the sugars are very readily soluble in aqueous solution even at relatively low temperatures.

2.4.1 Sweetness

Many mono- and oligosaccharides exhibit the characteristic property of sweetness. Typical values related to sucrose as the standard are shown in Table 2.1. The actual stereochemistry of the sugar is seen to be all-important, and theories of sweetness on this basis have been proposed. Mutarotation effects account for the difference between the values for the crystalline solids and those for solutions, and also for the range in reported values. For example, the sweetest sugar is β-D-fructopyranose, but after mutarotation, solutions are only just slightly sweeter than sucrose. As the different tautomeric forms obviously affect observed organoleptic properties, sweetness is a temperature-dependent phenomenon, *i.e.* a fructose solution is 40% sweeter than sucrose at 5°C, equal to it at at 40°C, and is only 80% as sweet at 60°C.

TABLE 2.1
THE RELATIVE SWEETNESS (SUCROSE = 1·0)
OF MONO- AND OLIGOSACCHARIDES

	Sweetness	
Sugar	in solution	crystalline
β-D-Fru p	1·00–1·75	1·8
Sucrose	1·0	1·0
α-D-Glu p	0·4–0·8	0·7
β-D-Glu p		0·8
α-D-Man p	0·6	0·3
β-D-Man p	bitter	bitter
α-D-Lactose	0·2–0·4	0·2
β-D-Lactose	0·5	0·3
Raffinose	0·2	0·01
Stachyose		0·10
Glucose syrups	< 1·00	–
Glucose–fructose syrup	> 1·00	–

2.4.2 Dehydration

2.4.2.1 Introduction

When heat is applied to mono- and oligosaccharides, *browning* occurs. The extent of such browning depends on a variety of factors such as the temperature, concentration, and presence of other materials. In general terms, the browning reaction is one of dehydration in the first instance, leading to a further complex series of reactions and end-products. These are not, as yet, fully understood, although recent work has shed some light on some likely pathways and some frequently encountered intermediates.

The effect of heat on simple sugars has often been considered as falling into three categories:

(1) caramelisation;
(2) pyrolysis; and
(3) the Maillard reaction.

'*Caramel*' was originally made by 'burning sugar', and its formation was said to result from loss of water from the sugar molecule to give 'anhydro sugars', perhaps followed by further unknown reactions to give brown-coloured degradation and polymerisation products.

Pyrolysis implies *severe heating* of sugar molecules, which again results in brown colourations, carbon–carbon linkages probably being broken.

The *Maillard reaction* occurs when carbohydrates are heated in the presence of amines: again browning occurs, and this is usually to a greater extent than when carbohydrates are heated alone, or in the presence of acid or alkali.

It appears that there is a common thread to these three categories in that they are all examples of dehydration of the carbohydrate molecules, followed by further complex reactions.

It should be said that the brown colourations present in such heat-induced reactions do differ considerably, although the reasons for these differences are not understood. Some may be pH-sensitive, for example, in their u.v. spectra, others not; some may be fat-soluble, others not, and so on. There is a sizeable world-wide industry in the commercial production of such brown colourations. Caramels are commonly used in the food and drink industries to impart acceptable colours to products along, in some cases, with suitable flavours and aromas. Although originally (and still in some specialised cases, as, for example, the production of caramel toppings for desserts) produced from heating sugar alone, most caramels today are produced in the presence of ammonia in some form (sugar alone does not usually give colourations of sufficient intensity). Thus most commercial caramelisations are really Maillard reactions, and therefore 'facilitated' dehydration reactions initially.

2.4.2.2 *The Dehydration Reaction*

Several common intermediate compounds have been identified in the various reaction mixtures of carbohydrate dehydrations. Two of the most important compounds are

5-hydroxymethyl-2-furfuraldehyde
(I)

2-(2-hydroxyacetyl)-furan
(II)

For example, D-glucose can lose three moles of water under acidic

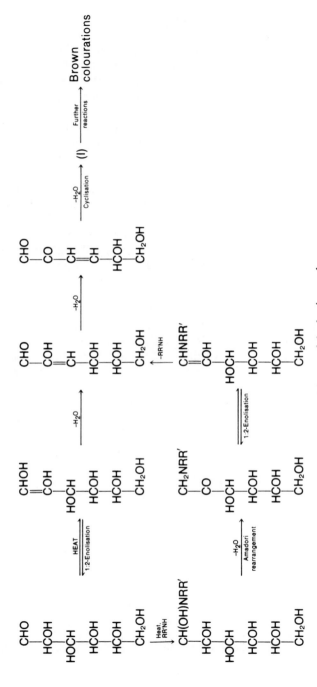

FIG. 2.5 D-Glucose dehydration pathways.

conditions of heating to yield (I), as it can also by heating with an amino compound. In both cases 1:2-enolisation is thought to take place (see Fig. 2.5).

Commonly occurring intermediates such as (I) and (II) are reactive, and clearly undergo a variety of further reactions to give the brown colourations. There is evidence of a build-up of such intermediates in these reactions, so that it is quite possible that some of the further stages may involve reactions of these available intermediates with even later reaction products to give quite large, coloured polymeric materials.

It should also be mentioned that the amino compound in the Maillard reaction does not fulfil a simple catalytic function: it is not usually recoverable in great yield. Thus, in the case of Maillard reaction in a foodstuff, protein damage can occur (see Section 2.4.2.5). 2:3-Enolisation can also take place, and it is thought that ketoses (which also exhibit browning on heating) and Amadori products form reactive intermediates through this mechanism. Thus, D-fructose forms (II), probably in the manner shown in Fig. 2.6.

Whilst 1:2-enolisation clearly contributes significantly to the

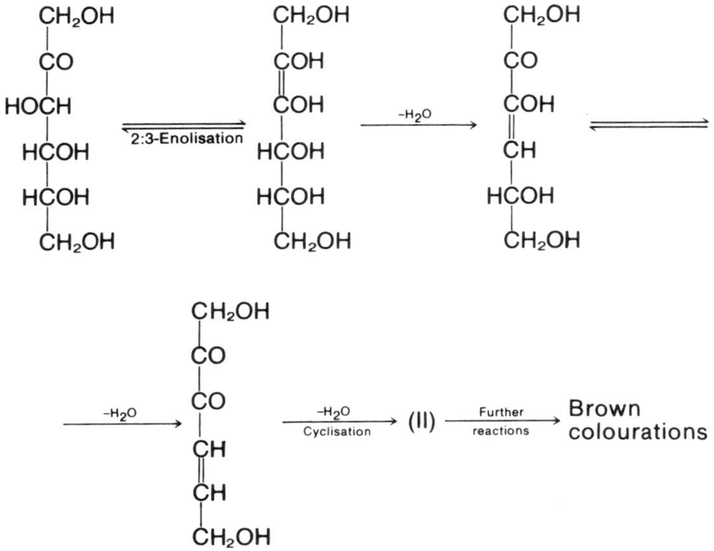

FIG.2.6   D-Fructose dehydration pathway.

development of browning, it is thought that 2:3-enolisation is mostly responsible for the formation of flavour and aroma compounds and their precursors. Thus, the 2:3-enolisation of D-fructose can also give rise to isomaltol (III) and its pyrone isomer, maltol (IV). These are components of bakery flavours.

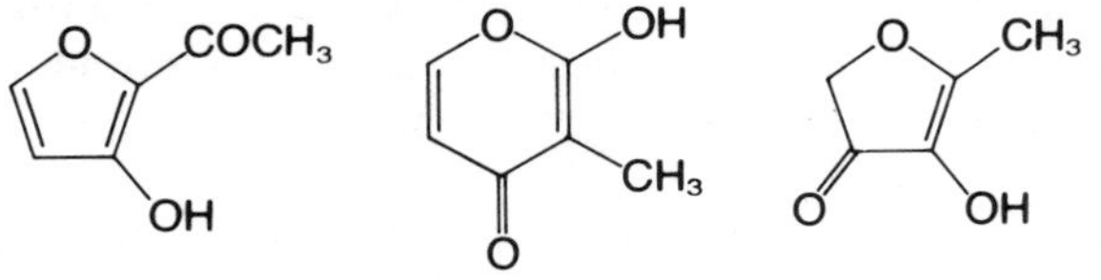

(III)   (IV)   (V)

Another well-known furan flavour component is 4-hydroxy-5-methyl-3(2H)-furanone (V), a principal component in cooked-beef flavour. This compound is formed when, for example, pentoses such as D-xylose or D-ribose are heated in aqueous solution in the presence of amino compounds, again almost certainly via 2:3-enolisation.

Browning also takes place when carbohydrates are heated under alkaline conditions. A variety of reactions can take place including, for example, the familiar 1:2-enolisation, but carbon–carbon bond damage must occur. With hexoses, for example, the 1:2-enol can give rise to glyceraldehyde and DL-lactic acid (Fig. 2.7):

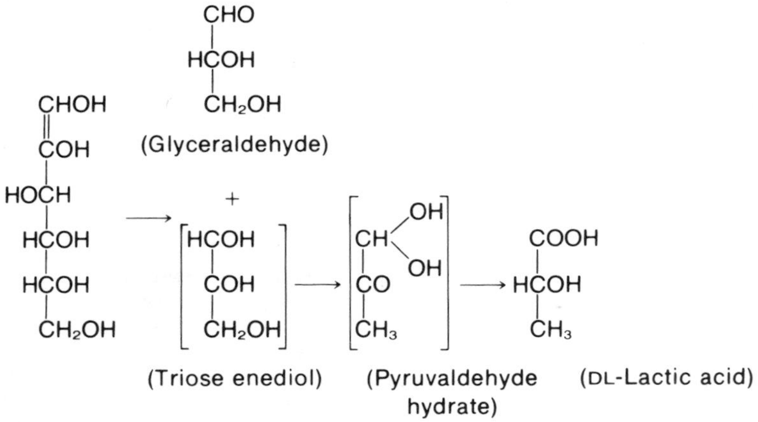

FIG. 2.7   Alkaline degradation of a hexose.

2.4.2.3 Factors Affecting the Reaction

The reaction and development of browning is dependent on a number of factors such as temperature, pH, concentration, water activity, oxygen supply, and the nature of the raw materials. The higher the temperature, the greater the extent of browning. The browning rate can quite commonly double or treble for a 10°C rise. The higher the pH, in general the faster the rate of browning. Casein–glucose browning rate, for example, is 10 times faster at pH 7 than at pH 3. Likewise, the storage stability of orange juice is better at lower pH values.

The reaction pathway can be much influenced by pH. It has been shown, for example, that a Maillard reaction of D-xylulose proceeds predominantly via 1:2-enolisation at pH 2 or less; 2:3-enolisation predominates at pH 2–7.

As would be expected, the higher the concentration of reactants, the greater the extent of reaction. Where, for example, the active concentration is higher, e.g. ingredients mixed as a wet paste and then freeze-dried, browning on heating is greater than where the ingredients have simply been mixed as powders.

Water activity can greatly affect the browning rate. Often there is an activity range over which browning proceeds optimally. Variation of relative humidity in the heated reaction of glucose with glycine, for example, shows a maximum browning in the equilibrium relative humidity (E.R.H.) region of 50–60%.

Oxygen supply is not vital for, but greatly facilitates the browning reaction. The nature of the raw materials is important, however, in that the brown-coloured end-products can be formed at different rates and with different properties. Suitable choice of carbohydrate, for instance, can determine late or early development of colour in a given process, fat- or water-solubility, and even pH-dependence of colour depth.

2.4.2.4 Inhibition of the Reaction

It has long been known that sulphites can inhibit or slow down the browning reactions, although how this happens is not yet understood. For example, the browning of glucose with glycine is inhibited, whilst that of ascorbic acid with glycine is slowed down. Further, the effects of adding sulphites once colour has developed are often quite different.

In commercial caramel production, sulphites are usually used to prevent mould growth on the end product: the reaction conditions commonly used, therefore, must take the inhibiting effect of the presence of sulphites into account.

In other areas of food production, inhibition of undesirable browning is achieved by consideration of some of the already described factors affecting browning. Thus, the storage stability of orange juice is much enhanced by having as low a pH as possible and by reducing oxygen supply to a minimum. The use of non-reducing sugars such as sucrose (and avoiding sugar inversion) in, and the removal of amino acids (where high nutritional quality is not important) from food formulations which are to be heated, are sometimes helpful in reducing browning.

2.4.2.5   *Damage to the Nutritional Value of the Food*
Whilst many dehydration or browning reactions in the preparation of a foodstuff are desirable, *e.g.* the production of desirable crust colour, aroma and flavour in the baking of a loaf of bread, such reactions can, especially when protein is present, damage the nutritional status of that product. When Maillard browning of a loaf of bread takes place, the lysine content can be reduced by 10–15%, this 'loss' occurring mainly through crust formation. Lysine and arginine, and to a lesser extent other amino acids such as tryptophan, cystine and histidine, are often 'lost' in such browning reactions.

There is also the possibility that browning reactions can give rise to toxic materials. It has been shown that the loss of important amino acids does not completely account for the loss of nutritional value of the food. Since our state of knowledge of the products of browning is at present imprecise, we can only conjecture as to what toxic materials, if any, are produced. Nevertheless, there is some concern in food legislation circles that the quantity and nature of caramels being used in food production should now be controlled.

2.4.2.6   *Commercial Caramels*
These are complex brown colouring materials derived from the heating of sugars, usually with ammonia, and often with sulphur dioxide and sodium hydroxide. Broadly, they fall into two categories, 'positive' and 'negative'*.

---

*These terms give an indication of the natural electrical charge of the caramel molecules at pH 2·5–6, the range of normal use of the caramel. The choice of suitable caramel for a particular food application depends on this charge and on the isoelectric point of the caramel, and its relation to the pH of the foodstuff. Clarity or cloudiness of drinks can, for example, result from suitable choice of the caramel used in their preparation.

'*Positive*' *caramels* are usually made by heating (by steam coil) high D.E. glucose syrups in a stainless-steel pan with ammonia liquor at atmospheric pressure. The pH of the reaction mixture falls to about 7 as the ammonia combines with the sugars. The mix is boiled, water is driven off, and the boiling point increases to about 130°C. Boiling is carried out until the required colour is reached, when the reaction is quenched with water. The pH of the caramel is typically 4–6 and the product is used for example, in beer.

'*Negative*' *caramels* are usually made in a steam-jacketted pressure kettle by boiling glucose syrups with a mixture of ammonia and sulphur dioxide, the pH of which has been adjusted with sodium hydroxide, at 40 p.s.i. and 140–150°C until the required colour is reached. The product is 'flashed off', cooled, and its pH adjusted to that required.

There is a third category of caramel, '*caustic soda* (or *spirit*) *caramel*'. This product is produced atmospherically from crystalline dextrose monohydrate which is dissolved in water, caustic soda solution added, and the caramel boiled and finished in a manner similar to that for 'positive' caramels. Its pH is about 4 and it is used in the production of spirits, where stability in high alcohol concentrations is required.

2.5 POLYSACCHARIDES

2.5.1 Introduction

This section outlines the essential structural features and the heat-dependent physicochemical behaviour of those polysaccharides which are of importance in foodstuffs. Polysaccharides occur in an infinite variety of different structural types which can be broadly classified for the purposes of this survey into *homopolysaccharides* and *heteropolysaccharides**.

Homopolysaccharides contain the same structural unit throughout,

---

*Another method of classification involves *periodic sequences* in which the sugar units are arranged in a pattern which repeats along the chain, for example, amylose and cellulose, *interrupted sequences* in which repeating sequences are separated, or interrupted, by departures from regularity, and *aperiodic sequences* which are characterised by irregular sequences of units, linkages and sometimes configurations.

for example, the glucans* (starch and glycogen), fructans, mannans, *etc.*, but these polymers can possess either simple linear structures, or branched structures of varying complexity with more than one type of inter-unit linkage.

Heteropolysaccharides contain two or more types of monomer units, for example, the arabinoxylans or glucomannans. Again, these biopolymers can be linear or branched to varying degrees, with different types of branch points.

Following the convention outlined above, the notation for indicating polysaccharide structure is exemplified for the two $(1 \rightarrow 4)$-linked D-glucose polymers as:

$$\rightarrow 4)\text{-}\alpha\text{-D-Glu } p \ (1 \rightarrow 4)\text{-}\alpha\text{-D-Glu } p \ (1 \rightarrow 4)\text{-}\alpha\text{-D-Glu } p \ (1 \rightarrow$$

and

$$\rightarrow 4)\text{-}\beta\text{-D-Glu } p \ (1 \rightarrow 4)\text{-}\beta\text{-D-Glu } p \ (1 \rightarrow 4)\text{-}\beta\text{-D-Glu } p \ (1 \rightarrow$$

Typical sugar units found in the polysaccharides which occur in food are shown in Table 2.2, whilst the parent biopolymers are classified as homo- and heteropolysaccharides in Tables 2.3 and 2.4.

Some of these polysaccharides are considered below, with an emphasis on starch.

2.5.2   Starch

2.5.2.1   *Introduction*
The importance of starch in food processing is based on the fact that this $\alpha,1 \rightarrow 4$-glucan provides a very high proportion of the world's food energy intake: over 80% of all food crops are composed of cereals and starchy-food crops. A vast amount of both academic and technologically-orientated work has been carried out on this biopolymer, but detailed knowledge of this material only advanced when it was realised that the starch granule was not chemically homogeneous and that a separation could be made into the simpler components, amylose and amylopectin. The basic problem in this subject is understanding the nature of the starch granule, particularly to determine its exact chemical composition and evaluate how the constituent polymers are organised to form the unique structural entity.

An inherent complication in this whole subject is that it is not

---

*The suffix *-ose* in the monosaccharide is changed to *-ans* to describe the corresponding polysaccharide.

TABLE 2.2

TYPICAL SUGAR UNITS FOUND IN POLYSACCHARIDES WHICH OCCUR IN FOOD

Name	Abbreviation	Name	Abbreviation
D-Fructose	Fru	D-Mannose	Man
D-Glucose	Glu	D-Mannuronic acid	ManA
D-Glucuronic acid	GluA	D-Xylose	Xyl
D-Galactose	Gal	L-Arabinose	Ara
D-Galacturonic acid	GalA	L-Rhamnose	Rha

TABLE 2.3

HOMOPOLYSACCHARIDES OCCURRING OR USED IN FOODSTUFFS

Type/Linkage	Structure	Polysaccharide	Occurrence
Glucans			
$\alpha,1 \rightarrow 4$-	linear	amylose	starchy materials
$\alpha,1 \rightarrow 4$-/$\alpha,1 \rightarrow 6$-	branched	amylopectin	starchy materials
		glycogen	animal liver
$\beta,1 \rightarrow 4$-	linear	cellulose	cell walls of all plants
$\beta,1 \rightarrow 3$-/$\beta,1 \rightarrow 4$-	linear	β-glucan	cereal grains (oats, barley)
Fructans			
$\beta,2 \rightarrow 6$-/$\beta,2 \rightarrow 1$-	branched	fructans	various plants (wheat endosperm)
$\beta,2 \rightarrow 1$-	linear	insulin	Jerusalem artichokes
Arabinans			
$\alpha,1 \rightarrow 3$/$\alpha,1 \rightarrow 5$-	branched	pectic substances	sugar beet, citrus pectins
Xylans			
$\beta,1 \rightarrow 4$-	linear	xylans	cell walls of plants

possible to make generalisations about starch. The starch granule possesses *individuality*, for not only is its external appearance sufficiently characteristic to allow its botanical source to be identified by optical microscopy, but each granule in a population may differ from its neighbours in both its fine structure and properties.

TABLE 2.4

HETEROPOLYSACCHARIDES OCCURRING OR USED IN FOODSTUFFS

Units*	Structure	Polysaccharides	Occurrence
Ara; Xyl	branched	arabinoxylans	plant cell walls (wheat flour)
GluA; Xyl	branched	glucuronoxylans	plant cell walls
Glu; Man	linear	glucomannans	seeds
Gal; Man	branched	guar/carob gum	leguminous seeds
GulA; ManA	linear	alginic acid	brown seaweeds
Gal sulphate: anhydro Gal	linear	carrageenan	brown seaweeds
GalA; Rha	linear	pectin materials	all plant material
Ara; Rha; Gal; GluA; Glu	branched	gum arabic	trees, *Acacia* spp.
GalA; Xyl; Gal; Fuc	branched	gum tragacanth	trees, *Astragalus* spp.

*Abbreviations follow the scheme in Table 2.2.

2.5.2.2   *The Starch Components*

In order to understand the architecture of the starch granule, it is necessary to evaluate the fine structure of the component polymeric material. Such fundamental studies entail (a) the isolation of the starch from plant tissues without any inadvertent modification, followed by (b) the separation and purification of the components by a non-degradative process. Methods of achieving these have now been developed, and it has been established that the starch granule is made up of at least three components—amylose, amylopectin, and intermediate material—the amounts of which vary from starch to starch.

Amylose is best described as being an essentially linear molecule in the sense that it is a mixture of completely linear chains of $\alpha,1 \rightarrow 4$-linked D-glucose units, together with molecules possessing a very limited amount of branching. The branch points appear to be $\alpha,1 \rightarrow 6$-linkages, and they occur only to the extent of one per several thousand glucose units. Undegraded amylose is a very large molecule with an average degree of polymerisation of many thousands.

Amylopectin is a highly ramified structure containing some 4–5% of $\alpha,1 \rightarrow 6$ branch points, which correspond to an average length of unit chain of 25–30 glucose units. Three model structures have been proposed for amylopectin: (a) the laminated structure of Haworth, which was the simplest consistent with methylation studies; (b) the 'herring-bone' structure of Staudinger in which one main chain carries all the branch linkages; and (c) the randomly branched structure of Meyer. Although, at first sight, all these models appear to be very different, there is a close relation which can be understood on the basis of the probability of growth. Indeed, by suitably altering the probabilities of growth of main- and side-chains, any structure between the above extreme models can be formed. Amylopectin is likely to be composed, in fact, of a variety of similar, but not identical, branched structures arising from variations in probabilities of the growth of side-chains—perhaps through steric factors occurring in biosynthesis. Unfortunately, our knowledge of the exact structure and physical size of amylopectin is limited, although measurements indicate it to be one of the largest molecules in nature, with a degree of polymerisation of many millions.

The amylopectin component from some starches—particularly those from roots and tubers—contains a small amount of ester phosphate bound to the C(6) position of the glucose ring. Although ranging in amount from only one ester group per 300–400 glucose residues, the substituent confers some degree of polyelectrolyte behaviour on the component when it is dispersed in aqueous solution. For example, the addition of salt will cause a decrease in the dimensions of the dissolved polymers.

The percentage of intermediate material varies from 5–10% in most cereal starches—although it is much higher in amylomaize—and its structure is currently not known, and may vary with the botanical source.

The apparent amylose content of a starch can vary considerably depending on the botanical species: it is not a well-defined quantity. Cereal starches typically contain, for example, around 25–28% of amylose, but in the so-called *waxy starches*, the amylose content is 0%. Conversely, there are varieties of maize, the *amylomaizes*, where the apparent amylose content ranges from 40–70%.

The molecular structure of the starch components is most easily investigated by studying the action of the specific, amylolytic enzymes α-amylase and β-amylase. β-Amylase hydrolyses alternate $\alpha,1 \to 4$ bonds sequentially from the non-reducing end of the polymer to yield maltose. In contrast, α-amylase randomly hydrolyses $\alpha,1 \to 4$ bonds within the molecular structure to yield ultimately a mixture of branched and linear glucose oligomers (see Fig. 2.8).

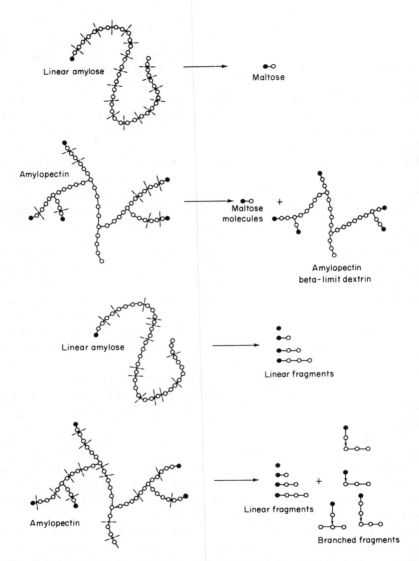

FIG. 2.8   Schematic representation of the action of α-amylase and β-amylase on amylose and amylopectin. O—O, Glucose units; ●, non-reducing chain end; ---- point of amylolytic attack.

The action of β-amylase on amylose and amylopectin is quite different, for this enzyme cannot by-pass $\alpha,1\rightarrow6$ branch points in a branched starch structure. Hence, whilst linear amylose is converted completely to maltose, amylopectin is only hydrolysed to within two or three glucose units of each of the $\alpha,1\rightarrow6$ branch points to yield maltose and a 'β-limit' dextrin of high molecular weight. The degree of conversion, *i.e.* the 'β-limit', readily differentiates between linear and branched material, and may be determined experimentally by estimation of the reducing power of a hydrolysate of the starch fraction after reaction with the enzyme.

2.5.2.3 The Starch Granule
Granule morphology
Starch granules vary in size from 2–100 μm and may be round, oval, or irregular in shape. In addition to the *simple type* of starch granule, in which a plastid gives rise to a single nucleus and consequently one granule, a second type of granule is also found. This is the *compound granule*, in the formation of which a plastid must contain several nuclei, with a consequent multipart granule and its characteristic morphology. In some cereals (*e.g.* wheat), the granule size distribution is bimodal.
Crystallinity and birefringence
Starch granules are *birefringent* in general, and show characteristic 'Maltese cross' patterns under the polarising microscope. They are also *crystalline* and exhibit an x-ray diffraction pattern. Different degrees of structural order are responsible for these properties. The fact that the starch granule is birefringent only implies that there is a high degree of molecular orientation within the granule without reference to any crystalline form. Indeed, not all granules exhibit any anisotropy. For example, many of the granules in high-amylose starch are non-birefringent.
Swelling and gelatinisation
Starch granules are insoluble in cold, but swell in warm, water. This swelling is reversible until at a certain temperature—the so-called 'gelatinisation temperature'—material is leached from the granule and structural order is irreversibly lost. Gelatinisation is one of the most important characteristics of starch when used in the food industry, and is dealt with in detail in Section 2.6.1.
Degradation by acids and enzymes
Starch granules are susceptible to degradation by mineral acids and

by certain enzymes, particularly those of the amylolytic type. The action of mineral acid on starch greatly reduces the viscosity of the resultant paste by hydrolysing the glycosidic bonds in the starch components in a random manner, and the resultant starch product has specialised uses in the food industry.

2.5.2.4   Commercial Native Starches

Sources of starch are cheap, readily-available, high starch-content plants from which the starch granules can be easily isolated and purified. For economic reasons, complete utilisation of the plant source is desirable, and by-products are often more important than the starch itself (e.g. wheat starch is a by-product of gluten manufacture).

There are two main sources of commercial starches, cereals, and roots and tubers. In cereals (e.g. maize, wheat and rice), the moisture content of the grain is low, and the starch granules are embedded in a hard, proteinaceous matrix which requires preliminary softening before starch extraction. Roots and tubers (e.g. potato and tapioca) have, in contrast, a much higher water content, and no preliminary softening process is required, for the starch granules are relatively loosely bound in the cellular plant structure.

2.5.2.5   Pre-Gelatinised Starches

In many food uses, a cold-water soluble starch is required. To achieve this objective, the granular structure of starch is destroyed by cooking, and the paste subsequently dried. On re-hydration, the starch readily forms a homogeneous viscous paste. Starch is cooked by either (i) heating to boiling point in a conventional vessel, or (ii) passage through a cooker in which a slurry of starch is pumped into a high-pressure steam jet. The granule is gelatinised and the structure disrupted in both cooking operations, resulting in a considerable reduction in the paste viscosity. The cooked paste may then be dried by spray drying or by drum drying.

2.5.2.6   Chemically Modified Starches

Starch esters and ethers can be synthesised with a complete range of physicochemical properties, particularly with regard to the heat stability of their paste, but use of such derivatives in food is restricted. Starch phosphates, which have a natural analogue in the branched fraction of potato starch, are suitable food additives. Two distinct classes of phosphate ester are produced: mono-starch esters and crosslinked phosphate esters.

The introduction of hydroxyalkyl substituents increases the solubility of starch and prevents molecular aggregation. In consequence, hydroxyalkyl starches (*e.g.* hydroxypropyl) gelatinise at lower temperatures than the parent starch, and pastes show little tendency to form gels or retrograde (see section 2.6.1.3). A range of product viscosity may be obtained by acid modification of a hydroxyalkyl starch, for the ether linkage of the substituent group is not cleaved by acid, and such products are used in foodstuffs.

2.5.3 Cellulose

Cellulose is a linear polymer of D-glucose units linked (1 → 4) in the β-configuration. It is, in fact, the most abundant polysaccharide in nature, since one-third of all higher plants consist of this biopolymer which functions as the main structural material.

The cellulose chains are unbranched, and may contain as many as 5000 glucose units. Because of the β-linkage, the glucose units in the chain alternate (see Fig. 2.9), and the molecule is effectively a rigid straight chain. As a result, cellulose molecules can readily align themselves side-by-side in an arrangement which is stabilised by intermolecular hydrogen bonding. Intermolecular bonding is so strong that cellulose is insoluble in water, and even in very strong sodium hydroxide. The cellulose molecules form fibres (microfibrils) of some 100-polymer chains. One theory is that these microfibrils are not structurally homogeneous, and consist of regions of crystalline micelles some 50–70 μm in width and about 60 μm in length, separated from each other by amorphous regions. In any case, the cellulose forms the effective framework for cells in the plant tissue, and the actual form of the plant is governed by the different ways in which the cellulose fibres are woven together. Other polysaccharides—the pectic substances and hemicelluloses—are laid down in the plant to cement the cellulose fibrils together.

In all foodstuffs prepared from plants, cellulose is responsible essentially for the form and gross texture. Being insoluble, it is little affected by any cooking process, and does not disperse. On ingestion, it is unaffected by enzymes in the digestive tract and does not hydrate.

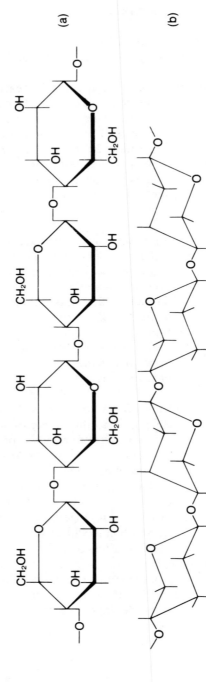

FIG. 2.9 The linear structure of the cellulose molecule shown in (a) the Haworth convention, and (b) in the most stable chair conformation.

2.5.4 Pectins, Gums and Mucilages

The *pectins* or *pectic substances* are found universally in the primary cell walls and intercellular layers in plants. They are most abundant in young tissue and are the characteristic constituent of fruits, *e.g.* citrus fruits contain 30% and fleshy roots such as sugar-beet pulp contain 25% pectin. The pectin content of lignified tissue is small. Pectic substances are a family of very closely associated polysaccharides which are, in fact, very difficult to separate. This term is used generally to refer to a group of substances in which D-galacturonic acid is the principal constituent, and the term 'pectin' is used in relation to water-soluble polysaccharides. The latter contain a high proportion of the D-galacturonic acid residues esterified as methyl esters, and they possess considerable gelling power. Galacturonans containing methyl groups are known as *pectinic acids*; those without such ester groups as *pectic acids*.

Although D-galacturonic acid is the main sugar constituent of pectic substances, other constituents include D-galactose, L-arabinose, D-xylose, L-rhamnose, and L-fucose. Three types of homopolysaccharides are also present—D-galacturonan, D-galactan, and L-arabinan—as well as heteropolysaccharides. Typical homopolysaccharide structures are: (1) for the *arabinan*, a chain of $(1 \to 5)$-linked arabinose units with side units of arabinose, *i.e.*

$$\to 5)\text{-}\alpha\text{-L-Ara } f \ (1 \to 5)\text{-}\alpha\text{-L-Ara } f \ (1 \to 5)\text{-}\alpha\text{-L-Ara } f \ (1 \to$$

$$
\begin{array}{ccc}
3 & & 3 \\
\uparrow & & \uparrow \\
1 & & 1 \\
\alpha\text{-L-Ara } f & & \alpha\text{-L-Ara } f
\end{array}
$$

(2) for the *galactans*, an essentially linear structure of $(1 \to 4)$-linked galactan units, *i.e.*

$$\to 4)\text{-}\beta\text{-D-Gal } p \ (1 \to 4)\text{-}\beta\text{-D-Gal } p \ (1 \to 4)\text{-}\beta\text{-D-Gal } p \ (1 \to$$

(3) for the *galacturonans*, an essentially linear chain of $(1 \to 4)$-linked galacturonic acid units, *i.e.*

$$\to 4)\text{-}\alpha\text{-D-GalA } p \ (1 \to 4)\text{-}\alpha\text{-D-GalA } p \ (1 \to 4)\text{-}\alpha\text{-D-GalA } p \ (1 \to$$

Typical heteropolysaccharides associated with pectic substances include the soyabean L-arabino-D-galactan represented by

→ 4)-β-D-Gal p (1 → 4)-β-D-Gal p (1 → 4)-β-D-Gal p (1 →

$$\overset{\displaystyle 3}{\underset{\displaystyle \underbrace{1}}{\uparrow}}$$

L-Ara f

$$\overset{\displaystyle 5}{\underset{\displaystyle \underbrace{1}}{\uparrow}}$$

L-Ara f

It is possible that the L-rhamnose is a constituent of many pectic acids where sequences of 4-O-substituted α-D-galacturonic acid residues are interrupted by sequences of the following type:

→ 4)-GalA p (1 → 2)-L-Rha p (1 → 4)-α-D-GalA p (1 → 4)-L-Rha p (1 →

Other neutral sugars may be attached as side chains to such a structure.

Plant gums, which may be formed spontaneously, or at the site of injury to the plant, are exuded as viscous fluids which become dehydrated to give hard, clear nodules consisting mainly of polysaccharides. Many such gums from tropical countries find uses in the food industry as thickening agents or emulsion stabilisers, *e.g.* gum arabic, gum tragacanth, gum ghatti, karaya gum, *etc.* These polysaccharides all possess complex highly-branched structures with D-glucuronic and/or D-galacturonic acids, together with two or more neutral sugars. The acidic residues are found naturally as salts, and some of the sugars are esterified with acetic acid.

As a group, the gums are probably the most complex of all natural polymers. Structural investigations are very difficult. Most likely, a gum is a group of closely related molecular species in which varying side-chains are attached to a main backbone. Figure 2.10 shows, as a typical example, the structural features for gum arabic. This polysaccharide has a branched backbone structure of galactose with a very wide variety of side groups.

Mucilages occur in many seeds, *e.g.* cereals, where it is probable that they function as reservoirs for the retention of water in the seed. Certainly, their hydration properties are of importance in foodstuffs, and many mucilages, *e.g.* guaran, or guar gum and carob gum, are used as thickening agents. Typical neutral polysaccharides of this

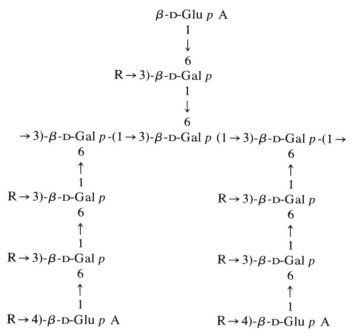

where R = L-Ara f-(1 → , L-Rha p-(1 → , α-D-Gal p-(1 → 3)-L-Ara f-(1 → , or, less frequently, β-L-Ara p-(1 → 3)-L-Ara f-(1 →

FIG. 2.10 The structure of gum arabic.

type are the D-galacto-D-mannans which occur in the seeds of leguminous plants, *e.g.* guar and carob. These polysaccharides consist of a backbone of (1 → 4)-linked β-D-mannopyranose units with single-unit side chains of α-D-galactopyranose at intervals, *i.e.*

$$\rightarrow 4)\text{-}\beta\text{-}\text{D-Man } p \text{ } (1 \rightarrow 4)\text{-}\beta\text{-}\text{D-Man } p \text{ } (1 \rightarrow 4)\text{-}\beta\text{-}\text{D-Man } p \text{ } (1 \rightarrow$$

```
         6                              6
         ↑                              ↑
         1                              1
    α-D-Gal p                       α-D-Gal p
```

The water-soluble polysaccharides of cereal endosperms—the 'cereal gums'—consist of linear β-D-glucans with (1 → 3)- and (1 → 4)-linkages, and highly branched L-arabino-D-xylans in which single

α-L-arabinofuranose residues are attached as random side chains to a $(1 \rightarrow 4)$-linked β-D-xylan backbone, *i.e.*

$\rightarrow$ 4)-β-D-Xyl p (1 $\rightarrow$ 4)-β-D-Xyl p (1 $\rightarrow$ 4)-β-D-Xyl p (1 $\rightarrow$ 4)-β-D-Xyl p (1 $\rightarrow$

3	3	3
↑	↑	↑
1	1	1
α-L-Ara f	α-L-Ara f	α-L-Ara f

2.5.5 Algal and Microbial Polysaccharides

Alginic acid is the most common algal polysaccharide. Found in brown seaweeds (*Laminaria* spp.), it is commonly used as a gelling and stabilising agent to improve the texture of products such as ice-cream, pie fillings and icings. This linear polysaccharide is composed of β-D-mannuronic acid and α-L-guluronic acid, both linked through the $(1 \rightarrow 4)$ positions. Evidence indicates that these monomer units do not occur randomly but are present in relatively long sequences of each type (see Fig. 2.11).

Another group of seaweed polysaccharides are the *carrageenans*, which are found in various species of red seaweeds (*Rhodophyseae* spp.). These polysaccharides have been used traditionally in foods for centuries, and have the ability, even when used at very low concentrations, to modify rheological properties, and are used as gelling agents, thickeners and stabilisers.

The term carrageenan covers a range of sulphated galactans which are linked alternatively by $(1 \rightarrow 3)$ and $(1 \rightarrow 4)$ glycosidic bonds. Recent work has shown that the carrageenans can be fractionated into six types which vary depending on the degree and manner of sulphation, and the presence or absence of 3:6-anhydrogalactose units. These types—lambda, kappa, iota, mu, nu, and theta—are shown in Fig. 2.12, and some may be chemically interconverted by treatment with alkali.

In practice, the various fractions do not occur together but different species of red seaweed contain essentially *one* structural type of polysaccharide, and the most important forms (lambda, kappa and iota) are prepared commercially on this basis. Evidence indicates that the polysaccharides have a high molecular weight in the range of 100 000 to 1 000 000, and they are regarded as being non-absorbable in the digestive tract of man.

The solubility properties of these polysaccharides depend on the

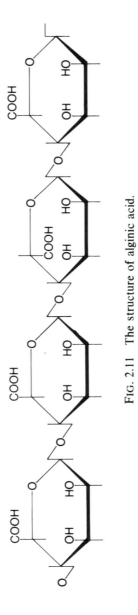

FIG. 2.11   The structure of alginic acid.

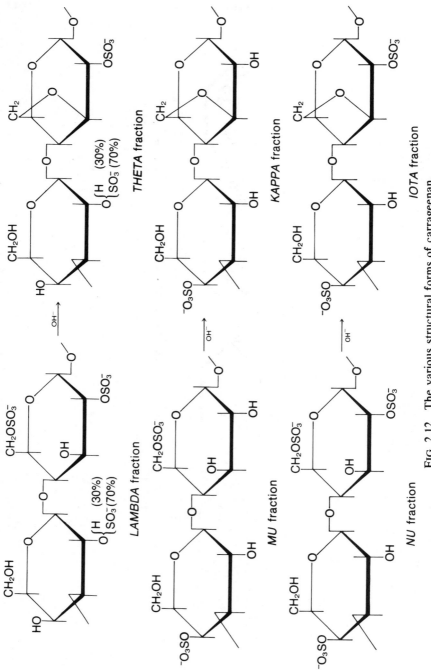

FIG. 2.12 The various structural forms of carrageenan.

proportion of sulphate groups, the nature of the cations associated with them, and the proportion of 3:6-anhydrogalactose residues— the latter being relatively hydrophobic. For example, the *lambda* fraction is easily soluble in water because of the high proportion of sulphate groups and the absence of anhydrogalactose, and is unaffected by the nature of the cations present. The *kappa* fraction contains a lower proportion of sulphate groups and some anhydro-galactose units, and as a result is only soluble in water in the form of the sodium salt. Other cations (K^+, Ca^{2+}) only allow swelling in cold water, and heating to 60°C is necessary to ensure solubilisation. Iota-carrageenan has an intermediate structure and properties.

Because of the presence of the strongly charged anionic sulphate groups, the carrageenans as a group are able to form a complex not only with cationic materials but also with amphoteric substances such as proteins. This unique property of carrageenan extracts can be utilised for example as a stabiliser for condensed milk.

One bacterial polysaccharide which can be used as a gelling agent in food is *xanthan gum* produced by *Xanthomonas campestris*. This heteropolysaccharide is composed of D-glucose (2·8 mole), D-mannose (2 mole) and D-glucuronic acid (2 mole). The xanthan gum backbone is identical to that of cellulose, but alternate an-hydroglucose units carry at the 3-position a trisaccharide branch consisting of a glucuronic acid residue between two mannose units.

The polysaccharide is complex, for the non-terminal mannose unit is acetylated at position 6, and about half the terminal mannose units carry a 4→6-linked pyruvate ketal group.

It is thought that the trisaccharide stubs are closely aligned to the glucan backbone—a conformation which is stabilised by hydrogen bonding—and it has been suggested that, in the native state, the essentially linear polymers exist as a two-stranded double helix. Such a rigid structure would account for the stability of xanthan gum to changes in ionic strength, pH and heat. In turn, these characteristics enable the gum to stabilise suspensions and provide body and mouth-feel to food products such as salad dressings, frozen foods, bakery fillings, sauces and gravies.

Xanthan gum also has the property of interacting strongly with galactomannans, *e.g.* locust bean gum, to form more viscous solutions at low concentrations or more viscoelastic gels at high concentrations than with either component alone. This property is made use of in the US in ice cream, cream cheese, and cottage cheese.

2.6   SOME HEAT-DEPENDENT PROPERTIES OF POLYSACCHARIDES

2.6.1   Starch in Food Processing

Textural qualities which arise from the presence of starch in any foodstuff result from changes which occur in the biopolymer during, or after, heating. The general changes which occur are outlined below, but as has been stressed above, every type of starch possesses its own characteristic properties. Consequently, the temperature–behaviour profile will depend on the species from which it is derived, the extent of any damage incurred by the granule, and the presence and interaction with other components present.

2.6.1.1   *Gelatinisation Temperature*

Although individual starch granules gelatinise over a range of $\sim 2°C$ and a typical sample of starch over a range of 4–10°C, certain general phenomena are observed. It is apparent that waxy varieties of starch gelatinise at temperatures not very different from those for their normal counterparts, and that starches of high amylose content have a significantly higher gelatinisation temperature range. As amylose content, gelatinisation and, presumably, intermolecular bonding increase, the intensity of the birefringence patterns diminishes. The relation between the properties of starch in granular form and the component properties is not yet fully understood.

The gelatinisation temperature is markedly altered by any physical or chemical modification which affects the strong intermolecular bonds in the granule's structure. For example, pregelatinised starches swell and disperse in cold water; granules which have been 'damaged' in the milling of cereals swell in cold water; the introduction of substituent groupings usually causes a marked reduction in the gelatinisation temperature, whilst a 'heat-moisture' treatment will cause an increase.

In food manufacture, the gelation properties of the starch present can be modified by interactions with other materials in the system. Starch interactions of this type are obviously of great practical importance, but are not fully understood.

Sucrose reduces the tendency of starch to swell in hot water and so increases the gelatinisation temperature. The effect of heating starch pastes in the presence of *salts* is complicated, but it is generally accepted that if starch is exposed to a series of anions (all having the same cation), the resultant changes in the gelatinisation temperature will occur in the same order as the anions occur in the Hofmeister lyotropic series. The salt concentration determines whether the gelatinisation temperature is raised (low concentration) or decreased (high concentration). Salt effects are more complex in the case of starches such as potato which contain phosphate groups.

The presence of *fat* or *surfactants* usually causes an increase in gelatinisation temperature which has been attributed to complex formation with the amylose.

Starch–protein interactions occur and affect the gelatinisation behaviour of a starch, for example in the batter stage and subsequent heating in cake production, but such phenomena are little understood.

2.6.1.2 *Paste Viscosity and Viscoelasticity*

The most desired textural quality when starch is incorporated into a food product is viscosity, and the commercial application of a starch is usually determined by its response to cooking in water. The maximum viscosity reached by a starch paste on heating determines the concentration at which it may be easily handled, and the subsequent behaviour on cooking determines the usefulness of the paste or gel. For example, it may be desirable to have certain gel characteristics, or a resistance to retrogradation (see section 2.6.1.3). The paste properties of starch, when subjected to a cooking cycle, yield much valuable information on the projected use of a starch.

A convenient measurement of the inherent paste viscosity and its subsequent behaviour on cooling is obtained by subjecting the starch to a cooking cycle in the Brabender amylograph. The following temperature programme is convenient: 1, start at 50°C; 2, heat at a rate of 1·5°C per minute until a temperature of 95°C is attained; 3, hold for 1 h at 95°C; 4, cool at a rate of 1·5°C per minute until a temperature of 50°C is attained; 5, hold at 50°C for 1 h.

The resultant amylograph gives quantitative values for: (a) the *peak viscosity*, the maximum viscosity achieved on heating the suspension; (b) the extent of breakdown of the paste structure on prolonged stirring at elevated temperature, *i.e.* its resistance to shear; and (c) the amount of setback, or the development of aggregated structures on cooling.

2.6.1.3 *Aggregation Phenomena*

On cooling an aqueous dispersion of starch, various molecular-aggregation phenomena can occur. *Amylose*, because of its essentially linear structure, may readily aggregate, the resulting structure depending on the rate of cooling. On rapid cooling, aggregates form in a haphazard way throughout the solution wherever segments of two or more molecules overlap in a sterically suitable manner. A gel network held together by small aggregated regions results, in which large quantities of solvent are entrapped between areas of disordered polymer molecules. If, however, the solution is cooled slowly, the polymer molecules may align themselves to form large, partly crystalline regions which exclude solvent as they grow, resulting in an essentially two-phase system of solid material and excluded solvent: this phenomenon is known as 'retrogradation' (see Fig. 2.13). The branch points in amylopectin inhibit molecular-aggregation phenomena. However, under certain conditions, such as alternate freezing and thawing of a concentrated solution, molecular aggregations do occur in amylopectin pastes.

The optical properties of a starch gel or paste depend on the size of such molecular aggregates. If, as is the case for normal maize starches, these aggregates are larger than the wavelength of light, i.e. 250 nm, then they will scatter light, and the gel or paste will appear opaque. The scattering bodies in, for example, waxy maize pastes, are, in contrast, smaller than the wavelength of light, and hence these pastes are translucent. Freezing and subsequent thawing of this paste, however, will induce retrogradation, with the subsequent formation of larger scattering bodies, which then render the paste opaque.

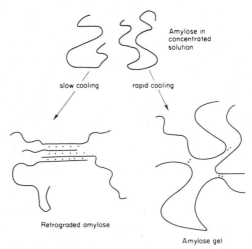

FIG. 2.13   Aggregation phenomena for amylose in solution.

2.6.1.4 *Dehydration*

When starch is heated, a series of dehydration reactions takes place, similar to those described above for mono- and oligosaccharides, and a brown solid is formed. α-1:6-Anhydroglucopyranose can be prepared by the pyrolysis of starch, and this dehydration and degradative reaction is accompanied by the formation of smaller degradation products such as carbon dioxide, carbon monoxide, furans, ketones, alcohols and aldehydes.

2.6.2 Gelation Phenomena

When a solid polymer is placed in contact with a limited amount of solvent, the first stage of the interaction is solvation of the material to form a *gel* before—in the presence of excess solvent—the gel disperses to form a *sol*. Polysaccharides, as biopolymers, are no exception, and the sequence

$$\text{polysaccharide} \rightleftarrows \text{gel} \rightleftarrows \text{sol}$$

is typical. This sol–gel transformation is reversible and is temperature dependent; generally a rise in temperature favours the formation of a sol. The essential feature of a gel is the formation of some type of three-dimensional, continuous structure (which resists the flow of liquid) through the formation of junction points which can vary from chemical crosslinks to hydrogen bonding (see Fig. 2.14a). If the crosslinkages are not chemical, then the formation of the gel structure depends upon the concentration as well as the temperature.

The formation of a starch gel has been discussed in the previous section in terms of hydrogen-bonding forces occurring to form 'junctions' between discrete parts of the starch molecule.

In the case of acidic polysaccharides such as alginic acid, the junction zones are likely to involve cations such as Ca^{2+} in 'calcium bridges'. It has been suggested that the regions of polygulonic acid or polygalacturonic acid in the polymer chain can adopt a zig-zag shape which is capable of coordinating the calcium ion (see Fig. 2.14b) in a precise stereochemical way.

Gels formed from alginate show considerable resistance to heat, but any breakdown is irreversible, presumably because the probability of reforming such well-coordinated junctions is limited.

For other seaweed polysaccharides, such as carrageenan, evidence is accumulating that the junction zones are regions where the randomly shaped polymer molecule converts to the helical state, and two helices or pairs of helices interact together (see Fig. 2.14c). Gels

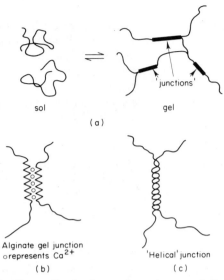

sol   gel

(a)

Alginate gel junction
o represents Ca^{2+}

(b)

'Helical' junction

(c)

FIG. 2.14   Generalised scheme for gel network formation.

of this type are melted by heating but reform on cooling—as do those of starch and pectin.

In the case of carrageenan, the characteristics of the gel depend on the fraction type (*i.e.* kappa gives strong rigid gels, iota gives weak elastic gels), the concentration (above a certain minimum concentration, the gel strength increases with concentration), the cations in solution (*i.e.* for kappa, Ca^{2+} forms a stronger gel than K^+), the pH and the temperature.

BIBLIOGRAPHY

Aspinall, G. O. (1970) *The Polysaccharides.* Oxford: Pergamon Press.

Banks, W. and Greenwood, C. T. (1975) *Starch and its Components.* Edinburgh: Edinburgh University Press.

Guthrie, R. D. & Honeyman, J. (1968) *Introduction to Carbohydrate Chemistry,* 3rd. edn. Oxford: Oxford University Press.

Pigman, W. & Horton, D. (eds.) (1970) *The Carbohydrates,* Vols. 1A, 1B, 2A and 2B. New York: Academic Press.

Rees, D. A. (1977) *Polysaccharide Shapes.* London: Chapman and Hall.

Whistler, R. L. & BeMiller, J. N. (eds.) (1959) *Industrial Gums.* New York: Academic Press.

CHAPTER 3

Pigments

M. L. WOOLFE

University of Strathclyde, Glasgow, Scotland*

The colour of foods has a great influence on their acceptability. Hence much research has been directed towards the identification and behaviour of food pigments. Investigations into the fate of pigments in food during processing have been made since modern food preservation began, yet our knowledge of these colour changes is still somewhat scanty. This is understandable when one considers how complex a phenomenon the colour and appearance of foods can be. A considerable proportion of these attributes certainly arises from the absorption of visible light by the pigments present in food. However, the pigments are themselves large organic molecules, which, although restricted to a relatively small number of chemical groups, can vary within each group in their chemical stability and susceptibility to heat processing. The occurrence of mixtures of pigments further complicates the situation by affecting their spectral properties; co-pigments and metal ions can also have marked effects.

The strength of colour is affected not only by the actual concentration of pigments, but also by the physical structure of the food and the way in which light is scattered from its surface. Heating can alter the physical structure, resulting in a brightening of colour as noticed, for example, when green vegetables are first brought to the boil. Pigments are not usually free and mobile, but are confined in the foodstuff within a physical system such as a membrane. Complexing of the pigment with other biological constituents will slightly modify its colour; heat processing will alter the complex and in turn affect the chemical changes which subsequently take place. Considering the intricacy of these interdependent reactions, it is not surprising to note that much of our present knowledge of pigment changes is derived

*Present address: Instituto de Nutrição, Universidade Federal de Pernambuco, C. P. 299, 50.000 Recife (PE), Brazil.

from studies on isolated pigments or model systems. The results of such studies may only account for some of the changes which are actually taking place in the food.

Pigment changes are generally undesirable, except in most flesh foods where the changes have become acceptable and desirable indicators of heat processing. Food processors attempt to minimise any undesirable changes which occur but, to satisfy the consumer, often have to disguise such changes which do occur by the use of more heat-stable synthetic food dyes.

One other major factor which must be borne in mind when considering colour changes during a heat process is the Maillard reaction, with its resulting brown-pigment formation. This directly affects the colour, and intermediate reaction products can accelerate chemical changes in the pigments. Since discussion of the Maillard reaction is covered elsewhere, this chapter will confine itself to changes in pre-existing food pigments.

3.1   TYPES OF FOOD PIGMENTS

Individual commodities are dealt with in other chapters and the discussion which follows is intended merely as background information.

It is usual to divide food pigments into three major groups and a fourth minor group (Mackinney and Little, 1962). The distribution of these groups in foods is summarised in Table 3.1. Many foods contain mixtures of groups of pigments, but usually the colour is derived from the contribution of one major group of pigments.

Tetrapyrroles are divided into two groups: the haems, which give the red colour to meat; and the chlorophylls, the green colour of leaves. Carotenoids are a large family of compounds, ranging from pale yellow to deep red. The anthocyanins are the only coloured compounds of the flavonoid family and range from red to blue.

3.2   COLOUR AND CHEMICAL STRUCTURE

Before examining the effects of heat processing on food pigments, it is useful to recall the fundamental relationship between colour and chemical structure. The understanding of this relationship helps to

TABLE 3.1
DISTRIBUTION OF PIGMENTS IN FOODS

1. *Tetrapyrroles*		2. *Carotenoids*	3. *Flavonoids*		4. *Betalains*
Haems	*Chlorophylls*		*Anthocyanins*	*Others*	
meat and fish	green vegetables and fruit	eggs, cereals, dairy products fruit, root vegetables, crustaceans and fish	fruits and root vegetables	root vegetables	beetroot

correlate the chemical changes taking place with the colour changes observed by the consumer.

Foods appear coloured because the pigments they contain absorb part of the white light falling on them and reflect or transmit the remainder (complementary colour). The human eye responds to a narrow region of the electromagnetic spectrum (400–750 nm), each colour corresponding to a range of wavelengths within this region as indicated in Table 3.2. The human eye is not equally sensitive to all colours, but has maximum sensitivity around the yellow–green region. Thus, a spectral shift in wavelength as small as 1·25 nm in this region is detectable by the human eye and will manifest itself as a change of colour (Murrell, 1971).

Of the naturally occurring organic compounds, only a small number have the ability to absorb strongly in the visible region and so act as pigments. Absorption of ultraviolet and visible light involves changes in the electronic distribution within molecules. Excitation of electrons from a ground-state orbital to an excited-state orbital requires large amounts of energy, up to $12\,560\,\text{kJ}\cdot\text{mol}^{-1}$, hence only the outer less strongly held electrons are involved in this process.

The molecular orbital transitions which are likely to be responsible

TABLE 3.2

THE COLOUR AND COMPLEMENTARY COLOUR OF ABSORBED LIGHT IN THE VISIBLE REGION (FROM MACLEOD, 1973)

Approximate wavelength region (nm)	Absorbed colour	Complementary colour
380–450	violet	yellow–green
450–480	blue	yellow
480–490	green–blue	orange
490–500	blue–green	red
500–530	green	red–purple
530–570	yellow–green	purple
570–575	green–yellow	violet
575–580	yellow	blue
580–590	yellow–orange	blue
590–595	orange	green–blue
595–620	red–orange	blue–green
620–780	red	blue–green

for electronic spectra of organic molecules are summarised in Table 3.3. Of the various possibilities indicated, only two have low enough energies to qualify as candidates for absorption in the visible region: these are $\pi \rightarrow \pi^*$ and $n \rightarrow \pi^*$ transitions. The remainder involve high-energy transitions and correspond only to absorption in the ultraviolet region.

There are certain selection rules which govern whether a particular transition is allowed. These are based on the compatibility of the symmetry of the bonding and anti-bonding orbitals. These rules in fact govern the intensity of absorption and are not strict when applied to large unsaturated molecules. Hence, a forbidden transition can still take place, but will be observed as having only weak intensity.

In order to achieve absorption in the visible region, the energy difference between the ground and excited states must be of the order of 146–293 kJ·mol^{-1}. The only way of reducing the energy difference to this low range is to have a large π-bonding system, where electrons are extensively delocalised along the molecule, *i.e.* a conjugated system. This can be illustrated by a series of α,β-unsaturated

TABLE 3.3

SUMMARY OF ORBITALS INVOLVED IN EXCITATION OF ELECTRONS IN ORGANIC MOLECULES, AND ELECTRONIC TRANSITIONS WITH THE CORRESPONDING ABSORPTION REGION

	Orbital	Symbol
Excited state	Anti-bonding single-bonding orbitals	σ^*
	Anti-bonding double-bonding orbitals	π^*
Energy	Non-bonding orbitals	n
	Double-bonding orbitals	π
Ground state	Single-bonding orbitals	σ

Electronic transition	Region of spectrum
(1) $\sigma \rightarrow \sigma^*$	Far u.v., *e.g.* methane, 125 nm.
(2) $\pi \rightarrow \pi^*$	U.v. and visible (if extensively delocalised), *e.g.* benzene, 203 nm.
(3) $n \rightarrow \pi^*$	U.v. and visible, low intensity, since symmetry-forbidden transition, *e.g.* acetone, 277 nm.
(4) $n \rightarrow \sigma^*$	Far u.v. and near u.v., *e.g.* methylamine, 213 nm.

aldehydes (Fig. 3.1). As there are non-bonding electrons on the carbonyl oxygen, both $\pi \to \pi^*$ transitions and $n \to \pi^*$ transitions can occur. The $n \to \pi^*$ transitions usually occur at longer wavelengths than $\pi \to \pi^*$ transitions but, since they are symmetry-forbidden, they are usually of much lower intensity (10–100 times lower). Thus two absorption maxima can be seen for the lower members of the series, corresponding to the two transitions (Fig. 3.1). As the number of double bonds increases, the n-orbital, being localised, remains independent of size, whereas the π-orbital is substantially lowered in

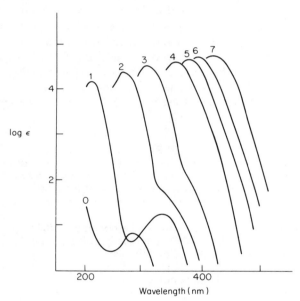

FIG. 3.1   Absorption spectra of a series of α,β-unsaturated aldehydes, $CH_3(CH{=}CH)_n CHO$

n	Colour
0	Colourless
1	Colourless
2	Colourless
3	Pale yellow
4	Yellow
5	Golden yellow
6	Red–orange
7	Deep red

energy due to the increased delocalisation of the π-electrons. The result is that the $\pi \rightarrow \pi^*$ transitions are shifted to longer wavelengths and swamp the less intense $n \rightarrow \pi^*$ transitions (Murrell, 1971). When there are four or more conjugated double bonds the molecule appears coloured. In discussing the transitions occurring in food pigments, it is the $\pi \rightarrow \pi^*$ transitions which are responsible for the intense absorptions in the visible region. The $n \rightarrow \pi^*$ transitions are responsible for producing weak colours in many organic compounds such as $\beta-\gamma$ unsaturated ketones, quinones, and some azobenzenes (Griffiths, 1976).

Figure 3.1 also illustrates another important feature of electronic spectra, namely, that absorption usually occurs as broad bands rather than sharp peaks. A large molecule has many vibrational and rotational energy levels, which are superimposed on any one electron energy level (Fig. 3.2). Electronic transitions are very rapid compared with the more sluggish vibrational and rotational movements in the molecule. Hence the position of the nuclei in the molecule remains unchanged during the period of electron excitation, a phenomenon which is referred to as the *Franck–Condon Principle* (Moore, 1963). Transitions take place not only between one electron energy level and another, but from one particular vibrational and rotational level in the ground state to a specific one in the excited state. A population of molecules will have a spread of vibrational and rotational energy in the ground state, which is governed by Boltzmann's distribution law;

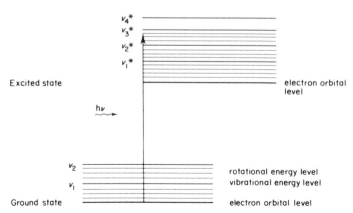

FIG. 3.2   Excitation of electron from ground to excited state with superimposition of vibrational and rotational energy levels.

therefore excitation of electrons will occur as an envelope around a maximum absorption (λ_{max}).

The interpretation of electronic spectra in terms of the molecular orbital theory has been one of the most exciting and difficult challenges to physical chemists. With the aid of computers, great advances have been made in recent years. Although the Quantum Theory enables molecular orbitals to be calculated in general terms, exact calculations of molecular orbitals, even for simple diatomic molecules, are extremely difficult. Examination of large conjugated molecules in terms of molecular orbital theory is almost impossible without the introduction of empirical approximations. Thus, only determination of the highest occupied (ground-state) and lowest vacant (excited-state) molecular orbitals are necessary for their correlation with transitions in electronic spectra. Two main approaches have been used. The first method attempts to calculate the molecular orbital by examining the motion of a free electron in the molecule as a series of stationary waves. Because of the fundamental approximations involved, this method is severely limited and only gives good agreement with experimental data if the bond lengths in a molecule are all equal. Linear combination of individual atomic orbitals to produce molecular orbitals is the other approach. There have been several methods developed to calculate the linear combination of atomic orbitals, all requiring the use of approximations and assumptions. One such method, which has been found suitable for calculating the ground states of large, conjugated molecules, was developed independently by Pople (1953) and Pariser and Parr (1953), and attempts to take some electronic interaction into consideration. Examination of these empirical methods in more detail is beyond the scope of this chapter and more specialised treatments should be consulted (Murrell, 1971; Griffiths, 1976; Jaffé and Orchin, 1962; Rao, 1975; Pople and Beveridge, 1970).

Certain terms will be used in the text which require explanation. The colour-producing system of a molecule is called a 'chromogen'. This is composed of conjugated, unsaturated functional groups known as chromophores, *e.g.* in Fig. 3.1, double bonds and the carbonyl group. The intensity and maximum absorption (λ_{max}) can be altered by addition of electron-donating or withdrawing groups, formerly termed 'auxochromes', which are not themselves coloured. A displacement to a longer wavelength is termed a *bathochromic shift* and to a shorter wavelength a *hypsochromic shift*.

3.3 ABSORPTION SPECTRA OF FOOD PIGMENTS

3.3.1 Carotenoids

These have a similar chromogen to the unsaturated aldehydes, namely, a long-chain conjugated polyene. Carotenes are hydrocarbons built from isoprene units; xanthophylls are their oxygenated derivatives. Most commonly occurring food carotenes have eleven conjugated double bonds (see Table 3.4), *e.g.* β-carotene (I) and lycopene (II), hence there is considerable delocalisation of the π-electrons. Figure 3.3 shows absorption spectra of lycopene and β-carotene, which are bright red and orange, respectively. The main $\pi \rightarrow \pi^*$ transition band is separated into three sub-bands (fine structure about 30 nm apart). These sub-bands arise because, being long flexible molecules, they have well-separated vibrational levels. Although lycopene and β-carotene have the same chromogen, their electronic spectra are quite different, producing different colours. β-Carotene has cyclic ends, which results in an increase in steric hindrance between the ring methyls and the polyene chain, rendering the molecule less planar and reducing delocalisation of the π-orbital (Moss and Weedon, 1976). Calculation of the ground- and excited-

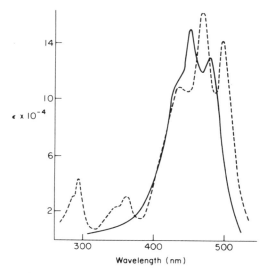

FIG. 3.3 Absorption spectra of β-carotene (——) and lycopene (– – – – –).

TABLE 3.4
STRUCTURES OF SOME CAROTENOID PIGMENTS

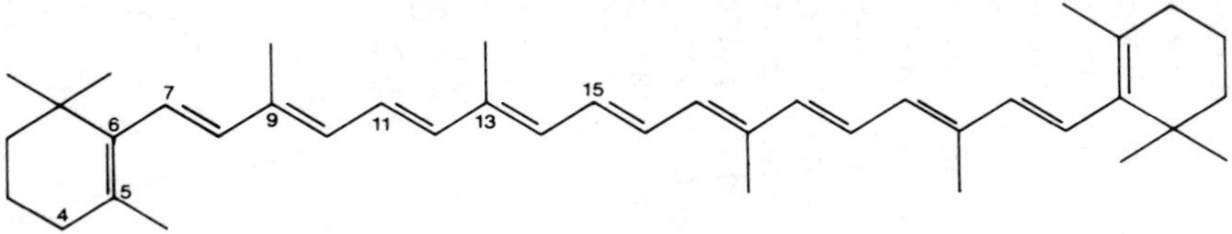

(I) β-Carotene

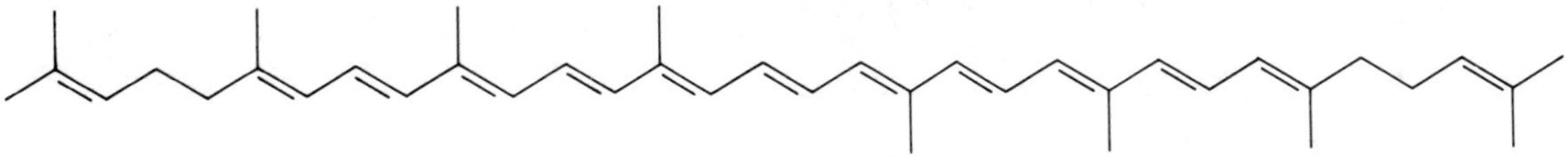

(II) Lycopene

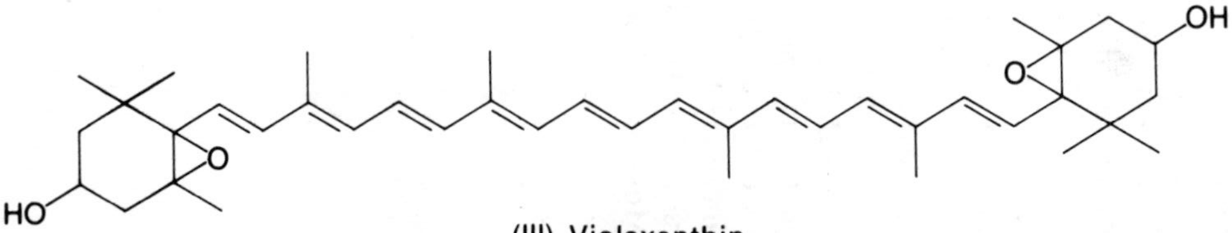

(III) Violaxanthin

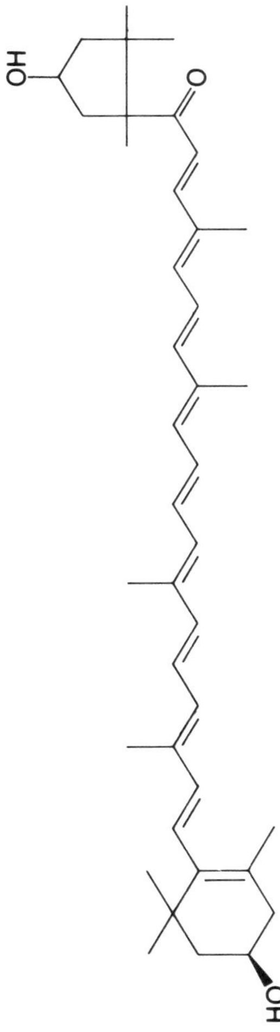

(IV) Capsanthin

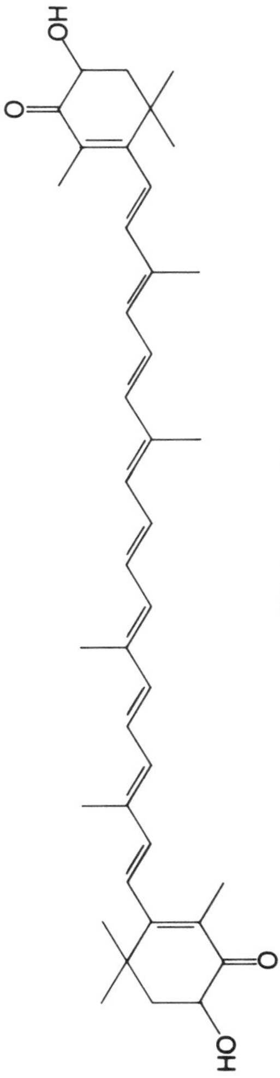

(V) Astaxanthin

energy states of β-carotene indicates that there is only a partial double-bond character to the alternating single bonds of the polyene. Also, in the excited state, the π-electron density decreases significantly in the central region of the polyene chain compared to the ends (Song *et al.*, 1972). Because the single bonds only have partial double-bond character, the electrons are not totally delocalised, which causes the absorption spectra of polyenes to converge, so that increasing the number of double bonds produces a progressively smaller bathochromic shift.

Carotenoids usually occur with the *all-trans* configuration, but minor quantities of mono-*cis* isomers are often present. Poly-*cis* isomers are rare, but do occur in certain fruits (Goodwin, 1976) and vegetables. *Cis* isomers absorb at shorter wavelengths than their corresponding *trans* isomers as a result of the change in molecular shape. Introduction of oxygenated groups also causes changes in electronic spectra. Conjugation of the polyene with a carbonyl group will cause a loss of fine structure and a bathochromic shift in the spectrum (Moss and Weedon, 1976). Formation of epoxide xanthophylls by oxidation of a carotene, *e.g.* violaxanthin (III), will decrease the length of the conjugated double bonds from eleven to nine and hence alter the colour.

3.3.2 Tetrapyrrole Pigments

Both haem and chlorophyll have as their chromogen a cyclic tetrapyrrole ring derived from the parent porphin (VI) (see Table 3.5), which is a symmetrical, planar molecule of four pyrrole rings joined by methine bridges. Porphyrins can be regarded as cyclic polyene systems. The main feature of their spectra is the occurrence of two main, well-separated $\pi \rightarrow \pi^*$ transitions. One is a moderately intense band in the visible region around 600 nm, and is called the Q-band; the other is a very intense band in the ultraviolet region, around 400 nm, called the B-band or more commonly the Soret band. Owing to their rôle in photosynthesis, porphyrins are probably the most extensively investigated of the food pigments in terms of prediction of the spectra from molecular orbitals, but even they are still not fully understood.

One remarkable feature of porphyrin spectra is that even if hydrogenation of the outer pyrrole double bonds occurs, the molecule still absorbs in the visible region. This implies that the chromogen of porphin (VII) can be considered as an inner delocalised pathway not

TABLE 3.5
STRUCTURES OF SOME TETRAPYRROLE PIGMENTS

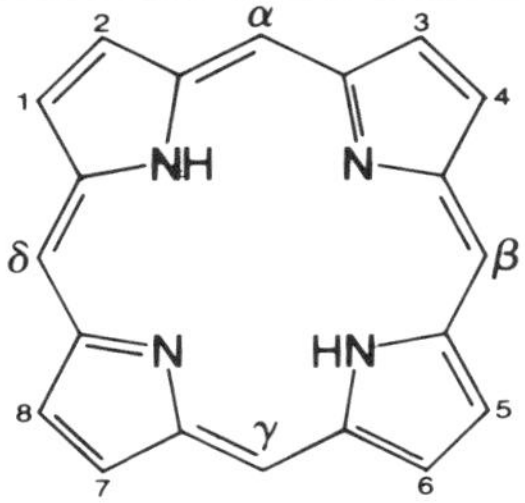

(VI) Porphin

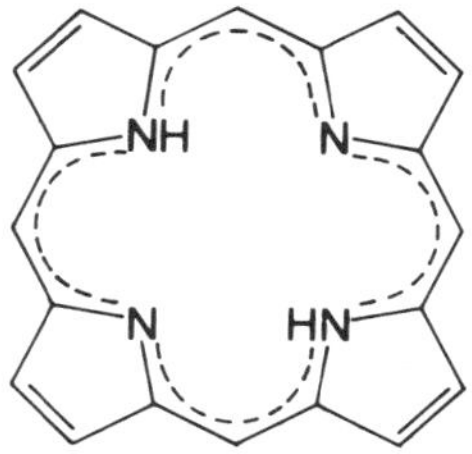

(VII) Chromogen of porphin

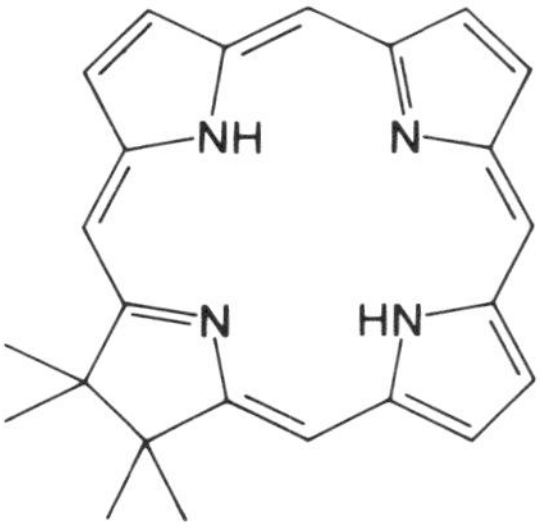

(VIII) Chlorin

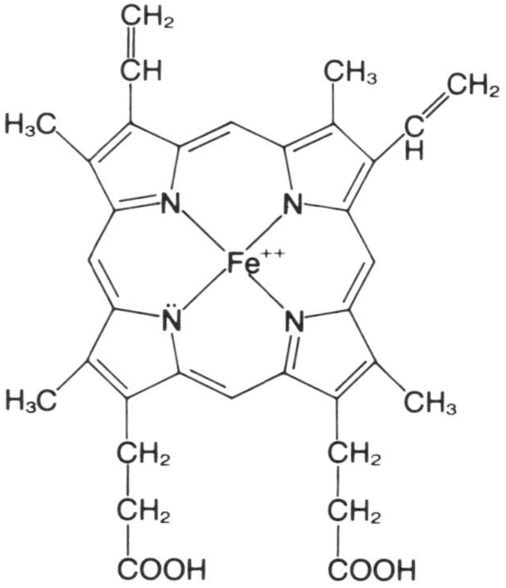

(X) Haem

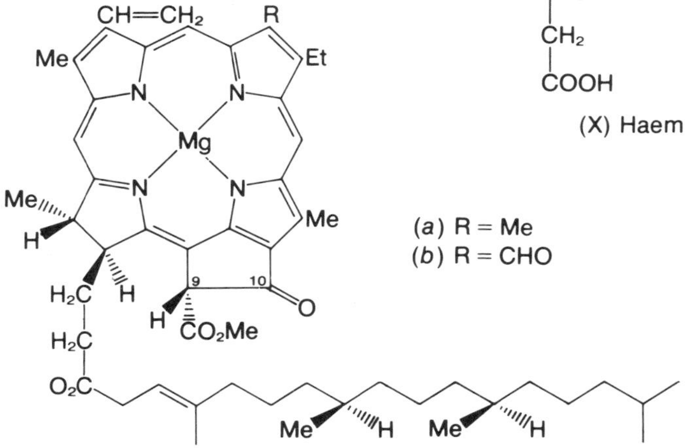

(a) R = Me
(b) R = CHO

(IX) Chlorophyll

containing the outer double bonds (Griffiths, 1976). Metal complexes of porphin have much simpler spectra than the free base because of the higher degree of symmetry. Hence the original molecular-orbital calculations were confined to symmetrical porphins (Longuet-Higgins *et al.*, 1950) with only partial success, but they have been subsequently refined (Weiss *et al.*, 1965) and applied to less symmetrical porphyrins (Song *et al.*, 1972; Weiss, 1972). Once the porphyrin ring is reduced as a chlorin (VIII), the ring becomes buckled and the molecule is no longer symmetrical. The effect of metal complexing is quite complicated as illustrated by the spectra of chlorophyll *a* (IX) and pheophytin *a*, the magnesium and free-base porphyrin, respectively; the B-band is shifted *hypsochromically* and the Q-band *bathochromically*. The bright green colour of chlorophyll, and the olive-green colour of pheophytin *a* result (Fig. 3.4).

3.3.3 Flavonoids

The relationship between delocalisation of the π-electrons and colour is further illustrated by flavonoid compounds. The common structural feature of the flavonoids is two (poly)phenol rings, A and B, linked by a 3-carbon heterocyclic oxygen ring (see Table 3.6). In Fig. 3.5, for

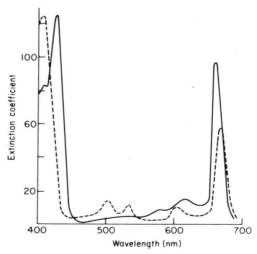

FIG. 3.4 Absorption spectra of chlorophyll *a* (——) and pheophytin *a* (- - - - - -). (From Smith and Benitz, 1955, by permission of Springer-Verlag.)

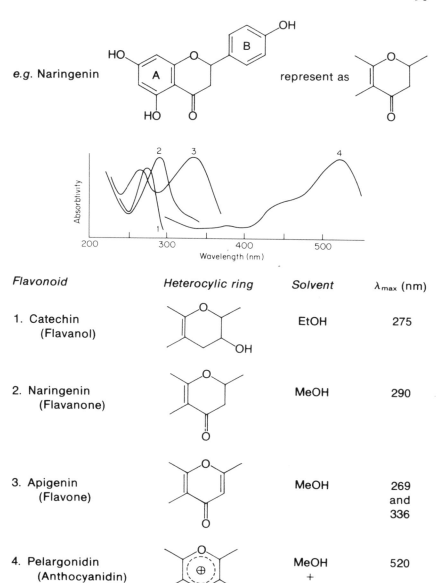

e.g. Naringenin   represent as

FIG. 3.5 Absorption spectra of four flavonoid compounds. (Adapted from Swain, 1976a,b.)

TABLE 3.6
STRUCTURES OF SOME ANTHOCYANINS

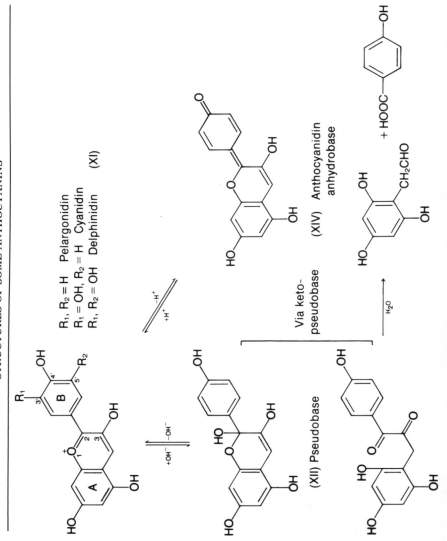

$R_1, R_2 = H$ Pelargonidin
$R_1 = OH, R_2 = H$ Cyanidin
$R_1, R_2 = OH$ Delphinidin   (XI)

(XII) Pseudobase

Via keto-pseudobase

(XIV) Anthocyanidin anhydrobase

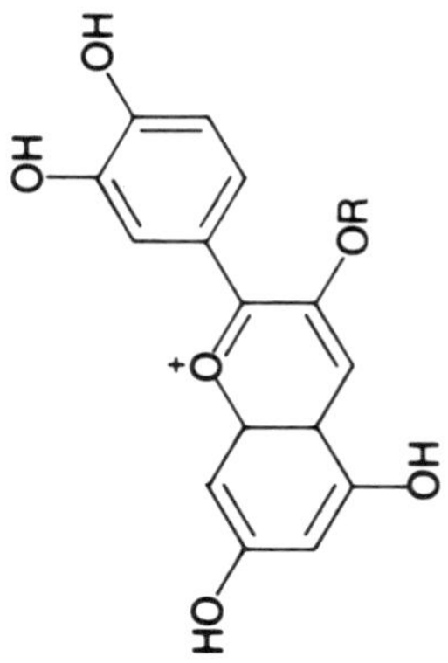

Anthocyanin

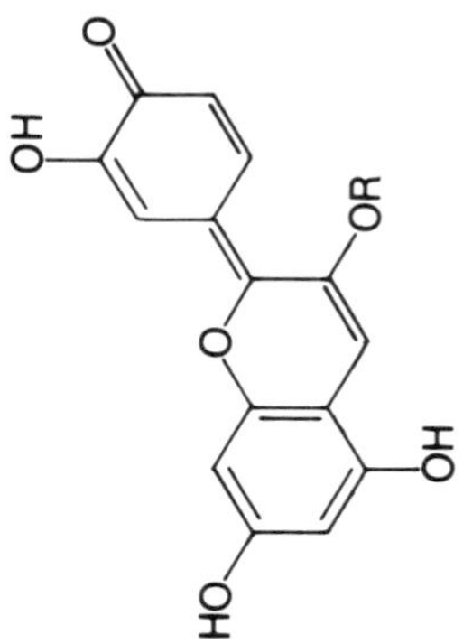

(XVI) Anthocyanin anhydrobase

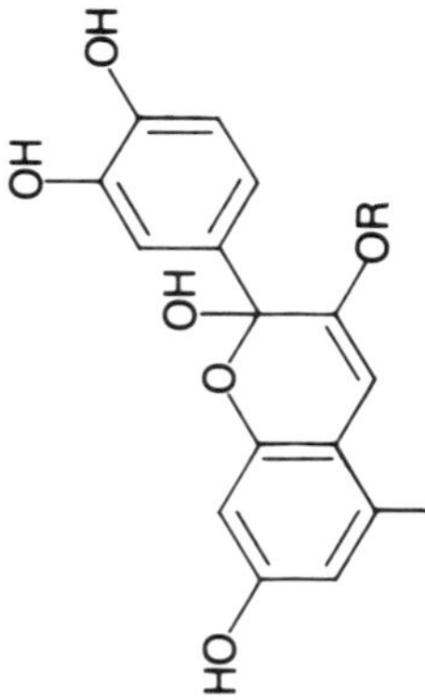

(XV) Chromenol

simplification, only the heterocyclic ring is shown for four compounds—a flavanol, a flavanone, a flavone and an anthocyanidin, with their corresponding spectra. Examination of the figure reveals why anthocyanidins are the only highly coloured group of the family. For the other compounds, the two aromatic rings are separated and unconjugated. Even in a flavone, where there is a limited delocalisation of π-electrons from ring B, this is insufficient for absorption in the visible region (Swain, 1976a,b). The formation of the flavylium cation in an anthocyanidin results in a dramatic change in the spectrum. Donation by the heterocyclic oxygen of its non-bonding electrons produces a ring with aromatic character. The positive charge on this oxygen can be delocalised on to other oxygen atoms in the molecule, especially the 4'-hydroxyl group. The molecular orbital system is unusual in that the cation gives rise to the highest occupied orbital, being a non-bonding molecular orbital (Griffiths, 1976), not to be confused with the non-bonding electrons of the heteroatom. This means that the energy of transition to the first anti-bonding orbital is small and there is strong absorption in the visible region, resulting in an orange–red colour for pelargonidin (Fig. 3.5). Comparison of transition energies calculated from theoretical molecular orbitals with those from experimental data indicates that ring B could be at an angle of 45° or more to the flavylium ring, although a co-planar configuration is not ruled out (Song et al., 1972). The three principal parent aglycones are pelargonidin, cyanidin and delphinidin (XI), which differ in the hydroxyl substitution of the B ring. Hydroxylation results in a bathochromic shift and the colour changes from orange–red to mauve, respectively. It is interesting that derivatives of these three parents can give such a wide range of colours in plant materials, varying from pink to dark purple. The spectra can be altered by the effect of substituents (Swain, 1976a; Stevenson, 1965; Markakis, 1974; Hrazdina, 1974; Harborne, 1976) and by interaction with other compounds. Thus methylation of the B-ring hydroxyl groups causes a hypsochromic shift and so reddens the colour. Anthocyanidins rarely occur in plant materials without one or more of the hydroxyl groups being glycosylated to form anthocyanins; the colour again will vary with the number and position of the sugar groups. Glycosylation also confers water solubility on the pigment, as well as stability and prevention of loss of colour.

Since the flavylium nucleus is in the cation form, it will remain so only in an acidic environment: pH is very important to colour and stability of anthocyanins. Modification of colour will also occur if the anthocyanins are present with other compounds such as flavones or other anthocyanins, or if the anthocyanin is complexed with a metal ion such as aluminium or tin (Harborne, 1976). The distribution within the plant material and the immediate environment around the anthocyanins can also alter the intensity and colour of these pigments (Nakayama and Powers, 1972).

3.4 EFFECTS OF HEAT PROCESSING ON FOOD PIGMENTS

3.4.1 Chlorophyll

3.4.1.1 *Location in Plant Materials*
As already mentioned, when examining the effects of heating it is important to consider not just the pigment itself but also the surrounding biological constituents. 'Chlorophyll' is a collective name for a group of green pigments which occur in the chloroplasts of plants and in some photosynthetic bacteria and algae; they are important for their primary rôle of converting sunlight into chemical energy. Although five different chlorophylls have been identified, only two are important in plants, namely, *a* and *b* (IX), which occur in approximately a ratio of between 2·5 and 3·5:1. The chemistry of the chlorophylls has been well reviewed (Aronoff, 1953; Jackson, 1976) and will only be discussed where relevant to heat processing.

In higher plants, the chlorophyll is located in the grana, which are densely packed regions of membrane lamellae distributed along the length of the chloroplast (Galston, 1961). The exact arrangement and location of chlorophyll in the chloroplast membrane has aroused much discussion through its bearing on photosynthesis, and also for its contribution to the stability and processing behaviour of chlorophyll. The insolubility of chlorophyll has long been attributed to its interaction with the chloroplast lipoprotein membrane. Anderson (1975) has made some tentative proposals as to the location of chlorophyll (Fig. 3.6). This is based on an assumed model of the membrane as consisting of a mosaic of intrinsic protein embedded in a lipid bilayer. The intrinsic protein has a hydrophilic region in contact with the membrane surface, and a hydrophobic region in contact with the fluid lipid bilayer. The chlorophyll molecule orientates itself such that its hydrophobic portion (the phytol chain and

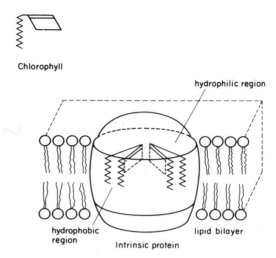

Chlorophyll

FIG. 3.6   Possible location of chlorophyll in chloroplast membrane. (From
Anderson, 1975, by permission of *Nature*.)

part of the porphyrin ring) will be in contact with the hydrophobic
region of the protein. The phytol chain runs perpendicular to the
membrane surface and acts as boundary lipid between the protein and
fluid lipid bilayer and is thus in contact with both. The porphyrin ring
is buried within the protein with its hydrophilic region (the cyclo-
pentanone ring and magnesium ion) in contact with the membrane
surface.

A further component of the chloroplast is the elusive enzyme
chlorophyllase, which appears to be present as a chlorophyll–lipoprotein complex (Ardao and Vennesland, 1960). The distribution of the
enzyme varies from one plant species to another and even between
varieties of the same plant. Chlorophyllase can also vary with the
time of year (Mackinney and Weast, 1940a). Its rôle in the chloroplast
is still little understood and even the evidence for its involvement
with chlorophyll synthesis is conflicting (Bogorod, 1976). The obvious
difficulty in studies on chlorophyllase is that both enzyme and substrate are insoluble in water. The action of chlorophyllase is to split
off the phytol chain to produce chlorophyllide; this no longer interacts
effectively with the lipoprotein membrane and can leach into the
aqueous phase.

3.4.1.2 *Heat Processing of Foods Containing Chlorophyll*

The consumer prefers his cooked or processed green vegetables, such as peas, beans, cabbage, and broccoli, to have a bright green colour, which is associated with a fresh, nutritious product of good flavour. It is not surprising, therefore, that much effort has been involved in the study of the nature and prevention of colour changes occurring during heat processing of green vegetables.

When green vegetables are cooked or simply blanched, there is an initial brightening of the green colour. This is a physical effect caused by a combination of the removal of air around the fine hairs on the surface of the plant and the expulsion of air between the cells (Mackinney and Weast, 1940b; Meyer, 1960), which alters the surface-reflecting properties. As further heating continues, the colour of vegetables gradually changes from bright green to olive green. Vegetables such as spinach, which contain significant quantities of carotenoids, are already dark green and after heating appear brown–green. Prolonged heating of green vegetables destroys the pigments and colour changes of olive green to brown–green, yellow–green and eventually yellow, take place.

Although the chlorin ring itself is fairly stable to heat, the central magnesium ion is very labile. The change of colour from bright to olive green has long been attributed to loss of magnesium caused by the release of organic acids from the plant tissues, thus converting chlorophyll to pheophytin (Mackinney and Weast, 1940b). In addition to pheophytin formation, isomeric chlorophylls *a'* and *b'* and their respective pheophytins are also produced in equilibrium with their parent compounds (Strain and Manning, 1942; Strain, 1954). The exact nature of these isomers is still unresolved (Jackson, 1976) but, since they are produced in very small quantities with similar spectral properties to chlorophyll and pheophytin *a* and *b*, their contribution to the overall colour change is not significant. As already noted, the shift in the Q- and B-bands to the spectrum of pheophytin *a* means an increased reflection of orange and blue light and gives an olive–green colour (Fig. 3.4).

The conversion of chlorophyll to pheophytin is regarded as an index of the severity of heat processing. Conversion can be measured directly using reflectance spectroscopy (Dutton *et al.*, 1943; Kapsalis *et al.*, 1965) and typical reflectance spectra of fresh and heat-processed peas are shown in Fig. 3.7. The broad bands are due to the presence of carotenoids with the chlorophyll, although any changes in

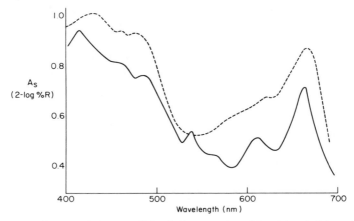

FIG. 3.7 Reflectance spectra of fresh (------) and heat-treated (——) peas. (From Kapsalis *et al.* (1965). Copyright © by the Institute of Food Technologists.)

these are insignificant compared to those in the latter. Extraction of the pigments followed by spectrophotometric measurement of the conversion is also widely used (Dietrich, 1958). Generally, it is necessary for more than 50% conversion of the chlorophyll to occur before a change of colour from bright green is noticed (Mackinney and Weast, 1940b).

The kinetics of the conversion of chlorophyll to pheophytin have been studied by several workers. The reaction is first order with respect to temperature (Mackinney and Joslyn, 1941), and pseudo-first order with respect to chlorophyll concentration (Joslyn and Mackinney, 1940; Cho, 1966; Haisman and Clarke, 1975). Chlorophyll *a* is roughly nine times more easily converted to the corresponding pheophytin than chlorophyll *b* (Joslyn and Mackinney, 1940). With regard to hydrogen-ion concentration, different orders of reaction have been found. Earlier work on chlorophyll solutions (Joslyn and Mackinney, 1938) gave the reaction as first order with respect to hydrogen-ion concentration. Cho (1966), on the other hand, found the reaction of chlorophyll in aqueous acetone solution to be second order, and was able to propose the following mechanism:

$$\text{chlorophyll} + 2\text{H}^+ \xrightleftharpoons{K_{eq}} [\text{chlorophyll } \text{H}_2]^{2+} \xrightarrow{K_1} \text{pheophytin} + \text{Mg}^{2+}$$

There is rapid equilibrium to form an intermediate protonated complex, which in a slower rate-determining step loses magnesium. The presence of a formyl group in chlorophyll b increases the positive charge on the pyrrole nitrogens and so reduces the equilibrium constant (K_{eq}) which could account for the slower conversion of chlorophyll b to pheophytin b.

The previous kinetic determinations were all performed on extracted chlorophyll. Haisman and Clarke (1975) converted chlorophyll *in situ* in green leaves before extraction of the pigments and found that the rate was porportional to the square root of the hydrogen-ion concentration, *i.e.* $[H^+]^{1/2}$. After comparing rates for different leaves, they suggested that, although pH was a very important factor, the wide variation of rates could only be explained by chemical differences in the environment around the chloroplast. Electron micrographs of chloroplasts in heated leaves revealed that above 60°C the chloroplast envelope disappeared and was converted into a denatured globular structure, consisting of multiple concentric lipoprotein membranes, similar in appearance to a dispersed smectic mesophase. These membranes would occlude the chlorophyll, and reaction with hydrogen ions would have to take place across a lipid–water interface. The natural pH conditions in the plant would result in the interface having a net negative charge, thus attracting hydrogen ions and accelerating pheophytin formation. This hypothesis affords an explanation for the wide variation in chlorophyll loss from different plants where the overall pH is the same.

Although pheophytin formation is the most important mechanism for change of colour in green vegetables, other mechanisms are also involved. The action of chlorophyllase, as already mentioned, is to split off the phytol chain from chlorophyll to produce chlorophyllide, which loses magnesium to form pheophorbide. Having lost the hydrophobic chain, these molecules no longer interact effectively with the membranes and pass into aqueous solution. Chlorophyllase is a heat-stable enzyme and may be active even at 80°C (Mackinney and Weast, 1940a; Jones *et al.*, 1963). After heat processing, chlorophyllides and pheophorbides can be detected, and may cause problems, for example in the preparation of leaf protein (Holden, 1974). Conversion of chlorophyll to chlorophyllides as a method of preserving the colour has been patented (Lesley and Shumate, 1937) and, although there seems evidence of greater stability to conventional heat processing, there is no significant gain on long-term storage (Clydesdale and Francis, 1968). The mechanism of fading of the colour in chlorophyll is oxidative and probably involves attack on the C_{10} β-keto-ester group, leading eventually to low molecular weight, colourless compounds (Simpson *et al.*, 1976). It is unlikely that such reactions occur during normal processing.

3.4.1.3 *Retention of Green Colour in Processed Vegetables*

The most widely used and well-established method of prevention of pheophytin formation is the addition of alkaline salts at all stages of processing. Canned vegetables present a particularly difficult problem and alkaline salts have been applied at one or more of the stages of soaking, blanching and sterilisation (Blair and Ayres, 1943; Gieseker, 1949). In the preparation of canned peas, sodium bicarbonate has been used at the soaking stage, calcium hydroxide during blanching and magnesium hydroxide added to the brine (Blair and Ayres, 1943). Other salts used during blanching prior to canning or freezing, or in the cooking water of frozen vegetables, include magnesium carbonate (Clydesdale and Francis, 1968; Gupte and Francis, 1964), ammonium hydroxide (Gieseker, 1949), a combination of magnesium carbonate and calcium acetate (Sweeney, 1970), and ammonium carbonate (Eheart and Odland, 1973a,b). The main disadvantage of using alkaline salts is the possibility of inducing undersirable changes in the texture of vegetables. Using a citrate–phosphate buffer in the cooking water of frozen vegetables, the most effective pH range for chlorophyll retention was pH 6·2–7·0; above pH 7 no further improvement in colour resulted and there was a marked deterioration in texture (Sweeney and Martin, 1961). Ammonium carbonate and the mixture of calcium acetate and magnesium carbonate used in blanching or cooking water at the appropriate levels had no significant effect on texture (Sweeney, 1970; Eheart and Odland, 1973a,b). Sodium chloride and other neutral salts, especially when used in hard water, help to retain chlorophyll without changes in texture of vegetables blanched prior to freezing (Hudson *et al.*, 1974). Apart from the simple neutralisation of organic acids, the reduction in pheophytin formation can be explained in terms of the hypothesis of Haisman and Clarke (1975) as a neutralisation or dilution of the negative charge at the lipid–water interface. Cationic surface-active agents, such as cetyltrimethylammonium bromide, also reduce chlorophyll loss by the latter mechanism (Haisman and Clarke, 1975).

The kinetics of pheophytin formation are first order with respect to temperature, whereas microbial destruction is logarithmic; hence there should be a distinct advantage in colour retention by processing vegetables for a short time at ultra-high temperature (UHT). UHT processing with pH adjustment did result in better colour retention (Gupte and Francis, 1964; Buckle and Edwards, 1970). However, chlorophyll conversion occurred rapidly during storage. Examination of pH-adjusted (pH 8·5) pea purée processed at 149°C for 68 seconds revealed other green pigments apart from chlorophyll and pheophytin, and these were similar to degradation products reported in certain ripening vegetables (Buckle and Edwards, 1969).

Re-greening of pheophytin can take place in the presence of copper and zinc ions, which form stable complexes, hence explaining the preference for copper cooking vessels in the past. This reaction can also cause a green discolouration in canned oysters since pheophytin and pheophorbide, present naturally in oysters, combine with metals such as magnesium, iron, zinc or copper, contained in the viscera during heat processing (Osada, 1974).

3.4.2 Haem Pigments (see also Section 5.4.4)

The two major pigments occurring in animal tissue are haemoglobin in blood and myoglobin in muscle tissue. Since most of the blood is removed from the animal after slaughter, myoglobin is the major pigment present in meat.

Myoglobin is composed of a prosthetic group, haem, which is a ferroporphyrin (X) based on protoporphyrin bound to a protein called globin. The tertiary structure of globin is very important; it folds in such a way as to form a cleft into which the haem fits so that non-polar groups on the porphyrin system and in the protein can interact (Kendrew, 1963). The central ferrous ion forms a square pyramidal complex, in which four pyrrole nitrogens are in the planar positions, the fifth ligand being the proximal histidine group from globin.

The function of myoglobin is to transport oxygen in the muscle for respiration and so has the capacity to weakly and reversibly bind oxygen. Oxygen becomes co-ordinated at the sixth position, stabilised possibly by a second histidine group interacting with the oxygen by hydrogen bonding (Givandarajan, 1973; Giddings, 1977a,b). Myoglobin must be in the ferrous form in order to complex with oxygen. Protoporphyrin is readily oxidised unless stabilised by globin and the presence of reducing agents.

The spectra of meat pigments are of the porphyrin type with Q- and B-bands. Myoglobin is purple in colour, since the Q-band absorbs in the green region; the Soret band (B-band) is much more intense but at 435 nm absorbs mainly in the violet region. Oxymyoglobin has the Q-band split into α- and β-bands (Fig. 3.8) and the Soret band is at 418 nm; the colour is bright red. Oxymyoglobin is responsible for the desirable colour of fresh meat, although the hue does vary with species of animal (Lawrie, 1974).

Although a freshly exposed surface of meat will be bright red in colour, as the supply of reducing agents decreases the central ferrous ion becomes oxidised to the ferric state to give metmyoglobin. Metmyoglobin has a brown colour of lower intensity than oxymyoglobin or myoglobin. The colour of meat is dictated by the inter-conversion of these three important pigments (Price and Schweigert, 1971; Lawrie, 1974; Givandarajan, 1973; Giddings, 1977a,b), but the physical state of the meat fibres is important too, especially to the brightness of the colour. Hence, the water-holding capacity of the meat will govern whether the fibres are in a closely packed structure, thus scattering little light and appearing dark, or in an open structure, appearing light in colour (Lawrie, 1974).

Heat processing of the pigment denatures the globin, but usually the haem nucleus remains intact. Oxidation of any reduced iron will be rapid after heating, unless reducing conditions prevail. The pigment formed is brown globin ferrihaemochromogen, although in the

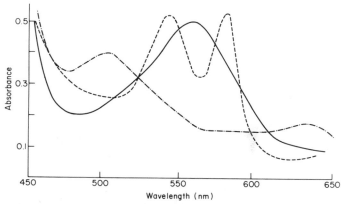

FIG. 3.8   Absorption spectra of beef muscle pigments. —— Myoglobin; ----- oxymyoglobin; –·–·– metmyoglobin.

centre of a large piece of meat the dull red pigment of globin ferrohaemochromogen, in which the iron is still in the ferrous state, can be seen. In most cases, the brown colour of heat-processed meat is acceptable.

The red or pink colour of fresh meat can be maintained in the cooked product if the meat is cured with salts containing nitrate and nitrite, resulting in the formation of nitric oxide myoglobin which has spectral properties similar to oxymyoglobin. Nitric oxide is a strong ligand which stabilises the ferrous form, the stable red pigment, nitric oxide haemochromogen, being formed on heating.

Overheating of meat pigments, especially in the presence of spoilage organisms, can give rise to green discolourations. Exposure to hydrogen sulphide, a product of severe protein degradation, in the presence of air will form green sulphmyoglobin, in which reduction of the porphyrin ring has probably occurred. Further severe conditions will eventually rupture the porphyrin ring and give rise to yellow or colourless bile pigments (Lawrie, 1974).

A serious discolouration, known as 'greening', which has caused financial loss in the tuna canning industry, occurs during the precooking of the fish. The discolouration is intermittent in its occurrence and has been linked to the level of trimethylamine oxide (TMAO) (Nagaoka and Suzuki, 1964; Yamagata et al., 1970). The exact nature of the green pigment is not known, but it has been produced by heating metmyoglobin, TMAO and cysteine together (Ok-Koo et al., 1967). The rôle of the TMAO is probably that of a mild oxidising agent, since it can be replaced by air. The presence of cysteine is necessary. The green pigment has been postulated as containing a new disulphide bond between the cysteine and denatured metmyoglobin (Ok-Koo et al., 1967).

3.4.3 Carotenoids

Carotenoids are the most widespread of all the food pigments and are present in nearly all biological materials. In plants, the carotenoids are either complexed with proteins as constituent parts of chloroplasts and chromoplasts in leaves and skin of fruits and vegetables, or present as esters of fatty acids in the flesh of fruits (Goodwin, 1976; Goodwin and Goad, 1970). Carotenoids are not synthesised in mammals, so any pigmentation arising from carotenoids is derived from ingestion of plant or animal carotenoids and their deposition in fatty tissues.

Since carotenoids are highly unsaturated molecules, they are susceptible to oxidation. Their distribution and dispersion in foods usually affords them protection to heat processing and under mild heat-processing conditions such as domestic cooking, little loss of carotenoids occurs (Martin *et al.*, 1960). Canning, a more severe heat process, can bring about changes which continue during storage as a result of redistribution of food constituents, mainly acids (Adams and Blundstone, 1971; Blundstone *et al.*, 1971; Chichester and McFeeters, 1971; Borenstein and Bunnell, 1966).

3.4.3.1 *Cis–Trans Isomerisation*

Under conditions of heat and acid, isomerisation occurs of one or more double bonds from the predominant *all-trans* carotenoids to mixed *cis–trans* isomers, often in the 9 or 13 position (Moss and Weedon, 1976). The resulting loss of planarity of the polyene chain causes a small hypsochromic shift, as illustrated by the spectra of fresh and canned mango (Fig. 3.9). The effect on overall colour is usually quite small and the shifts are not distinguished by the human eye. *Cis–trans* isomerisation has been followed in boiled and canned carrots (Kemmerer *et al.*, 1945; Weckel *et al.*, 1962) and in heated oils containing β-carotene (Borenstein and Bunnell, 1966).

In those foods which contain poly-*cis*-carotenoids, such as swede (Joyce, 1954), the reverse process takes place during heat processing. The deepening of the yellow colour in cooked swede is a result of isomerisation of the poly-*cis*-carotenoids to *trans*-isomers (Hanson, 1953).

3.4.3.2 *Epoxide Isomerisation*

Many fruits, including orange, pineapple, peach and papaya, contain significant quantities of epoxide carotenoids. The most commonly occurring epoxides are of the 5,6 type, *e.g.* violaxanthin (III) and, in the presence of acid, they can isomerise to 5,8-epoxides:

5,6-epoxide $\xrightarrow{\text{H}^+}$ 5,8-epoxide

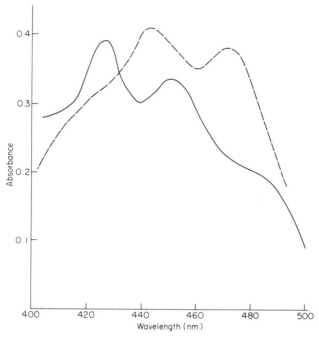

FIG. 3.9 Absorption spectra of carotenoids extracted from fresh mango (------) and canned mango (———) stored 10 months at 2°C. (From Ranganna and Siddappa, 1961. Copyright © by The Institute of Food Technologists.)

The isomerisation results in the loss of one conjugated double bond, hence causing a hypsochromic shift in the spectrum. Heating is not essential to the reaction, but it will accelerate and assist the release of acid from the fruit. Epoxide isomerisation has been clearly demonstrated in canned orange juice (Curl and Bailey, 1956), canned pineapple (Singleton *et al.*, 1961) and processed papaya (Chan *et al.*, 1975). Poor handling of the fruit prior to processing will assist in the release of acid and promote isomerisation (Gortner and Singleton, 1961). Significant changes in carotenoid spectra have been noted in canned pineapple, but the consumer perceives these only as a minor lightening of the yellow colour (Singleton *et al.*, 1961). Both types of isomerisation will continue during storage and the temperature of storage has a more significant effect on the extent of isomerisation than the initial heat process (Dalal and Salunkhe, 1964).

3.4.3.3 *High-Temperature Treatments*

Carotenoids rely on their association with lipids or proteins to protect them from oxidation. Conditions which involve a phase change can expose carotenoids to oxidation or cause the lipids around them to oxidise. Hence, during any dehydration process, precautions must be taken to prevent carotenoid losses. Overheating of tomato purée can cause browning of lycopene, probably by oxidation (Adams and Blundstone, 1971). In the manufacture of popcorn, where temperatures of around 200°C are reached, there is nearly total loss of the β-carotene present in the maize unless antioxidants are added (Borenstein and Bunnell, 1966).

Oxidation of carotenoids is a complex process and, since it is not the major degradation process, it will not be discussed in detail. The few studies undertaken have been of isolated pigments in model systems rather than in food systems. Oxidation of β-carotene showed that epoxide formation occurred and that 5,6- and 5',6'-epoxides were the main end products (El-Tinay and Chichester, 1970). However, in the oxidation of capsanthin (IV), the major xanthophyll in red pepper and paprika, oxidation and loss of end groups occurred to form an apocarotenal as an intermediate product (Philip and Francis, 1971). Similar intermediate products have been found to occur during enzymic degradation of carotenoids (Simpson *et al.*, 1976).

3.4.3.4 *Heat Processing of Crustaceans*

One of the most spectacular colour changes during a heat process is that which takes place when crustaceans, such as crab and lobster, are boiled. Their natural colour is blue or blue–grey, which rapidly turns to a bright red when they are dropped into boiling water.

The major carotenoid present in marine life is the red xanthophyll astaxanthin (V). *In vivo*, it exists as a water-soluble protein complex, termed 'carotenoprotein', present in the exoskeleton of some crustaceans and their eggs (Cheesman *et al.*, 1967). The carotenoprotein in lobster carapace is crustacyanin (Cheesman *et al.*, 1967; Buchwald and Jencks, 1968; Kuhn and Kühn, 1967). This pigment is a stoichiometric combination of astaxanthin and a simple protein; three blue components, α-, β- and γ-crustacyanin, and a yellow component have been isolated. β-Crustacyanin is the smallest component and contains a protein complexed with two astaxanthin molecules and it is equivalent to one-eighth the size of α-crustacyanin (Buchwald and Jencks, 1968). The formation of the protein–astaxanthin complex, which is reversible under mild conditions, causes a considerable bathochromic shift in the spectrum to produce a blue colour (Fig. 3.10). Denaturation of the carotenoprotein by heat releases the astaxanthin from its complex and the colour reverts back to bright red (Fig. 3.10). Hence the configuration of protein is essential to the formation of the complex. The nature of the xanthophyll–protein interaction which is able to produce a 200-nm shift in the spectrum has caused some interest and two mechanisms have been proposed (Cheesman *et al.*, 1967; Buchwald and Jencks, 1968).

The presence of the 4,4'-keto groups is essential for the formation of the carotenoprotein: since the behaviour of this group is little changed by complexing, a covalent bond is ruled out (Buchwald and Jencks, 1968). Polarisation of the polyene system is one explanation for the shift, and could arise if ionised basic groups on the protein interacted with the carbonyl groups of the xanthophyll allowing further interaction between electron-deficient centres on the polyene chain with nucleophilic groups on the protein. The resulting polarisation of the conjugated system would make the double and single bonds of the polyene chain of more or less equal length, increase delocalisation of the π-electrons, and reduce the energy of transition to the excited state (Cheesman *et al.*, 1967). The second mechanism

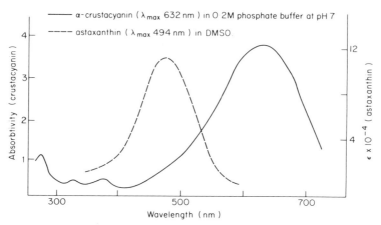

FIG. 3.10 Absorption spectra of α-crustacyanin (from Cheesman *et al.*, 1967) and astaxanthin (from Kuhn and Kühn, 1967) by permission of Cambridge University Press and the Federation of European Biochemical Societies, respectively.

proposes that the stereochemical interaction between the two molecules is such as to produce distortion in the polyene system. If the apoprotein is able to immobilise the methyl groups on the polyene chain and attach to the keto groups on the β-ionone rings, twisting them out of plane, this would cause a strain specifically in the double bonds of the polyene system. This strain would raise the ground state and lower the excited-state energy levels and produce a bathochromic shift (Buchwald and Jencks, 1968).

Shrimps also turn pink when boiled although their initial colour is off-white or grey–pink. It has been suggested that shrimps contain a colourless carotenoprotein containing astaxanthin (Fox, 1955). Astaxanthin appears to be non-degradable by marine-scavenging microorganisms and so is deposited on the sea bed, which can lead to a pink discolouration in the flesh of some demersal fish (Borgstrom, 1968).

3.4.4 Anthocyanins
In general anthocyanins are not stable pigments, plant material easily losing colour both on standing and when processed. The factors which govern the stability of anthocyanins are many and are usually interrelated.

3.4.4.1 *pH and Oxygen*
The colour of both anthocyanins and anthocyanidins is pH-dependent and is only stable in acid solution, since the normal colour is dependent on the presence of the flavylium cation (Markakis, 1974; Hrazdina, 1974; Simpson *et al.*, 1976; Jurd, 1972; Shrikhande, 1976). The aglycone is much less stable to pH changes than anthocyanins. The structures of some anthocyanins are shown in Table 3.6. Studies with pelargonidin have shown that, as the pH is increased in the range 3 to 7, there is a reversible conversion of the flavylium ion to produce a colourless pseudobase (XII) in equilibrium with a diketone (XIII) (Harper, 1968). Other work has shown the diketone to be unstable and it irreversibly hydrolyses to *p*-hydroxybenzoic acid and a phloroglucinol derivative (Jurd, 1972). A rapid increase in pH turns the anthocyanidin solution blue, caused by ionisation of the anhydrobase (XIV), but the colour is very rapidly lost on standing (Harper, 1968). Glycosylation of the 3-hydroxyl group prevents formation of the α-diketone below pH 5 and so stabilises the colour of anthocyanins. Although fading of anthocyanins takes place on standing, the colour

can be regenerated by addition of acid. The colour change will differ from one anthocyanin to another, pelargonidin-3-glucoside giving minimum, and delphinidin-3-glucoside maximum, change of hue. If the pH is raised above 6, the colour will fade, although the mechanism of this loss is disputed. The flavylium glycoside has been reported as existing in equilibrium with the colourless chromenol (XV) (Timberlake and Bridle, 1966). The loss of colour is attributed to either formation of the colourless chromenol via the anhydrobase (XVI) (Jurd and Asen, 1966; Jurd, 1972), or anhydrobase (XVI) production via the chromenol (XV) (Timberlake and Bridle, 1967).

Canning of fruit causes redistribution of constituents; anthocyanins and acid will leach into the syrup. Changes in the environmental pH of the anthocyanin can take place as the pH in the vacuole may be different from the remainder of the fruit tissue (Nakayama and Powers, 1972). The lower the pH of the fruit and syrup, the greater the stability of the pigments during canning: for example, pH 1·8 was found to be optimum for strawberry colour (Meschter, 1953). Usually the range of pH in fruits is such that the effect of pH variation is small and is only important where aerobic conditions prevail (Markakis, 1974; Shrikhande, 1976).

Destruction of the colour during heating is much more rapid when oxygen is present (Lukton et al., 1956; Tinsley and Bockian, 1960; Adams, 1973a,b); the rate of anthocyanin breakdown is independent of pH under anaerobic conditions (Lukton et al., 1956). The presence of oxygen appears to affect the mechanism of destruction of anthocyanins. Whereas heating a solution of pelargonidin-3-glucoside gives a brown precipitate under aerobic conditions, under nitrogen the solution becomes pale yellow (Lukton et al., 1956; Adams, 1973a,b). The presence of oxygen in the headspace of stored canned raspberries (Daravingas and Cain, 1965) and stored cranberry juice (Starr and Francis, 1968) greatly accelerates anthocyanin degradation.

3.4.4.2 Interaction with Other Fruit Constituents

Many workers have shown that ascorbic acid will accelerate anthocyanin breakdown in fruits and wines (Meschter, 1953; Tinsley and Bockian, 1960; Starr and Francis, 1968; Markakis et al., 1957; Timberlake, 1960), yet in blackcurrant juice the ascorbic acid is particularly stable (Clegg and Morton, 1968). The degradation is thought to be a result of the production of hydrogen peroxide from the reaction of ascorbic acid with metal ions and oxygen (Sondheimer and Kertesz, 1952; Harper *et al.*, 1969). Hydrogen peroxide has been shown to cause opening of the heterocyclic ring of anthocyanins (Hrazdina, 1974). However, it has been pointed out that hydrogen peroxide has never been detected in fruits such as strawberry (Meschter, 1953). Also, ascorbic acid and anthocyanins can react even when oxygen is totally removed (Markakis *et al.*, 1957). A condensation type of reaction, similar to that occurring with dimedone, has been suggested to account for the loss of colour (Jurd, 1972). In blackcurrant juice, moreover, anthocyanins in the presence of copper ions exert an antioxidant effect on ascorbic acid (Clegg and Morton, 1968; Harper *et al.*, 1969) rather than destroying it; the flavonols and flavonones also present in the juice are even more effective antioxidants (Clegg and Morton, 1968).

The presence of sugars has been found to increase the rate of anthocyanin breakdown in strawberry products (Meschter, 1953; Tinsley and Bockian, 1960; Daravingas and Cain, 1965); fructose, arabinose, lactose and sorbose were more effective than sucrose. This observation has been attributed to the production of aldehydes such as furfural and hydroxymethylfurfural formed during heat processing (Meschter, 1953).

3.4.4.3 *Temperature and Time*

In comparison to the other factors mentioned, time and temperature of processing and storage are the most important and account for the greatest proportion of loss of colour. Kinetics of anthocyanin thermal degradation in model systems or pigments extracted from fruits show a first-order relationship (Daravingas and Cain, 1965; Markakis *et al.*, 1957). During the canning of strawberries, pigment losses as a result of exhausting and sterilising, which are short processes, are small in comparison with those taking place during storage (Adams and Ongley, 1973). This confirmed earlier work on strawberry preserves, which had shown a logarithmic relationship between temperature and colour loss (Meschter, 1953). So, for example, in the storage of this preserve, the time for a 50% loss of anthocyanin increases from 10 days at 38°C to 11 months at 0°C. This has meant a general recommendation of preserving anthocyanin colour by low processing temperatures (Decareau *et al.*, 1956) and, more especially, keeping the storage temperatures as low as possible (Dalal and Salunkhe, 1964; Adams and Ongley, 1973).

The mechanism of thermal breakdown of anthocyanins has proved difficult to elucidate mainly because the intermediate products are unstable and not easily identifiable. Earlier workers (Lukton *et al.*, 1956; Daravingas and Cain, 1965; Markakis *et al.*, 1957; Keith and Powers, 1965; Powers *et al.*, 1960) proposed that the main pathway was opening of the pyrylium ring to give a colourless chalcone glycoside. The aglycone was not detected (Markakis *et al.*, 1957) and the chalcone glycoside was considered to degrade further giving products such as hydroxybenzoic acid (Powers *et al.*, 1960), or coumaryl glycosides (Jurd, 1972). Recent work by Adams (1973a) has indicated that, under anaerobic conditions, glycosidic hydrolysis is the main rate-determining step in the thermal breakdown of pelargonidin-3-glucoside. This conclusion was based on the observation that the rate of sugar formation was similar to the rate of colour loss. An intermediate colourless product, thought to be either the hydroxyketone or the diketone form of the chalcone, since it appeared relatively stable in the absence of oxygen, was also detected. Under aerobic conditions, the chalcone glycoside rapidly degrades at high temperature, shifting the mechanism in favour of that pathway. Hence a scheme of thermal degradation was proposed incorporating both principal pathways (Fig. 3.11), but it seems that this is an area that requires further experimental investigation.

Colour loss of processed fruit products is a problem which is difficult to overcome. Although attempts are made to reduce losses during processing and storage, long-term storage would require refrigeration (Adams, 1973b). The addition of extra anthocyanins from other natural sources has been suggested and used (Markakis, 1974). Several synthetic flavylium salts have shown potential usage as colourants and have greater stability than anthocyanins (Markakis, 1974; Jurd, 1972). Addition of certain reagents to anthocyanins to augment and intensify colour is another possibility (Timberlake and Bridle, 1977), but the problem of their safety still has to be considered.

3.4.4.4 *Discolouration by Other Flavonoids after Heat Processing*

Although anthocyanins and, to a lesser extent, flavonols, are the only coloured flavonoid compounds, it is possible that, as a result of heat processing, a colourless polyphenol can be converted into a coloured compound. Normally these pigments, which are often metal complexes, are regarded as undesirable.

The occurrence of a pink discolouration can cause problems in the

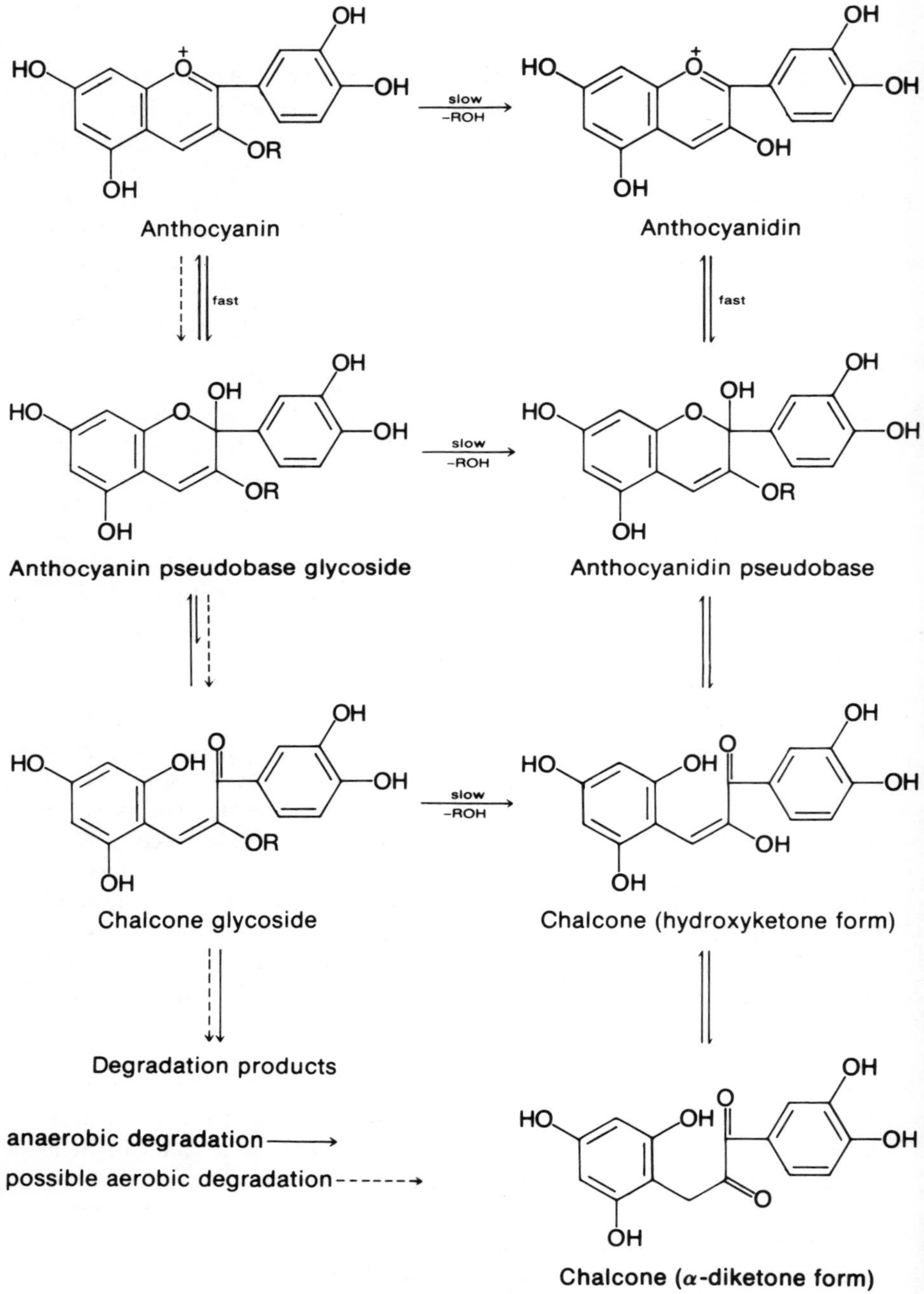

FIG. 3.11 Proposed mechanism for anthocyanin degradation. (From Adams, 1973a.)

canning of fruits such as gooseberries, apples, peaches, pears, grapes and bananas (Adams and Blundstone, 1971). It also appears in canned quinces, but in this case a pink colour is desired and conditions are set to optimise pigment production. The fruits prone to discolouration contain leucoanthocyanins or leucoanthocyanidins (flavonols) which, under conditions of acid and heat, give rise to anthocyanin or anthocyanidin complexes with tin or iron. The spasmodic appearance of the pink discolouration of Bartlett pears has been investigated (Luh *et al.*, 1960; Chandler and Clegg, 1970a) and attributed to the formation of a purple-pink insoluble stannous-anthocyanidin complex. Its occurrence is most common during excessive heating and delayed cooling of the canned pears (Chandler and Clegg, 1970a) and arises only where plain cans are used. The addition of tin ions prior to heat processing prevented formation of the pink complex by reversal of the first step in the oxidation of the leucoanthocyanidin (Chandler and Clegg, 1970b). If the fruits susceptible to pink discolouration are processed in lacquered cans, a brown discolouration is produced, which is thought to be due to the polymerisation of the leucoanthocyanins (Adams and Blundstone, 1971).

Black discolourations can also be formed in cooked or processed vegetables as a result of reaction of iron with flavonols and some flavones (Herrmann, 1976). One example which is of economic importance is blackening which takes place shortly after canned green asparagus is opened. Green asparagus has a very high content of the flavonol rutin (3-rutinoside of quercetin), which itself can precipitate out after heat processing and give a yellow ring on the surface of the asparagus container. In the presence of iron, which arises from the metal container, and oxygen when the can is opened, a black ferric–rutin complex is formed. The presence of stannous ions competes with the iron to form a soluble yellow complex. Hence, if tin is in excess, the discolouration will be prevented (Davis *et al.*, 1961; Hernandez and Vosti, 1963; Lueck, 1970) and the addition of citric acid gives a similar result (Davis *et al.*, 1961).

A similar reaction is the dark grey discolouration which develops after certain varieties of potatoes have been cooked (Charley, 1972). During cooking a colourless ferrous–chlorogenic acid complex is formed which, on standing, slowly oxidises to the black ferric complex. The discolouration is prevented by the presence of citric acid in the potato. Both chlorogenic acid and citric acid vary in their distribution in the tuber, the concentration of the former being higher at the stem end and that of the latter at the bud end. Hence blackening tends to be more prevalent at the stem end of the tuber. However, the concentration of chlorogenic acid also varies with potato variety and growing conditions and that of citric acid with soil composition.

3.4.5 Betalains

Plants of the order *Centrospermae* contain two groups of water-soluble pigments distributed in the cell vacuoles, collectively named 'betalains'. The red pigments are betacyanins and the yellow ones betaxanthins, so named because they were thought to be related to red anthocyanins and yellow flavonoid pigments. The structure and chemistry of these pigments have only recently been determined (Piatelli, 1976).

The most important pigment in the family is the red–violet glucoside from red beetroot called betanin (XVII), which contains a mixture of two isomeric aglycones, betanidin and isobetanidin, that differ only in the configuration at C_{15}. With the increasing restriction in the use of artificial food colours, betanin has recently come into prominence as an alternative red food dye. It is less sensitive to pH change than anthocyanins, and has maximum stability at pH 4–5 (von Elbe *et al.*, 1974a). Addition of alkali destroys the red colour and causes degradation of the product.

When beets are boiled, the cell membranes break down and the pigment leaches into the cooking water. There is fading of colour but usually the pigment is so intense that very little change is noticed; excessive heating turns the pigment brown. Studies on betanin solution and beet juice (von Elbe *et al.*, 1974a) showed that they were most

$R_1 = $ O-Glucose, $R_2 = $ OH, betanin
$R_1, R_2 = $ OH, betanidin

(XVII)

stable to boiling at pH 5·0. However, betanin is easily destroyed by heat; the half-life for the pigment is 90 ± 10 minutes at 75°C, and $14·5 \pm 2$ minutes at 100°C (von Elbe *et al.*, 1974a). There does seem to be a protective effect exerted by beet juice and other food systems which reduce degradation. The presence of oxygen and ultraviolet light increases pigment loss.

The stability of the pigment is greatly increased at lower water activities (a_w), being four times more stable at $a_w = 0·37$ than at $a_w = 1·0$ (Pasch and von Elbe, 1975). This indicates that the pigment would find best use in dried foods or foods stored at low temperatures or for short periods, such as meat substitutes, sausages, gelatin desserts and dairy products (von Elbe *et al.*, 1974b; von Elbe and Maing, 1973).

Our fundamental knowledge of the structure and chemistry of naturally occurring food pigments has increased in recent years. The fate of individual pigments during heat processing is also reasonably well known from studies on model systems. However, pigments occur as part of a complex physical and chemical system in foodstuffs. So it is now more apparent that the behaviour of the pigments is only partly explained by changes in the individual pigments, and that interactions with the other components of the system are taking place. It is in this area that future investigations into changes of food pigments brought about by processing will be concentrated.

REFERENCES

Adams, J. B. (1973a) *J. Sci. Fd. Agric.*, **24**, 747.

Adams, J. B. (1973b) *Fd. Mfr.*, **48**(2), 19.

Adams, J. B. & Blundstone, H. A. W. (1971) In: *The Biochemistry of Fruits and their Products*, ed. Hulme, A. C. Vol. 2, p. 513. London & New York: Academic Press.

Adams, J. B. & Ongley, M. H. (1973) *J. Fd. Technol.*, **8**, 139.

Anderson, J. M. (1975) *Nature*, **253**, 536.

Ardao, C. & Vennesland, B. (1960) *Plant Physiol., Lancaster*, **35**, 368.

Aronoff, S. (1953) *Advan. Fd. Res.*, **4**, 133.

Blair, J. S. & Ayres, T. B. (1943) *Ind. Eng. Chem.*, **35**, 85.

Blundstone, H. A. W., Woodman, J. S. & Adams, J. B. (1971) In: *The Biochemistry of Fruits and their Products*, ed. Hulme, A. C. Vol. 2, p. 546. London & New York: Academic Press.

Bogorod, L. (1976) In: *Chemistry and Biochemistry of Plant Pigments*, ed. Goodwin, T. W. 2nd edn., vol. 1, p. 118. London & New York: Academic Press.

Borenstein, B. & Bunnell, R. H. (1966) *Advan. Fd. Res.*, **15**, 195.

Borgstrom, G. (1968) *Principles of Food Science*, Vol. 2. New York: Macmillan.

Buchwald, M. & Jencks, W. P. (1968) *Biochemistry*, **7**, 844.

Buckle, K. A. & Edwards, R. A. (1969) *Phytochemistry*, **8**, 1901.

Buckle, K. A. & Edwards, R. A. (1970) *J. Fd. Technol.*, **5**, 173.

Chan, H. T., Kuo, M. T. H., Cavaletto, C. G., Nakayama, T. O. M. & Brekke, J. E. (1975) *J. Fd. Sci.*, **40**, 701.

Chandler, B. V. & Clegg, K. M. (1970a) *J. Sci. Fd. Agric.*, **21**, 315.

Chandler, B. V. & Clegg, K. M. (1970b) *J. Sci. Fd. Agric.*, **21**, 323.

Charley, H. (1972) In: *Food Theory and Applications*, ed. Paul, P. C. & Palmer, H. H., p. 298. New York: John Wiley.

Cheesman, D. F., Lee, W. L. & Zagalsky, P. F. (1967) *Biol. Rev.*, **42**, 132.

Chichester, C. O. & McFeeters, R. (1971) In: *The Biochemistry of Fruits and their Products*, ed. Hulme, A.C. Vol. 2, p. 707. London & New York: Academic Press.

Cho, D. H. (1966) Ph.D. Dissertation, University of California, Davis.

Clegg, K. M. & Morton, A. D. (1968) *J. Fd. Technol.*, **3**, 227.

Clydesdale, F. M. & Francis, F. J. (1968) *Fd. Technol.*, **22**, 793.

Curl, A. L. & Bailey, G. F. (1956) *J. Agric. Fd. Chem.*, **4**, 156.

Dalal, K. B. & Salunkhe, D. K. (1964) *Fd. Technol.*, **18**, 1198.

Daravingas, G. & Cain, R. F. (1965) *J. Fd. Sci.*, **30**, 400.

Davis, R. B., Guyer, R. B., Daly, J. J. & Johnson, H. T. (1961) *Fd. Technol.*, **15**, 212.

Decareau, R. V., Livingston, G. E. & Fellers, C. R. (1956) *Fd. Technol.*, **10**, 125.

Dietrich, W. C. (1958) *Fd. Technol.*, **12**, 428.

Dutton, H. J., Bailey, G. F. & Kohake, E. (1943) *Ind. Eng. Chem.*, **35**, 1173.

Eheart, M. S. & Odland, D. (1973a) *J. Fd. Sci.*, **38**, 202.

Eheart, M. S. & Odland, D. (1973b) *J. Fd. Sci.*, **38**, 954.

El-Tinay, A. H. & Chichester, C. O. (1970) *J. Org. Chem.*, **35**, 2290.

Fox, H. M. (1955) *Endeavour*, **14**, 40.

Galston, A. W. (1961) *Life of the Green Plant*. New Jersey: Prentice-Hall.

Giddings, G. G. (1977a) *J. Fd. Sci.*, **42**, 288.

Giddings, G. G. (1977b) *CRC Crit. Rev. Fd. Sci. Nutr.*, **9**, 81.

Gieseker, L. F. (1949) *US Pat.* 2 473 747.

Givandarajan, S. (1973) *CRC Crit. Rev. Fd. Technol.*, **4**, 117.

Goodwin, T. W. (1976) In: *Chemistry and Biochemistry of Plant Pigments*, ed. Goodwin, T. W. 2nd edn., vol. 1, p. 247. London & New York: Academic Press.

Goodwin, T. W. & Goad, L. J. (1970) In: *The Biochemistry of Fruits and their Products*, ed. Hulme, A. C. Vol. 1, p. 305. London & New York: Academic Press.

Gortner, W. A. & Singleton, V. L. (1961) *J. Fd. Sci.*, **26**, 52.

Griffiths, J. (1976) *Colour and Constitution of Organic Molecules*. London & New York: Academic Press.

Gupte, S. M. & Francis, F. J. (1964) *Fd. Technol.*, **18**, 1645.

Gupte, S. M., El-Bisi, H. M. & Francis, F. J. (1964) *J. Fd. Sci.*, **29**, 379.

Haisman, D. R. & Clarke, M. W. (1975) *J. Sci. Fd. Agric.*, **26**, 1111.

Hanson, S. W. (1953) Quartermaster Food and Container Institute. Surv. Progr. Military Subsistence Problems. Ser. 1, No. 5, 136.

Harborne, J. B. (1976) In: *Chemistry and Biochemistry of Plant Pigments*, ed. Goodwin, T. W. 2nd edn., vol. 1, p. 736. London & New York: Academic Press.

Harper, K. A. (1968) *Australian J. Chem.*, **21**, 221.

Harper, K. A., Morton, A. D. & Rolfe, E. J. (1969) *J. Fd. Technol.*, **4**, 255.

Hernandez, H. H. & Vosti, D. C. (1963) *Fd. Technol.*, **17**, 95.

Herrmann, K. (1976) *J. Fd. Technol.*, **11**, 433.

Holden, M. (1974) *J. Sci. Fd. Agric.*, **25**, 1427.

Hrazdina, G. (1974) *Lebensm.-Wiss. u. Technol.*, **7**, 193.

Hudson, M. A., Sharples, V. J. & Gregory, M. E. (1974) *J. Fd. Technol.*, **9**, 105.

Jackson, A. H. (1976) In: *Chemistry and Biochemistry of Plant Pigments*, ed. Goodwin, T. W. 2nd edn., vol. 1, p. 1. London & New York: Academic Press.

Jaffé, H. H. & Orchin, M. (1962) *Theory and Application of U.V. Spectroscopy*. New York: John Wiley.

Jones, I. D., White, R. C. & Gibbs, E. (1963) *J. Fd. Sci.*, **28**, 437.

Joslyn, M. A. & Mackinney, G. (1938) *J. Am. Chem. Soc.*, **60**, 1132.

Joslyn, M. A. & Mackinney, G. (1940) *J. Am. Chem. Soc.*, **62**, 231.

Joyce, A. E. (1954) *Nature*, **173**, 311.

Jurd, L. (1972) In: *The Chemistry of Plant Pigments. Advances in Food Research*, ed. Chichester, C. O. Suppl. 3, p. 123. London & New York: Academic Press.

Jurd, L. & Asen, S. (1966) *Phytochemistry*, **5**, 1263.

Kapsalis, J. G., Driver, M., Johnson, K. R., Nii, I. T. & Henick, A. A. (1965) *Fd. Technol.*, **19**, 1149.

Keith, E. S. & Powers, J. J. (1965) *J. Agric. Fd. Chem.*, **13**, 577.

Kemmerer, A. R., Fraps, G. S. & Meinke, W. W. (1945) *Fd. Res.*, **10**, 66.

Kendrew, J. (1963) *Science*, **139**, 1259.

Kuhn, R. & Kühn, H. (1967) *Eur. J. Biochem.*, **2**, 349.

Lawrie, R. A. (1974) *Meat Science*, 2nd edn. Oxford: Pergamon Press.

Lesley, B. E. & Shumate, J. W. (1937) *US Pat.* 2 097 198.

Longuet-Higgins, H. C., Rector, C. W. & Platt, J. R. (1950) *J. Chem. Phys.*, **18**, 1174.

Lueck, R. H. (1970) *J. Agric. Fd. Chem.*, **18**, 607.

Luh, B. S., Leonard, S. J. & Patel, D. S. (1960) *Fd. Technol.*, **14**, 53.

Lukton, A., Chichester, C. O. & Mackinney, G. (1956) *Fd. Technol.*, **10**, 427.

Mackinney, G. & Joslyn, M. A. (1941) *J. Am. Chem. Soc.*, **63**, 2530.

Mackinney, G. & Little, A. C. (1962) *Colour of Foods*, p. 212. Westport, Conn.: Avi. Publ. Co.

Mackinney, G. & Weast, C. A. (1940a) *J. Biol. Chem.*, **133**, 551.

Mackinney, G. & Weast, C. A. (1940b) *Ind. Eng. Chem.*, **32**, 392.

MacLeod, A. J. (1973) *Instrumental Methods of Food Analysis*. London: Elek Science.

Markakis, P. (1974) *CRC Crit. Rev. Fd. Sci. Nutr.*, **4**, 437.

Markakis, P., Livingston, G. E. & Fellers, C. R. (1957) *Fd. Res.*, **22**, 117.
Martin, M. E., Sweeney, J. P., Gilpen, G. L. & Chapman, V. J. (1960) *J. Agric. Fd. Chem.*, **8**, 387.
Meschter, E. E. (1953) *J. Agric. Fd. Chem.*, **1**, 574.
Meyer, L. M. (1960) *Food Chemistry.* New York: Reinhold Publ. Corp.
Moore, W. J. (1963) *Physical Chemistry,* 4th edn. London: Longmans Green & Co. Ltd.
Moss, G. P. & Weedon, B. C. L. (1976) In: *Chemistry and Biochemistry of Plant Pigments,* ed. Goodwin T. W. 2nd edn., vol. 1, p. 149. London & New York: Academic Press.
Murrell, J. N. (1971) *The Theory of Electronic Spectra of Organic Molecules,* 2nd edn. London: Chapman & Hall.
Nagaoka, C. & Suzuki, N. (1964) *Fd. Technol.*, **18**, 777.
Nakayama, T. O. M. & Powers, J. J. (1972) In: *The Chemistry of Plant Pigments. Advances in Food Research,* ed. Chichester, C. O. Suppl. 3, p. 193. London & New York: Academic Press.
Ok-Koo, G., Cobb, B. F., Mebine, B. & Brown, W. D. (1967) *J. Fd. Sci.*, **34**, 404.
Osada, H. (1974) *Abstr. IV Int. Congr. Fd. Sci. Technol.*, Madrid **1b**, 104.
Pariser, R. & Parr, R. G. (1953) *J. Chem. Phys.*, **21**, 466 & 767.
Pasch, J. H. & von Elbe, J. H. (1975) *J. Fd. Sci.*, **40**, 1145.
Philip, T. & Francis, F. J. (1971) *J. Fd. Sci.*, **36**, 96.
Piatelli, M. (1976) In: *Chemistry and Biochemistry of Plant Pigments,* ed. Goodwin, T. W. 2nd edn., vol. 1, p. 560. London & New York: Academic Press.
Pople, J. A. (1953) *Trans. Faraday Soc.*, **49**, 1375.
Pople, J. A. & Beveridge, D. L. (1970) *Approximate Molecular Orbital Theory.* New York: McGraw-Hill.
Powers, J. J., Somaatmadja, D., Pratt, D. E. & Handy, M. K. (1960) *Fd. Technol.*, **14**, 626.
Price, J. F. & Schweigert, B. S. (1971) *The Science of Meat and Meat Products.* 2nd edn. San Francisco: Freeman.
Ranganna, S. & Siddappa, G. S. (1961) *Fd. Technol.*, **15**, 204.
Rao, C. N. R. (1975) *U.V. and Visible Spectroscopy—Chemical Applications.* 3rd edn. London: Butterworths.
Shrikhande, A. J. (1976) *CRC Crit. Rev. Fd. Sci. Nutr.*, **7**, 193.
Simpson, K. L., Lee, T. C. Rodriguez, D. B. & Chichester, C. O. (1976) In: *Chemistry and Biochemistry of Plant Pigments,* ed. Goodwin, T. W. 2nd edn., vol. 1, p. 780. London & New York: Academic Press.
Singleton, V. L., Gortner, W. A. & Young, H. Y. (1961) *J. Fd. Sci.*, **26**, 49.
Smith, H. C. & Benitz, A. (1955) *Modern Methods in Plant Analysis,* ed. Paech, K. & Tracey, M. V. Vol. IV. Berlin: Springer-Verlag.
Sondheimer, E. & Kertesz, Z. I. (1952) *Fd. Res.*, **17**, 288.
Song, P. S., Moore, T. A. & Sun, M. (1972) In: *The Chemistry of Plant Pigments. Advances in Food Research,* ed. Chichester, C. O. Suppl. 3, p. 33. London & New York: Academic Press.
Starr, M. S. & Francis, F. J. (1968) *Fd. Technol.*, **22**, 1293.
Stevenson, P. E. (1965) *J. Mol. Spectrosc.*, **18**, 51.

Strain, H. H. (1954) *J. Agric. Fd. Chem.*, **2**, 1222.

Strain, H. H. & Manning, W. M. (1942) *J. Biol. Chem.*, **146**, 275.

Swain, T. (1976a) In: *Chemistry and Biochemistry of Plant Pigments*, ed. Goodwin, T. W. 2nd edn., vol. 1, p. 425. London & New York: Academic Press.

Swain, T. (1976b) In: *Chemistry and Biochemistry of Plant Pigments*, ed. Goodwin, T. W. 2nd edn., vol. 2, p. 185. London & New York: Academic Press.

Sweeney, J. P. (1970) *Fd. Technol.*, **24**, 490.

Sweeney, J. P. & Martin, M. E. (1961) *Fd. Technol.*, **15**, 263.

Timberlake, C. F. (1960) *J. Sci. Fd. Agric.*, **11**, 268.

Timberlake, C. F. & Bridle, P. (1966) *Nature*, **212**, 158.

Timberlake, C. F. & Bridle, P. (1967) *J. Sci. Fd. Agric.*, **18**, 473.

Timberlake, C. F. & Bridle, P. (1977) *J. Sci. Fd. Agric.*, **28**, 539.

Tinsley, I. J. & Bockian, A. H. (1960) *Fd. Res.*, **25**, 161.

von Elbe, J. H. & Maing, I.-Y. (1973) *Cereal Sci. Today*, **18**, 263.

von Elbe, J. H., Maing, I.-Y. & Amundson, C. H. (1974b) *J. Fd. Sci.*, **39**, 334.

von Elbe, J. H., Klement, J. T., Cassens, R. G. & Lindsay, R. C. (1974a) *J. Fd. Sci.*, **39**, 128.

Weckel, K. G., Santos, B., Hermon, E., Lafferriere, L. & Gabelman, W. H. (1962) *Fd. Technol.*, **16**(8), 91.

Weiss, C. (1972) *J. Mol. Spectrosc.*, **44**, 37.

Weiss, C., Kobayashi, H. & Goutermann, M. (1965) *J. Mol. Spectrosc.*, **16**, 415.

Yamagata, M., Horimoto, K. & Nagaoka, C. (1970) *Fd. Technol.*, **24**, 198.

CHAPTER 4

Vitamins

R. J. PRIESTLEY

National Food Research Institute, Pretoria, South Africa

Because of their essential nature, the extent of destruction of vitamins is often the main criterion by which the popular media judge the quality of processed foods. But it is not often realised that home cooking generally leads to much greater losses than those encountered in industrial processing. Most vitamins break down to some extent on heating, the most labile under conditions normally encountered in food processing being ascorbic acid and thiamine. A rough guide to the relative stability of the vitamins is shown in Table 4.1. In this chapter, where available, information is given regarding the mechanism of thermal destruction, particularly of the more labile vitamins. Consequently, less space is available for citation of actual losses of vitamins and for the important subject of storage losses which is outside the scope of this review. Fortunately, excellent coverage of these areas is available (Harris and von Loesecke, 1960; Harris and Karmas, 1975).

It is necessary to view vitamin losses in perspective. For instance, loss of vitamin C during milk processing may be high but is of marginal importance compared to losses in citrus juices, which have a high vitamin C content, and in potato products which, although containing relatively small quantities of ascorbic acid, may constitute a large proportion of the vitamin C intake in Western diets.

Despite the volume of literature published on vitamin losses in foods, for several reasons it is not possible to make much more than an informed guess as to the vitamin content of a processed foodstuff which has undergone a heating operation. For instance, other operations such as pre-process handling and method of blanching also have a considerable influence. Often, variations due to genetic, climatic and

TABLE 4.1

STABILITY OF THE VITAMINS UNDER VARIOUS CONDITIONS (FROM HAR-
RIS AND KARMAS, 1975, BY PERMISSION OF THE AVI PUBLISHING CO.)

Vitamin	Condition[a]					
	pH 7	Acid	Alkaline	Air	Light	Heat
Vitamin A	S	U	S	U	U	U
Vitamin D	S		U	U	U	U
Vitamin E	S	S	S	U	U	U
Vitamin K	S	U	U	S	U	S
Vitamin C	U	S	U	U	U	U
Vitamin B_1	U	S	U	U	S	U
Vitamin B_2	S	S	U	S	U	U
Vitamin B_6	S	S	S	S	U	U
Vitamin B_{12}	S	S	S	U	U	S
Niacin	S	S	S	S	S	S
Pantothenic acid	S	U	U	S	S	U
Biotin	S	S	S	S	S	U
Folic acid	U	U	S	U	U	U

[a]S = stable; U = unstable.

maturity differences affect the vitamin content of the final product
more than the processing itself. Carrots, for example, may vary
100-fold with respect to their carotene content and ascorbic acid
content may vary 20-fold for melons (Senti, 1971), 35-fold for grapes
(Bell et al., 1942) and 16-fold for tomato juice (Anderson et al., 1954).
Variations of pH and metal and enzyme concentrations may also be
significant.

Apart from the above factors, the main obstacle to the prediction of
vitamin losses on heating is a lack of adequate published kinetic data.
In order to make such predictions the reaction rate must be known as
a function of temperature. In many cases, vitamin destruction can be
described in terms of a first-order reaction

$$A \xrightarrow{k} B$$

k being the reaction rate constant and

$$\log_{10} k = [(-E_a/2 \cdot 303 \, R)1/T] + C \qquad \text{(Arrhenius' equation)}$$

where E_a = energy of activation; R = universal gas constant; T =

absolute temperature; and C = constant. If this equation holds, a plot of log (% nutrient retained) versus time yields a straight line. The result is generally quoted as the rate constant, k, but may be given as a half-life time $\theta_{1/2} = \log_e 2/k$ or as the decimal reduction time, $D = 2 \cdot 303/k$. In either case, results obtained can be used to estimate losses under similar conditions. The rate constant, k, is also a function of temperature, depending on the activation energy, E_a. As E_a increases, then an increase in temperature has a greater effect on reaction rate. The effect of temperature can be easily determined by measuring k at three or more different temperatures since a plot of log k versus $1/T$ gives a straight line. Thus, merely recording the vitamin content of foods before and after heating gives information of very limited value.

4.1 FAT-SOLUBLE VITAMINS

These are generally more stable than the water-soluble vitamins but are prone to degradation at high temperatures in the presence of oxygen. They interact with the products of lipid oxidation and thus measures used to protect lipids will also improve the retention of these vitamins. Labuza (1971) has reviewed the kinetics of lipid oxidation.

4.1.1 Vitamin A

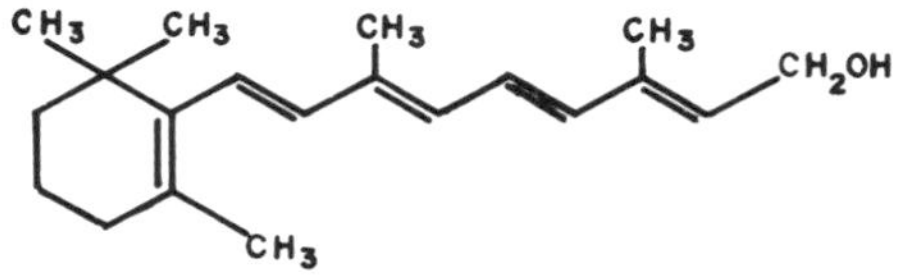

VITAMIN A (RETINOL)

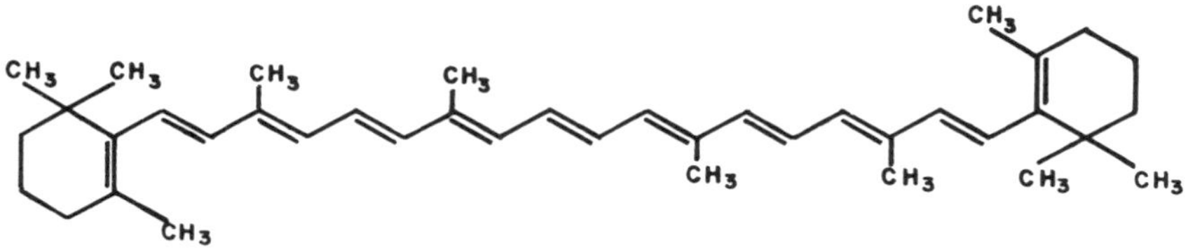

β – CAROTENE

Preformed vitamin A (retinol) is an alcohol but occurs mainly as a fatty acid ester, vitamin A palmitate, and is found almost exclusively in animals. Good sources are the liver of fish and animals, butter and eggs. In plants, vitamin A activity occurs only as provitamin A carotenoids which are converted in the animal body to vitamin A. The most important is β-carotene, which has similar properties to vitamin A but is more stable. Good sources are vegetables such as carrots and spinach, and fruits such as apricots and oranges.

The unsaturation of vitamin A renders it vulnerable to oxidation by heat, ultraviolet light and oxygen, catalysed by some mineral ions such as copper and iron. Vitamin A is quite stable in food processing, although losses may occur in the presence of oxidised oils (Aylward and Haisman, 1969). In liver braised with an internal temperature of 77°C, 90–100% of the vitamin was retained (Kizlaitis et al., 1964). There is no loss on spray or drum drying or evaporation of milk (Hartman and Dryden, 1965) and excellent stability was reported in the production of various baked products (Guttikar et al., 1965).

Only slight or no losses of carotenoids have been reported on cooking fresh or frozen broccoli (Sweeny et al., 1959, 1960; Chapman et al., 1960), frozen carrots (Ang et al., 1975) or peas (Eheart and Gott, 1964) by various methods. Hewston et al. (1948) found that carotene was extremely stable and during the preparation of 20 common foods, retentions approaching 100% were found in most cases.

Significant destruction of carotene may occur during dehydration. Della Monica and McDowell (1965) found that the losses of total β-carotene from carrots by tray, explosion-puff and freeze-drying were 26%, 19% and 15%, respectively. Corresponding losses were even higher for trans-β-carotene at 40%, 40% and 20%, such high losses indicating that thermal destruction as well as free-radical oxidation took place. Sweeney and Marsh (1971) also reported a 13% loss of β-carotene during freeze-drying of carrots and found that packing under low oxygen conditions reduced the rate of destruction on storage by a factor of ten. Loss of carotenoids in freeze-dried shrimp was found to follow a first-order reaction and increased water activity decreased the loss, as is the case for lipid oxidation (Martinez and Labuza, 1968).

4.1.2 Vitamin D

The two common compounds of the vitamin D group, vitamin D_2 (ergocalciferol) and vitamin D_3 (cholecalciferol), are sterols. Vitamin

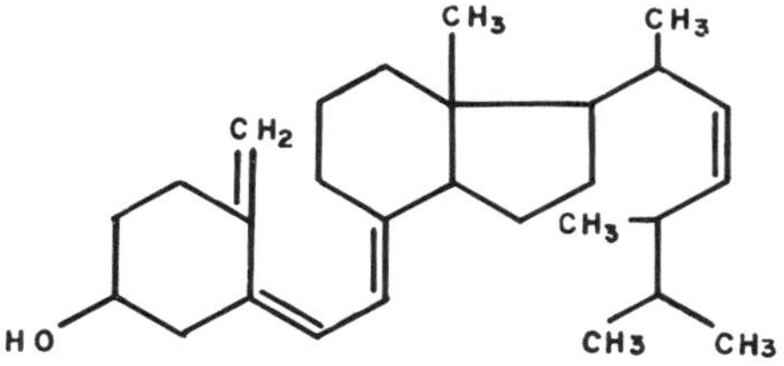

VITAMIN D₂

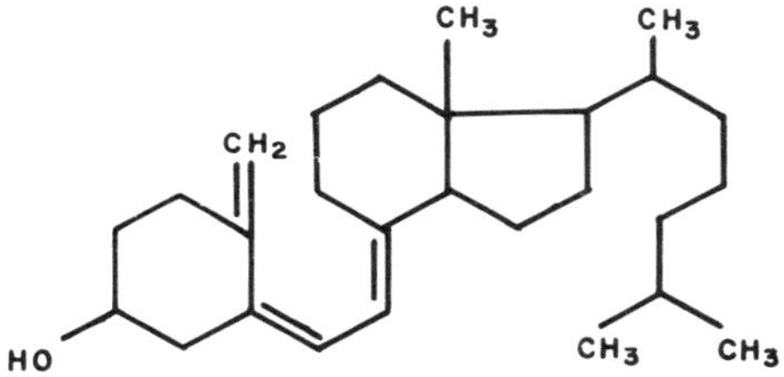

VITAMIN D₃

D is sensitive to the same factors as vitamin A but is generally more stable. Vitamin D_2 is more labile than vitamin D_3, possibly because of its extra double bond. The most widely distributed is vitamin D_3, which is found in large quantities in fish liver oils and fatty tissues and to a lesser extent in eggs, milk and butter.

Few reports are available on losses of vitamin D due to heating. No losses occur during pasteurisation or sterilisation of milk (Thompson, 1969) or during production of spray-dried, drum-dried or evaporated milk (Hartman and Dryden, 1965). But, like vitamin A, it was found to be unstable during the production of breakfast cereals (Anderson *et al.*, 1976) although no figures were given.

4.1.3 Vitamin E

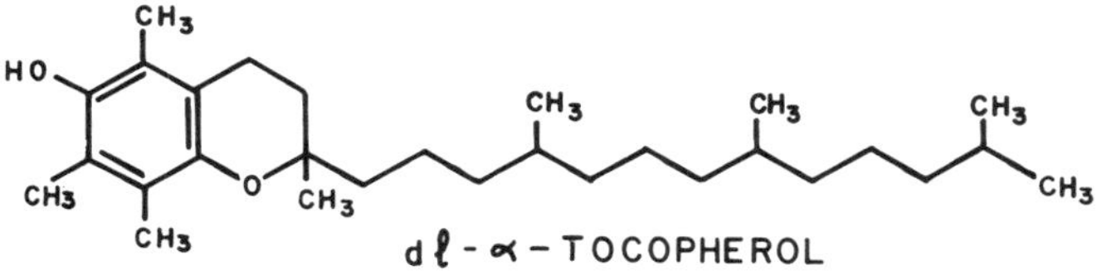

dℓ - α - TOCOPHEROL

Vitamin E consists of a series of compounds called tocopherols of which only the D-isomers are found in nature. The most important is α-tocopherol, rich sources being wheat germ and vegetable oils. Significant amounts are also found in fish, meat, eggs, dairy products and leafy vegetables. Bauernfeind (1977) has recently reviewed data relating to the tocopherol content of foods and factors influencing their retention.

Tocopherols are quite heat resistant. The losses during food processing are mainly due to oxidation which, since α-tocopherol is a powerful antioxidant, occurs readily, especially in the presence of oxygen and catalysts at high temperatures. Bunnel et al., (1965) reported that α-tocopherol is not destroyed to any great extent during normal cooking procedures. Although the loss from oils used to fry potato products was only 11%, large losses were found from the oils in these foods on storage, even at −12°C. They suggested that at low temperatures, hydroperoxides are still formed and preferentially react with tocopherol rather than decomposing to produce rancid-smelling products as they do at normal temperatures.

Anderson et al. (1976) obtained variable results for tocopherol destruction in the manufacture of breakfast cereals. Losses of 10–40% were found but in some cases apparent gains occurred. Between 4°C and 25°C destruction of tocopherols in seaweed was found to follow a first-order reaction with an activation energy of 10 kcal mol^{-1} (Jensen, 1969).

4.1.4 Vitamin K

VITAMIN K$_1$

Vitamin K is a group of 2-methyl-1,4-naphthaquinone derivatives with a side-chain in the 3-position. Vitamin K$_1$, which occurs in green vegetables, potatoes, some fruits and liver oils, is the predominant form in foodstuffs.

Vitamin K compounds are stable to heat but sensitive to light. Canning of vegetables was found to have no significant effect on vitamin K content (Richardson et al., 1961).

4.2 WATER-SOLUBLE VITAMINS

Losses of these vitamins into processing water during operations such as washing or blanching often far exceed losses due to thermal destruction. In order to reduce such losses, steam blanching is preferred and, if water is necessary in an operation, minimum quantities should be used.

4.2.1 Vitamin C

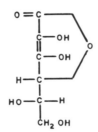

ASCORBIC ACID

The most important compound possessing vitamin C activity is L-ascorbic acid which is the enolic form of 3-keto-L-gulofuranolactone. It is widely distributed in varying concentrations in fruits and vegetables.

The enediol group on carbon atoms 2 and 3 of L-ascorbic acid is readily oxidised to a diketo group. The resulting dehydro-L-ascorbic acid (DHA) forms a redox system with L-ascorbic acid and has full vitamin C activity. However, DHA is more labile than L-ascorbic acid and further oxidation to 2,3-diketogulonic acid (DKGA) is irreversible and activity is lost.

The route and rate of oxidation of ascorbic acid in foods is influenced by several factors including pH, trace metals (particularly copper and iron), enzymes, oxidation–reduction potential, presence of oxygen as well as time and temperature. Bauernfeind and Pinkert (1970) have devised a reaction scheme which accounts for many of the known products of ascorbic acid oxidation (Fig. 4.1). The aerobic oxidation of ascorbic acid produces DHA and hydrogen peroxide, the latter leading to further oxidation. Traces of copper catalyse the reaction and the effect is enchanced by iron (Timberlake, 1960; Spanyar *et al.*, 1963, 1964a,b). Enzymes containing copper and iron in

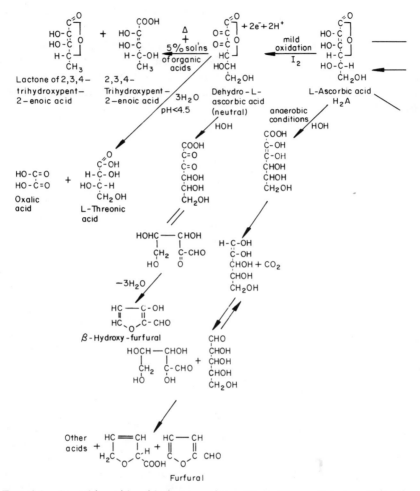

FIG. 4.1   Ascorbic acid oxidation reactions. (From Bauernfeind and Pinkert, 1970, by permission of Academic Press Inc.)

their prosthetic groups are even more active catalysts. Ascorbic acid oxidase, with molecular oxygen, causes direct destruction of the vitamin. Quinones, resulting from the action of phenolase on mono- and dihydroxyphenols, and oxidised cytochrome c produced by cytochrome oxidase, both react directly with ascorbic acid. Peroxidase, together with phenolic compounds cause oxidation by means of hydrogen peroxide.

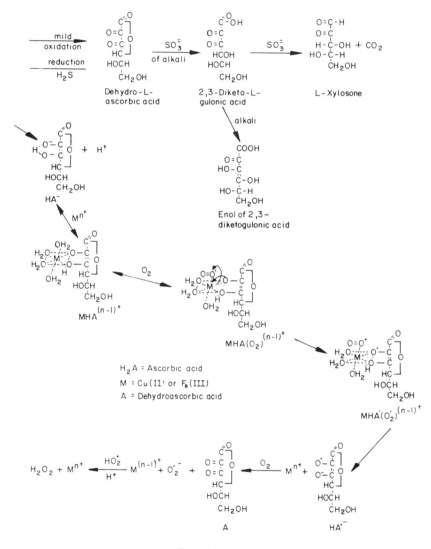

FIG. 4.1—cont.

For the copper-catalysed reaction, the amount of oxygen consumed can vary from one or two atoms per molecule of ascorbic acid oxidised whereas in the enzyme-catalysed reaction, the value is always unity. Otherwise, the reactions are similar (Scaife, 1959; Butt and Hallaway, 1961; Dawson, 1960). The oxidation involves an electron transfer in two stages, the first product being an unstable semiquinone-like free radical, monodehydroascorbic acid (Yamazaki *et al.*, 1959). The transfer of a further electron results in the formation of DHA which is also unstable and can be converted to DKGA by the opening of the lactone ring, a change which is rapid at neutral pH, instantaneous in alkali and slow at pH 3–4. The oxidation of ascorbic acid in sugar solutions in the presence of dissolved oxygen was found to follow first-order kinetics (Joslyn and Miller, 1949a) but under conditions of limited oxygen supply the initial rate of oxidation was reduced (Joslyn and Miller, 1949b). Singh *et al.* (1976) reported that degradation of ascorbic acid and oxygen uptake on storage of infant formula in the presence of limited dissolved oxygen followed a second-order reaction.

Numerous ascorbic acid degradation products have been identified. After heating in aqueous solution, Tatum *et al.* (1969) isolated 10 furan-type compounds, two lactones, three acids and 3-hydroxy-2-pyrone, the major product being furfural. Mikova and Davidek (1974) found 49 degradation products containing between one and ten carbon atoms. Other workers have identified 4-hydroxy-5-methyl-3(2H)-furanone at pH 4·3 (Anderegg and Neukom, 1972), 2-furancarboxylic acid at pH 1 (Mooser and Neukom, 1974), and from DHA heated at pH 2·2, 3-keto-4-deoxypentose and 3-hydroxy-2-pyrone (Kurata and Fujimaki, 1976a,b). Velisek *et al.* (1976) heated aqueous solutions of DHA and found the major volatile products were acetic acid, furfural, 2-acetylfuran, 3-hydroxy-2-pyrone and 2-furancarboxylic acid. The main product at pH 2 and 4 was 3-hydroxy-2-pyrone and at pH 6 and 8, acetic acid. The composition of the products was not affected by the presence of oxygen.

In the absence of free oxygen, or when it has been used up, anaerobic destruction takes over (Kefford *et al.*, 1959). It is much slower than aerobic degradation and is not catalysed by copper. Other metals such as lead, zinc and aluminium catalyse the reaction but at much higher levels than those encountered in foodstuffs (Finholt *et al.*, 1966). It is accelerated by fructose, particularly in the furanose form, and by sucrose, probably due to the formation of fructose on hydrolysis (Huelin, 1958). Unlike the aerobic reaction, the rate of anaerobic degradation is virtually independent of pH, except for a small maximum at pH 4, suggestive of a complex between ascorbic acid and its monohydrogen ion (Finholt *et al.*, 1963). The anaerobic decomposition of ascorbic acid in acidic aqueous solutions has been shown to produce furfural and carbon dioxide, L-xylose and several organic acids, primarily 2,5-dihydro-2-furoic acid (Huelin, 1953; Cier *et al.*, 1959; Anet and Reynolds, 1955; Coggiola, 1963). Yields of furfural and carbon dioxide were found in approximately equimolecular amounts (Yamamoto and Yamamoto, 1964; Finholt *et al.*, 1965a,b) with intermediate formation of 3-deoxy-L-pentosone (Kurata and Sakurai, 1967).

Finholt *et al.* (1965b) suggested that ascorbic acid decomposes via two parallel first-order reactions, one leading to the formation of furfural and one leading to the formation of other products. According to Huelin *et al.* (1971), three reactions may take place: the reaction involving unionised ascorbic acid and catalysed by hydrogen ions, with furfural as the major product; a reaction involving both the unionised form and the monovalent ascorbate ion with an optimum pH near pK_1 (4·2); and a reaction promoted by fructose, particularly at higher pH values.

Ascorbic acid is very stable in some fruit juices containing flavones and flavonones with a 3-hydroxyl-4-carbonyl group in the pyrone ring or a 3'4'-dihydroxy group in the B-ring (Spanyar *et al.*, 1964a,b; Clegg and Morton, 1968). This effect has been associated with their ability to complex with metal ions (Clements and Anderson, 1966). However, Harper *et al.* (1969) believe this is only a secondary function and that the protective action of flavonoids depends on their ability to act as free-radical acceptors.

The effect of water activity on the stability of ascorbic acid has received some attention. Several workers have shown that the destruction rate in foods increases with increasing water activity (Karel and Nickerson, 1964; Jensen, 1969; Vojnovich and Pfeifer, 1970; Lee and Labuza, 1975), although the effect on the activation energy is not consistent.

Ascorbic acid is relatively stable in fruit juices owing to the low pH and high citrate content. But since DHA is very labile it is essential that, during the processing of fruits and fruit juices, the material be kept in a deaerated condition, glass-lined or stainless-steel containers be used, and that enzyme activity be arrested. For example, unless tomato juice is produced by the 'hot-break' method to inactivate enzymes, much of the ascorbic acid is lost, and apple juice will rapidly lose its vitamin C and darken if not deaerated.

Very little breakdown of ascorbic acid occurs in canned-fruit products during the actual heating process and the loss is often used as an index of the degree of mishandling of the product. Cameron *et al.* (1955) reported that commercial practice used at that time resulted in the retention of 92–97% of the ascorbic acid in canned citrus juices. Escher and Neukom (1970) found that, for apple flakes, there was an 8% loss of vitamin C after slicing, 62% loss on blanching, 10% loss after purée preparation and only a 5% loss in the drum-drying process.

Sulphur dioxide is frequently used to protect ascorbic acid from oxidation during pasteurisation of fruit juices. It has also been used to inhibit peroxidase in tomato pulp (Chmielnicka, 1965) and to protect both vitamin C and β-carotene in dried apricots (Bolin and Stafford, 1974).

Although little loss of vitamin C occurs during the production of fruit juices, losses during storage can be high and storage at 10°C or below is preferred. Greater amounts are also retained in plain rather than lacquered cans or glass jars since oxygen reacts preferentially with the tin-plate (Khan *et al.*, 1963).

The ascorbic acid content of milk is reduced by pasteurisation, losses of 10% (Kon, 1961) and 20% (Hartman and Dryden, 1974) being reported. Significant destruction of ascorbic acid may occur in the preparation of mashed potatoes, ranging from 30% (Hellstrom, 1952–1953) to 80% (Wertz and Weir, 1946). Bring *et al.* (1963) reported losses of 57–63·5% in potato flakes reconstituted in water and losses of 27–29% were found by Cording *et al.* (1961) for both natural and added vitamin C in the production of potato flakes using an antioxidant. Jadhav *et al.* (1975) found that, in the production of dehydrated mashed potatoes, the major loss occurred at the mashing step. By the addition of sodium pyrophosphate, which complexes copper, the oxidation rate was reduced by 80%.

Domah *et al.* (1974) showed that the retention of total vitamin C in potatoes when fried at 140–180°C was better than when boiled. Apparently, although ascorbic acid is oxidised more rapidly to DHA during frying, further breakdown to DKGA is slower due to the dehydration effect.

The loss of vitamin C in cooked or processed vegetables is very variable due to both product and process variations. As with other water-soluble vitamins, large losses occur during water-blanching owing to leaching. Care must also be taken that the temperature of the blanch water does not drop to a level which temporarily accelerates enzyme activity. Overall losses in a range of canned vegetables reported by Watt and Merrill (1963) varied so widely that generalisations are impossible. Comprehensive data have been collected on the influence of cooking methods (boiling, steaming, pressure cooking), state of subdivision, volume of water used and hot-holding on vitamin C retention in a wide range of vegetables (Harris and von Loesecke, 1960; Harris and Karmas, 1975). Hot-holding of cooked vegetables is particularly detrimental, losses commonly exceeding 50% after one hour. A rough guide to the extent and source of losses to be expected in household cooking of vegetables is shown in Table 4.2.

TABLE 4.2

EFFECT OF HOUSEHOLD COOKING ON ASCORBIC ACID CONTENT OF VEGETABLES[a] (FROM OLLIVER, 1967, BY PERMISSION OF ACADEMIC PRESS, INC.)

Method	% Ascorbic acid		
	destroyed	extracted	retained
Green Vegetables			
Boiling A[b]	10–15	45–60	25–45
Boiling B[c]	10–15	15–30	55–75
Steaming	30–40	< 10	60–70
Pressure cooking	20–40	< 10	60–80
Root Vegetables[d]			
Boiling	10–20	15–25	55–75
Steaming	30–50	< 10	50–70
Pressure cooking	45–55	< 10	45–55

[a]Typical values; [b]ratio of water to vegetable high, long cooking time; [c]ratio of water to vegetable low, short cooking time; [d]whole or large pieces.

Despite the number of publications dealing with vitamin C losses in heated foodstuffs, there are very little kinetic data available. However, there are some data available concerning destruction at storage temperatures and Labuza (1972) has tabulated a useful summary of this, activation energies ranging from 8·8 to 45 kcal mol^{-1}.

4.2.2   Vitamin B₁ (Thiamine)

THIAMINE

Vitamin B₁ is also known as thiamine because of the thiazole and pyrimidine rings in its structure. It occurs in foods either in the free form or in a combined form as a protein complex, phosphorus–protein complex, or as its pyrophosphoric acid ester (cocarboxylase). Good sources are lean pork, kidney, liver, beans, peas, nuts and cereals.

Thiamine is more stable than ascorbic acid but is the most heat labile of the B vitamins, particularly under alkaline conditions. Many thermal breakdown products of thiamine have been reported. A comprehensive review of the chemistry of thiamine degradation has been given by Dwivedi and Arnold (1973) who devised the breakdown scheme shown in Fig. 4.2. It was recognised very early that heating could split the thiamine molecule (Williams, 1938; Obermeyer and Chen, 1945). At pH 6·0 and below there is a preferential cleavage of the methylene 'bridge' with 4-methyl-5-(β-hydroxyethyl)thiazole as the major sulphur-containing product (Dwivedi and Arnold, 1972). According to the same authors the small amounts of the pseudo base and/or thiol forms of thiamine which exist above pH 6·0 may account for the production of hydrogen sulphide and various other products since the energy of activation for the breakdown of the thiazole ring in these forms is lower than that for cleavage of the methylene 'bridge'.

Morfee and Liska (1971, 1972) studied thiamine breakdown products in heated model milk systems and evaporated milk at slightly acid or basic pH. Sulphur was a major degradation product and a large proportion of the sulphur-containing products were reversibly bound to protein. They suggested this was due either to disulphide bonding or reaction with the free –NH₂ groups of the protein. The most important factors governing thiamine loss in heated foodstuffs are temperature, time of heating and pH. Other important factors are the presence of metal ions, particularly copper, the form of the vitamin and the absence of protective agents.

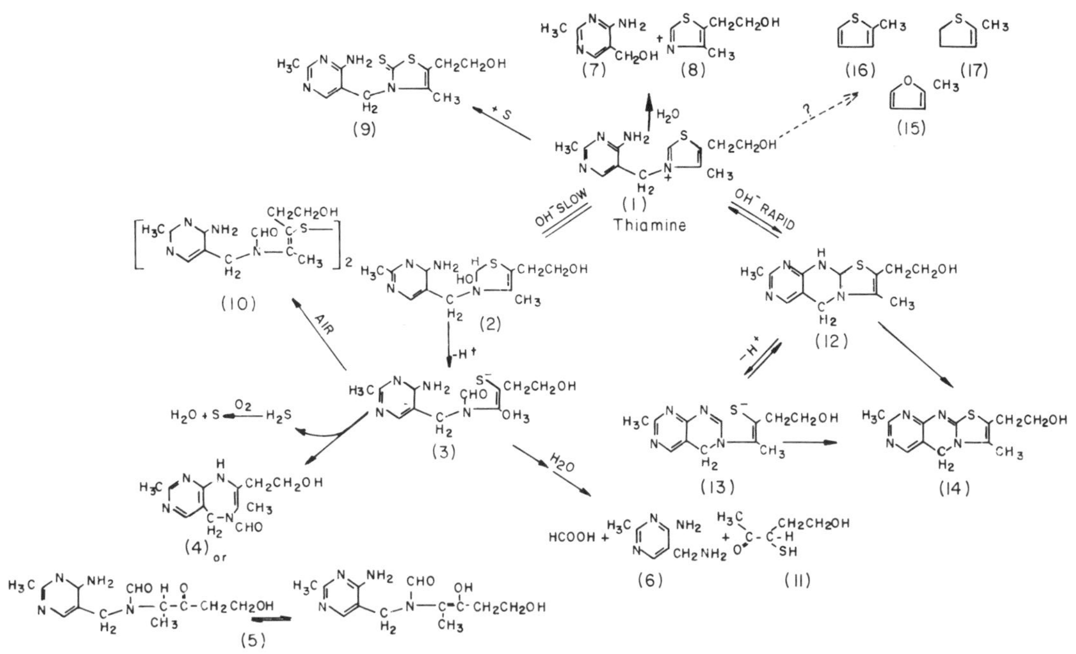

FIG. 4.2 Thiamine degradation reactions: (1) thiamine; (2) carbinol form of thiamine; (3) thiol form of thiamine; (4) dethiothiamine; (5) dethiothiamine; (6) 2-methyl-4-amino-5-aminomethyl pyrimidine; (7) 2-methyl-4-amino-5-hydroxymethyl pyrimidine; (8) 4-methyl-5-(β-hydroxyethyl) thiazole; (9) thiothiazolone; (10) thiamine disulphide; (11) thioketone; (12) dihydrothiochrome; (13) yellow form of thiamine; (14) thiochrome; (15) 2-methylfuran; (16) 2-methylthiophene; (17) 2-methyl-4, 5-dihydrothiophene. (From Dwivedi and Arnold, 1973. Reprinted with permission. Copyright by the American Chemical Society.)

It is generally accepted that cocarboxylase is less stable than thiamine. Mulley *et al.* (1975b) suggested the reason was connected with the pyrophosphoric acid group since this is the only difference between the two molecules. According to Farrer (1955) different proportions of cocarboxylase in meats are likely to be the main variable affecting thiamine loss.

The susceptibility of thiamine to breakdown in the presence of alkali is well known. According to Harris (1960) no loss of thiamine is suffered when it is boiled in acid for several hours, yet the loss approaches 100% when boiled at pH 9 for 20 min. Mulley *et al.* (1975b) found a sharp drop in stability of thiamine hydrochloride above pH 6, which corresponded roughly to neutralisation of the hydrochloride. Apparently, at low pH, the protonated form predominates, being less heat-labile than thiamine (Dwivedi and Arnold, 1972).

Metals capable of forming complex anions with thiamine will accelerate its rate of destruction (Farrer, 1947). A thiamine–copper complex has been isolated (Tanaka, 1966a,b) and it has been proposed that such complexes are constantly being formed and degraded, resulting in the gradual destruction of thiamine (Tanaka, 1969).

Thiamine participates in a Maillard-type reaction with glucose (van der Poel, 1956; Lhoest, 1958) but it is not known to what extent this affects its loss during processing. Other studies have shown that fructose, mannitol and inositol actually reduce the rate of thiamine destruction (Ache and Ribeiro, 1945; Wai *et al.*, 1962).

Numerous reports have indicated that thiamine in natural products is more stable to heat than in either aqueous or buffer solution. Proteins retard the rate of destruction of thiamine but the mode of action is not clear. Wada and Suzuki (1965) suggested that the sulphydryl groups are involved, and reversible bonding between thiamine and protein was noted by Morfee and Liska (1971). Leichter and Joslyn (1969) found that casein and also soluble starch protected thiamine and suggested that the effect is associated with some macromolecular property. Adsorption may play a rôle in this respect.

Sulphite can split thiamine into free thiazole base and pyrimidylmethane sulphuric acid. For this reason sulphur dioxide is usually not permitted as an additive to foods which contribute significant quantities of thiamine to the diet. According to de Ritter (1976) the reaction is very slow at pH 3, very rapid at pH 5 and instantaneous at pH 6. As in the case of ascorbic acid, thiamine losses are greater at higher moisture contents (Rice *et al.*, 1944; Hollenbeck and Obermeyer, 1952).

There is a possibility that some of the degradation products of thiamine may contribute to the flavour of food systems. Heated thiamine solutions have been reported to give rise to food-like odours (Arnold *et al.*, 1969; Morfee and Liska, 1972) and certain known breakdown products have been identified as flavour constituents (Merritt *et al.*, 1963; Nonaka *et al.*, 1967). However, in the case of hydrogen sulphide, a quantitative study has shown that the amounts produced would be unlikely to play a significant rôle in influencing flavour (Dwivedi and Arnold, 1971).

Farrer (1955) has made an extensive review of thiamine stability in foods and showed that in almost all cases from which kinetic data could be calculated, the rate of destruction followed a first-order reaction. Data for the decimal reduction time, and energy of activation for thiamine destruction from various sources, are given in Table 4.3. The data obtained from Farrer (1955), however, has been corrected as indicated by Labuza (1972).

Thiamine losses in bread making were reviewed by Farrer (1955). These ranged from 3–35% with an average of about 20%. Toasting for periods of 30–70 s has been shown to result in the destruction of 10–30% of the thiamine (Downs and Meckel, 1943).

Several reports have demonstrated the marked effect of pH on thiamine retention in cereal products. White *et al.* (1946) found that whole wheat cooked for 5 min at pH 6·2 lost 8·5% of its thiamine whereas a sample of enriched farina at pH 6·9 lost 33·9%. Briant and Klosterman (1950) found that, in muffins, thiamine destruction increased from 27 to 64% as the pH was raised from 6·9 to 7·5 by the addition of baking powder. Other work on scones (Barackman, 1942; Briant and Hutchins, 1946), bread (Wilson, 1942; Kawasaki and Kani, 1949), corn bread and muffins (Pace and Whitacre, 1953a,b) demonstrated similar effects.

Steaming rice results in thiamine losses of about 5% (Kik, 1945; Leong and Strahan, 1952) but losses may be much higher on boiling, particularly if the water is alkaline. Roy (1953) found 60–70% loss at pH 9–10 and 5–8% loss at pH 4–5 and Roy and Rao (1963) found a 36% loss using well water compared to zero loss in distilled water.

The losses of thiamine in meat will depend on several factors such as the size of the cut, fat content and thermal gradient. Reported retentions have ranged from 90% in fried beef (Tucker *et al.*, 1946) to

TABLE 4.3

KINETIC PARAMETERS FOR THE DESTRUCTION OF THIAMINE

Medium	Temperature °C	D value[a]	E_a^b	Reference
Yeast extract (natural B₁)	Storage		23·5	Farrer (1955)
Yeast extract (mononitrate)	Storage		22·8	
Cheese (natural B₁)	Storage		19·4	
Cheese (mononitrate)	Storage		18·5	
Peanut butter	Storage		15·0	
Orange juice	Storage		15·5	
Dehydrated pork	27	209 days	22	Rice et al. (1944)
Dehydrated pork	37	54		
Dehydrated pork	49	10·7		
Dehydrated pork	63	4·0		
Phosphate buffer pH 3	100	2879 min		Farrer (1955)
Phosphate buffer pH 5	100	1535		
Phosphate buffer pH 7	100	144		
Phosphate buffer pH 8	100	16·5		
Aqueous solution	100	799	30	Dwivedi & Arnold (1971)
Aqueous solution	120	100		
Fresh pork	99	920	18·5	Farrer(1955)
Fresh pork	110	406		
Fresh pork	118·5	200		
Fresh pork	126·5	105		

	Temperature	Decimal reduction time[a]	Energy of activation[b]	Reference
Lean pork	99	480		Rice & Beuk (1945)
Lean pork	98	800		Greenwood et al. (1943)
Beef stew	82	1201		Kahn & Livingston (1970)
Pea purée	100	1100		
Carrot purée	100	1060		Farrer (1953)
Cabbage purée	100	860		
Potato purée	100	1160, 720		
Carrot purée	121	158	27	
Green bean purée	121	145	27	
Pea purée	121	163	27	
Spinach purée	121	134	27	
Beef heart purée	121	115	27	Feliciotti & Esselen (1957)
Beef liver purée	121	124	27	
Lamb purée	121	120	27	
Pork purée	121	157	27	
Whole peas	121	164	21·2	Bendix et al. (1951)
Phosphate buffer	121	157	29·4	
Pea purée	121	247	27·5	
Beef purée	121	254	27·4	Mulley et al. (1975a)
Peas-in-brine	121	227	27·0	

[a]Decimal reduction time at temperature stated; [b]energy of activation (kcal mol^{-1}).

29% in pressure-cooked lamb stews (Cover and Dilsaver, 1947). However, much of the vitamin lost in moist cooking methods is recoverable in the drip. As a rough guide it would appear that losses are about 15–40% on boiling, 40–60% on roasting, 50–75% on canning, 40–45% on braising and 40–50% on frying, pork generally giving the highest retention (Harris and von Loesecke, 1960; Farrer, 1955; Engler and Bowers, 1976).

Boiling, pressure cooking or steaming fresh vegetables generally results in thiamine retentions above 75%, although large losses may occur on hot-holding or on boiling due to leaching (Harris and Karmas, 1975). Losses on canning may also be very high, sometimes in excess of 80% (Watt and Merrill, 1963). Re-cooking frozen vegetables resulted in an average loss of 16% but over half of this was recoverable in the cooking water (Teply and Derse, 1958). Kon (1941) found the following losses during milk processing: pasteurising, 10%; sterilising, 30%; spray-drying, 10%; roller-drying, 15%; and condensing 40%. Subsequent reports are in rough agreement with these figures.

Losses of thiamine on cooking eggs by various methods range from 9–26% with an average of about 15% (Stamberg and Peterson, 1946; Lane *et al.*, 1942; Everson and Souders, 1957). High losses occur in peanuts during roasting. Fournier *et al.* (1949) found that over 90% thiamine was destroyed after roasting at 155–160°C for 20 min.

4.2.3 Vitamin B$_2$ (Riboflavin)

RIBOFLAVIN

Riboflavin consists of the flavin pigment, lumichrome, and the reduced form of ribose, from which its name is derived. It is present in most living cells, usually as a dinucleotide, phosphate ester or bound to protein. Important sources are milk, liver, kidney, all meats, tomatoes, yeast and leafy green vegetables.

Riboflavin is heat stable in acid solution, relatively stable at neutral pH but destroyed rapidly under alkaline conditions. It is stable in the presence of oxidising agents but is very sensitive to light, being converted to lumiflavine.

Losses in canning vegetables range from about 25 to 70% but these include leaching losses (Watt and Merrill, 1963; Harris and Karmas, 1975). Boiling vegetables generally results in retentions of over 60% and in steaming of over 80%, although holding on a steam table may result in extensive destruction of riboflavin (Hewston et al., 1948; Harris and von Loesecke, 1960). Re-heating frozen vegetables rarely gives losses above 20%, of which about two-thirds is due to leaching (Ang et al., 1975; Teply and Derse, 1958).

Cooking meat only results in small losses of riboflavin, retentions in excess of 90% being common (Engler and Bowers, 1976). Negligible losses were reported by Hodson (1941) for chicken cooked by various methods or for cooked turkey (Bowers and Fryer, 1972). Pre-cooking chicken under conditions which led to a 50% loss of thiamine resulted in complete retention of riboflavin and niacin (Rowe et al., 1963).

There is no loss of riboflavin during pasteurisation or sterilisation of milk (Thompson, 1969). In cases where destruction occurs, this is probably due to insufficient protection from light.

Little destruction of riboflavin occurs during the baking of cereal goods. At pH 6·6 there was an 11% loss in corn bread but complete retention at pH 5·4 (Thomas et al., 1952). Losses of up to 15% were noted during the severe conditions employed in breakfast-cereal manufacture (Anderson et al., 1976). In corn grits extruded at 300 or 380°F and 13% moisture content, retention of riboflavin was complete but increasing the moisture content to 16% gave a retention of only 53·6%. Deep-fat frying may cause significant destruction of riboflavin, a loss of 23% being recorded for doughnuts cooked in this way (Everson and Smith, 1945).

4.2.4 Vitamin B₆ (Pyridoxine)

CH₂OH

HO — CH₂OH

CH₃   N
       H

PYRIDOXINE (PYRIDOXOL)

Vitamin B_6 activity is shown by three substituted pyridine derivatives differing only in the functional group in the 4-position. These are pyridoxine (pyridoxol), which is also used to denote the B_6 group, its aldehyde, pyridoxal, and its amine, pyridoxamine.

The three forms are widely distributed in low concentrations in all plant and animal tissues, good sources being meat, fish, liver, egg-yolk, milk, yeast, cereals and green vegetables.

Pyridoxine is stable to heat in acidic and alkaline solution but is decomposed by light at neutrality and alkaline pH. The other forms are significantly less stable and Orr and Watt (1972) have pointed out the lack of information concerning shifts among the forms on cooking.

Vitamin B_6 is fairly stable in most foods, although early studies on cooked meat indicated the reverse. McIntyre et al. (1944) found losses of about 70% by roasting or boiling and 80% by braising or stewing with only about 5% recoverable in the drip. Henderson et al. (1941) found losses of 60%, 50% and 30%, respectively, on boiling, roasting or frying pork ham. Lushbough et al. (1959) reported 42–67% retention in meat cooked by several methods with up to 13% accounted for in the drip. High retentions were recorded by Meyer et al. (1969). For oven-roasted beef loin, a 28% loss was found including 16% in the drip and for oven-braised round, a 51% loss with 34% in the drip. Losses on canning meat or seafoods averaged 43–49% but were negligible in dried meats (Schroeder, 1971). The reason for the wide variations in apparent stability is not clear but may be partly accounted for by differences in methodology.

Large losses of vitamin B_6 occur as a result of canning vegetables, ranging from 40 to 77% (Richardson et al., 1961; Schroeder, 1971) while in canned fruit, losses averaged 38% (Schroeder, 1971). Reheating frozen vegetables resulted in an average loss of 29% with about one-third of this due to leaching (Teply and Derse, 1958).

Baking appears to result in little destruction of vitamin B_6 since Hennessy et al. (1960) found complete retention of pyridoxine hydrochloride added to bread, although this is more stable than the natural form of the vitamin (Hassinen et al., 1954).

In milk products, pyridoxine destruction can be quite serious. Attention was drawn to this when symptoms of pyridoxine deficiency were observed in infants fed on canned liquid milk products (Coursin, 1954). The vitamin B_6 activity of fresh milk is largely due to pyridoxal (Rabinowitz and Snell, 1948). During processing and storage of evaporated milk this may be converted to pyridoxamine. Reaction may also take place with cysteine producing a sulphur-containing product of lowered activity (Bernhart *et al.*, 1960). Hassinen *et al.* (1954) found losses of 50–67% of the natural vitamin B_6 in processed liquid infant formula but only 16% of added pyridoxine hydrochloride was destroyed. Spray-drying only resulted in 17–31% loss. Davies *et al.* (1959) studied the evaporation and sterilisation of whole milk. Assays using *S. carlsbergensis*, chick and rat growth gave retentions of 30, 55 and 65%, respectively. Thompson (1969) reported no destruction in milk pasteurised or sterilised conventionally or by rapid-heating methods.

Some idea of the heat lability of pyridoxine can be gained from the work of Everson *et al.* (1964a,b). For thiamine, the loss in canned strained lima beans and strained beef were 40·3 and 21·6%, respectively. Comparable figures for pyridoxine were 10·1 and 2·9%. High-temperature–short-time (HTST) processing more than halved the thiamine loss while pyridoxine was virtually unchanged, indicating that pyridoxine destruction is less temperature dependent. It is apparent that data for vitamin B_6 destruction are limited and inconsistent and a great deal more work is needed.

4.2.5 Vitamin B_{12}

The compounds in this group have a complicated structure with a central 'corrin' ring similar to the porphyrins but containing a cobalt atom. The most important is cyanocobalamin.

Only small amounts of vitamin B_{12} are found in foods, the main dietary sources being entirely of animal origin such as liver, kidney and egg-yolk.

The optimum stability of cyanocobalamin is at pH 4·5–5·0 (Bartilucci and Foss, 1954) and it is stable to retorting in this region. It is slightly unstable in mild alkaline or acid solutions and can be cleaved by dilute acids to the inactive corrin nucleus (Moore and Folkers, 1968). Oxidising and reducing agents, and exposure to light may cause destruction which is catalysed by ferrous salts (Shenoy and Ramasarma, 1955) although ferric salts enhance its stability.

The few reported studies available indicate that vitamin B_{12} is fairly stable in heated foodstuffs. Hartman *et al.* (1956) found that pasteurisation and 3-day storage of milk had no effect on its vitamin B_{12} content. Thompson (1969) reported no loss in pasteurising milk by HTST treatment but the holder method resulted in a loss of about

CYANOCOBALAMIN

10%. In-bottle sterilisation destroyed 30% of the vitamin B_{12} which was reduced to 10% by using an ultra-high temperature (UHT) method. Karlin *et al.* (1969) found a similar loss using UHT sterilisation whereas the in-bottle method at 119–120°C for 13–15 min resulted in a loss of 77%. In breakfast-cereal manufacture, only about 15% of the vitamin B_{12} was destroyed (Anderson *et al.*, 1976) and small losses of between 0 and 21% were also observed in the oven heating of frozen meals containing meat and fish (de Ritter *et al.*, 1974).

4.2.6 Nicotinic Acid and Nicotinamide

NICOTINIC ACID   NICOTINAMIDE

Nicotinic acid (niacin) is pyridine β-carboxylic acid and nicotinamide (niacinamide), the corresponding amide, possesses equal vitamin activity. Nicotinic acid is widely distributed in foods, rich sources being yeast, meat, liver, fish, peanuts and legumes. Potatoes and whole wheat are also good sources. In some foods, particularly maize, it is unavailable but can be released by treatment with mild alkali.

Niacin is probably the most stable of all the vitamins and is not appreciably affected by heat or light in the normal pH range of foods. Thus, very little is destroyed during the cooking of meat but up to one-half may be lost in the drip (Engler and Bowers, 1976), the losses being greater in braising or stewing than frying or roasting. Retentions during microwave or conventional cooking of ground beef or frozen pork patties averaged over 90% (Thomas et al., 1949; Causey et al., 1950).

Leaching is probably the major cause of niacin losses from vegetables during canning operations, being as high as 75% (Watt and Merrill, 1963). Destruction is only slight on boiling or steaming and retentions greater than 90% are not uncommon (Harris and Karmas, 1975). Page and Hanning (1963) tested 58 samples of boiled and baked potatoes, losses averaging 18% and 4%, respectively. Losses on re-heating frozen vegetables averaged 12% and in some cases were as high as 26% but two-thirds of the loss was due to leaching (Teply and Derse, 1958). A 20% loss of niacin was reported by Miller et al. (1973) for drum-dried bean powders but acidification to pH 3·5 reduced this to only 1%.

Losses are usually negligible during the baking of cereal products, regardless of pH (Anderson et al., 1976; Harris and von Loesecke, 1960) and during the pasteurisation or sterilisation of milk (Hartman and Dryden, 1974; Thompson, 1969; Kon, 1961).

4.2.7 Pantothenic Acid

$$CH_2OH - \underset{\underset{CH_3}{|}}{\overset{\overset{CH_3}{|}}{C}} - CHOH - CO - NH - CH_2 - CH_2 - COOH$$

PANTOTHENIC ACID

Chemically, pantothenic acid is an α,δ-dihydroxy-β,β-dimethyl-butyryl-β'-alanide, and only the dextro-rotary form has vitamin activity. It is not often found in the free state but is widely distributed as a component of coenzyme-A. Rich sources are liver, kidney and lean meat, egg-yolk and yeast. Cereals and some green plants, especially legumes, are also good sources.

Stability of pantothenic acid is very pH-dependent but, unlike thiamine, it is more stable as pH increases, with an optimum around pH 6–7 (Frost and McIntyre, 1944).

Several workers have studied the retention of pantothenic acid during the cooking of meat. In general, the vitamin has good thermal stability, similar to that of riboflavin or niacin, with most of the losses caused by transference to the drip. Losses of 12–37% were reported in various cooked meats (Cheldelin and Williams, 1943) and 7–25% in fried steak or liver (Meyer et al., 1947). Schweigert and Guthneck (1953) found losses of 15–50% in pork, beef and lamb, greater losses occurring in roasting than in broiling. Cover et al. (1947) found that stewing beef and lamb resulted in about 25% loss which was increased by 10% if the meat was browned. Over 50% of the vitamin was leached into the broth when large volumes of water were used. Work by Meyer et al. (1969) on beef roasts indicated that thermal destruction of pantothenic acid is neglibible but large amounts were transferred to the drip, 19% in the case of oven-roasted loin and 44% for oven-braised round.

The data reported by Schroeder (1971) indicate the losses of pantothenic acid in canned foods of animal origin to range from 20 to 35% and in canned vegetables from 46 to 78%. In canned fruits and juices, the average loss was 50%. The high losses in canned vegetables are probably more a reflection of operations such as washing and blanching rather than thermal destruction in the can, since the losses in producing frozen vegetables were also high. Steaming vegetables only results in small losses of around 10% (Harris and von Loesecke, 1960). An average loss of 40% was found in re-cooked frozen vegetables but almost one-half of this was recoverable in the cooking water (Teply and Derse, 1958). Little data are available for retention of pantothenic acid in other foodstuffs but the indications are that it is relatively stable.

4.2.8 Biotin

Biotin is a cyclic derivation of urea with an attached thiophene ring. Since it contains three asymmetric carbon atoms, there are eight possible stereoisomers, of which only the so-called d-biotin is found in nature and has vitamin activity.

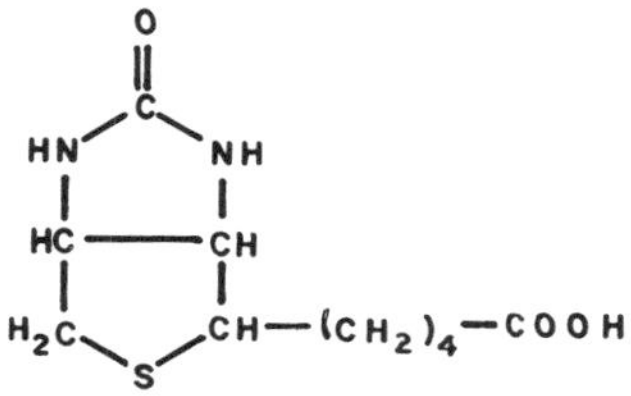

BIOTIN

Biotin is widely distributed in foods in small concentrations. It is found partly in the free state (vegetables, fruit, milk, rice bran) and partly in a form bound to protein (animal tissue, plant seeds, yeast). Relatively high concentrations are found in yeast, liver and kidney.

Biotin is stable to heat and light, but is unstable in strong acids and alkalis. Although few studies have been made on biotin stability in foods, the little evidence available indicates good stability. Retentions of biotin in cooked meats averaged 77% (Schweigert *et al.*, 1943) and it was found to be stable during the production of breakfast cereals (Anderson *et al.*, 1976). In canned vegetables, however, losses ranged from 0 to 78% with an average of 51% (Schroeder, 1971) but, as with other water-soluble vitamins, leaching probably accounted for a considerable proportion of this loss.

4.2.9 Folic Acid

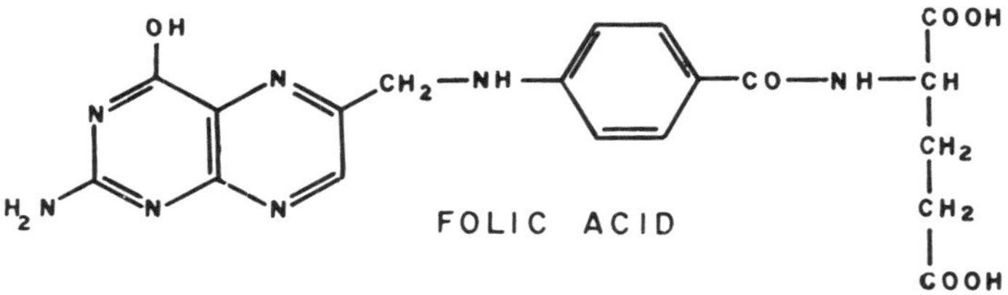

FOLIC ACID

Folic acid or folacin is used as the group name to denote compounds with folic acid activity. These always contain one or more linked molecules of glutamic acid which are essential for their biological activity. The basic form is pteroylmonoglutamic acid (PGA) which is a combination of the pteridine nucleus, *p*-aminobenzoic acid and glutamic acid. Further addition of glutamate to the γ-carboxy group of the glutamic acid yields pteroylglutamic acid. More complex forms such as dihydro-, tetrahydro-, methyl- and formylfolates exist in foods, usually in far greater quantities than PGA (Butterworth *et al.*, 1963; Santini *et al.*, 1964; Perry, 1971).

Compounds with folic acid activity are widely distributed in foods in minute concentrations. Folic acid conjugates are present in liver, kidney, lean meat, milk, cheese, dark-leaf vegetables (in the free state in spinach), cauliflower, legumes and wheat germ. Perloff and Butrum (1977) have presented figures for the folacin content of almost 300 foodstuffs.

In microbiological assays 'free folacin' denotes that which can promote growth in unmodified form whereas 'total folacin' refers to the vitamin available after treatment with a conjugase enzyme. Differences in methodology are often responsible for variations in test results.

There has been evidence to suggest that folacin deficiency is the most widespread vitamin deficiency in humans (Leevy *et al.*, 1965; Herbert, 1968). Surveys indicating low intakes of folic acid (Walker and Page, 1975) and low serum folate levels (Baker *et al.*, 1975) have highlighted the seriousness of folacin destruction in foodstuffs.

According to Borenstein (1968) the monoglutamate is moderately heat-stable in acid solution and at neutrality. It is stabilised by ascorbate but destruction is accelerated by copper, air and sunlight in the presence of riboflavin. The data reported by Perloff and Butrum (1977) indicate that losses during cooking vary greatly among foods and are due to both thermal destruction and leaching into the cooking water. Free folacin appears to be more labile than the conjugate forms. After boiling a wide range of foods for 5 min, 50–90% of the free folacin and 10–80% of the total folacin was lost (Taguchi *et al.*, 1973). When the boiling period was increased to 15 min the respective figures were 90–95% and 60–80%. Another study using a wide range of foods gave an average loss of 73% for free folacin and 45% for total folacin after cooking (Huskisson and Retief, 1970).

Cheldelin *et al.* (1943) found that, of the B vitamins, folic acid was the most seriously affected by cooking. Losses among meats and fish ranged from 95% for pork chops to 46% for halibut. No loss was found by Hurdle *et al.* (1968) in boiled or fried liver, or fried chicken. Losses in the cooked meats examined by Schweigert *et al.* (1946) ranged from 33 to 92%, and beef, pork or chicken boiled for 15 min retained less than one-half of their free or total folic acid (Taguchi *et al.*, 1973). A 70% loss of folate was found by Hurdle *et al.* (1968) in egg-yolk after boiling but only 29% after frying.

In canned vegetables, losses ranged from 35 to 84% (Schroeder, 1971). Boiling cabbage and potatoes for as little as 5 min resulted in losses of free folic acid of 68% and 50%, respectively, and losses of total folic acid of 46% and 8% (Taguchi *et al.*, 1973). In the same study, it was found that boiling rice for 15 min gave a retention of only 10% of the total folic acid. In re-cooked frozen vegetables losses averaged 22%, two-thirds being due to leaching (Teply and Derse, 1958). Leaching was also the major reason for the loss of folic acid in canned chickpeas (Lin *et al.*, 1975) or pinto beans (Miller *et al.*, 1973).

Keagy *et al.* (1975) investigated the stability of natural and added folic acid in flour. During bread making almost one-third of the natural folic acid was destroyed compared to only 11% for synthetic pteroylglutamic acid. Losses of up to 15% were found in processed breakfast cereals (Anderson *et al.*, 1976).

Serious destruction of folic acid may occur in milk processing. It is stable during pasteurisation but some losses may occur during dehydration (Ghitis and Candanosa, 1966). Boiling or sterilisation however, may result in destruction of up to 97% of the vitamin (Karlin, 1960).

4.3 MODERN HEATING PROCESSES

The following processes have been mentioned separately on account of their relatively recent development and their increasing popularity.

4.3.1 Microwave Heating

There appears to be no consistent trend regarding vitamin retention in foods processed by microwave energy compared to conventional heating methods. Engler and Bowers (1976) reviewed the effects of microwave heating on the retention of B vitamins in meat. In some cases retention was improved but in others conventional methods were superior. Reviews by Livingston *et al.* (1973) and Ang and Livingston (1974) indicated a similar situation for the retention of thiamine, riboflavin and ascorbic acid in various foods.

Goldblith *et al.* (1968) showed that the destruction of thiamine in buffered solutions by microwave energy was due solely to the temperature effect, and van Zante and Johnson (1970) could find no significant difference in the retention of thiamine and riboflavin heated electrically or by microwaves. Thus, no great benefits with respect to vitamin retention can be expected from the use of microwave energy for heating processes.

4.3.2 High-Temperature–Short-Time (HTST) Processes

Since higher processing temperatures have a greater effect on bacterial kinetics than many reactions leading to destruction of vitamins and flavours, HTST methods of heating are receiving increased attention.

HTST processes generally result in improved vitamin retention for pasteurisation treatments (Hartman and Dryden, 1965; Thompson, 1969), or for sterilisation aseptically or in convection packs (Feaster et al., 1949; Clifcorn et al., 1950; Everson et al., 1964a,b). In most cases, a markedly improved vitamin retention is obtained, particularly in the case of thiamine. In processes where enzymes must be destroyed, however, there are limitations to the heating regime which can be employed owing to the similar temperature response of nutrients, quality factors and enzymes (Lund, 1975).

In conduction-heating packs, HTST methods do not necessarily result in greater retention of vitamins. Whereas in aseptic processing or sterilisation of convective-heating packs it is possible to subject the entire food material to a similar heating cycle, in conduction packs the material at the periphery of the container is subjected to a much more severe treatment than that required to achieve commercial sterility. Various methods for calculating the average destruction of nutrients in conduction-heating packs have been presented (Hayakawa, 1969; Jen et al., 1971; Manson et al., 1970; Teixeira et al., 1969), and attempts have been made to optimise the processes used. Teixeira et al. (1969) found that HTST treatment for canned green-bean purée was not the best method to be employed for maximising thiamine retention. It was also found, using a simulated computer system representing sterilisation of canned pork (Teixeira et al., 1975), that little significant advantage was to be gained by using time-varying surface-temperature policies of equal sterilising value rather than a constant-temperature policy.

Methods of designing thermal processes for maximising nutrient retention have recently been reviewed in detail by Lund (1977). For optimisation, each heating process and product must be considered individually. It is only possible to do this if the temperature response of the nutrient of interest is known. This means that kinetic data for the thermal destruction of vitamins in food materials must be obtained. Unfortunately, with the exception of thiamine, little useful information of this nature is available.

REFERENCES

Ache, L. & Ribeiro, O. F. (1945) *Rev. Fac. Med. Vet. Univ. Sao Paulo*, **3**, 27. *Chem. Abstr.* (1946) **40**, 7525.

Anderegg, P. & Neukom, H. (1972) *Mitt. Gebiete Lebensm. Hyg.*, **63**, 81.

Anderson, E. E., Fagerson, I. S., Hayes, K. M. & Fellers, C. R. (1954) *J. Am. Dietet. Assoc.*, **30**, 1250.

Anderson, R. H., Maxwell, D. L., Mulley, A. E. & Fritsch, C. W. (1976) *Fd. Technol.*, **30**(5), 110.

Anet, E. F. L. J. & Reynolds, T. M. (1955) *Australian J. Chem.*, **8**, 267.

Ang, C. Y. W. & Livingston, G. E. (1974) In: *Nutritional Qualities of Fresh Fruits and Vegetables*, eds. White, P. L. & Silvey, N., p. 51. Mount Kisco, N.Y.: Futura Publ. Co.

Ang, C. Y. W., Chang, C. M., Frey, A. E. & Livingston, G. E. (1975) *J. Fd. Sci.*, **40**, 997.

Arnold, R. G., Libbey, L. M. & Lindsay, R. C. (1969) *J. Agric. Fd. Chem.*, **17**, 390.

Aylward, F. & Haisman, D. R. (1969) *Advan. Fd. Res.*, **17**, 1.

Baker, H., Frank, O., Thompson, A. D., Langer, A., Munves, E. D., de Angelis, B. & Kaminetzky, H. A. (1975) *Am. J. Clin. Nutr.*, **28**, 59.

Barackman, R. A. (1942) *Cereal Chem.*, **19**, 121.

Bartilucci, A. & Foss, N. E. (1954) *J. Am. Pharm. Assoc. (Sci. Edn.)*, **43**, 159.

Bauernfeind, J. C. (1977) *CRC Crit. Rev. Fd. Sci. Nutr.*, **8**, 337.

Bauernfeind, J. C. & Pinkert, D. M. (1970) *Advan. Fd. Res.*, **18**, 219.

Bell, T. A., Yarbrough, M., Clegg, R. E. & Satterfield, G. H. (1942) *Fd. Res.*, **7**, 144.

Bendix, G. H., Heberlein, D. G., Ptak, L. R. & Clifcorn, L. E. (1951) *J. Fd. Sci.*, **16**, 494.

Bernhart, F. W., D'Amato, E. & Tomarelli, R. M. (1960) *Arch. Biochem. Biophys.*, **88**, 267.

Bolin, H. R. & Stafford, A. E. (1974) *J. Fd. Sci.*, **37**, 1034.

Booth, R. G. (1943) *Biochem. J.*, **37**, 518.

Borenstein, B. (1968) In: *Handbook of Food Additives*, ed. Furia, T. E., p. 107. Cleveland, Ohio: The Chemical Rubber Co.

Bowers, J. A. & Fryer, B. A. (1972) *J. Am. Dietet. Assoc.*, **56**, 133.

Briant, A. M. & Hutchins, M. R. (1946) *Cereal Chem.*, **23**, 512.

Briant, A. M. & Klosterman, A. M. (1950) *Trans. Am. Assoc. Cereal Chem.*, **8**, 69.

Bring, S. V., Grassl, C., Hofstrand, J. T. & Willard, M. J. (1963) *J. Am. Dietet. Assoc.*, **42**, 320.

Bunnell, R. H., Keating, J., Quaresimo, A. & Parman, G. K. (1965) *Am. J. Clin. Nutr.*, **17**, 1.

Butt, V. S. & Hallaway, M. (1961) *Arch. Biochem. Biophys.*, **92**, 24.

Butterworth, C. E., Jr., Santini, R. & Frommeyer, W. B., Jr. (1963) *J. Clin. Invest.*, **42**, 1929.

Cameron, E. J., Clifcorn, L. E., Esty, J. R., Feaster, J. F., Lamb, F. D., Monroe, K. H. & Royce, R. (1955) *Retention of Nutrients during Canning.* Washington D.C.: National Canners Association.

Causey, K., Andrearsen, E. G., Hausrath, M. E., Along, C., Ramstad, P. E. & Fenton, F. (1950) *Fd. Res.*, **15**, 237.

Chapman, V. J., Pritz, J. O., Gilpin, G. L., Sweeney, J. P. & Eisen, J. N. (1960) *J. Home Econ.*, **52**, 161.

Cheldelin, V. H. & Williams, R. R. (1943) *J. Nutr.*, **26**, 417.

Cheldelin, V. H., Woods, A. A. & Williams, R. J. (1943) *J. Nutr.*, **26**, 477.

Chmielnicka, J. (1965) *Nutr. Abstr. Rev.*, **35**, 77.

Cier, A., Nofre, C., Drevon, B. & Lefier, A. (1959) *Bull. Soc. Chim. Fr.*, 74.

Clegg, K. M. & Morton, A. D. (1968) *J. Fd. Technol.*, **3**, 277.

Clements, C. A. B. & Anderson, L. (1966) *Ann. N.Y. Acad. Sci.*, **136**, 339.

Clifcorn, L. E., Peterson, G. T., Boyd, J. M. & O'Neil, J. H. (1950) *Fd. Technol.*, **4**, 450.

Coggiola, I. M. (1963) *Nature*, **200**, 954.

Cording, J, Jr., Eskew, R. K., Salinard, G. J. & Sullivan, J. F. (1961) *Fd. Technol.*, **15**, 279.

Coursin, D. B. (1954) *J. Am. Med. Assoc.*, **154**, 406.

Cover, S. & Dilsaver, E. M. (1947) *J. Am. Dietet. Assoc.*, **23**, 613.

Cover, S., Dilsaver, E. M. & Hays, R. M. (1947) *J. Am. Dietet. Assoc.*, **23**, 693.

Davies, M. K., Gregor, M. E. & Henry, K. M. (1959) *J. Dairy Res.*, **26**, 215.

Dawson, C. R. (1960) *Ann. N.Y. Acad. Sci.*, **88**, 353.

de Ritter, E. (1976) *Fd. Technol.*, **30**(2), 48.

de Ritter, E., Osadca, M., Scheiner, J. & Keating, J. (1974) *J. Am. Dietet. Assoc.*, **64**, 391.

Della Monica, E. S. & McDowell, P. E. (1965) *Fd. Technol.*, **19**, 141.

Domah, A. A. M. B., Davidek, J. & Velisek, J. (1974) *Z. Lebensm. Unters. -Forsch.*, **154**, 270.

Downs, D. E. & Meckel, R. B. (1943) *Cereal Chem.*, **20**, 352.

Dwivedi, B. K. & Arnold, R. G. (1971) *J. Agric. Fd. Chem.*, **19**, 923.

Dwivedi, B. K. & Arnold, R. G. (1972) *J. Fd. Sci.*, **37**, 886.

Dwivedi, B. K. & Arnold, R. G. (1973) *J. Agric. Fd. Chem.*, **21**, 54.

Eheart, M. S. & Gott, C. (1964) *J. Am. Dietet. Assoc.*, **44**, 116.

Engler, P. P. & Bowers, J. A. (1976) *J. Am. Dietet. Assoc.*, **69**, 253.

Escher, F. & Neukom, H. (1970) *Trav. Chimie Aliment. Hyg.*, **61**, 339.

Everson, G. J. & Smith, A. H. (1945) *Science*, **101**, 338.

Everson, G. J. & Souders, H. J. (1957) *J. Am. Dietet. Assoc.*, **33**, 1244.

Everson, G. J., Chang, C., Leonard, S. & Luh, B. S. (1964a) *Fd. Technol.*, **18**, 84.

Everson, G. J., Chang, C., Leonard, S. & Luh, B. S. (1964b) *Fd. Technol.*, **18**, 87.

Farrer, K. T. H. (1947) *Biochem. J.*, **41**, 162.

Farrer, K. T. H. (1953) *Austral. J. Sci.*, **16**, 62.

Farrer, K. T. H. (1955) *Advan. Fd. Res.*, **6**, 257.

Feaster, J. F., Tompkins, M. D. & Ives, M. (1949) *Fd. Inds.*, **20**, 14.

Feliciotti, E. & Esselen, W. B. (1957) *Fd. Technol.*, **11**, 77.

Finholt, P., Paulssen, R. B. & Higuchi, T. (1963) *J. Pharm. Sci.*, **52**, 948.
Finholt, P., Paulssen, R. B., Alsos, I. & Higuchi, T. (1965a) *J. Pharm. Sci.*, **54**, 124.
Finholt, P., Alsos, I. & Higuchi, T. (1965b) *J. Pharm. Sci.*, **54**, 181.
Finholt, P., Kristiansen, H., Krowczynski, L. & Higuchi, T. (1966) *J. Pharm. Sci.*, **55**, 1435.
Fournier, S. A., Beuk, J. F., Chornock, F. W., Brown, L. C. & Rice, E. E. (1949) *Fd. Res.*, **14**, 413.
Frost, D. V. & McIntyre, F. C. (1944) *J. Am. Chem. Soc.*, **66**, 425.
Ghitis, J. & Candanosa, C. (1966) *Am. J. Clin. Nutr.*, **18**, 452.
Goldblith, S. A., Tannenbaum, S. R. & Wang, D. I. C. (1968) *Fd. Technol.*, **22**, 1266.
Greenwood, D. A., Beadle, B. W. & Kraybill, H. R. (1943) *J. Biol. Chem.*, **149**, 349.
Guttikar, N. N., Panemangalore, M., Rao, M. N., Rajagopalan, R. & Swaminathan, M. (1965) *J. Nutr. Dietet.*, **2**, 21.
Harper, K. A., Morton, A. D. & Rolfe, E. J. (1969) *J. Fd. Technol.*, **4**, 255.
Harris, R. S. (1960) In: *Nutritional Evaluation of Food Processing*, eds. Harris, R. S. & von Loesecke, H., p. 1. New York: John Wiley. Reprinted in 1971 by Avi. Publ. Co., Westport, Conn.
Harris, R. S. & von Loesecke, H. (eds.) (1960) *Nutritional Evaluation of Food Processing*. New York: John Wiley. Reprinted in 1971 by Avi. Publ. Co., Westport, Conn.
Harris, R. S. & Karmas, E. (eds.) (1975) *Nutritional Evaluation of Food Processing*, 2nd edn. Westport, Conn.: Avi. Publ. Co.
Hartman, A. M., Dryden, L. P. & Riedel, G. H. (1956) *J. Nutr.*, **59**, 77.
Hartman, A. M. & Dryden, L. P. (1965) *Vitamins in Milk and Milk Products*. Washington D.C.: ADSA, USDA.
Hartman, A. M. & Dryden, L. P. (1974) In: *Fundamentals of Dairy Chemistry*, eds. Webb, B. H., Johnson, A. H. & Alford, J. A., 2nd edn. Westport, Conn.: Avi. Publ. Co.
Hassinen, J. B., Durbin, G. T. & Bernhart, F. W. (1954) *J. Nutr.*, **53**, 249.
Hayakawa, K. (1969) *Can. Inst. Fd. Technol.*, **2**, 165.
Hellstrom, V. (1952–3) *Z. Vitamin-, Hormon-, Fermentforsch.*, **5**, 98.
Henderson, L. M., Wasiman, H. A. & Elvehjem, C. A. (1941) *J. Nutr.*, **21**, 589.
Hennessy, D. J., Steinberg, A. M., Wilson, G. S. & Keaveney, W. P. (1960) *J. Assoc. Offic. Agric. Chem.*, **43**, 765.
Herbert, V. (1968) *Am. J. Clin. Nutr.*, **21**, 115.
Hewston, E. M., Dawson, E. H., Alexander, L. M. & Orentkeiles, E. (1948) *Vitamin and Mineral Content of Certain Foods as Affected by Home Preparation*, misc. publ. No. 628. Washington, D.C.: USDA.
Hodson, A. Z. (1941) *Fd. Res.*, **6**, 175.
Hollenbeck, C. M. & Obermeyer, H. E. (1952) *Cereal Chem.*, **29**, 82.
Huelin, F. E. (1953) *Fd. Res.*, **18**, 633.
Huelin, F. E. (1958) *Indian Fd. Packer*, **12**(12), 11.
Huelin, F. E., Coggiola, I. M., Sidhu, G. S. & Kennett, B. H. (1971) *J. Sci. Fd. Agric.*, **22**, 540.

Hurdle, A. D. F., Barton, D. & Searles, I. H. (1968) *Am. J. Clin. Nutr.*, **21**, 1202.

Huskisson, Y. J. & Retief, F. P. (1970) *S. Afr. Med. J.*, **44**, 362.

Jadhav, S., Steele, L. & Hadziyer, D. (1975) *Lebensm. -Wiss. u. Technol.*, **8**, 225.

Jen, Y., Manson, J. E., Stumbo, C. R. & Zahradnik, J. W. (1971) *J. Fd. Sci.*, **36**, 692.

Jensen, A. (1969) *J. Sci. Fd. Agric.*, **20**, 622.

Joslyn, M. A. & Miller, J. (1949a) *Fd. Res.*, **14**, 325.

Joslyn, M. A. & Miller, J. (1949b) *Fd. Res.*, **14**, 340.

Kahn, L. N. & Livingston, G. E. (1970) *J. Fd. Sci.*, **35**, 349.

Karel, M. & Nickerson, J. T. R. (1964) *Fd. Technol.*, **18**, 104.

Karlin, R. (1960) *Ann. Nutr.*, **14**, 53.

Karlin, R., Hours, C., Vallier, C., Bertoye, R., Berry, N. & Morand, H. (1969) *Int. Z. Vitaminforsch.*, **39**, 359.

Kawasaki, C. & Kani, T. (1949) *J. Pharm. Soc. Japan*, **69**, 216.

Keagy, P. M., Stokstad, E. L. R. & Fellers, D. A. (1975) *Cereal Chem.*, **52**, 348.

Kefford, J. F., McKenzie, H. A. & Thompson, P. C. O. (1959) *J. Sci. Fd. Agric.*, **10**, 51.

Khan, S. A., Ahmad, M. & Khan, S. (1963) *West Pakistan J. Agric. Res.*, **1**(3), 27.

Kik, M. C. (1945) *Arkansas Expt. Stn. Bull.*, 458.

Kizlaitis, L., Deibel, C. & Siedler, A. J. (1964) *Fd. Technol.*, **18**, 103.

Kon, S. K. (1941) *Nature*, **148**, 607.

Kon, S. K. (1961) *Federation Proc.*, **20**, 209.

Kurata, T. & Sakurai, Y. (1967) *Agric. Biol. Chem.*, **31**, 170.

Kurata, T. & Fujimaki, M. (1976a) *Agric. Biol. Chem.*, **40**, 1287.

Kurata, T. & Fujimaki, M. (1976b) *Agric. Biol. Chem.*, **40**, 1429.

Labuza, T. P. (1971) *CRC Crit. Rev. Fd. Technol.*, **2**, 355.

Labuza, T. P. (1972) *CRC Crit. Rev. Fd. Technol.*, **3**, 217.

Lane, R. L., Johnson, E. & Williams, R. R. (1942) *J. Nutr.*, **23**, 613.

Lee, S. H. & Labuza, T. P. (1975) *J. Fd. Sci.*, **40**, 370.

Leevy, C. M., Cardi, L., Frank, O., Gelleve, R. & Baker, H. (1965) *Am. J. Clin. Nutr.*, **17**, 259.

Leichter, J. & Joslyn, M. A. (1969) *J. Agric. Fd. Chem.*, **17**, 355.

Leong, P. C. & Strahan, J. H. (1952) *Med. J. Malaya*, **7**, 39.

Lhoest, W. J. (1958) *J. Pharm. Belg.*, **13**, 519.

Lin, K. C., Luh, B. S. & Schweigert, B. S. (1975) *J. Fd. Sci.*, **40**, 562.

Livingston, G. E., Ang, C. Y. W. & Chang, C. M. (1973) *Fd. Technol.*, **27**, 28.

Lund, D. B. (1975) In: *Nutritional Evaluation of Food Processing*, eds. Harris, R. S. & Karmas, E., 2nd edn., p. 205. Westport, Conn.: Avi. Publ. Co.

Lund, D. B. (1977) *Fd. Technol.*, **31**(2), 71.

Lushbough, C. H., Weichman, J. M. & Schweigert, B. S. (1959) *J. Nutr.*, **67**, 451.

Manson, J. E., Zahradnik, J. W. & Stumbo, C. R. (1970) *Fd. Technol.*, **24**, 1297.

Martinez, F. & Labuza, T. P. (1968) *J. Fd. Sci.*, **33**, 241.
McIntyre, J. M., Schweigert, B. S. & Elvehjem, C. A. (1944) *J. Nutr.*, **28**, 219.
Merritt, C. B., Bazinet, M. L., Sullivan, J. H. & Robertson, D. H. (1963) *J. Agric. Fd. Chem.*, **11**, 152.
Meyer, B. H., Hinman, W. F. & Halliday, E. G. (1947) *Fd. Res.*, **12**, 203.
Meyer, B. H., Mysinger, M. A. & Wodarski, L. A. (1969) *J. Am. Dietet. Assoc.*, **54**, 122.
Mikova, K. & Davidek, J. (1974) *Chem. Listy.*, **68**, 715.
Miller, C. F., Guadagni, P. & Kow, S. (1973) *J. Fd. Sci.*, **38**, 493.
Moore, H. W. & Folkers, K. (1968) In: *The Vitamins*, eds. Sebrell, W. H., Jr. & Harris, R. S. Vol. 2. New York: Academic Press.
Mooser, O. & Neukom, H. (1974) Work documents of the *4th Int. Congr. Fd. Sci. Technol.*, Madrid, **1b**, 60.
Morfee, T. D. & Liska, B. J. (1971) *J. Dairy Sci.*, **54**, 1082.
Morfee, T. D. & Liska, B. J. (1972) *J. Dairy Sci.*, **55**, 123.
Mulley, E. A., Stumbo, C. R. & Hunting, W. M. (1975a) *J. Fd. Sci.*, **40**, 985.
Mulley, E. A., Stumbo, C. R. & Hunting, W. M. (1975b) *J. Fd. Sci.*, **40**, 989.
Nonaka, M., Black, D. R. & Pippen, E. L. (1967) *J. Agric. Fd. Chem.*, **15**, 713.
Obermeyer, H. G. & Chen, L. (1945) *J. Biol. Chem.*, **159**, 117.
Olliver, M. (1967) In: *The Vitamins*, eds. Sebrell, W. H., Jr. & Harris, R. S. Vol. 1, p. 359. New York: Academic Press.
Orr, M. L. & Watt, B. K. (1972) *Am. J. Clin. Nutr.*, **25**, 647.
Pace, J. K. & Whitacre, J. (1953a) *Fd. Res.*, **18**, 231.
Pace, J. K. & Whitacre, J. (1953b) *Fd. Res.*, **18**, 239.
Page, E. & Hanning, F. M. (1963) *J. Am. Dietet. Assoc.*, **42**, 42.
Perloff, B. P. & Butrum, R. R. (1977) *J. Am. Dietet. Assoc.*, **70**, 161.
Perry, J. (1971) *Brit. J. Haematol.*, **21**, 435.
Rabinowitz, J. C. & Snell, E. E. (1948) *J. Biol. Chem.*, **176**, 1157.
Rice, E. E. & Beuk, J. F. (1945) *Fd. Res.*, **10**, 99.
Rice, E. E., Beuk, J.F., Kaufman, F. L., Shultz, H. W. & Robinson, H. E. (1944) *Fd. Res.*, **9**, 491.
Richardson, L. R., Wilkes, S. & Ritchey, S. J. (1961) *J. Nutr.*, **73**, 363.
Rowe, D. M., Mountrey, G. J. & Prudent, I. (1963) *Fd. Technol.*, **17**, 111.
Roy, J. K. (1953) *J. Indian Chem. Soc., Ind. News Edn.*, **16**, 50.
Roy, J. K. & Rao, R. K. (1963) *Indian J. Med. Res.*, **51**, 533.
Santini, R., Brewster, C. & Butterworth, C. E., Jr. (1964) *Am. J. Clin. Nutr.*, **14**, 205.
Scaife, J. F. (1959) *Can. J. Biochem. Physiol.*, **37**, 1049.
Schroeder, H. A. (1971) *Am. J. Clin. Nutr.*, **24**, 562.
Schweigert, B. S., Nielsen, E., McIntyre, J. M. & Elvehjem, C A. (1943) *J. Nutr.*, **26**, 65.
Schweigert, B. S., Pollard, A. E. & Elvehjem, C. A. (1946) *Arch. Biochem.*, **10**, 107.
Schweigert, B. S. & Guthneck, B. T. (1953) *J. Nutr.*, **51**, 283.
Senti, F. R. (1971) In: *Symposium on Vitamins and Minerals in Processed Foods*, p. 61. Chicago: American Medical Association.
Shenoy, K. G. & Ramasarma, G. B. (1955) *Arch. Biochem. Biophys.*, **55**, 293.
Singh, R. P., Heldman, D. R. & Kirk, J. R. (1976) *J. Fd. Sci.*, **41**, 304.

Spanyar, P., Kevei, E. & Blazovich, M. (1963) *Z. Lebensm. Unters. -Forsch.*, **120**, 1.

Spanyar, P., Kevei, E. & Blazovich, M. (1964a) *Z. Lebensm. Unters. -Forsch.*, **123**, 418.

Spanyar, P., Kevei, E. & Blazovich, M. (1964b) *Z. Lebensm. Unters. -Forsch.*, **126**, 10.

Stamberg, O. E. & Peterson, C. F. (1946) *J. Am. Dietet. Assoc.*, **22**, 315.

Sweeney, J. P., Gilpen, G. L., Statey, M. G. & Martin, M. E. (1959) *J. Am. Dietet. Assoc.*, **35**, 354.

Sweeney, J. P., Gilpen, G. L., Martin, M. E. & Dawson, E. H. (1960) *J. Am. Dietet. Assoc.*, **36**, 122.

Sweeney, J. P. & Marsh, A. A. (1971) *J. Am. Dietet. Assoc.*, **59**, 238.

Tuguchi, H., Hara, K., Hasei, T. & Sanada, H. (1973) *Bitamin*, **47**, 513.

Tanaka, A. (1966a) *Bitamin*, **33**, 19.

Tanaka, A. (1966b) *Bitamin*, **33**, 497.

Tanaka, A. (1969) *Bitamin*, **39**, 330.

Tatum, J. H., Shaw, P. E. & Berry, R. E. (1969) *J. Agric. Fd. Chem.*, **17**, 38.

Teixeira, A. A., Dixon, J. R., Zahradnik, J. W. & Zinsmeister, G. F. (1969) *Fd. Technol.*, **23**, 845.

Teixeira, A. A., Zinsmeister, G. E. & Zahradnik, J. W. (1975) *J. Fd. Sci.*, **40**, 656.

Teply, L. J. & Derse, P. H. (1958) *J. Am. Dietet. Assoc.*, **34**, 836.

Thomas, K., Pace, J. K. & Whitacre, J. (1952) *Texas Agric. Exptl. Stn. Bull.*, 753.

Thomas, M. H., Brenner, S., Eaton, A. & Craig, V. (1949) *J. Am. Dietet. Assoc.*, **25**, 39.

Thompson, S. Y. (1969) In: *Ultra-High Temperature Processing of Dairy Products*. London: Society of Dairy Technology.

Timberlake, C. F. (1960) *J. Sci. Fd. Agric.*, **11**, 258.

Tucker, R. E., Hinman, W. F. & Halliday, E. G. (1946) *J. Am. Dietet. Assoc.*, **22**, 877.

van der Poel, G. H. (1956) *Voeding*, **14**, 452.

van Zante, H. J. & Johnson, S. K. (1970) *J. Am. Dietet. Assoc.*, **56**, 133.

Velisek, J., Davidek, J., Kubelka, V., Zelinkova, Z. & Pokorny, J. (1976) *Z. Lebensm. Unters. -Forsch.*, **162**, 285.

Vojnovich, C. & Pfeifer, V. F. (1970) *Cereal Sci. Today*, **19**, 317.

Wada, S. & Suzuki, H. (1965) *Kaseigaku Zasshi*, **16**, 322.

Wai, K., Dekay, H. G. & Banker, G. S. (1962) *J. Pharm. Sci.*, **51**, 1076.

Walker, M. A. & Page, L. (1975) *J. Am. Dietet. Assoc.*, **66**, 146.

Watt, B. K. & Merrill, A. L. (1963) *Composition of Foods. Handbook 8*. Washington, D.C.: Consumer Fd. Econ. Res. Div. ARS. USDA.

Wertz, A. W. & Weir, C. E. (1946) *Fd. Res.*, **11**, 319.

White, E. G., Murray, M. & Maveety, D. J. (1946) *J. Am. Dietet. Assoc.*, **22**, 770.

Williams, R. R. (1938) *J. Am. Med. Assoc.*, **110**, 727.

Wilson, E. C. G. (1942) *New Zealand J. Sci. Technol.*, **B24**, 35.

Yamamoto, R. & Yamamoto, E. (1964) *Yakuzaigaku*, **24**, 309; (1965) *Chem. Abstr.* **63**, 1663e.

Yamazaki, I., Mason, H. P. & Pitts, L. (1959) *Biochem. Biophys. Res. Commun.*, **1**, 336.

CHAPTER 5

Meat

D. A. LEDWARD

University of Nottingham, Loughborough, UK

In most societies, it is usual to subject meat to some form of heat treatment prior to consumption and it is readily apparent to even the most naïve consumer that the quality of the cooked product varies markedly with the type of heat treatment. Thus, in domestic cooking several heating methods may be employed, the regime being dictated by the nature of the meat and the desired organoleptic properties of the final product. Flavour, colour and texture are all important attributes of cooked-meat quality but it is well established that texture (tenderness) is of paramount importance and this quality factor usually dictates the method of cooking. Normally only inherently tender meat is cooked by heating for a relatively short time (grilling, roasting and frying) and, in such cases, it is usual to cook to a desired colour and flavour by varying the time of heating to give, for example, rare, medium or well-done steaks. In meat that is inherently tough, the main aim is to obtain a reasonably tender cooked product and this is usually achieved by heating at a relatively low temperature, often in the presence of water, for several hours (braising, stewing). Sometimes in this type of cooking a short, initial treatment at a high temperature, such as flash-frying, is used to seal the outside surfaces and prevent loss of soluble, low molecular-weight nutrients and flavour precursors during subsequent heating.

In conventional cooking, heat is transferred by conduction from the outside of the sample to the interior. This gives rise to a temperature gradient through the meat so that, in the high-temperature–short-time cooking methods, different degrees of 'doneness' occur through the sample. Very rapid cooking with a relatively uniform degree of 'doneness' throughout can be achieved by microwaves.

Although texture, flavour and colour are the main factors involved in selecting the mode of domestic cooking, for several commercial processes a heating regime may be used primarily to control bacterial growth. For example, a relatively mild heat treatment may be employed to pasteurise fresh or cured meat or a more intense heat treatment may be applied to sterilise canned meats. These treatments will also cook the meat and so affect its quality.

Before one can understand how these various heating regimes affect the properties of meat it is necessary to have some knowledge of the composition and structure of meat and the inherent differences that may occur between muscles.

5.1   COMPOSITION AND STRUCTURE OF MEAT

Meat is defined as the flesh of animals consumed for food and, as is the case with most biological material, it is rather variable in composition.

It is not the intention in this chapter to dwell too long on the composition and structure of meat as there are several excellent texts and reviews available which treat this subject in depth (Lawrie, 1974; Forrest et al., 1975; Briskey et al., 1966). Typical values for the concentration of the different components to be found in skeletal muscle (lean) are given in Table 5.1; the actual composition for a given muscle will vary with the breed, age, sex and diet of the animal as well as its anatomical location, as discussed later.

All skeletal muscle contains fat depots and the amount and composition of the fat varies quite markedly with the type of animal. However, most of the lipids in the depots are neutral triglycerides, i.e. glycerol esters of fatty acids. Typical values for the fatty acid and triglyceride composition of some animal fats are shown in Table 5.2. It can be seen that the most abundant triglyceride contains one palmitic and two oleic fatty acid residues and the next most abundant contains one residue each of oleic, palmitic and stearic acid.

Most skeletal muscles are attached directly to bone although a few are attached to ligaments, fascia, cartilage and skin. A muscle can be physically divided into successively smaller longitudinal units, each of which is surrounded by a sheath of connective tissue. The muscle itself is surrounded by the *epimysium*, the fibre bundle by the *perimysium* and the fibre by the *endomysium* and *sarcolemma* (Fig. 5.1).

TABLE 5.1

APPROXIMATE COMPOSITION OF MAMMALIAN SKELETAL MUSCLE (PERCENT FRESH-WEIGHT BASIS)

Component	Composition (%)	Component	Composition (%)
Water (range 65–80%)	75·0	*Non-protein nitrogenous substances*	1·5
Protein (range 16–22%)	18·5	Creatine and creatine phosphate	0·5
Myofibrillar	9·5	Nucleotides (adenosine triphosphate, ATP; adenosine diphosphate, ADP; etc.)	0·3
myosin	5·0	Free amino acids	0·3
actin	2·0	Peptides (anserine, carnosine, etc.)	0·3
tropomyosin	0·8	Other non-protein substances (creatinine, urea, inosine monophosphate, IMP; nicotinamide adenine dinucleotide, NAD; nicotinamide adenine dinucleotide phosphate, NADP)	0·1
troponin	0·8	*Carbohydrates and non-nitrogenous substances* (range 0·5–1·5)	1·0
M protein	0·4	Glycogen (variable range 0·5–1·3)	0·8
C protein	0·2	Glucose	0·1
α-actinin	0·2	Intermediates and products of cell metabolism (hexose and triose phosphates, lactic acid, citric acid, fumaric acid, succinic acid, acetoacetic acid, etc.)	0·1
β-actinin	0·1	*Inorganic constituents*	1·0
Sarcoplasmic	6·0	Potassium	0·3
soluble sarcoplasmic and mitochondrial enzymes	5·5	Total phosphorus (phosphates and inorganic phosphorus)	0·2
myoglobin	0·3	Sulphur (including sulphate)	0·2
haemoglobin	0·1	Chlorine	0·1
cytochromes and flavoproteins	0·1	Sodium	0·1
Stromal	3·0	Others (including magnesium, calcium, iron, cobalt, copper, zinc, nickel, manganese, etc.)	0·1
collagen and reticulin	1·5		
elastin	0·1		
other insoluble proteins	1·4		
Lipids (variable range 1·5–13·0%)	3·0		
Neutral lipids (range 0·5–1·5)	1·0		
Phospholipids	1·0		
Cerebrosides	0·5		
Cholesterol	0·5		

TABLE 5.2
FATTY ACID AND TRIGLYCERIDE COMPOSITION (PERCENT BY WEIGHT) OF SOME ANIMAL FAT DEPOTS

Component	Pig			Cattle		Sheep	
	subcutaneous[a] outer	subcutaneous[a] inner	perirenal[b]	subcutaneous[a]	perirenal[b]	subcutaneous[a]	perirenal[b]
Fatty acids							
Saturated fatty acids							
lauric	trace	trace	trace	0·1	0·2	0·1	0·1
myristic	1·3	0·1	4·0	4·5	2·7	3·2	2·6
palmitic	28·3	30·1	28·0	27·4	27·8	28·0	28·0
stearic	11·9	16·2	17·0	21·1	23·8	24·8	26·8
arachidic	trace	trace	trace	0·6	0·6	1·6	2·6
Total	41·5	46·4	49·0	53·7	55·1	57·7	60·1
Unsaturated fatty acids							
palmitoleic	2·7	2·7	2·0	2·0	2·2	1·3	1·9
oleic	47·5	40·9	36·0	41·6	40·1	36·4	34·2
linoleic	6·0	7·1	11·8	1·8	1·8	3·5	4·0
linolenic	0·2	0·3	0·2	0·5	0·6	0·5	0·6
archidonic plus chipandonic	2·1	1·7	1·0	0·4	0·2	0·6	0·8
Total	58·5	52·7	51·0	46·3	44·9	42·3	41·5
Approximate triglyceride composition							
Fully saturated							
tripalmitin	1			3		trace	
dipalmitostearin	2			8		3	
palmitodistearin	2			6		2	
tristearin	–			–		–	
Mono-oleo-disaturated							
oleodipalmitin	5			15		13	
oleopalmitostearin	27			32		28	
oleodistearin	–			2		1	
Dioleo-monosaturated							
palmitodiolein	53			23		46	
stearodiolein	7			11		7	
triolein	3			0		0	

[a] Fat from the dorsal, thoracic and lumbar regions.
[b] Fat around the kidneys.

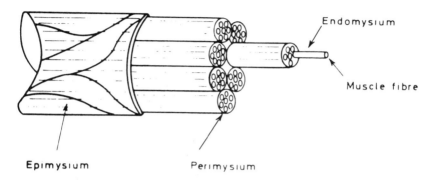

FIG. 5.1   Longitudinal units of a muscle.

Muscle fibres are often several centimetres long, taper slightly at the ends, and may vary in diameter from 100–1000 nm. Each muscle fibre is composed of several long, thin cylindrical rods (about 10–20 nm in diameter) known as *myofibrils*. Thus, a muscle fibre of diameter 500 nm is composed of between 100–200 myofibrils. These myofibrils are the essential contractile units of muscle and are separately enwrapped in the *sarcoplasmic reticulum*, a highly specialised mesh of tubules concerned with calcium ion control and hence the initiation and arrest of contraction. The myofibrils are bathed in an aqueous fluid (*sarcoplasm*) which is about 75–80% water and contains lipid droplets, glycogen granules, ribosomes, numerous proteins, non-protein nitrogen substances and a number of inorganic constituents. Within the myofibril, and still strictly in line with the fibre direction, the filaments are arranged as shown schematically below:

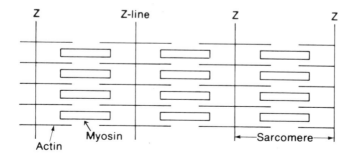

The I or thin filaments that extend longitudinally from the transverse Z-lines are composed mainly of the protein actin, and at rest length their free tips extend just less than half-way along the sarcomeres. The thick A or myosin filaments span the gap between the tips of the opposing actin units, interdigitating with their free ends.

In living muscle, energy for the contractile process is supplied by the calcium activated enzymic dephosphorylation of adenosine triphosphate (ATP). This essentially involves a shortening of the sarcomere produced by the relative movement of the two filament types. The actin filaments advance towards each other as the result of a co-ordinated forming and breaking of cross-bridges between the myosin and actin filaments, *i.e.* actomyosin forms. On relaxation the reverse process occurs. This contractile movement would be confined to the myofibrillar level were it not for the supportive, adhesive and force-transmissive abilities of the connective tissue. Connective tissue consists of a structureless mass called the *ground substance* in which are embedded cells and extracellular fibres of collagen, elastin and reticulin. The ground substance is a viscous solution containing soluble glycoproteins, often referred to as mucoproteins or muco-polysaccharides. However, in the context of muscle as a food, the connective-tissue components of most interest are the fibrous proteins, since they are of major importance in determining the textural proper-ties of meat. Of these, reticulin and elastin fibres are of relatively minor importance as, compared to collagen, they are usually only present in relatively low concentrations. For this reason, it is the structure and chemistry of collagen that has received the greatest attention with respect to the effect of connective tissue on meat quality.

The basic structural unit of a collagen fibre is the tropocollagen molecule, the structure of which has already been described in Chapter 1. The inextensible collagen fibres are composed of precisely aligned tropocollagen molecules in a quarter stagger arrangement (see p. 163). These units are bonded at intervals by intermolecular crosslinks and, although these crosslinks are heat labile in young animals, on maturation they gradually transform to thermostable bonds (see Chapter 1). It is the formation of these stable bonds that is undoubtedly the major cause of the increased toughness in meat from older animals.

The epimysium, perimysium and endomysium are all collagenous materials but the sarcolemma which, as well as the endomysium, surrounds the muscle fibre, is not. However, this relatively elastic

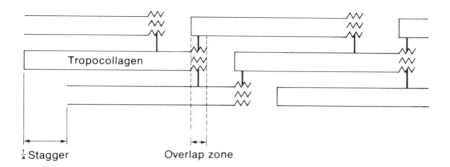

¼ Stagger   Overlap zone

material is not considered to be a major factor in determining meat quality and so will not be discussed here.

5.2 CONVERSION OF MUSCLE TO MEAT

The most important single change during the conversion of muscle to meat is post-mortem glycolysis—the process whereby glycogen is converted to lactic acid. As the lactic acid accumulates in meat there is a concomitant decrease in pH from the *in vivo* value of a little over 7. The rate and extent of pH fall following slaughter are both highly variable. A normal pH-decline pattern for pork muscle is shown schematically in Fig. 5.2. It is seen that within 6–8 h post-mortem, the pH falls to 5·6–5·8 and reaches an ultimate value (after about 24 h) of about 5·5. However, in some animals, the pH drops only a few tenths of a unit in the first hour after slaughter and then remains relatively

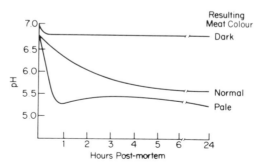

FIG. 5.2   Types of post-mortem pH curves found in different pork muscles.

stable giving an ultimate pH of 6·5–6·8. In other animals, the pH drops rapidly to around 5·4–5·5 and yields an ultimate pH of 5·3–5·6. As will be seen later, these differences in the rate and extent of pH fall markedly affect the ultimate quality of the meat.

As well as the decrease in glycogen and increase in lactic acid concentrations, post-mortem glycolysis gives rise to many other changes in the muscle and the most important of these, from the viewpoint of meat quality, will be briefly considered. For post-mortem glycolysis to occur, inorganic phosphate (P_i) must be available to enable phosphorylase to convert glycogen to glucose-1-phosphate, the first product of glycolysis. The P_i arises from the splitting of adenosine triphosphate (ATP),

$$ATP \rightarrow ADP + P_i$$
$$\text{adenosine}$$
$$\text{diphosphate}$$

Thus, even in death the muscle attempts to maintain its structural integrity and temperature by energy derived from this reaction. In many muscles there is a store of creatine phosphate (CP) which is used to re-synthesise ATP via

$$ADP + CP \rightarrow ATP + \text{creatine}$$

Thus, from the moment of death the CP level in muscle falls and ultimately there is a point at which it is no longer possible to re-synthesise ATP and the level of ATP itself begins to fall. As ATP disappears, the muscle ceases to be elastic and tends to stiffen, *i.e.* *rigor mortis* occurs. This change occurs because ATP, apart from being a source of energy, is also a plasticiser which prevents the myofibrillar proteins—actin and myosin—from crosslinking to form the inextensible actomyosin.

During post-mortem glycolysis the temperature of the muscle will slowly change from 37°C to ambient. The rate at which post-mortem glycolysis occurs is a marked function of the environmental temperature, decreasing with decreasing temperature down to 5°C. However, rather unexpectedly, the rate appears to increase slightly as the temperature decreases from 5 to 0°C (Newbold and Scopes, 1967).

There is obviously an inter-relationship between rigor mortis and pH decline as both are consequences of the process of post-mortem glycolysis, although the relationship is not necessarily simple. For example, for the three muscles depicted in Fig. 5.2 the time for rigor mortis to reach completion will be slower in the normal muscle than in either the high pH or low pH samples. In the muscle in the upper curve of Fig. 5.2 the onset and completion of rigor mortis will be rapid because the energy supply is limited. The sample represented by the bottom curve will also rapidly enter rigor mortis because either the energy supply is rapidly metabolised or the low pH conditions curtail important reactions in the energy metabolism.

Since actomyosin formation during rigor mortis is the same as in muscle contraction, rigor mortis will usually lead to muscle shortening or, if the muscle is restricted from shortening, tension is developed. The amount of shortening undergone by the muscle is a marked function of temperature. This will be discussed later in Section 5.3. Other changes which accompany the conversion of muscle to meat and affect its quality are as follows:

(a) The natural antibacterial defence mechanisms of the body are destroyed and thus the growth of microorganisms is encouraged.

(b) As the pH decreases enzymes (cathepsins) may be released from the lysosomes and degrade the tissue.

(c) Some of the compounds formed may well modify the intrinsic flavour associated with the meat. For example, the pattern of nucleotides changes via

$$\text{ATP} \longrightarrow \text{ADP} \longrightarrow \text{IMP} \longrightarrow \text{inosine} \longrightarrow \text{hypoxanthine}$$

$$+ \qquad \begin{array}{c}\text{inosine} \\ \text{monophosphate}\end{array} \qquad + \qquad \downarrow$$

$$P_i \qquad + P_i + NH_3 \qquad P_i \qquad \text{ribose}$$

Most of the breakdown of IMP occurs during and after rigor mortis.

(d) Fats solidify.

(e) Proteins denature.

5.3 FACTORS AFFECTING MEAT QUALITY

As with the previous sections it is not the intention in this chapter to give a comprehensive review of the factors affecting meat quality. This aspect of meat science has been extensively researched and documented, and readers requiring further details are advised to consult standard texts and also recent reviews which deal with the relationships between meat quality and animal physiology (Cassens *et al.*, 1975), and the effect of recent advances in processing on meat quality (Locker *et al.*, 1975).

It is the intention in this section to briefly outline the causes of variability in meat quality to serve as a background for the effects of heat on the quality of the final product. The factors affecting meat quality can be conveniently separated into four sections, *viz.* type of animal, pre-slaughter treatment, pre-rigor processing and post-rigor treatment.

5.3.1   Effect of Animal Type

Species
It is readily apparent that the composition and quality of meat from different species, both before and after cooking, is markedly different. Important examples of these variations are as follows:
(i) Differences in myoglobin concentration in the muscles: cattle and sheep have about 5 to 10 times more myoglobin than pigs and rabbits, causing the meat to be darker (redder).
(ii) Differences in flavour volatiles give rise to the characteristic flavours of the different meats: present evidence suggests that most of the species-specific character of meat flavour resides in the fat (Patterson, 1975).
(iii) Ruminants, such as cattle and sheep, tend to hydrogenate unsaturated dietary fats so that the composition of the depot fats is usually more saturated than in non-ruminants such as pigs, which tend to deposit unchanged dietary fat (see Table 5.2).
(iv) Differences in enzyme activity lead to variations in rates of post-mortem glycolysis and to the stability, or not, of post-rigor colour and texture.
(v) Differences in the texture of meat from different species presumably indicate that the nature of the connective tissues differs.

Breed
Significant differences in meat quality may also occur between breeds of the same species. Examples are as follows:
(i) The myoglobin concentrations of the same muscles may vary.
(ii) The proportion of intramuscular fat may vary, *e.g.* Friesian cattle (a predominantly dairy breed) have less intramuscular fat than Herefords (a beef breed).
(iii) The rates of post-mortem glycolysis may vary with breed. This

phenomenon has been extensively studied in pigs, in which very rapid post-mortem glycolysis gives rise to inferior PSE (pale, soft and exudative) meat.

Sex
In general, males have less intramuscular fat than females while castrated animals tend to have more fat than either males or females. Other differences owing to sex tend to be minimal except that entire males may yield meat of undesirable odour and flavour (*e.g.* 'boar' taint in pigs).

Age
With increasing animal age there is an increase in concentration of most components other than water (although there is also an apparent decrease in the total collagen content). With regard to meat quality, important differences are as follows:

(i) The concentration of intramuscular fat increases with age. For example, a 12-day-old calf has about 0·5% while a 3-year-old steer has about 3·7%. Also, the degree of unsaturation tends to decrease with age.

(ii) The increased concentration of myoglobin leads to darker (redder) meat in older animals, *cf.* veal and beef.

(iii) The increased concentration of flavour volatiles causes the meat from older animals to taste 'meatier', *cf.* veal and beef.

(iv) Although the total concentration of collagen and elastin decreases with age, the number of stable, intermolecular crosslinks increases leading to increased toughness.

Anatomical Location
Although muscles may be broadly classified as 'red' or 'white' according to whether they carry out sustained action or operate in short bursts, the diverse functions of the 300 or so muscles (and hence the meat) cannot be so simply differentiated. For example, in a beef carcase, moisture content ranged from 62·5 to 76%, fat from 18·1 to 1·5% and ultimate pH from 5·4 to 6·0 for different muscles (Standine, 1948, as reported by Lawrie, 1974). The whole gamut of the differences found for muscles from the same carcase are too numerous to discuss in detail in this chapter and readers requiring further information should consult one of the standard texts (*e.g.*

Lawrie, 1974). The main differences, as reflected in meat quality, are
(i) the concentration of connective tissue in different muscles may
vary by a factor of 5 or more leading to the well established variations
in texture (toughness);
(ii) the myoglobin concentration of different muscles may vary by a
factor of 2 or more leading to variations in colour intensity; and
(iii) the enzymic constitution varies and thus any post-mortem
changes involving enzymes will occur at different rates.

Differences in composition and constitution may also occur within
a single muscle and this may be very pronounced in some pig
muscles. For example, areas only 1-cm apart have been found to have
ultimate pH values differing by 0·7 of a pH unit in pig *m. semimem-
branosus*.

Regular Exercise

Sustained and frequent exercise will alter the constitution of muscle.
The two main differences as far as meat quality is concerned are the
increased myoglobin concentration, leading to darker meat, and increased glycogen stores, leading to a lower ultimate pH, in exercised
muscles.

Nutrition

Good nutrition generally increases the level of intramuscular fat and
decreases the level of moisture in muscles whilst under-nutrition
causes a significant increase in moisture. The nature of the depot fats
may be influenced by the level of nutrition and in pigs, but not
ruminants, diets high in unsaturated fats will lead to the laying down
of increased concentrations of unsaturates in the depots. Another
important aspect of nutrition on meat quality is that the composition
of the forage can lead to flavour variations, especially in lambs,
although cattle seem relatively resistant to flavour adulteration by
feedstuffs. Tainted swill or the use of feed additives may affect the
flavour of pig meat.

Before leaving this section, it is worth noting that even muscles
obtained from littermates of the same sex may differ in composition.
The reasons for this are not fully understood and, until they are, it is
unlikely that carcases of uniform quality will be obtained by even the
most selective of breeding programmes.

5.3.2 Effect of Pre-Slaughter Handling on Meat Quality

The stress associated with the conversion of living tissue to meat can lead to changes in the muscle metabolites and hence differences in the ultimate properties of the meat.

Different animals have variable degrees of resistance to the stresses imposed by the pre-slaughter environment. Stress-susceptible animals generally have higher post-mortem muscle temperatures and undergo very rapid post-mortem glycolysis (and pH fall). The combination of high temperature and low pH encourages protein denaturation with concomitant loss of water-holding capacity (WHC) and colour so that, after rigor, the meat is PSE. This condition is a major problem in pig processing.

If an animal survives stress applied over a relatively long term, it may do so at the expense of its glycogen reserves. Thus, some stress-susceptible animals and all stress-resistant ones which survive stress associated with fatigue, exercise, fasting, fighting, *etc.*, and are slaughtered before their glycogen reserves are replenished, can only undergo limited post-mortem glycolysis. The resultant high pH gives rise to dark, firm meat (*e.g.* dark cutting beef), which, as well as being unpopular with the consumer on account of its appearance, is hygienically undesirable since the environment for bacterial growth is more favourable than in meat of normal pH. The marked effect of pH on meat appearance (colour) can be explained thus: at high pH, the WHC of the muscle fibres is maximal resulting in a dry, relatively compact structure which reflects little light, while at normal pH values the decreased WHC of the fibres leads to a more open structure, with which is associated some relatively free water, capable of reflecting more light. Also, the surviving oxygen-utilising enzymes in the tissue are more active at high than at low pH values so that oxygen cannot penetrate to any appreciable depth in the tissue, causing the dark-purple colour of reduced myoglobin to be visible as opposed to the bright-red colour of oxymyoglobin seen at the surface of meat of normal pH. In PSE meat, the changes are exaggerated owing to increased loss of WHC associated with the protein denaturation and may be even more marked if some acid denaturation of myoglobin occurs or if the denatured proteins precipitate to mask the natural colour of myoglobin.

As well as leading to changes in the rate of post-mortem glycolysis, poor handling can cause some more obvious defects in the final meat quality, such as bruising during transportation, but these will not be discussed in this review.

5.3.3 Pre-Rigor Processing

When free to do so, muscle will contract (shorten) after death. If rigor mortis occurs while the muscle is in this state then marked changes in the properties of the meat occur which, as will be seen later, are still manifest in the cooked state. Even if a muscle is restrained from shortening by its mode of attachment to the carcase, localised areas of 'shortened' meat may still occur. The amount of shortening undergone by a muscle is very temperature dependent, being minimal at about 15°C (Fig. 5.3).

The generally accepted explanation of the increased shortening observed at temperatures below 15°C (*i.e.* cold shortening) is that the ATP-driven calcium pump, responsible for the control of muscle contraction, fails at the low temperature so that the muscle is continuously stimulated to contract. Rigor shortening observed at temperatures above 20°C is probably due to the rapid depletion of ATP which is needed to drive the calcium pump.

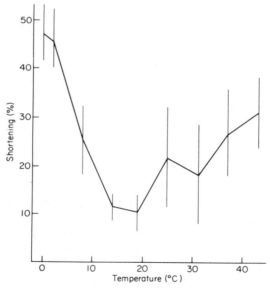

FIG. 5.3 Mean ultimate shortenings of muscles at various storage temperatures. (From Locker and Hagyard, 1963, by permission of the authors.)

If meat is frozen pre-rigor and rapidly thawed, massive shortening occurs (up to 80% of the rest length) accompanied by a copious loss of fluid or 'drip' (up to 30% of the total weight). This phenomenon of *thaw-rigor* is obviously undesirable and probably results from the gross disruption of the calcium pump on freeze-thawing.

Because of the problems associated with cold shortening, it is usual to leave meat on the carcase until rigor is completed. This is wasteful of time and space and recently techniques whereby the meat is butchered pre-rigor have been developed. In this 'hot-boning' process, great care must be exercised to minimise shortening by maintaining the temperature at 10–15°C and, as the process thereby involves delayed chilling, a good standard of hygiene is also essential. (Pre-rigor meat, mainly on account of its high pH, has good emulsifying and water-holding properties, and thus is increasingly being used in some meat products such as sausage and ham.) Even if muscles are not excised pre-rigor, some will still be able to shorten considerably, the extent of shortening being very dependent on the posture of the carcase as it enters rigor. Recent work (summarised by Locker *et al.*, 1975) has shown that considerable improvements in the quality of some cuts can be achieved by altering the posture of the carcase prior to and during rigor. The results all indicate that conventional hanging by the Achilles tendon is far from ideal.

Another recent innovation is the use of electrical stimulation immediately following slaughter, effectively accelerating rigor and allowing rapid chilling to be employed without shortening.

5.3.4 Post-Rigor Treatment

It is common practice to 'age' meat for several days following rigor to allow changes to occur which result in 'tenderising' the meat. This process of ageing has been the subject of several comprehensive reviews (Bate-Smith, 1948; Whitaker, 1959; Laakkonnen, 1973) but there is still controversy over the actual mechanism involved. It is generally agreed that the changes are brought about by enzymes, released during the conversion of muscle to meat, which attack the myofibrillar and/or connective-tissue components. Several studies have failed to demonstrate any major changes in the nature of the connective tissue (Ledward *et al.*, 1975; Chizzolini *et al.*, 1975) although the degree of change necessary to affect textural properties is open to question. Most recent work has been focused on the changes in myofibrillar structure.

There are two main schools of thought regarding the structural changes undergone during ageing, *viz.* a weakening of the linkages between actin and myosin in the filament, and disintegration of the Z-lines of the sarcomere. A recent study by Davey and Graafhuis (1976) indicates that the important structural changes may occur in the thin, elastic, 'gap filaments' which are believed by Locker and Leet (1975) to form a structural skeleton to the sarcomere. These filaments are claimed to reside in the core of the thick filaments (A-band) and are attached to, or pass through, the Z-lines. Davey and Graafhuis (1976) suggest that ageing represents either the weakening of these filaments or the rupture of their attachment to the Z-lines.

Although the structural changes brought about by shortening and ageing appear to be related primarily to change in the myofibrils, the measured effects on meat quality must be seen as a composite property. This arises from the complex interaction of the myofibrils and connective tissue for, as the dimensions of the sarcomere change, so the structural arrangement of the connective tissue must also change.

Although ageing brings about structural changes which, as will be seen later, improve the tenderness of meat when cooked, other changes also occur which may not be so desirable. For example, freshly cut myoglobin-rich meat is purple in colour as the haemoproteins (myoglobin plus some haemoglobin) are in their reduced form. But, in the presence of oxygen, the meat rapidly blooms to the bright-red colour of oxymyoglobin which consumers associate with freshness. However, on prolonged storage, the colour changes to brown metmyoglobin which consumers consider to be undesirable. As described in Chapter 1, myoglobin consists of a protein moiety, globin, and a prosthetic group, haematin (iron protoporphyrin IX), and it is the interaction of this prosthetic group with the environment that is primarily responsible for the colour of myoglobin, and hence also of meat. The structure of haematin is shown below:

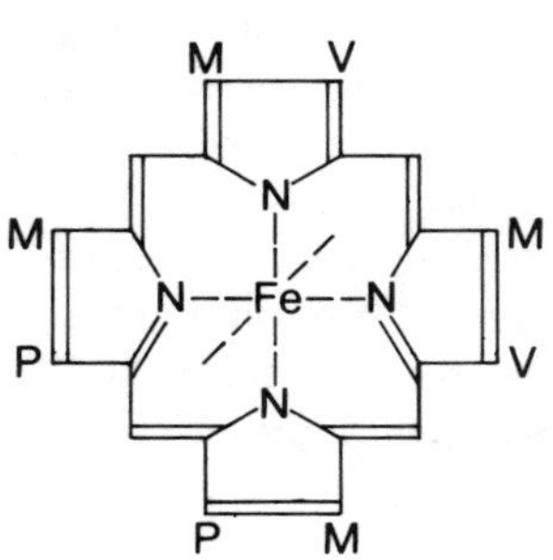

M = Methyl ($-CH_3$)
P = Propionate ($-CH_2CH_2COO^-$)
V = Vinyl ($-CH=CH_2$)

The central iron atom may bind up to six ligands. Four of these ligands are N atoms of the porphyrin ring while the N of an imidazole residue of the protein chain is the 5th ligand. In reduced myoglobin the iron atom is in the ferrous state and the 6th-ligand position is unoccupied; in oxymyoglobin, O_2 binds to the 6th position and the electronic configuration is probably best represented as $Fe^{3+}-O_2^-$ (Wittenberg et al., 1970). In metmyoglobin, the iron is in the ferric state and a water molecule occupies the 6th position. The formation of metmyoglobin is markedly dependent on the storage conditions (temperature, relative humidity, gaseous environment, and pH) but discussion of these are outside the scope of this review and readers requiring further information are advised to read a review by Govindarajan (1973). Obviously myoglobin can undergo many more reactions than those described above but these also will not be discussed here.

During the storage of fresh meat, bacteria will proliferate at rates dependent on the temperature, relative humidity and gaseous environment. This is a critical consideration in choosing the temperature and time for meat ageing. Also during storage, the enzymes of raw meat continue to act on meat components forming potential flavour precursors and Dwivedi (1975), in his review on meat flavour, has summarised these reactions. During air storage, lipid oxidation may occur giving rise to undesirable flavour compounds but, in chilled meat, this is not normally a problem since the factor determining shelf-life is usually bacterial growth. However, in frozen meat, lipid oxidation is usually the limiting factor.

5.4 EFFECT OF HEAT TREATMENT ON MEAT

The complex nature and composition of meat gives rise to numerous chemical reactions and physical transitions during heating, including the following: protein denaturation, aggregation and degradation; fat liquefaction and subsequent breakdown reactions; enzyme and microbial destruction; loss of some trace nutrients; reaction between sugars and amines; and interactions between flavour precursors. The relative importance of these different reactions will vary with the type of heat treatment; for example, low-temperature treatment may increase enzymic activity while high temperatures will result in loss of activity. Also, owing to the variability in composition and structure between muscles, the relative importance of these reactions will vary with the type of muscle. Thus, reactions undergone by collagen will be more important in muscles of high connective-tissue contents.

Such changes as protein denaturation and melting of fats are endothermic and so it is not surprising that a thermogram of meat exhibits heat absorption over a relatively wide temperature range (Fig. 5.4). Figure 5.4 also indicates that most of the reactions giving rise to the thermogram are virtually irreversible since on re-heating cooked meat there is little re-absorption of heat. However, care must be taken in interpreting these thermograms as some important reactions may be reversible but, because of the low concentration of reactant(s) or small enthalpy of reaction, are not detected by the calorimeter. For example, the denaturation of collagen is partially reversible but the low concentration in muscle (1–2%) makes it difficult to detect, although it is apparent in the collagen-rich tissues of isolated intramuscular connective tissue and tendon (Fig. 5.5).

In this review no attempt will be made to discuss the microbiology of heat processing (which is extensively reviewed in standard texts) or to discuss in detail recommended cooking regimes for domestic or research needs as reviews are available on these aspects (Paul, 1975; Harrison, 1975). The discussion will be mainly directed at the fundamental changes which occur during the different types of heating and their effect on final quality (texture, flavour, colour and nutritive value).

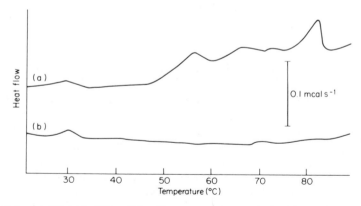

FIG. 5.4 (a) Thermogram of fresh meat (pork); (b) thermogram obtained on re-heating the sample. (From Ledward and Lawrie, 1975, by permission of the authors.)

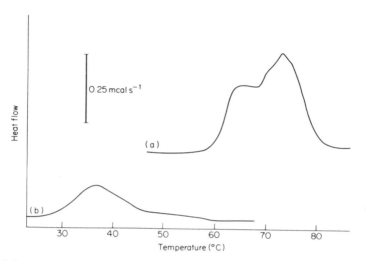

FIG. 5.5   (a) Thermogram of fresh tendon (sheep); (b) thermogram obtained
on re-heating the sample. (From Ledward and Lawrie, 1975, by permission of
the authors.)

5.4.1   Tenderness

Since muscle structure is determined by the organisation of the
myofibrillar and connective-tissue proteins, it is not surprising that
cooked-meat texture is determined primarily by the response of these
components to heat. However, the sarcoplasmic proteins and
intramuscular lipids may also play minor rôles in determining the
overall texture of cooked meat. Meat toughness is usually measured
in terms of the resistance to shear across the fibres, these determinations correlating well with taste panel data (Bouton *et al.*, 1971).
Bouton and Harris (1972b) have compared some of the commonly
used objective methods and found reasonable agreement between
them.

Hamm (1966) states that at temperatures below 40°C only minor
changes occur in myofibrillar proteins but at 40–50°C marked changes
occur which affect the WHC, rigidity, pE, dye-binding capacity and
number of available sulphydryl groups. At 50–55°C, even more
marked changes occur including the formation of some relatively
stable crosslinks, and at 65°C most of the myofibrillar proteins are
coagulated.

Giles (1969) studied the ultrastructural changes undergone by the myofibrils during heating and observed that, even after 100 min at 60°C, the main features of the sarcomere were still visible and little shrinkage of the fibres occurred. However, the actin filaments coagulated with time at 60°C and the Z-line rapidly lost all trace of fine structure. After 45 min at 70°C the filaments could still be discerned but after longer periods they became very indistinct. After 20–45 min at 70°C the junction between the A and I bands became discontinuous and after 100 min a break was seen at the junction of the I band and Z-line. Throughout the heating period at 70°C the actin filaments became increasingly coagulated while the Z-lines, which lost their fine structure immediately at this temperature, became more ill-defined and disorganised on further heating. After 100 min at 70°C the fibres had shrunk by about 20% of their original length. Landmann (1967) and Hostetler and Landmann (1968) followed the shrinkage of isolated muscle fibres at several temperatures and found that it appeared to occur in two stages: at temperatures of 50°C and below the fibres slowly decreased in diameter with little change in length; at temperatures from 50–70°C there was an appreciable decrease in length.

The above sets of results are not incompatible as one would anticipate that the denaturation of the proteins would lead to aggregation and shrinkage across the fibres at temperatures of 50°C and below, while the lengthwise shrinkage observed at the higher temperatures presumably relates to the denaturation of the collagen of the connective tissue. The fact that the decrease in length occurred at a lower temperature in the washed, isolated fibres than in the muscle sections studied by Giles (1969) may be due to the different environments of the connective tissue as it is well established that the denaturation temperature of collagen is very dependent on the conditions (Finch and Ledward, 1973).

Heat, as well as causing aggregation of the myofibrillar proteins and consequent hardening (toughening) also allows the connective tissue to swell and denature with resultant softening (tenderising) of the texture. The denaturation of intramuscular connective-tissue collagen, which is accompanied by shrinkage, usually occurs in the range 56–60°C (Machlik and Draudt, 1963) although, as mentioned earlier, the actual temperature may vary with the environment. During the thermal contraction of collagen, some soluble fragments are released from the fibre into solution (Verzar, 1964) and Field *et al.* (1970) found that 'tender' muscles yielded the most soluble fragments. This hydrolysis of collagen is aided by the presence of excess water and thus, for muscles relatively rich in connective tissue, moist cooking methods are recommended. These are preferably carried out at low temperatures to minimise myofibrillar hardening even though Paul *et al.* (1973) and Penfield and Meyer (1975) found that higher cooking temperatures yielded greater amounts of soluble collagen. The structure of the other major constituent of connective tissue, elastin, is little affected by heat although a slight hardening may occur (Lawrie, 1968) and thus prolonged cooking will not tenderise samples rich in elastin. Fortunately, elastin-rich muscles are not commonly encountered.

The effects of cooking time and temperature on meat tenderness have been widely studied ever since Bramblett *et al.* (1959) suggested that softening of connective tissue without toughening of myofibrillar proteins could be achieved by cooking meat at 57°–60°C. This suggestion was apparently verified by Machlik and Draudt (1963) who studied the effect of various heat treatments on beef muscle. Figure 5.6 summarises their findings and it can be seen that at 56–58°C, 62–64°C and 72–74°C there is an initial decrease in toughness due to collagen softening, the rate of tenderisation increasing with temperature. However, at the higher temperature range of 72–74°C, the tenderising is followed by a toughening phase related to the so-called protein hardening of the myofibrillar proteins. Continued heating results in collagen degradation and further tenderisation. These

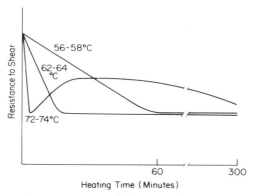

FIG. 5.6   Effect of temperature and time on the tenderness of beef. (Summarised from Machlik and Draudt, 1963. Copyright © by the Institute of Food Technologists.)

findings were confirmed by Bouton *et al.* (1974) who observed a
marked reduction in adhesion values (which they regard as an index
of connective-tissue strength) with increasing cooking temperature
from 50 to 60°C or with increasing cooking time at 90°C. At the same
time, shear-force values (which they associate with the condition of
the myofibrillar proteins) increased significantly from 60 to 90°C with
only a small decrease on prolonged cooking at 90°C.

Davey and Gilbert (1974) determined the relationship between
toughness and cooking temperature of beef *m. sternomandibularis*
cooked for 1 h. They observed a two-phase relationship between
resistance to shear and temperature (Fig. 5.7). Bouton *et al.* (1972b,
1974) obtained similar profiles to those shown in Fig. 5.7 for several
different muscles. However, the two phases of increasing toughness
between 40 and 50°C and between 65 and 75°C were not as clearly
defined and, as mentioned earlier, they usually observed decreasing
toughness from 50 to 60°C. This decrease in toughness appeared to be
more marked in meat from young animals and muscles rich in
connective tissue.

Davey and Gilbert claim that the three- to four-fold toughening

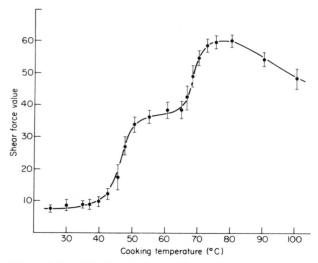

FIG. 5.7 The relationship between cooking temperature and shear force
value ($\propto$ toughness) for beef *m. sternomandibularis*. (From Davey and Gilbert, 1974, by permission of the authors.)

observed between 40 and 50°C (Fig. 5.7) is associated with general denaturation of the contractile system, while the second phase, between 65 and 75°C is 'loosely' associated with collagen shrinkage and concomitant fibre shortening. These conclusions appear to conflict with the accepted view of collagen shrinkage leading to a softening of meat and also, the second toughening phase appears to occur at temperatures slightly above that normally associated with collagen shrinkage. An explanation that may reconcile these apparently conflicting views is that, at all temperatures above about 40°C, aggregation of the myofibrillar (and sarcoplasmic) proteins occurs leading to the hardening reaction. When one considers that the mode of aggregation of denatured proteins can vary quite markedly with temperature yielding structures ranging from gels, which tend to be favoured at lower temperatures, to compact precipitates (Chapter 1) it does not seem unreasonable that the hardness of meat increases with temperature. Due to the loss in rigidity of the connective-tissue network accompanying the shrinkage of collagen, a tenderisation is superimposed on this hardening reaction giving rise to the discontinuity observed around 55–65°C (Fig. 5.7). However, in samples rich in collagen crosslinked with thermally stable bonds, the collagen denaturation may also lead to a further increase in toughness owing to the tension generated as it attempts to shrink. This tightening of the connective-tissue network will squeeze water out from the muscle fibres leading to increased myofibrillar hardening. If the above explanation of the effect of collagen denaturation on toughness is correct then the muscles of young animals, rich in connective tissue in which the collagen possesses few thermally stable crosslinks, should exhibit the maximum increase in tenderisation following the shrinkage reaction. The results of Bouton *et al.* (1972b, 1974) appear to demonstrate this.

The decreased toughness observed at very high temperatures (Fig. 5.7) presumably corresponds to the degradation of the denatured collagen.

Not only collagen but other muscle proteins, mainly sarcoplasmic, are increasingly solubilised as the temperature is raised from 45 to 60°C (Paul *et al.*, 1966) and such increases were attributed to endogenous proteolytic activity. Lutalo-Bosa and Macrae (1969) and Laakkonen *et al.* (1970a,b) demonstrated that enzymes with proteolytic activity were active at low cooking temperatures, and Penfield and Meyer (1975) found a significant correlation between proteolytic activity and tenderness in slowly heated meat. Thus Laakkonen's claim (1973) that 'sarcoplasmic proteins, exhibiting proteolytic activity, may play a role in tenderizing meat before they are coagulated by heat during cooking' seems justified.

In all studies reported above, meat tenderness was assessed at 20°C or less, and only recently have data become available on the effect of the temperature of measurement on the measured toughness (Ledward and Lawrie, 1975). These authors found that the toughness of meat cooked at a temperature below the collagen-shrinkage temperature (55°C) was independent of the temperature of measurement, while meat cooked at 80°C toughened significantly on cooling. They explained these observations in terms of the partial renaturation of collagen: on cooling, hydrogen bonds forming between the denatured polypeptide chains of collagen yield a more rigid structure in much the same way a gelatin solution gels on cooling.

Obviously the texture of cooked meat will also depend on the nature of the product prior to cooking as well as the time–temperature regime, and it is apparent from the preceding discussions that the texture will be very dependent on the nature and quantity of the connective tissue present. However, even in muscles where the connective-tissue components are similar, wide variations can occur. One of the most marked effects is the dependence on sarcomere length, as it is well established that cold-shortened meat gives rise to toughness. Marsh and Carse (1974) evaluated the toughness of meat cooked at 80°C as a function of sarcomere length and found the relationship shown in Fig. 5.8. In these experiments, different degrees of shortening were induced by chilling to −0·5°C at various post-slaughter times and different degrees of stretching were induced by allowing stretched, pre-rigor muscle strips to enter rigor at 15°C. The relationship between shortening and toughening found for meat cooked at 80°C is also found for meat cooked at 60°C (Davey and Gilbert, 1975). However, for raw meat, the texture of which is primarily determined by the connective tissue, there is an inverse relationship between sarcomere length and toughness, i.e. toughness decreases with shortening and increases with stretching (Rhodes and Dransfield, 1974).

Marsh and Carse (1974) claim that the effect of shortening on toughness can be explained solely in terms of changes in the organisation of the myofibrillar proteins, the connective-tissue contribution being almost independent of sarcomere length. Thus, the minor peak

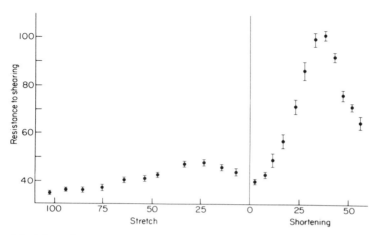

FIG. 5.8 The effect of extension or shortening before rigor completion on the toughness of meat cooked in rigor. Length change as percent initial excised length ±s.e. (From Marsh and Carse, 1974, by permission of the Institute of Food Science and Technology, UK.)

at about 24% stretch occurs at the point where the tips of the thin filaments first contact one another and the major peak at about 35% shortening coincides with the point at which interaction could occur between thin filaments and those thick filaments successfully penetrating the Z-line from the adjacent sarcomere. If this explanation is correct then the toughening associated with the myofibrils must completely override the connective-tissue effects observed in raw meat (Rhodes and Dransfield, 1974) at both 60°C, where collagen shrinkage is minimal (Davey and Gilbert, 1975), and at 80°C where shrinkage has occurred.

The paradoxical tenderising observed with highly shortened (> 40%) muscle has been explained in terms of widespread structural damage (fibre fracturing) associated with super-contraction (Marsh et al., 1974).

For several years the explanation of the toughness associated with shortening arising solely from changes in the myofibrillar proteins has been questioned (Bendall and Voyle, 1967; Voyle, 1969). An electron-microscopic study by Rowe (1974) certainly suggests that extensive changes in the arrangement of the connective-tissue collagen occur during shortening, and rheological measurements by Bouton et al., (1973a,b) indicate that the connective-tissue strength of cold-shortened muscle is increased compared to normal muscle. Rhodes and Dransfield (1974) and Dransfield and Rhodes (1976) also state that the connective-tissue elements must contribute to the observed relationship.

The interdependence of the myofibrillar and connective-tissue components in cooked-meat texture is further illustrated by a recent study (Davey and Gilbert, 1976). These authors found that prolonged cooking of meat (24 h as opposed to 40 min) at 80°C caused a marked decrease in toughness in both normal and shortened muscle. Thus, the tenderisation owing to collagen degradation did not eliminate the effect of shortening. Also, prolonged cooking of meat aged at 15°C for 3 days led to a further increase in tenderness, at least up to 40% shortening, without destroying the dependence of toughness on shortening. As these effects were additive, it suggests that ageing and prolonged cooking affect different structural elements, neither of which is solely responsible for the observed shortening/toughening relationship (Fig. 5.8).

On the basis of their results on prolonged cooking, Davey and Gilbert (1976) claim that myofibrillar proteins are solely responsible for the observed shortening–toughness relationship. From the brief survey given above, however, it is apparent that this view is not universally held.

The above discussion has been concerned with meat of normal pH (5·4–5·7) although pH is an obvious parameter that will affect any property dependent on protein structure. When proteins denature, buried ionic groups may become exposed to the solvent and, if the pH is appropriate, they ionise, resulting in a small pH change. In meat of normal pH, the pH rises on heating, at 40°C by 0·1, at 45–65°C by 0·2–0·3 and at 70–80°C by about 0·4 pH units (Paul et al., 1966). Hamm (1966) has suggested that the release of buried imidazole groups could account for these increases. Meat of high ultimate pH exhibits less increase in pH than given above; for example, at pH 7·0 the increase is below 0·1 units even after heating at 90°C (Bouton et al., 1971). On denaturation, the release of buried ionic groups shifts the isoelectric point, pE, of meat to higher pH; the increase being greater at higher temperatures (Hamm and Deatherage, 1960).

Several studies have demonstrated a marked dependence of cooked-meat toughness on pH and the studies by Bouton et al., (1971, 1972b, 1973b) and Miles and Lawrie (1970) are typical. Toughness decreases with increasing pH for meat cooked at all temperatures from 60 to 100°C and, in all muscles, the decrease from pH 6 to 7 is very marked. However, Bouton *et al.* found that, in a few muscles— but by no means all—the dependence between pH 5·5 and 6·0 was small. It is interesting to note that these workers found that the tensile strength of the fibres (regarded as an index of myofibrillar toughness) was very pH dependent, being 4–5 times greater at pH 5·5 than at pH 7·0. At the same time, adhesion values (regarded as an index of connective-tissue strength) were less dependent on pH, being only about twice as high at pH 5·5 than pH 7·0. In fact, at 60°C, where shrinkage was minimal, the adhesion values were *not* pH dependent suggesting that it is mainly the denatured myofibrillar (and possibly sarcoplasmic) proteins which are affected by the pH of the environment. This is reasonable as it is well established that the properties of collagen fibres (Finch and Ledward, 1972) and denatured collagen systems (gelatin gels) (Veis, 1964) have little or no pH dependence in this range.

Ageing meat tends to decrease the dependence of toughness on pH. Bouton and Harris (1972a,c) and Bouton *et al.* (1973b) found that whereas the tensile strength of unaged meat was 4–5 times greater at pH 5·5 than pH 7·0, the tensile strength of aged samples only differed by about a factor of 2 over the same pH range. However, adhesion values changed little on ageing (Bouton and Harris, 1972c; Bouton *et al.*, 1973b) and this was taken as evidence that ageing mainly affects the myofibrillar proteins.

While ageing appears to decrease the pH dependence of meat toughness, cold-shortening increases this dependence (Bouton and Harris, 1972c; Bouton *et al.*, 1973a) since after cooking at 70°C for 1 h, cold-shortened and normal meat of pH 7·0 were of similar toughness while at pH 5·5 the contracted samples were over twice as tough.

From the above survey it would appear that the pH dependence of cooked-meat toughness is primarily related to the effect of pH on the mode of aggregation of the myofibrillar (and possibly sarcoplasmic) proteins and, as such, is related to the interactions between these proteins and solvent, *i.e.* their ability to hold water. As well as being related to toughness, WHC will also affect the 'juiciness' and loss in weight on cooking of meat.

5.4.2 Water-Holding Capacity (WHC)

As WHC and tenderness are related it is not surprising that factors affecting tenderness also affect WHC. Thus, as meat toughens with

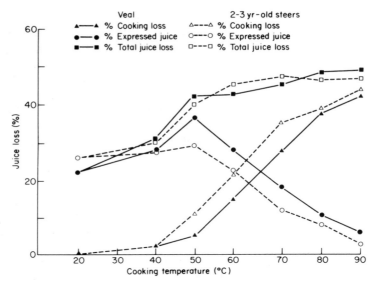

FIG. 5.9 Changes in cooking loss, centrifugally expressible juice and total juice loss for deep *m. pectoralis* from veal and 2–3-year-old steers (at pH 5·4–5·6) cooked at different temperatures for 1 h. (From Bouton and Harris, 1972a. Copyright © by the Institute of Food Technologists.)

increasing cooking temperature, so the WHC decreases. Typical results are summarised in Fig. 5.9, where it can be seen that the cooking loss increases almost linearly with temperature between about 30–80°C. The fluid lost tends to be the loosely bound, 'free' water which can be squeezed or centrifuged out. It appears that the denaturation of the myofibrillar proteins, at 40–50°C, leads to increases in 'free' water. The increased toughness associated with increasing temperature correlates with the squeezing out of the 'free' water from the meat matrix by the hardening reaction associated with the myofibrillar (and sarcoplasmic) proteins and the tightening of the connective-tissue network following collagen shrinkage. Earlier results by Laakkonnen (1970a) and Ritchey and Hostetler (1964) are in general agreement with those shown in Fig. 5.9.

The tenderisation of meat associated with collagen softening at about 60°C, and collagen degradation on prolonged heating at higher temperatures, have little effect on the WHC (Fig. 5.9). This may, however, merely be a reflection of the relatively low concentration of collagen in meat.

As with texture, one of the most significant factors affecting WHC is the pH of the meat (Hamm, 1975) and several studies have demonstrated that, for raw meat, increasing pH leads to increased WHC (Bouton *et al.*, 1971, 1972a, 1973a,b; Hatton *et al.*, 1972). The apparently linear relationship between pH 5·4 and 7·0 is still operative on cooking meat to temperatures of 80°C or less (Bouton *et al.*, 1971, 1972a). However, when cooked to 80–90°C the relationship between WHC and pH is curvilinear (Bouton *et al.*, 1971, 1972a; Hamm and Deatherage, 1960).

The close relationship between WHC and tenderness is further demonstrated by the relative effects of some post-mortem treatments on these parameters. Thus, cold- and thaw-shortened meats, which are very tough, have low WHC as demonstrated by the large amounts of 'drip' associated with these phenomena, while post-rigor storage of meat is associated with both tenderisation and increased WHC as the myofibrillar system degrades (Hamm, 1975).

The fluid exuded from meat during heating will contain some of the readily soluble meat components, in proportions related to the amount of water released. Obviously, if chemical changes occur in the nature of these components during heating, altering their solubility, then this will be reflected in the composition of the exudate. For instance, aggregation of proteins will lead to a decreased nitrogen content while protein degradation will increase its nitrogen content. This expressed 'juice' should not be confused with moisture that may be lost by evaporation in dry heating as this will merely concentrate the meat components.

A further parameter which has been associated with meat juiciness is 'marbling'. Well-marbled meat contains a high proportion of intramuscular fat and it has been claimed that this is a desirable attribute as it leads to a succulent product when cooked. However, studies have failed to show such a correlation (Campion *et al.*, 1975) and, in view of the supposed health risk associated with diets containing animal fats, it is unlikely that consumers will continue to pay a premium for such meats.

The time–temperature regimes discussed cover the types of heating usually used for meat cookery. However, in cases where microbial sterility is desired, high-temperature–long-time treatment is necessary and, owing to massive protein degradation, this leads to a 'bitty' texture associated with a low WHC. It has been claimed that microwave heating may permit microbial inactivation with minimum loss of organoleptic quality as the desired temperature is rapidly achieved, thus minimising any time dependence of the protein denaturation reactions (Roberts and Lawrie, 1974). However, for conventional heating procedures, the limited data available suggest that the effects of temperature rise on tenderness and WHC are small (Laakkonnen, 1973).

Practical guides to meat cookery can be developed on the basis of time and temperature influences on tenderness. For example, temperatures may be selected to minimise protein hardening while permitting collagen softening, although for full flavour and colour development other criteria must also be considered.

5.4.3 Flavour

It is apparent from the reviews by Patterson (1975) and Dwivedi (1975) that the chemistry of meat flavour is not fully understood. Cooking is necessary to develop meat flavour since raw meat has little odour and only a blood-like taste.

Flavour precursors are distributed between the lean and fat, the species-specific elements probably residing in the fat. Over 100 compounds, of at least 10 chemical classes, have been identified. Although many of these have little or no meaty odour, synergistic and antagonistic effects may prevail thus causing these apparently ineffective substances to become important flavour modifiers (Patterson, 1975). The majority of flavour studies on meat have been concerned with the volatile aroma compounds; this may be misleading as the fulsome and satisfying sensation of juice in the mouth plays an important part in the appreciation of meat flavour (Patterson, 1975).

Wasserman (1972) has reviewed the reactions which contribute to meat flavour as follows:

1. *Amino acids* may degrade to volatile products, *e.g.* 3-methyl- and 2-methyl-butanol from leucine and isoleucine; 2-methyl-propanol from valine; benzene, toluene and ethylbenzene from phenylalanine; H_2S from cysteine; NH_3 from lysine; and other examples discussed in Chapter 1.

2. *Carbohydrates* may caramelise to highly odoriferous substances, *e.g.* furan derivatives, carbonyl compounds and aromatic hydrocarbons.

3. *Maillard browning reactions* will occur between amino acids or protein material and carbohydrates (especially sugars). These types of

reactions are probably of major importance in determining meat flavour since the above reactions only occur at relatively high temperatures (> 100°C) while amino acids and sugars will readily react at normal cooking temperatures. The ultimate products of these reactions are the brown melanoidins but innumerable intermediates are formed which can contribute to flavour.

4. *Lipids* will contribute to flavour when heated. Watanabe and Sato (1971) identified 70 non-acid volatiles in beef fat; these consisted of aldehydes, ketones, lactones, alcohols, esters, hydrocarbons and pyrazines, some or all of which could contribute to flavour. Several of the compounds are volatilised by heat and involve no chemical change in the fat; however, oxidative changes are accelerated at higher temperatures, giving rise to some of the volatiles. In *very severe* heat treatment, pyrolysis of the fat may yield carcinogenic hydrocarbons (Lawrie, 1968).

5. *Volatiles containing nitrogen, oxygen and sulphur* will be formed or released during heating. Although their full relevance to flavour is not established, the nitrogen-containing pyrazines and several sulphur- and oxygen-containing volatiles found in cooked meat have such low odour thresholds that they are believed to play a significant part in the formation of a meaty aroma (Patterson, 1975).

6. *5'-Ribonucleotides* formed following slaughter may contribute to flavour but most recent studies have shown that inosine-5'-mono-phosphate and other nucleotides modify existing flavours rather than contribute intrinsic notes (Patterson, 1975).

As discussed earlier in this chapter, the intrinsic meat flavour can be modified by pre-slaughter factors. It is also apparent that the final flavour will depend on the heating regime, but present knowledge does not allow these differences to be related to specific compounds just as it does not allow the compounds responsible for the species differences to be identified.

5.4.4 Colour

As outlined earlier, one of the major factors affecting fresh meat colour is the concentration and nature of the haemoproteins and thus it is not surprising that the response of these pigments to heat is important in determining the colour of cooked meats.

In aqueous solution of pH 5·5–6·0 myoglobin, the haemoprotein mainly responsible for meat colour, remains in its native state to temperatures of 80°C or more while, in meat, it precipitates at temperatures of 60–70°C (Bernofsky *et al.*, 1959). This phenomenon is believed to be due to reaction between myoglobin and some of the heat-denatured proteins present in cooked meat; a pre-denaturation transition undergone by myoglobin partially exposes the haematin to the environment, allowing it to react (Ledward, 1971). Thus, cooked-meat haemoprotein is essentially a mixture of haematin-bound denatured protein complexes where the denatured protein is not necessarily globin but may be any of several of those found in meat. The concentration and type of bound protein is dependent on the thermal history of the meat. For example, beef-muscle extracts held at a lower temperature prior to heating at a higher temperature (but still below the denaturation temperature of myoglobin) form less cooked-meat haemoprotein than extracts heated directly to the higher temperature (Ledward, 1971). The relative proportions of the different reactant proteins in the two systems also differ. Subsequent studies (Ledward, 1974) suggested that the major products are ferric di-imidazole complexes formed by the 5th and 6th co-ordinated positions of the ferric ion in the porphyrin ring system being bound to histidine residues of the denatured proteins. Further stabilisation is afforded by salt-linkages and hydrogen and hydrophobic bonds between the protein(s) and porphyrin.

If meat is heated to temperatures below 60°C, little cooked-meat haemoprotein forms and the meat merely acquires a greyish tinge due to precipitation of the less stable proteins. There is also some loss of WHC and, in some regards, low-temperature heating can be thought of as giving PSE meat.

The importance of cooked-meat haemoprotein formation is diminished, and the denaturation of the other proteins proportionately increased, in meat of low myoglobin content (*e.g.*, pork) compared to myoglobin-rich meats (*e.g.*, beef), but there is no reason to believe the reactions involved differ.

Obviously the amount of cooked-meat haemoprotein formed will be temperature dependent and the dependence is used to assess the degree of 'doneness' of meat. For example, beef cooked to an internal temperature of 60°C is considered rare, 71°C medium and 77°C well-done (Paul, 1975). It appears that the unreacted myoglobin in rare meat is in the red, oxygenated form (Tappel, 1957) but the reason for this is not clear since, at zero or very low oxygen tensions at the centre of a meat sample, one would expect the pigment to be either in the purple, reduced form or, as seems more likely, in the oxidised, brown form (Ledward, 1970). A possible explanation is that there is a powerful reducing system present in meat which, at these higher temperatures, effectively maintains the iron of the porphyrin in the ferrous state.

As well as the changes related to the reactivity of the haemoproteins, cooked-meat colour may be influenced by other chemical effects. Chief among these are Maillard browning reactions between amino groups and sugars and, at very high temperatures (> 100°C), caramelisation of sugars. Also, the fibrous nature of a cooked-meat surface can act as a diffraction grating leading to iridescence as the incident white light is split up (Walters, 1975). This 'mother-of-pearl' effect is usually only seen with cooled, cooked-meat slices.

5.4.5 Nutritive Value

The biological value (BV) of fresh uncooked meat is about 74 (62–78) (Bender, 1975) and traditional cooking procedures lead to negligible decreases. For example, even after 3 h at 100°C, losses of essential amino acids were only of the order of 6% (Bognar, 1971). It is generally recognised that, in meat, the sulphur-containing amino acids and/or tryptophan are limiting and thus, the Maillard reactions undergone by lysine, which contribute to the flavour of cooked meat, do not significantly affect its BV since a considerable reduction in availability must occur before this amino acid becomes limiting.

Excessive heat treatment will lead to an appreciable loss of BV as essential amino acids are made unavailable by thermally induced chemical reactions. For example, lysine undergoes Maillard reactions, methionine oxidises and cysteine breaks down with the elimination of H_2S (Chapter 1). Donoso et al. (1962) found that when pork was cooked in water at 110°C for 24 h then dried at 100°C for 6 h, the net protein utilisation, NPU (= BV × digestibility) decreased from 76 to 41, available lysine fell by 34% and 20% was destroyed while 16% of the methionine and 44% of the cysteine were destroyed. Addition of methionine partly restored the NPU to 60 suggesting that lysine destruction was responsible for the rest of the damage.

Although meat is usually thought of as a good-quality protein food it is also an excellent source of readily available iron. Much dietary iron is poorly absorbed but meat is a good source of easily absorbed iron and also assists the absorption of iron from other foods. It is not clear to what extent cooking affects the availability of iron in meat although it is apparent that both cooked and raw meat are excellent sources of this essential nutrient.

Meat is also a useful source of several vitamins and numerous studies have shown that cooking leads to some loss. General figures are that the concentrations of vitamins B_1, B_6, B_{12} and pantothenic acid decrease by about one-third while vitamin B_2 and niacin decrease in concentration by one-tenth or less. Bender (1975) has summarised some of the experimental data pertaining to the effect of cooking on the vitamin content of some meats.

Wood *et al.* (1962) found that heated meat extracts, and therefore cooked meat (Bender, 1975) contain a factor which stimulates the secretion of gastric juice. They suggest that this may be one of the reasons why meat is so highly regarded as a food.

REFERENCES

Bailey, A. J. & Sims, T. J. (1977) *J. Sci. Fd. Agric.*, **28**, 565.

Bate-Smith, E. C. (1948) *J. Soc. Chem. Ind.*, **67**, 83.

Bendall, J. R. & Voyle, C. A. (1967) *J. Fd. Technol.*, **2**, 259.

Bender, A. E. (1975) In: *Meat*, eds. Cole, D. J. A. & Lawrie, R. A., p. 433. London: Butterworths.

Bernofsky, C., Fox, J. B., Jr. & Schweigert, B. S. (1959) *Fd. Res.*, **24**, 339.

Bognar, A. (1971) *Ernähr. -Umsch.*, **18**, 200.

Bouton, P. E. & Harris, P. V. (1972a) *J. Fd. Sci.*, **37**, 140.

Bouton, P. E. & Harris, P. V. (1972b) *J. Fd. Sci.*, **37**, 218.

Bouton, P. E. & Harris, P. V. (1972c) *J. Fd. Sci.*, **37**, 539.

Bouton, P. E., Harris, P. V. & Shorthose, W. R. (1971) *J. Fd. Sci.*, **36**, 435.

Bouton, P. E., Harris, P. V. & Shorthose, W. R. (1972a) *J. Fd. Sci.*, **37**, 351.

Bouton, P. E., Harris, P. V. & Shorthose, W. R. (1972b) *J. Fd. Sci.*, **37**, 356.

Bouton, P. E., Carroll, F. D., Harris, P. V. & Shorthose, W. R. (1973a) *J. Fd. Sci.*, **38**, 404.

Bouton, P. E., Carroll, F. D., Harris, P. V. & Shorthose, W. R. (1973b) *J. Fd. Sci.*, **38**, 816.

Bouton, P. E., Harris, P. V., Shorthose, W. R. & Ratcliff, D. (1974) *J. Fd. Sci.*, **39**, 869.

Bouton, P. E., Ford, A. L., Harris, P. V., Macfarlane, J. J. & O'Shea, J. M. (1977a) *J. Fd. Sci.*, **42**, 132.

Bouton, P. E., Harris, P. V. & Shorthose, W. R. (1977b) *J. Text. Studies*, **7**, 179.

Bouton, P. E., Harris, P. V. & Shorthose, W. R. (1977c) *J. Text. Studies*, **7**, 193.

Bramblett, V. D., Hostetler, R. L., Vail, G. E. & Draudt, H. N. (1959) *Fd. Technol.*, **13**, 707.

Briskey, E. J., Cassens, R. G. & Trautman, J. C. (eds.) (1966) *Physiology and Biochemistry of Muscle as Food*. Madison: University of Wisconsin Press.
Campion, D. R., Crouse, J. D. & Dikeman, M. E. (1975) *J. Fd. Sci.*, **40**, 1225.
Cassens, R. G., Marple, D. N. & Eikelenboom, G. (1975) *Advan. Fd. Res.*, **21**, 71.
Cheng, C. S. & Parrish, F. C., Jr. (1976) *J. Fd. Sci.*, **41**, 1449.
Chizzolini, R., Ledward, D. A. & Lawrie, R. A. (1975) *Proc. 21st Eur. Meeting Meat Res. Workers*, Berne, p. 29.
Davey, C. L. & Gilbert, K. V. (1974) *J. Sci. Fd. Agric.*, **25**, 931.
Davey, C. L. & Gilbert, K. V. (1975) *J. Fd. Technol.*, **10**, 333.
Davey, C. L. & Gilbert, K. V. (1976) *J. Sci. Fd. Agric.*, **27**, 251.
Davey, C. L. & Graafhuis, A. E. (1976) *J. Sci. Fd. Agric.*, **27**, 301.
Donoso, G., Lewis, O. A. M., Miller, D. S. & Payne, P. R. (1962) *J. Sci. Fd. Agric.*, **13**, 192.
Dransfield, E. & Rhodes, D. N. (1976) *J. Sci. Fd. Agric.*, **27**, 483.
Dwivedi, B. K. (1975) *CRC Crit. Rev. Fd. Technol.*, **5**, 487.
Field, R. A., Pearson, A. M. & Schweigert, B. S. (1970) *J. Agric. Fd. Chem.*, **18**, 280.
Finch, A. & Ledward, D. A. (1972) *Biochim. Biophys. Acta*, **278**, 433.
Finch, A. & Ledward, D. A. (1973) *Biochim. Biophys. Acta*, **295**, 296.
Forrest, J. C., Aberle, E. D., Hedrick, H. B., Judge, M. D. & Merkel, R. A. (1975) *Principles of Meat Science*. San Francisco. W. H. Freeman.
Giles, B. G. (1969) *Proc. 15th Eur. Meeting Meat Res. Workers*, Helsinki, p. 289.
Govindarajan, S. (1973) *CRC Crit. Rev. Fd. Technol.*, **4**, 117.
Hamm, R. (1966) *Fleischwirtschaft*, **46**, 856.
Hamm, R. (1975) In: *Meat*, eds. Cole, D. J. A. & Lawrie, R. A., p. 321. London: Butterworths.
Hamm, R. & Deatherage, F. E. (1960) *Fd. Res.*, **25**, 587.
Harrison, D. L. (1975) *Proc. 28th Ann. Recipr. Meat Conf. Am. Meat Sci. Assoc.*, p. 340.
Hatton, M. W. C., Lawrie, R. A., Ratcliff, P. W. & Wayne, N. (1972) *J. Fd. Technol.*, **7**, 443.
Hostetler, R. L. & Landmann, W. A. (1968) *J. Fd. Sci.*, **33**, 468.
Jones, S. B., Carroll, R. T. & Cabanaugh, J. R. (1977) *J. Fd. Sci.*, **42**, 125.
Laakkonnen, E. (1973) *Advan. Fd. Res.*, **20**, 257.
Laakkonnen, E., Sherlon, J. W. & Wellington, G. H. (1970a) *J. Fd. Sci.*, **35**, 175.
Laakkonnen, E., Sherlon, J. W. & Wellington, G. H. (1970b) *J. Fd. Sci.*, **35**, 181.
Landmann, W. A. (1967) *Proc. 13th Eur. Meeting Meat Res. Workers*, Rotterdam, DZ.
Lawrie, R. A. (1950) *J. agric. Sci., Camb.*, **40**, 356.
Lawrie, R. A. (1968) *J. Sci. Fd. Agric.*, **19**, 233.
Lawrie, R. A. (1974) *Meat Science*, 2nd edn. Oxford: Pergamon Press.
Ledward, D. A. (1970) *J. Fd. Sci.*, **35**, 33.
Ledward, D. A. (1971) *J. Fd. Sci.*, **36**, 883.

Ledward, D. A. (1974) *J. Fd. Technol.*, **39**, 59.
Ledward, D. A. & Lawrie, R. A. (1975) *J. Sci. Fd. Agric.*, **26**, 691.
Ledward, D. A., Chizzolini, R. & Lawrie, R. A. (1975) *J. Fd. Technol.*, **10**, 349.
Locker, R. H. & Carse, W. A. (1976) *J. Sci. Fd. Agric.*, **27**, 891.
Locker, R. H. & Hagyard, C. J. (1963) *J. Sci. Fd. Agric.*, **14**, 787.
Locker, R. H. & Leet, N. G. (1975) *J. Ultrastruct. Res.*, **52**, 64.
Locker, R. H., Daines, G. J., Carse, W. A. & Leet, N. G. (1977) *Meat Sci.*, **1**, 87.
Locker, R. H., Davey, C. L., Nottingham, P. M., Haughey, D. P. & Law, N. H. (1975) *Advan. Fd. Res.*, **21**, 157.
Lutalo-Bosa, A. J. & Macrae, H. F. (1969) *J. Fd. Sci.*, **34**, 401.
Machlik, S. M. & Draudt, H. N. (1963) *J. Fd. Sci.*, **28**, 711.
Marsh, B. B. & Carse, W. A. (1974) *J. Fd. Technol.*, **9**, 129.
Marsh, B. B., Leet, N. G. & Dickson, M. R. (1974) *J. Fd. Technol.*, **9**, 141.
Miles, C. L. & Lawrie, R. A. (1970) *J. Fd. Technol.*, **5**, 325.
Newbold, R. P. & Scopes, R. K. (1967) *Biochem. J.*, **105**, 127.
Patterson, R. L. S. (1975) In: *Meat*, eds. Cole, D. J. A. & Lawrie, R. A., p. 359. London: Butterworths.
Paul, P. C. (1975) In: *Meat*, eds. Cole, D. J. A. & Lawrie, R. A., p. 403. London: Butterworths.
Paul, P. C., Butcher, L. & Wierenga, A. (1966) *J. Agric. Fd. Chem.*, **14**, 490.
Paul, P. C., Macrae, S. E. & Hofferber, L. M. (1973) *J. Fd. Sci.*, **38**, 66.
Penfield, M. P. & Meyer, B. H. (1975) *J. Fd. Sci.*, **40**, 150.
Rhodes, D. N. & Dransfield, E. (1974) *J. Sci. Fd. Agric.*, **25**, 1163.
Ritchey, S. J. & Hostetler, R. L. (1964) *J. Fd. Sci.*, **29**, 413.
Roberts, P. C. B. & Lawrie, R. A. (1974) *J. Fd. Technol.*, **9**, 345.
Rowe, R. W. D. (1974) *J. Fd. Technol.*, **9**, 501.
Rowe, R. W. D. (1977) *Meat Sci.*, **1**, 205.
Tappel, A. L. (1957) *Fd. Res.*, **22**, 404.
Veis, A. (1964) *Macromolecular Chemistry of Gelatin.* New York: Academic Press.
Verzar, F. (1964) *Intern. Rev. Connect. Tissue. Res.*, **2**, 243.
Voyle, C. A. (1969) *J. Fd. Technol.*, **4**, 275.
Walters, C. L. (1975) In: *Meat*, eds. Cole, D. J. A. & Lawrie, R. A., p. 385. London: Butterworths.
Watanabe, K. & Sato, Y. (1971) *Agric. Biol. Chem.*, **35**, 756.
Wassermann, A. E. (1972) *J. Agric. Fd. Chem.*, **21**, 737.
Whitaker, J. R. (1959) *Advan. Fd. Res.*, **9**, 1.
Wittenberg, J. B., Wittenberg, B. A., Peisach, J. & Blumberg, W. E. (1970) *Proc. Natl. Acad. Sci.*, **67**, 1846.
Wood, T., Adams, E. P. & Bender, A. E. (1962) *Nature*, **195**, 1207.

Since this chapter was completed, a number of papers have appeared (included in the References, above) dealing with the effect of heat on meat texture. It has not been possible to include reviews on these articles but, for

the benefit of readers who wish to study this topic in more detail, they are listed as follows:
Bailey, A. J. & Sims, T. J. (1977); Bouton, P. E. *et al.* (1977a,b,c); Cheng, C. E. & Parrish, F. C., Jr. (1976); Jones, S. B. *et al.* (1977); Locker, R. H. & Carse, W. A. (1976); Locker, R. H. *et al.* (1977); and Rowe, R. W. D. (1977).

CHAPTER 6

Poultry Meat

RUTH E. BALDWIN and OWEN J. COTTERILL

University of Missouri, Columbia, Missouri 65211, USA

Chickens, turkeys, ducks, geese, guinea fowl or pigeons are all classified as poultry. However, this review is focused on effects of heating on chicken and turkey meat since most of the published research deals with these two species.

6.1 COMPOSITION OF CHICKEN AND TURKEY

Edible meat varies from 34·4 to 39·1% for roast turkey, of which approximately 60% is light and 40% is dark (Goertz *et al.*, 1962). The yield of edible meat may be as low as 28·4% from chicken wings and as high as 62·3% from breast and thigh (Smith and Vail, 1963). Edible yield of poultry is influenced by age, size, strain, processing techniques, phosphate treatment and cooking methods (Carlson *et al.*, 1975).

Of the specific constituents in poultry, moisture exerts the greatest influence on yield of cooked meat (Swanson *et al.*, 1964). Raw chicken and turkey average 65·2% and 64·2% moisture, respectively, when all classes are considered (Table 6.1). Water content may be affected by absorption of moisture during the chilling process (Froning *et al.*, 1960; Swanson *et al.*, 1962), and by phosphate treatment which favours moisture retention (Schermerhorn and Stadelman, 1964).

Other components of poultry which influence yield are protein and fat. On a raw basis over all classes, protein content averages 18·1% for chicken and 20·1% for turkey (Table 6.1). Thus, turkey contains slightly more protein than chicken, beef or pork, but its amino acid composition is similar to that of beef and pork (Scott, 1959).

TABLE 6.1
MOISTURE, PROTEIN AND FAT CONTENT[a] OF CHICKEN AND TURKEY

Species and description	Moisture (%)		Protein (%)		Fat (%)	
	raw	cooked	raw	cooked	raw	cooked
Chicken						
Fryers	75·7	53·3	18·6	30·7	4·9	11·8
Roasters	63·0	53·5	18·2	25·2	17·9	20·2
Hens and cocks	56·9	45·9	17·4	24·0	24·8	29·5
Mean	65·2	50·9	18·1	26·6	15·9	20·5
Turkey						
All classes	64·2	55·4	20·1	27·0	14·7	16·4

[a]Watt and Merrill, 1963.

Fat content averages 15·9% for raw chicken and 14·7% for raw turkey (Table 6.1). The lipids of both turkey and chicken are relatively rich in unsaturated fats (Scott, 1959; Marion and Woodroof, 1963, 1965) and are influenced by diet, age and sex of the birds (Marion and Woodroof, 1963; Moran *et al.*, 1973; Salmon, 1976; Schuler and Essary, 1971). Cholesterol content is low (8–50 mg/g) in raw turkey with the least amount in the breast meat (Scott, 1959).

6.2 METHODS OF COOKING

Cooking procedures may be classified as follows:
   (i) roasting or baking in a closed oven;
   (ii) broiling by exposure to direct heat;
   (iii) braising or heating in moisture;
   (iv) frying in either shallow or deep fat; and
   (v) pressure cooking.

6.2.1 Roasting

The most common temperature for roasting is about 163°C (Deethardt *et al.*, 1971; Fulton and Davis, 1974; Fulton *et al.*, 1967; Heine *et al.*, 1973; MacNeil and Dimick, 1970). Temperatures of 205°C and 190°C were found to reduce yield of edible meat as compared to 163°C, but eating quality of turkey was not affected by these temperatures (Hoke, 1968; Hoke *et al.*, 1967). According to the data on turkey, roasting may be started from either the frozen or thawed state without influencing yield or eating quality (Fulton et al., 1967).

The practice of pre-roasting turkeys at 135°C, holding for several hours, then re-heating at 163°C until brown, should be discouraged owing to the possibility of a decline in temperature to a range conducive to microbial growth during the holding period. However, continuous cooking of poultry (maximum weight 8 lb) at low temperature for 8–10 h is recommended by the manufacturers of an oven-broiler appliance with slow-cook setting (McGraw-Edison Co., Columbia, MO 65201, USA). With the slow-cook setting, 1 h is required to achieve temperatures of 64°C and 81°C, and 6 h to heat the oven-broiler to 90°C and 105°C near the bottom and top shelves, respectively (Korschgen and Baldwin, 1977). However, Marshall's (1975) study with meat loaf suggested that potential microbiological problems are minimal in using the oven-broiler on the slow-cook setting for periods of several hours.

6.2.2 Braising

For braising, the liquid in which poultry is cooked is maintained at a temperature of 85–99°C. This may be accomplished by using a closed container in an oven heated to temperatures ranging from 205 to 233°C as reported by Fulton and Davis (1974) and Deethardt et al. (1971), or by placing the container in direct contact with the source of heat. Electric casseroles (93°C) have also been used for braising (Engler and Bowers, 1975). The foil-covered roasting procedure reported by Deethardt et al. (1971) was essentially a braising technique although the foil was opened during the latter stage of cooking. The use of oven-proof film, paper bags with small openings, and loose foil cover, as reported by Heine et al. (1973), conformed more closely to the procedure for braising than to that for roasting.

6.2.3 Frying

Temperatures selected for frying poultry range from 125 to 152°C. Fulton and Davis (1974) fried chicken pieces at 127°C in only 15 g fat, whereas the skillet temperature was adjusted from 150 to 125°C by Funk et al. (1971) when cooking chicken pieces in 500 g fat. The chicken was completely immersed in fat at 152°C in the work of Hale and Goodwin (1968). Coating chicken with hydroxypropylmethylcellulose or carboxymethylcellulose before frying had no beneficial effects (Hale and Goodwin, 1968; Funk et al., 1971).

Funk *et al.* (1971) investigated pre-cooking by microwaves as a means of reducing the frying time, but panel scores indicated that this treatment was detrimental to flavour of the fried chicken. Combining frying with steam under pressure (15 p.s.i.), however, minimised cooking losses and maximised moisture retention in poultry (Mostert and Stadelman, 1964).

6.2.4 Pressure Cooking

Pudelkewicz *et al.* (1963) and Yingst *et al.* (1971) employed pressure in cooking poultry. This, of course, is moist heat, as in braising, but temperatures of 115°C and 121°C are achieved, respectively, at 10 and 15 lb pressure. In a comparison of steam plus pressure with cooking in water, Yingst *et al.* (1971) found a reduction in fat content with steam cooking, but no alteration in yield or in moisture content. Pressure further reduced the amount of fat in the skin.

6.2.5 Cooking Intensity

Of greater concern than method or temperature is intensity of cooking, for it is the combination of temperature and time that determines the ultimate effect. Martinsen and Carlin (1968) monitored the temperature change in turkey roasts cooked at different temperatures. A 0·56°C/min rise occurred with an oven temperature of 177°C and a 0·22°C/min rise was observed with a temperature of 107°C.

Cooking to a specific internal temperature is a means of controlling cooking intensity. Temperatures of 71–90°C have been reported in various studies as final internal temperatures in breast and thigh muscles of poultry, the latter temperature being considered a better indicator of 'doneness' (Goertz and Watson, 1964). Hoke *et al.* (1967) concluded that any oven temperature between 121 and 204°C could be used for cooking turkey roasts provided internal temperature was used to determine length of cooking. Wilkinson and Dawson (1967) found that light-meat turkey rolls were juicier and less tough when cooked to an internal temperature of 71°C rather than 88°C. Tenderness and juiciness of dark-meat turkey rolls, however, were not adversely affected by the higher internal temperatures. In contrast, Goodwin *et al.* (1962) observed no significant difference in shear values for turkey meat roasted to internal temperatures of 77, 82, 88 and 94°C.

6.3 INFLUENCE OF HEAT ON VARIOUS PROPERTIES OF POULTRY

6.3.1 Appearance

A brown exterior, as obtained with roasting or frying, contributes to appetite appeal of poultry. Cooking in oven-proof film or foil wrap is less conducive to browning than cooking in a paper bag with small openings (Heine *et al.*, 1973). Microwave heating also results in less browning than other cooking methods, particularly if cooking time is less than 20 min. Improved external appearance of microwave-cooked poultry can be accomplished by surface treatment with ingredients such as brown gravy mix. This procedure is a more satisfactory means of browning poultry than the use of utensils designed for browning foods which are cooked by microwaves (Baldwin and Brandon, 1973).

Internally, cooked poultry meat should appear coagulated; and, as doneness of the meat increases, the juice released upon slicing is less pink (Hoke, 1968). Pinkness of the meat, which sometimes appears near the surface of poultry cooked uncovered, has been attributed to the combining of haemoglobin with carbon monoxide and nitric oxide (Anon., 1956). Discolouration of meat next to the bones also occurs occasionally during cooking of frozen young fowl. This is due to haemoglobin which is released from the bone marrow by the freezing and thawing process (Ellis and Woodroof, 1959).

6.3.2 Flavour

Lineweaver and Pippen (1961) reviewed the early research on poultry flavour which revealed that flavour precursors can be extracted from raw chicken by cold water. Subsequent application of heat to these precursors results in typical cooked-meat flavour. Muscle is the best source of flavour, but fat contributes to aroma of chicken broth which is enhanced by a low pH during heating (Pippen *et al.*, 1965).

Wasserman (1972) summarised and discussed research on the rôle of thermal degradation products of amino acids, sugars, lipids, and vitamins in flavour of both red meats and poultry. In addition to these products of heat degradation, the importance of sulphur compounds, particularly hydrogen sulphide, to cooked-chicken flavour was stressed. Sulphur compounds are also prominent in the listing of specific components of poultry flavour prepared by Wilson and Katz (1972).

In contrast, Janney and Hale (1974) identified thiophene as the only sulphur-containing compound in the volatiles obtained from fried chicken.

A full, natural flavour in both light and dark meat of poultry is favoured by roasting (Fulton and Davis, 1974). Cooking poultry meat on or off the bone also influences flavour. The data of Baker *et al.* (1973) clearly indicated a preference for poultry cooked on the bone prior to formation into rolls or loaves.

Pre-cooking adversely affects flavour, and significant flavour changes may occur in less than 2 h after the initial cooking (Harris and Lindsay, 1972). Injections of antioxidants or pre-treatment with a phosphate solution protect flavour of poultry against adverse changes owing to storage and re-heating (Johnson and Bowers, 1974; Klinger and Stadelman, 1975) but meaty flavour of phosphate-treated chicken decreases during storage at $-18°C$ (Landes, 1972). Although protection against warmed-over flavour is exerted by phosphates, an objectionable soapy or baking-soda-type flavour is imparted to the meat (Johnson and Bowers, 1974; Landes, 1972).

6.3.3 Tenderness
Excessive scalding increases toughness of poultry. This effect is a function of the temperature of the poultry tissue in the early post-mortem period (Stadelman and Wise, 1961).

Poultry cooked soon after death is more tender than meat allowed to age one hour before cooking. The onset of rigor is rapid in poultry, and the meat remains tough until rigor passes (de Fremery and Pool, 1963).

Chicken may be cooked from either the thawed or frozen state without significant effects on tenderness, as indicated by shear values. This is also true for hen turkeys. However, breast and thigh of tom turkeys are tougher and give higher shear values when roasted from the thawed state or when braised from the frozen state (Fulton and Davis, 1974).

Cooking poultry on the bone appears to be preferable to de-boning prior to cooking. In addition to the superior flavour, mentioned earlier, a trend toward lower shear values was found by Baker *et al.* (1973).

In comparing effects of the cooking method on tenderness of poultry, roasting resulted in lower shear values than braising (Fulton and Davis, 1974). Also, dark meat of turkey was more tender when cooked in an open pan or paper bag than when cooked in oven-proof film or foil (Heine *et al.*, 1973). Sensory scores indicated greater tenderness in breast of turkey cooked 8–10 h at 93°C than in turkey breast cooked to 80°C in an oven heated to 177°C (Engler and Bowers, 1975). However, no difference in tenderness of turkey roasts was attributed to oven temperatures of 121, 177 or 204°C. Tuomy *et al.* (1969) evaluated the cooking process for freeze-drying and demonstrated a maximum toughening effect in light meat of turkey by heating to 71°C, whereas holding at specific temperatures less than 71°C resulted in little change in toughness from its initial value.

Tuomy *et al.* (1969) observed that tenderness of turkey meat increased if an internal temperature above 71°C was achieved. Wilkinson and Dawson (1967) reported greater tenderness in dark turkey meat as internal temperature increased from 60 to 88°C. Light meat, however, was more tender when cooked to 77 or 82°C and became tougher when cooked to 88°C. This may, in part, explain the difference observed by Culotta and Chen (1973) in microwave-cooked turkey. These researchers chose a final internal temperature of 88°C. They found no difference in dark meat, but light turkey meat was less tender when cooked by microwaves than when simmered in water.

Phosphate treatment has little effect on tenderness of poultry as indicated by shear values. However, panel scores indicated that such a treatment increased tenderness (Baker and Darfler, 1968).

6.3.4 Juiciness

Light meat of turkey becomes very dry when cooked to an internal temperature of 88°C. Wilkinson and Dawson (1967) recommended that, for light meat, an internal temperature of 82°C should not be exceeded. Engler and Bowers (1975) cooked turkey breast to only 80°C and found no difference in juiciness between meat cooked at 93°C and at 177°C. Likewise, turkey breast roasted at 177°C and heated by microwaves did not differ in juiciness when final internal temperatures ranged from 70 to 85°C (Bowers and Heier, 1970). Light meat of chicken cooked to an internal temperature of 88°C was more juicy when braised than when roasted, whereas dark meat was juicier when roasted (Fulton and Davis, 1974). Yet light meat of turkey cooked to 85°C in an open pan or foil wrap was juicier than that cooked to the same internal temperature in oven film or a paper bag (Heine *et al.*, 1973).

A microwave–steam combination treatment was recommended by

Dawson and Sison (1973) for processing frozen fried chicken because re-heating losses were lower while yield and eating quality were similar to chicken fried under pressure. Phosphate treatment was suggested as a means of increasing yield of chicken processed by this method. Pre-treating poultry by immersing in a 4–8% phosphate solution successfully reduced cooking losses but concentrations in excess of 12% increased losses (Schermerhorn and Stadelman, 1964).

Sensory response to juiciness may be influenced by total moisture, expressible moisture, and fat content. Changes in moisture and fat content owing to cooking are illustrated in Table 6.1. Rogers et al. (1967) conducted an intensive investigation of heat-induced changes in moisture of turkey muscle roasted at 176°C. Loose water, that which is expressible from tissues by pressure alone, increased in breast tissue as the end-point temperature increased from 25 to 65°C. In contrast, immobilised moisture, that which requires heat in addition to pressure for release, increased in the thigh muscle as end-point temperature increased.

6.3.5 Cooking Losses

Total cooking losses vary among strains of turkeys, but size appears to exert little effect. Losses also differ according to the piece, and MacNeil and Dimick (1970) observed greater losses in roasts of turkey breasts than in roasts of thigh meat.

Table 6.2 is a summary of selected studies concerned with cooking losses of poultry. According to Engler and Bowers (1975), roasting (177°C) caused greater total and volatile losses and less drip than slow cooking at 93°C. In a comparison of roasting temperatures, 177°C resulted in smaller total losses for half turkeys than 163°C or 149°C (Goertz and Stacy, 1960). Similar total losses were observed for whole turkeys roasted at these three temperatures. Greater volatile losses for whole turkey occurred at a temperature of 163°C but no effect on drip losses was noted. During the cooking process (176°C), the greatest total and volatile losses in turkey pieces occurred between 55 and 65°C, whereas drip losses increased at the fastest rate between temperatures of 45 and 55°C. These losses bore no relationship to amounts of expressible juice or to moisture components requiring heat for release (Rogers et al., 1967).

Heine et al. (1973) observed that foil wrapping of turkey halves resulted in less total cooking losses than cooking in an open pan, in oven-proof film, or in a paper bag, but volatile losses were greater with the open pan.

Several studies have shown that microwave heating causes greater total and volatile losses, and less drip than conventional heating (Bowers and Heier, 1970; Wing and Alexander, 1972; Cipra *et al.*, 1971; Bowers *et al.*, 1974). When turkey was re-heated by microwaves, no significant difference occurred in drip, but volatile losses were greater (Cipra *et al.*, 1971).

6.3.6 Protein and Fat Content

The nutritional quality of turkey protein is not damaged by heating even for as long as 120 min at 163°C. However, heating in an autoclave for 24 h decreased the protein efficiency ratio, apparent biological value, digestibility, and weight gain of rats (Liu and Ritchey, 1970). In the study on fowl by Pudelkewicz *et al.* (1963) the amino acids, lysine and methionine, were not significantly affected by cooking under pressure (10 p.s.i.).

Salt-soluble and surface proteins are responsible for binding strength in heated comminuted products. Cooking at low temperatures of 65 and 75°C for 40–50 min favours good binding power and minimal cooking losses in comminuted poultry meat (Vadehra *et al.*, 1970). Binding strength also increases as tissue rupture increases in the comminution process (Acton, 1972).

Diet and age of the bird influence the original fatty acid composition of the lipids (Schuler and Essary, 1971). Subsequent cooking alters the fat content (Table 6.1) and modifies the composition of the lipids. During cooking and re-heating, oils are absorbed by the tissue as well as by any batter coating the poultry tissue (Berry and Cunningham, 1970; Heath *et al.*, 1971). Myristic, palmitic, oleic, and linoleic acids in the tissue increase with frying time (Heath *et al.*, 1971). Deep-fat frying increases total fat content of tissue more than skillet frying (Smith and Vail, 1963). Cooking also causes fat hydrolysis (Harris and Lindsay 1972) and reduction in phosphorus content of phospholipids (Lee and Dawson, 1976). Fat hydrolysis is more extensive with microwave than with deep-fat pre-heating (Harris and Lindsay, 1972).

6.3.7 Vitamin Content

Thiamine content of microwave-cooked and conventionally roasted (177°C) turkey does not differ significantly, but slow-cooked (93°C)

TABLE 6.2

SUMMARY OF SELECTED STUDIES ILLUSTRATING EFFECTS OF HEATING ON COOK-
ING LOSSES OF POULTRY

Heating process	Cooking losses	Reference
Turkey roasts, 163°C; internal temperature 77°C	Higher for breast than for thigh	MacNeil & Dimick (1970)
Turkey breast, 177°C; internal temperature 80°C	Greater total and volatile losses, less drip with roasting than with slow cooking	Engler & Bowers (1975)
Turkey hen halves and whole turkey hens, 149°C 163°C, 177°C; internal temperature, breast 90°C	Total losses for halves least at 177°C. No difference in total losses for whole birds. Greatest volatile losses for half turkeys 163°C and for whole turkeys 177°C. Drip not affected	Goertz & Stacy (1960)
Turkey pieces, 176°C	Greatest increase in total and volatile losses between 55°C and 65°C internal temperature. Greatest increase in drippings between 45°C and 55°C	Rogers et al. (1967)

Conditions	Results	Reference
Turkey halves, 163°C; internal temperature, breast 85°C	Less total and volatile losses with aluminium foil than with oven-proof film, open pan or paper bag. Greatest drip loss with oven-proof film	Heine et al. (1973)
Turkey breasts, 177°C and microwave; internal temperatures 75°C, 85°C	Total and volatile losses less and drip greater for roasting than for microwave heating. Losses similar for internal temperatures	Bowers et al. (1974)
Turkey breasts, 177°C and microwave; internal temperatures 70°C, 75°C 80°C, 85°C	Trends same for three higher internal temperatures as reported by Bowers et al. (1974).	Bowers & Heier, (1970)
Chicken breasts, 163°C and microwave; internal temperature 88°C for conventional oven and 96°C for microwave heating	Greater drip, less weight loss with roasting	Wing & Alexander (1972)
Turkey breast, 163°C and microwave; internal temperature 85°C; re-heated to 70°C by the two methods	Greater total and volatile losses, less drip for microwave heating	Cipra et al. (1971)

turkey contains less thiamine than when cooked conventionally (Engler and Bowers, 1975; Bowers and Fryer, 1972). Thiamine content averaged 0·475 µg/g and 0·58 µg/g, respectively, for slow-cooked and roasted turkey (Engler and Bowers, 1975); 0·38 µg/g and 0·36 µg/g, respectively, for microwave and conventionally cooked turkey (Bowers and Fryer, 1972); and 1·1 µg/g for pressure-cooked (10 p.s.i.) fowl (Pudelkewicz et al., 1963).

Bowers and Fryer (1972) found that riboflavin content of microwave and conventionally (177°C) cooked turkey did not differ on a wet-weight basis, although on a dry-weight basis the value for the conventionally cooked product was significantly higher. On a wet-weight basis, average values for riboflavin content were 1·93 µg/g for conventionally roasted turkey, 1·84 µg/g for microwave cooked turkey (Bowers and Fryer, 1972) and 0·72 µg/g for pressure-cooked (10 p.s.i.) fowl (Pudelkewicz et al., 1963).

Pyridoxine content tends to be higher for microwave-heated than for conventionally heated poultry. Average amounts of this vitamin in microwave-cooked turkey and chicken were 5·80 µg/g and 6·38 µg/g, respectively. Conventionally heated turkey and chicken contained 5·15 µg/g and 5·43 µg/g, respectively (Bowers et al., 1974; Wing and Alexander, 1972).

Destruction of the B vitamins by heating poultry appears to be minimal, although pressure cooking (10 p.s.i.) resulted in a mean retention of only 45% for thiamine in chicken (Pudelkewicz et al., 1963). Retention of thiamine in turkey roasted (177°C) and cooked by microwaves averaged 79% (Bowers and Fryer, 1972). Riboflavin retention averaged 82% in pressure-cooked (10 p.s.i.) chicken (Pudelkewicz et al., 1963) and 86% in microwave and 92% in conventionally roasted turkey (Bowers and Fryer, 1972). Pyridoxine retention for microwave and conventionally cooked (163°C) chicken was 91% and 83%, respectively (Wing and Alexander, 1972).

6.4 IMPLICATIONS

Poultry is compatible with a variety of preparation and processing techniques. With the exception of thiamine destruction by pressure cooking, the nutrients in poultry are relatively stable. Heating to internal temperatures in excess of 82°C is detrimental to juiciness. Roasting is conducive to a full, natural flavour, and re-heating by microwaves is superior to other methods of re-heating.

Various species of poultry may be expected to be prominent sources of protein for human consumption in the future since they are more efficient than either cattle or swine in converting animal feeds to high-protein food.

REFERENCES

Acton, J. C. (1972) *J. Fd. Sci.*, **37**, 240.

Anon. (1956) *Poultry Proc. Marketing*, **62**(1), 29.

Baker, R. C. & Darfler, J. (1968) *Poultry Sci.*, **47**, 1590.

Baker, R. C., Darfler, J. M. & Nath, K. R. (1973) *Poultry Sci.*, **52**, 1574.

Baldwin, R. E. & Brandon, M. (1973) *Microwave Energy Appl. Newsletter*, **6**(5), 3.

Berry, J. G. & Cunningham, F. E. (1970) *Poultry Sci.*, **49**, 1236.

Bowers, J. A. & Fryer, B. A. (1972) *J. Am. Dietet. Assoc.*, **60**, 399.

Bowers, J. A. & Heier, M. C. (1970) *Microwave Energy Appl. Newsletter*, **3**(6), 3.

Bowers, J. A., Fryer, B. A. & Engler, P. P. (1974) *Poultry Sci.*, **53**, 844.

Carlson, C. W., Marion, W. W., Miller, B. F. & Goodwin, T. L. (1975) *South Dakota Agric. Expt. Stn. Tech. Bull.*, 630.

Cipra, J. E., Bowers, J. A. & Hooper, A. S. (1971) *J. Am. Dietet. Assoc.*, **58**, 38.

Culotta, J. T. & Chen, T. C. (1973) *J. Fd. Sci.*, **38**, 860.

Dawson, L. E. & Sison, E. C. (1973) *J. Fd. Sci.*, **38**, 161.

Deethardt, D., Burrill, L. M., Schneider, K. & Carlson, C. W. (1971) *J. Fd. Sci.*, **36**, 624.

de Fremery, D. & Pool, F. (1963) *J. Fd. Sci.*, **28**, 173.

Ellis, C. & Woodroof, J. G. (1959) *Fd. Technol.*, **13**, 533.

Engler, P. P. & Bowers, J. A. (1975) *J. Am. Dietet. Assoc.*, **67**, 43.

Froning, G. W., Swanson, M. H. & Benson, H. N. (1960) *Poultry Sci.*, **39**, 373.

Fulton, L. & Davis, C. (1974) *J. Am. Dietet. Assoc.*, **64**, 505.

Fulton, L. H., Gilpin, G. L. & Dawson, E. H. (1967) *J. Home Econ.*, **59**, 728.

Funk, K., Yadrick, M. K. & Conklin, M. A. (1971) *Poultry Sci.*, **50**, 634.

Goertz, G. E. & Stacy, S. (1960) *J. Am. Dietet. Assoc.*, **37**, 458.

Goertz, G. E. & Watson, M. A. (1964) *Poultry Sci.*, **43**, 812.

Goertz, G. E., Hooper, S. & Fry, J. L. (1962) *Poultry Sci.*, **41**, 1295.

Goodwin, T. L., Bramblett, V. D., Vail, G. E. & Stadelman, W. J. (1962) *Fd. Technol.*, **16**, 101.

Hale, K. K. & Goodwin, T. L. (1968) *Poultry Sci.*, **47**, 739.

Harris, N. D. & Lindsay, R. C. (1972) *J. Fd. Sci.*, **37**, 19.

Heath, J. L., Teekell, R. A. & Watts, A. B. (1971) *Poultry Sci.*, **50**, 219.

Heine, N., Bowers, J. A. & Johnson, P. G. (1973) *Home Econ. Res. J.*, **1**, 210.

Hoke, I. M. (1968) *J. Home Econ.*, **60**, 661.

Hoke, I. M., McGeary, B. K. & Kleve, M. K. (1967) *Fd. Technol.*, **21**, 773.

Janney, C. G. & Hale, K. K., Jr. (1974) *Poultry Sci.*, **53**, 1758.

Johnson, P. G. & Bowers, J. A. (1974) *Poultry Sci.*, **53**, 343.

Klinger, S. D. & Stadelman, W. J. (1975) *Poultry Sci.*, **54**, 1278.

Korschgen, B. & Baldwin, R. E. (1977) Unpublished data. Missouri Agric. Expt. Stn.

Landes, D. R. (1972) *Poultry Sci.*, **51**, 641.
Lee, W. T. & Dawson, L. E. (1976) *J. Fd. Sci.*, **41**, 598.
Lineweaver, H. & Pippen, E. L. (1961) Chicken flavour. Presented at *Flavour Chemistry Symposium*, Camden, N.J.
Liu, E. H. & Ritchey, S. J. (1970) *J. Am. Dietet. Assoc.*, **57**, 38.
MacNeil, J. H. & Dimick, P. S. (1970) *J. Fd. Sci.*, **35**, 184.
Marion, J. E. & Woodroof, J. G. (1963) *Poultry Sci.*, **42**, 1202.
Marion, J. E. & Woodroof, J. G. (1965) *J. Fd. Sci.*, **30**, 38.
Marshall, R. T. (1975) Unpublished data. Missouri Agric. Expt. Stn.
Martinsen, C. S. & Carlin, A. F. (1968) *Fd. Technol.*, **22**, 109.
Moran, E. T., Jr., Larmond, E. & Somers, J. (1973) *Poultry Sci.*, **52**, 1942.
Mostert, G. C. & Stadelman, W. J. (1964) *Poultry Sci.*, **43**, 896.
Pippen, E. L., de Fremery, D., Lineweaver, H. & Hanson, H. L. (1965) *Poultry Sci.*, **44**, 816.
Pudelkewicz, C., Gordon, H., Whitworth, L., Caldwell, H. M. & Kahlenberg, O. J. (1963) *Missouri Agric. Expt. Stn. Tech. Bull.*, 819.
Rogers, P. J., Goertz, G. E. & Harrison, D. L. (1967) *J. Fd. Sci.*, **32**, 298.
Salmon, R. E. (1976) *Poultry Sci.*, **55**, 201.
Schermerhorn, E. P. & Stadelman, W. J. (1964) *Fd. Technol.*, **18**, 101.
Schuler, G. A. & Essary, E. O. (1971) *J. Fd. Sci.*, **36**, 431.
Scott, M. L. (1959) *J. Am. Dietet. Assoc.*, **35**, 247.
Smith, A. A. & Vail, G. E. (1963) *J. Am. Dietet. Assoc.*, **43**, 541.
Stadelman, W. J. & Wise, R. G. (1961) *Fd. Technol.*, **15**, 292.
Swanson, M. H., Carlson, C. W. & Fry, J. L. (1964) *Minnesota Agric. Expt. Stn. Tech. Bull.*, 476.
Swanson, M. H., Froning, G. W. & Richards, J. F. (1962) *Poultry Sci.*, **41**, 272.
Tuomy, J. M., Schlup, H. T. & Helmer, R. L. (1969) *Fd. Technol.*, **23**(3), 60.
Vadehra, D. V., Schnell, P. G. & Baker, R. C. (1970) *Poultry Sci.*, **49**, 1447.
Wasserman, A. E. (1972) *J. Agric. Fd. Chem.*, **20**, 737.
Watt, B. K. & Merrill, A. L. (1963) *Agriculture Handbook No. 8*, USDA, Washington, D.C.
Wilkinson, R. J. & Dawson, L. E. (1967) *Poultry Sci.*, **46**, 15.
Wilson, R. A. & Katz, I. (1972) *J. Agric. Fd. Chem.*, **20**, 741.
Wing, R. W. & Alexander, J. C. (1972) *J. Am. Dietet. Assoc.*, **61**, 661.
Yingst, L. D., Wyche, R. C. & Goodwin, T. L. (1971) *J. Am. Dietet. Assoc.*, **59**, 582.

CHAPTER 7

Eggs

RUTH E. BALDWIN and OWEN J. COTTERILL

University of Missouri, Columbia, Missouri 65211, USA

Considerable attention has been focused on changes in physical and functional properties of eggs, induced by heat. These changes are a major concern to both processors and consumers (Cunningham, 1970).

7.1 INFLUENCE OF HIGH-TEMPERATURE STORAGE ON QUALITY OF SHELL EGGS

When storage times are limited to a few days, shell eggs should be stored at temperatures ranging from 10 to 16°C to maintain high quality (Swanson, 1973). The rate of thinning in egg white, moisture loss and the weakening of the vitelline membrane surrounding the yolk are quality attributes that are affected by heat. All can be controlled by proper refrigeration. High temperatures (above room temperature) increase the rate of degradation. The white becomes thin and watery, the yolk enlarges and the membrane is easily broken. The mechanism of degradation is not understood but pH is important. Initially, the pH of egg white is near 8·0. It increases to around 9·3 when stored at high temperatures, which enhance the loss of carbon dioxide. Funk (1950) discovered that the rate of thinning is reduced by a thermostabilisation process which involves heating shell eggs at 54°C for 14 min.

Low temperature is especially important for protecting the flavour of eggs. Dawson *et al.* (1956) indicated that shell eggs stored at 7°C and at 24°C had comparable flavour losses after 16–24 and 1–2 weeks, respectively. Oiled eggs developed off-flavours faster than untreated eggs when held at the lower temperature, but the reverse was true for the higher temperature. Banwart *et al.* (1957) also observed that off-flavours became more evident in oiled and thermostabilised eggs than in untreated eggs at a storage temperature of 1°C. In contrast, Hard *et al.* (1963) found that untreated and thermostabilised eggs remained acceptable in flavøur longer than those treated by oil, oil plus carbon dioxide, or silicone when stored at 0 or 13°C. These treated eggs, however, were the first to be rejected when the storage temperature was raised to 22°C.

7.2   INFLUENCE OF HEAT ON FUNCTIONAL PROPERTIES

Eggs are utilised in foods because of their functional properties such as foaming, coagulation, emulsifying, nutritive value, colour, crystallisation control, and flavour (Baldwin, 1973). The foaming property of egg white is very sensitive to heat. Even the mild heat treatment (57°C for 3·5 min) used in pasteurisation causes considerable damage. Heat causes the whip-time to increase, while foam volume and stability are decreased. On the other hand, heat sensitivity of egg proteins is a desirable property where coagulation is involved. The ability to coagulate is responsible for the many forms in which eggs can be prepared and served. The nutritional and emulsifying properties are not damaged by the heat treatments normally used in processing and cooking. In fact, heating may result in some improvement to both of these properties. The biological activity of ovomucoid, avidin and conalbumin is reduced by heat. These proteins complex with trypsin, biotin and iron, respectively. Cotterill *et al.* (1976) observed some improvement in the emulsifying properties of salted egg-yolk and whole egg on heating. Colour and flavour of eggs are grossly affected by heat and, although these changes are commonly recognised, they have received little attention.

7.3   HEAT SENSITIVITY OF EGG PROTEINS

Prior to 1950, work on the heat sensitivity of individual egg proteins was restricted primarily to two types: (1) general observations on the heat coagulability of protein isolates; and (2) basic studies on the heat-denaturation process (egg-white was frequently the protein used in these studies).

After 1950, food scientists became more concerned with the heat labilities of individual proteins, particularly with respect to the effects of processing. Cotterill and Winter (1954) observed that thermo-stabilisation did not decrease the lytic activity of lysozyme in the white of shell eggs, whereas higher temperatures did. Ovomucin was found to be very heat stable. However, Cotterill (1954) showed evidence that the interaction of lysozyme with ovomucin, and perhaps some other proteins in egg-white, is affected by heat. While studying the effect of pH on egg-white coagulation, Seideman et al. (1963) reported that lysozyme could be selectively immobilised (electrophoretically) by heating at pH 9·0, whilst conalbumin was immobilised at pH 7·0. Conalbumin complexed with iron or aluminium is more heat stable than the dissociated protein. Cunningham and Lineweaver (1965) developed a pasteurisation process involving these two concepts. Lineweaver et al. (1967) estimated that heating egg-white adjusted to pH 9 for 3·5 min at 62°C altered 3–5% of the ovalbumin, 90–100% of the lysozyme and more than 50% of the conalbumin. Lowering the pH to 7 reduced the amount of ovalbumin altered by the heat treatment to less than 0·1% and the amount of lysozyme altered to less than 6%, but increased the amount of conalbumin altered to 100%. Later, Cunningham (1974) reported that the heat-labile component designated as 'line 18' on starch-gel electrophoretograms is not protected by the $Al_2(SO_4)_3$–pH 7·0 process.

The effects of heat on yolk fractions are less well defined than on egg-white. However, the ion-exchange chromatograms of Seideman and Cotterill (1969) and McBee (1974) showed that yolk fractions are affected by heat treatments. Also, Chang et al. (1970) noted alterations of gel patterns due to pasteurisation of yolk samples.

7.4   EFFECTS OF HEATING ON LIPIDS OF YOLK

Schiller et al. (1973) extracted lipids from yolk and found that heating to 80°C caused no change in fatty acid composition of the lipids. TBA numbers, however, were higher in samples heated in a conventional electric oven than in samples heated by microwaves with a frequency of 2450 MHz, and these TBA numbers were higher than for samples heated by microwaves with a frequency of 915 MHz. The mean TBA number for the latter samples did not differ from that for uncooked eggs. The researchers postulated that microwaves at the higher frequency exerted a catalytic effect on autoxidation but to a lesser degree than conventional cooking.

7.5   FORMATION OF HYDROGEN SULPHIDE DURING HEATING

Hydrogen sulphide is produced by non-enzymic reactions when eggs or egg products are heated to temperatures exceeding 60°C. Production of this compound involves both sulphydryl and disulphide groups, and requires the presence of oxygen. The reaction is preceded by denaturation of proteins and is favoured by alkaline pH. When egg-white is heated, both hydrogen sulphide and lanthione, a thio-ether, are formed (Germs, 1973).

7.6 METHODS OF COOKING AND THEIR EFFECTS ON QUALITY

Regardless of method of cooking, the important consideration for successful egg cookery is the relationship between time and temperature. Over-coagulation may result from either high temperature or excessively long cooking. Rate of coagulation increases as temperature increases and is almost instantaneous at high temperatures (Lowe, 1955). The speed of coagulation of albumen is increased approximately 191 times for every 1°C rise in temperature and 635 times for every 10°C rise (Chick and Martin, 1910).

Cooking results in an average loss of 7·7% riboflavin and 15·0% thiamine. Loss of thiamine is rather consistent regardless of method of cookery. Stamberg and Peterson (1946) observed the greatest loss of riboflavin in poached egg and the smallest loss in scrambled eggs.

When eggs are cooked in the shell, temperatures of 85–90°C for 25–30 min are recommended to achieve a uniform hard-cooked consistency. At temperatures of 98–100°C the time can be reduced to 12 min (Paul and Palmer, 1972). Temperatures from 75 to 85°C, with subsequent rapid cooling, minimise green-colour formation on the surface of the yolk of hard-cooked eggs. The green colour is due to a reaction between H_2S from the albumen and iron from the yolk (Tinkler and Soar, 1920; Baker *et al.* 1967). The rapid cooling after the cooking process also prevents carbonyl–amino browning which occasionally occurs in the albumen of eggs which have been hard-cooked in the shell (Baker and Darfler, 1969).

Temperatures near boiling favour rapid coagulation and improved shape in poached eggs. However, for fried eggs, temperatures of 126–137°C promote optimum coagulation. Excessive spreading occurs with lower temperatures and over-coagulation with higher cooking temperatures (Andross, 1940).

Since dilution of egg protein elevates the temperature for coagulation, Andross (1940) recommended addition of 10–25 ml of milk per egg for scrambled eggs. Greater dilution is conducive to curdling, and insufficient dilution yields a rubbery consistency (Griswold, 1962). Increasing the proportion of egg in custard lowers the temperature at which thickening occurs since coagulation is due mainly to the protein supplied by egg (Paul and Palmer, 1972). Optimum and over-coagulation are separated by only 3°C when custards are cooked over boiling water, but these two conditions are separated by a temperature span of 5°C when custards are surrounded by water not exceeding 90°C during cooking (Andross, 1940).

Stable egg-white foams are the basis of meringues, soufflés and angel cakes. Stability of foams is not affected by pre-heating albumen for as long as 30 min at 50°C (Barmore, 1934). Heating at temperatures as high as 58°C is not detrimental if the albumen is not held at the elevated temperature (Slosberg et al., 1948). However, research has demonstrated that holding albumen for 3 min at 54°C or above decreases foam stability and volume of angel cakes (Brown and Zabik, 1967; Slosberg et al., 1948; Barmore, 1934).

Selection of an appropriate temperature for baking angel cakes depends to a large extent on the volume and shape of the container. Excessively high temperatures will cause rapid coagulation of an outer crust, limiting the volume of the cake, and low temperatures require unduly long times to complete baking (Paul and Palmer, 1972). Both insufficient coagulation of the interior and over-coagulation on the surface contribute to undesirable leakage of soft meringue. Gillis and Fitch (1956) recommended baking soft meringues at 163°C to achieve good overall quality. These researchers indicated that the amount of sugar and conditions of beating are as important as baking temperature in obtaining satisfactory soft meringues. For hard meringues, long, slow baking at 100–110°C is essential to develop a crisp, tender product (Paul and Palmer, 1972).

7.7 PASTEURISATION

Kline *et al.* (1965) found that egg-white can be pasteurised for 2 min at 56·1–56·7°C without physical changes in the product. The treatment increased beating time, but this can be counteracted by the addition of triethyl citrate. Adjusting the egg-white to pH 7 improves the stability of conalbumin, lysozyme, and ovomucoid. Addition of iron or aluminium salts stabilises conalbumin. These treatments stabilise the product sufficiently to permit pasteurisation at 60–62°C for 3·5–4 min, but increase whipping time (Cunningham and Lineweaver, 1965). Lactic acid, as well as aluminium salts, minimise heat denaturation but do not restore whipping quality (Meyer and Potter, 1974). Addition of sodium polyphosphate (0·75%) permits pasteurisation at 52–55°C for 3·5 min without detrimental effects on functional properties of albumin (Kohl, 1971).

A hot-pack process was devised by Cotterill *et al.* (1974) for pasteurisation of whole egg and yolk containing 10% salt. This method requires heating to 52°C and holding at that temperature for 72 h, which is not detrimental to emulsifying properties of the yolk. Later, Cotterill *et al.* (1976) determined that temperatures as high as 78°C for 5 min or 52°C for eight days can be applied to salted yolk without deleterious effects on emulsifying properties. It was suggested that storage may be more damaging to emulsifying properties than pasteurisation. Also, pasteurisation at 60–64°C had little effect on functional properties of yolk in the investigation conducted by Palmer *et al.* (1969). Freezing and frozen storage, however, were detrimental to performance of both pasteurised and unpasteurised sugared yolk in sponge cakes. These researchers stated that careful selection of processing and storage conditions would make it possible to control changes in viscosity of sugared egg yolk.

McCready *et al.* (1971) evaluated the effects of pasteurisation on composition and performance of the supernatant fraction of centrifuged whole egg. Pasteurisation at 60, 62, or 64°C caused an increase in viscosity in all samples except those at pH levels of 8·5–9·0 heated at 60 or 62°C. There was little difference in relative viscosity between heated and unheated samples of supernate, all of which were less viscous than whole egg. Volume of sponge cakes was not affected by prior heating of the supernate with which they were made.

7.8 DEHYDRATION

Most egg products are spray-dried with an air inlet temperature of about 121°C and an exhaust temperature of about 66°C. Evaporative cooling prevents the particles from exceeding the latter temperature. However, in addition to heat, damage may be caused by factors such as shear forces, dehydration, oxidation, *etc*. Foaming is the functional property most often affected, but this can be partially controlled by the use of additives (Bergquist, 1973). Funk *et al.* (1970) found that layer cakes prepared with frozen, freeze-dried, foam-spray-dried and spray-dried eggs did not differ in sensory properties. A previous study (Zabik *et al.*, 1969) indicated that foam-spray-dried, spray-dried and frozen eggs were superior to freeze-dried eggs in sponge and chiffon cakes. The layer cakes were similar in specific gravities, but batters containing spray-dried eggs were the most viscous and the least stable (Funk *et al.*, 1970).

Custards prepared with frozen, foam-spray-dried, freeze-dried and spray-dried eggs were found to differ in mouth-feel but not in other sensory qualities. Highly significant differences occurred with respect to colour, but penetrometer values and the amount of drained liquid did not differ among the custards (Funk *et al.*, 1969).

Dehydration does not destroy vitamin A, thiamine, or riboflavin in whole eggs. However, storage of dried eggs, particularly at a warm temperature (38–41°C) is detrimental to vitamin A and to thiamine (Whitford *et al.*, 1951).

Hill *et al.* (1965) found that the use of albumen, spray-dried at pH 8·5, resulted in angel cakes with larger volumes compared to cakes made with egg-white dried at pH levels ranging from 4 to 10. Albumen spray-dried at pH 8·5 was also more susceptible to heat coagulation.

Brown and Zabik (1967) attributed decreased apparent surface tension, increased specific gravity of albumen foam and angel-cake batter, decreased foam stability and decreased volume of angel cakes, to exposure of the albumen to pre-heating, spray-drying, or high-temperature storage. In studies of storage of spray-dried albumen at temperatures of 54, 60, 71 or 82°C, Cotterill *et al.* (1967) observed decreased lysozyme mobility, iron–conalbumin complexing, and solubility. Also, evolution of ammonia increased under these conditions. However, storage at these elevated temperatures for 60 days reduced the detrimental effects of yolk in albumen (Baldwin *et al.*, 1967).

7.9   IMPLICATIONS

Maintenance of high quality in shell eggs is dependent upon continuous refrigeration, and optimum sensory properties in cooked products require careful control of cooking time in relation to temperature of cooking. Improved functional properties of processed eggs can be expected to continue as knowledge is expanded concerning sensitivity of individual egg proteins to heat, pH and additives.

REFERENCES

Andross, M. (1940) *Chem. & Ind.*, **59**, 449.

Baker, R. C. & Darfler, J. (1969) *Fd. Technol.*, **23**, 77.

Baker, R. C., Darfler, J. & Lifshitz, A. (1967) *Poultry Sci.*, **46**, 664.

Baldwin, R. E. (1973) In: *Egg Science and Technology*, eds. Stadelman, W. J. & Cotterill, O. J., p. 241, Westport, Conn.: Avi Publ. Co.

Baldwin, R. E., Cotterill, O. J., Thompson, M. M. & Myers, M. (1967) *Poultry Sci.*, **46**, 1421.

Banwart, S. F., Carlin, A. F. & Cotterill, O. J. (1957) *Fd. Technol.*, **11**, 200.

Barmore, M. A. (1934) *Colorado Expt. Stn. Bull.*, 9.

Bergquist, D. H. (1973) In: *Egg Science and Technology*, eds. Stadelman, W. J. & Cotterill, O. J., p. 190. Westport, Conn.: Avi Publ. Co.

Brown, S. L. & Zabik, M. E. (1967) *Fd. Technol.*, **21**, 87.

Chang, P., Powrie, W. D. & Fennema, O. (1970) *J. Fd. Sci.*, **35**, 774.

Chick, H. & Martin, C. J. (1910) *J. Physiol.*, **40**, 404.

Cotterill, O. J. (1954) Ph.D. Thesis, Ohio State University, Columbus.

Cotterill, O. J. & Winter, A. R. (1954) *Poultry Sci.*, **33**, 1183.

Cotterill, O. J., Baldwin, R. E. & Myers, M. (1967) *Poultry Sci.*, **46**, 1431.

Cotterill, O. J., Glauert, J. & Bassett, H. J. (1976) *Poultry Sci.*, **55**, 544.

Cotterill, O. J., Glauert, J., Steinhoff, S. E. & Baldwin, R. E. (1974) *Poultry Sci.*, **53**, 636.

Cunningham, F. E. (1970) *World's Poultry Sci. J.*, **26**, 783.

Cunningham, F. E. (1974) *Poultry Sci.*, **53**, 1866.

Cunningham, F. E. & Lineweaver, H. (1965) *Fd. Technol.*, **19**, 136.

Dawson, E. H., Miller, C. & Redstrom, R. A. (1956) *Cooking Quality and Flavour of Eggs, Inform. Bull.*, No. 164. USDA.

Funk, E. M. (1950) *Missouri Agric. Expt. Stn. Bull.*, 467.

Funk, K., Conklin, M. T. & Zabik, M. E. (1970) *Cereal Chem.*, **47**, 732.

Funk, K., Boyle, M. A., Downs, D. M. & Zabik, M. E. (1969) *J. Am. Dietet. Assoc.*, **55**, 522.

Germs, A. C. (1973) *J. Sci. Fd. Agric.*, **24**, 7.

Gillis, J. N. & Fitch, N. K. (1956) *J. Home Econ.*, **48**, 703.

Griswold, R. M. (1962) *The Experimental Study of Foods.* Boston, Mass.: Houghton Mifflin Co.

Hard, M. M., Spencer, J. V., Locke, R. S. & George, M. H. (1963) *Poultry Sci.,* **42**, 815.

Hill, W. M., Cotterill, O. J., Funk, E. M. & Baldwin, R. E. (1965) *Poultry Sci.,* **44**, 1155.

Kline, L., Sugihara, T. F., Bean, M. L. & Ijichi, K. (1965) *Fd. Technol.,* **19**, 105.

Kohl, W. F. (1971) *Fd. Technol.,* **25**, 102.

Lineweaver, H., Cunningham, F. E., Garibaldi, J. A. & Ijichi, K. (1967) Heat stability of egg white proteins under minimal conditions that kill salmonellae, USDA ARS 74–39.

Lowe, B. (1955) *Experimental Cookery,* 4th edn. New York: John Wiley.

McBee, L. E. (1974) Ph.D. Thesis, University of Missouri, Columbia.

McCready, S. T., Norris, M. E., Sebring, M. & Cotterill, O. J. (1971) *Poultry Sci.,* **50**, 1810.

Meyer, R. & Potter, N. N. (1974) *Poultry Sci.,* **53**, 761.

Palmer, H. H., Ijichi, K. & Roff, H. (1969) *Fd. Technol.,* **23**(12), 85.

Paul, P. C. & Palmer, H. H. (1972) *Food Theory and Applications.* New York: John Wiley.

Schiller, E. A., Pratt, D. E. & Reber, E. F. (1973) *J. Am. Dietet. Assoc.,* **62**, 529.

Seideman, W. E. & Cotterill, O. J. (1969) *Poultry Sci.,* **48**, 894.

Seideman, W. E., Cotterill, O. J. & Funk, E. M. (1963) *Poultry Sci.,* **42**, 406.

Slosberg, H. M., Hanson, H. L., Stewart, G. F. & Lowe, B. (1948) *Poultry Sci.,* **27**, 294.

Stamberg, O. E. & Petersen, C. F. (1946) *J. Am. Dietet. Assoc.,* **22**, 315.

Swanson, M. H. (1973) In: *Egg Science and Technology,* eds. Stadelman, W. J. & Cotterill, O. J., p. 6. Westport, Conn.: Avi Publ. Co.

Tinkler, C. K. & Soar, M. C. (1920) *Biochem. J.,* **14**, 114.

Whitford, C., Pickering, C., Summers, K., Weis, A. & Bisbey, B. (1951) *Missouri Agric. Expt. Stn. Bull.,* 483.

Zabik, M. E., Anderson, C. M., Davey, E. M. & Wolfe, N. J. (1969) *Fd. Technol.,* **23**(3), 85.

CHAPTER 8

Fish*

A. AITKEN and J. J. CONNELL
Torry Research Station, Aberdeen, UK

Fish, which will be taken to include shellfish, is unique as a food commodity in two ways. First, many hundreds of different species are eaten; among these there are wide variations in composition and response to processing. Secondly, there is a great variation within individual species in these respects, particularly if post-harvesting handling is taken into account. Thus, it would be unwise to generalise from the specific examples quoted here.

During handling and processing of fish, heat is applied for a number of reasons. In its use as a human food these include:

   (i) sterilisation in a hermetically sealed container which may be preceded by a cooking, smoking or drying stage;

  (ii) various home-cooking methods such as frying, grilling, steaming, baking or boiling;

 (iii) steaming or pressure cooking prior to incorporation into fish cakes, pasta, fish-balls or spreads;

 (iv) steaming of jellied products such as Japanese Kamaboko;

  (v) frying of battered 'fish-fingers', sticks or portions before freezing;

 (vi) smoking;

(vii) drying;

(viii) pasteurisation;

 (ix) thawing of frozen fish; and

  (x) heating to prevent autolysis in shellfish.

Usually only the body musculature (flesh) of fish is eaten by humans, although significant quantities of skin, bone, gonad and viscera are also consumed. Because little is known about the effects of heat on these individual minor components, this review will be concerned mainly with the flesh when dealing with fish as a food for direct human consumption.

In addition to the above, about one-third of the world catch of fish is utilised as meal for animal feeding and as oil, mostly destined for human consumption. The process here involves cooking, usually accompanied by pressing, in order to coagulate protein and release water and oil, followed by drying of the press cake and usually the water phase (*i.e.* stick water) to about 10% moisture content. In this case, the raw material is either the whole fish or components of it that are not used for direct human consumption. Discussion of fish meal, therefore, relates to the effects of heat on a rather heterogeneous material.

Only some of the heat treatments outlined above have been studied and even then systematic examinations under completely well-defined conditions, which include moisture content and rate of heating, are infrequent. In this chapter only effects occurring at temperatures higher than about 30°C will be included; this restriction is particularly important with respect to the production of volatile compounds.

8.1 STRUCTURE AND COMPOSITION OF FISH

Before discussing the effects of heat, an outline will be given of structure and composition of fish as compared to meat. A comprehensive review of many aspects of structure and composition of true fish is available (Love, 1970). Specialised aspects of the structure of fish (Patterson and Goldspink, 1972; Jarenbäck and Liljemark, 1975), crustacea (Atwood, 1972) and molluscs (Hanson and Lowy, 1960; Tanaka, 1958), and of the nature of their proteins (Tsuyuki, 1974), lipids (Ackman, 1974) and other low molecular-weight compounds (Jones, 1967) have been covered fairly recently.

8.1.1 Structure
All true fish, and some crustacean and molluscan, muscle is typical striated muscle although, in each case, the cells are arranged in special configurations. In most true fishes the ends of the typically short, striated cells are inserted into sheets (myocommata) of

connective tissue, arranged in a complicated pattern which, on heating, break down and give rise to the characteristic flaky appearance of coagulated blocks (myotomes) of cells. Two main types of muscle exist, red or dark, and white, the former being disposed laterally along the body in discrete strips or blocks between the skin and the backbone. Different species of fish contain different proportions of red and white muscle, the latter generally predominating. In crustacea the blocks of striated cells are somewhat similarly segmented whilst in molluscs, the cells, which are predominantly of a specialised smooth type, run in a complex pattern for much of the length of the muscle. At the electron-microscopic level also, fish (Love, 1970; Patterson and Goldspink, 1972; Jarenbäck and Liljemark, 1975) and crustacean muscle (Atwood, 1972) is typical of other striated muscle but mollusc adductor and other muscles (Migata, 1953; Tanaka, 1958; Hanson and Lowy, 1960) have special features.

8.1.2 Proximate Composition

The major feature of the proximate composition of fish and shellfish is the great variability in lipid content (Murray and Burt, 1969; Sidwell et al., 1974). Lean species contain typically 0·3–1·0% lipid, most of which is phospholipid and the remainder triglyceride, whereas the total amount in fatty species can be as much as 30%. In the latter, the amount of lipid varies seasonally within a species and may fall to as low as 1%; these changes are accounted for entirely by changes in the proportion of triglycerides. As the amount of lipid increases, the amount of water falls in almost linear proportion, whilst the amount of protein remains fairly constant. In lean fish and crustacea, the amount of water is generally slightly greater than that in meat or chicken; in fatty fish of high lipid content it is often less. Several molluscs (mussel, oyster) have a high water content. The proportion of protein, as in meat and chicken, is in most cases in the range of 15–18%, the remaining content of nitrogenous substances (1–3%) being made up of a multiplicity of low molecular-weight compounds. Elasmobranch fish (sharks, skates, rays) are characterised by a high proportion (about 30% of the total nitrogen content) of these compounds.

8.1.3 Detailed Composition

The lipids of fish are amongst the most unsaturated of animal-muscle lipids. Whether as phospholipids or triglycerides, they contain high proportions of polyunsaturated fatty acids (Ackman, 1974) which in most fish are very susceptible to oxidation by atmospheric oxygen during handling and processing. In some species, the presence of natural antioxidants retards this tendency. The immediate products of oxidation are hydroperoxides which readily break down to a series of carbonyls, several of which have rancid odours and flavours. Such reactions are among the reasons why fish is so perishable.

Fish and crustacea contain the normal types of muscle proteins (Tsuyuki, 1974). Some mollusc muscles contain a special form of myofibrillar protein known as paramyosin (Hanson and Lowy, 1960). The proportion of connective-tissue proteins is lower than in meat, being 3–5% of the total protein in many species and 8–10% in elasmobranchii. This is likely to be one of the reasons why fish is much more tender than meat. To the food scientist and technologist, the special feature of the main fish-muscle proteins, including enzymes, is their instability *vis-à-vis* their meat counterparts. Thus, fish myosins, either when isolated or when in the intact tissue, denature much more rapidly than beef or chicken myosins kept under the same conditions (Connell, 1964). Also, the thermal shrinkage or denaturation temperatures of fish connective-tissue (myocommata) collagen are much lower than those of the corresponding beef protein (Mohr, 1971). This finding is probably connected with the fact that it is possible to separate the 'flakes' of some white fish after a brief period at a low temperature. Fish and shellfish muscle are not richly vasculated and therefore the concentration of blood chromoproteins is lower than that in meat. In the white and dark muscles of fish, the concentrations of myoglobin are very low and moderate, respectively.

The array of low molecular-weight compounds in fish and shellfish is, in general, typical of any muscle (Jones, 1967). Of particular note are the high concentrations of certain nitrogenous compounds peculiar to some species. Thus, marine species normally contain high concentrations (up to 1% of the total weight of the flesh) of trimethylamine oxide (TMAO). This compound is of considerable significance as an odour precursor in that it is reduced by spoilage bacteria or otherwise degraded during processing to trimethylamine (TMA), dimethylamine (DMA) and monomethylamine (MMA). TMA is a prominent contributor to the odour of stale fish. Elasmobranchii are unusual in containing high concentrations of urea (up to 2%) and the main spoilage odour of these is attributable to ammonia produced from this compound by bacteria.

A factor of importance when considering the effect of heat on flesh foods is the post-mortem pH. This is almost invariably higher in fish and shellfish than in meat and is usually in the range 6·4 to 6·8. Since the nutritional status of individual species changes markedly with season, there is considerable variation in pH and concentration of the various low molecular-weight compounds. In addition, the activities of spoilage bacteria and changes during frozen storage can result in large alterations to these concentrations, although relatively less change of pH occurs.

8.2   CHANGES DURING HEATING

8.2.1   Thermophysical Properties

A knowledge of the thermophysical properties of fish tissue is valuable in understanding the changes taking place during heating and in predicting the temperature distribution under a particular set of circumstances. Fish behaves, as far as is known, as a solid in respect of heat transfer, which takes place within the fish by conduction. Methods of calculating heat transfer across the surface of, and within, foodstuffs are well documented (Charm, 1971). Heat transfer across the surface is primarily a function of the properties of the heating fluid, whereas heat transfer by conduction within a food is controlled by the thermophysical properties of the food. These properties are the thermal conductivity, k, the heat capacity, c, and the density, ρ; a composite quantity, K, the thermal diffusivity, is defined as

$$K = \frac{k}{\rho c}$$

and can be determined directly.

While there are many measurements of these quantities at ambient and freezing temperatures, there are few at higher temperatures. The thermal conductivity, in J/cm·sec·°C, for a mince of mackerel varied from about 4×10^{-3} at room temperature to about $6·5 \times 10^{-3}$ at 80°C (Fujita and Kishimoto, 1956); similar values for other species were obtained earlier (Kawakami, 1934) and values of 5·8 and 6·0 $\times 10^{-3}$ were reported for mackerel and sardine minces at 45–50°C (Annamma and Rao, 1974). Measurements on cod, not minced, gave $5·4 \times 10^{-3}$ at 30°C and $5·8 \times 10^{-3}$ at 70°C (Aitken and Campbell, 1969). The heat capacity of fish above 30°C is available only for cod (Aitken and Campbell, 1969). The average value, varying little with temperature, was 3·65 J/g·°C over the range 30–90°C. It is common practice to estimate the heat capacity by adding the heat capacities of the water and other components (Lamb, 1976); this procedure gave good agreement with the experimental value (Aitken and Campbell, 1969). The density of fish at heat-processing temperatures does not appear to have been measured.

The composite thermal diffusivity can be calculated from the component quantities or can be measured directly. Direct measurement gave $1·33 \times 10^{-3}$ cm^2·sec^{-1} for minced mackerel and $1·14$ cm^2·sec^{-1} for minced sardine (Annamma and Rao, 1974) and, earlier, $1·6 \times 10^{-3}$ cm^2·sec^{-1} for various species (Cooper, 1937). The calculated value for cod was $1·47 \times 10^{-3}$ cm^2·sec^{-1} (Aitken and Campbell, 1969).

This is, perhaps, the place to point out that very often measurements carried out on flesh foods during heating do not relate to one particular temperature since the relatively low thermal conductivity results in temperature gradients through the portion. For instance, it can be calculated that, in a 3-cm thick slab of fish, initially at 20°C, which is immersed in water at 100°C, the temperature at the centre of the slab is less than 40°C after 5 min, 85°C after 20 min and near equilibrium (99°C) only after about 50 min.

8.2.2   Gross Appearance, Colour, Odour, Flavour and Texture
Heating converts the translucent, jelly-like cellular mass into an opaque, friable, slightly firm and springy form. Synaeresis or shrinkage occurs and fluid is released, the proteins in which may coagulate to form curd separately from the main solid mass. As noted above, the connective tissue holding the cells together is easily degraded and blocks of cells or the cells themselves become readily separated from one another. Thus, unlike many meats, cooked fish easily falls apart and becomes palatable on mild heating (Parry, 1970). Heating strips of fish of the cod family for 30 min at a temperature as low as 37°C reduced the tensile strength to zero (Forbes, 1927). Fish with a higher connective-tissue content, such as dogfish, required a temperature of 45°C to achieve the same effect whilst beef was unaffected even after heating for 1 h at 92°C. Tests on cod showed that visible softening of the connective tissue occurs after 15 min at 35°C but heating at temperatures below this had no effect (Aitken and Campbell, 1969). When cod is partially dried at a low temperature it can be heated to higher than the normal hydrolysis

temperature of the connective tissue before falling apart (Jason, 1963; Forbes, 1927).

On boiling, squid muscle contracts, particularly lengthwise. If the process is continued too far excessive contraction and hardening occur (Takahashi, 1965). Thus, good control of heating is necessary in order to produce an acceptable texture.

The increased opacity of cooked fish has been examined more closely (Aitken and Campbell, 1969). When fish is heated from one direction only, by placing the edge of a thin layer (held between glass plates) on a heated surface, three distinct changes of opacity can be discerned, moving away from the heated edge (Fig. 8.1). An initial increase in translucence is followed by two successive increases in opacity. The second increase in opacity is due to precipitation of the thermally denatured sarcoplasmic proteins, which appears to begin about 45°C. The initial increased translucence followed by the first opaque band begin at lower temperatures and are not unequivocally explained.

FIG. 8.1   Changes in translucence of fish tissue heated from the lower edge.

Heating under some conditions causes Maillard-type browning or the formation of orange pigments (Yamanaka *et al.*, 1973), both of which are undesirable in some species. Browning reactions are, on the whole, of little consequence in the processing of dark-fleshed species, but are one of the main reasons why few white-fleshed species are canned.

The reddish-brown colour of normal tuna and mackerel changes on heating to a darker brown or tan shade sometimes perfused with pink. The main reaction here is the formation of a metmyochromogen from myoglobin (Koizumi and Matsuura, 1967) as has been observed for mammalian muscle (Tarladgis, 1962). On occasions this desirable colour change is marred by a greenish hue. The cause is a reaction between denatured metmyoglobin and cysteine under oxidising conditions to form a disulphide derivative (Grosjean *et al.*, 1969).

Crab meat, when canned, can suffer from a blueish or blueish-black discolouration. The possible causes of this and other discolourations have been reviewed (Babbitt, 1973; Boon, 1975). Similarly, canned oysters can become green as a result of chemical changes in the porphyrin pigments (Osada, 1974), and canned shrimps can become blackened as a result of metal–pigment reactions (Nandakumaren *et al.*, 1969).

No systematic analysis appears to have been carried out of the odour and flavour profiles of different species heated in various ways. Common observation refers to raw fish as slightly salty, bland, metallic, iodine-like, seaweedy or sometimes unpleasant. These descriptions are different from those of the odours and flavours of fresh fish which develop on heating: mildly meaty, bland, characteristic of the species, mouth-filling, seaweedy or sweet. Some species, when cooked in the pre-rigor state, taste metallic (Jones, 1967). Different methods of heating can undoubtedly give rise to differences in odour and flavour; in particular, commercial heat sterilisation produces an overall character unlike that produced by other forms of heating. Heating to an internal temperature of 70°C in about 16 min leaves 200 g salmon steaks underdone and with less flavour than heating at temperatures up to 85°C (Charley, 1952). Cooking by baking, steaming or frying produced little difference in taste or palatability of cod, although the first method resulted in slightly better discrimination between different qualities (Dyer *et al.*, 1964). On the other hand, compared to steaming, frying was found to accentuate certain flavours of haddock (Connell and Howgate, 1971). The presence of bones (and skin) did not affect the palatability of fried or baked freshwater fish (Baldwin *et al.*, 1962).

Fish bones are quite often eaten together with flesh and the question of their rate of softening under different conditions is of interest but appears not to have been studied. As an extreme example, however, heat sterilisation for 1 h at 115°C in flat 200-g cans is sufficient to soften vertebrae in mackerel or herring.

8.2.3 Release of Water, Oil and Other Components

Most fish, like meat but unlike egg, releases a watery 'cook liquor' on heating. However, there are exceptions: cod roe does not lose liquor on cooking (McCance and Shipp, 1933), and it has been shown that extra water can be absorbed by cod roe during canning with advantage to the texture of the product (Bannerman, 1975). Little fundamental work has been carried out on the mechanism of the release of liquor; a review (Wagenknecht and Tülsner, 1974) of water binding in fish muscle relied on studies of meat when dealing with the effect of heat on water binding. There is, however, a significant amount of work on measurement of liquor loss for a wide variety of species heated in different ways. Three practical problems have stimulated most of this work:

1. the dietician's need for information on the composition of cooked fish;
2. the importance of adequate pre-cooking of fish for canning; and
3. cooking for fish-meal manufacture in order to achieve the most efficient expression of oil and water.

The classic work on the first requirement is that of McCance and Shipp (1933), who measured cooking losses of a range of species. (The range of species examined was later extended (McCance and Widdowson, 1960), although less usefully as the tables now give only the net differences in weight between the raw fish and the cooked edible product; these differences include waste and other quantities along with the cooking loss.) McCance and Shipp (1933) did not describe their cooking procedures in detail, a practice that has been almost universally followed by others. The amount of cook liquor varied greatly from one species to another and from one cooking method to another. In dry-cooking methods, such as grilling or frying, evaporation of water from the food made analysis difficult; only cooking in a saturated atmosphere, by boiling or steaming, allowed the true cooking loss to be studied. The average loss on steaming marine non-fatty fish species was 18·6%. Within this group, round fish lost more weight (20·7%) than flat fish (14·3%). Fatty fish lost only a little more weight (21·1%) than round, non-fatty fish. This suggests that the loss of fat is not high. A study devoted to the pre-cooking of sardines for canning confirmed that little fat is lost in steaming (Meesemaecker and Sohier, 1959). These authors noted total weight losses of 20–30%, in agreement with McCance and Shipp. A number of other limited studies have shown similar weight losses (Tarr, 1941; Dollar *et al.*, 1967; Deschacht and Vansevenant, 1968; Barnett *et al.*, 1969; Chappell, 1954; Andross, 1941; Cutting *et al.*, 1956; Young and Sidaway, 1943; Hamm *et al.*, 1944).

McCance and Shipp, in addition to the study of the effects of normal cooking, examined to a limited extent the effects of some of the factors that control cooking loss. Their results and those of others will be discussed under these factors.

Time

In Fig. 8.2, drawn from the data of McCance and Shipp (1933), the effect of steaming time on 50–60-g pieces can be seen for four species of fish, plus beef for comparison. From the point of view of eating quality, these pieces would be fully cooked after no more than 20 min. Loss of weight appears to continue, in some species at least, beyond

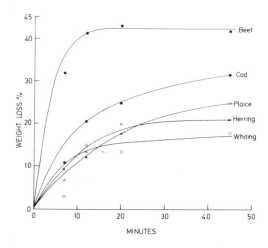

FIG. 8.2   Loss of weight of fish and beef by steaming for different periods.

45 min. This observation emphasises the importance of describing cooking procedures very closely if the results are to be of value for comparison purposes.

Temperature
For a given heating time, the amount of cooked-out liquor increases with temperature (Meesemaecker and Sohier, 1959; Lassen, 1965b; Ward *et al.*, 1975; Hanover *et al.*, 1973), although certain irregularities have been observed (Simidu and Takeda, 1951; Kushtalov and Saduakasov, 1971; Tülsner and Wagenknecht, 1976). The loss increases with temperature above 100°C (Tarr, 1941). It has not been shown, apparently, that the final cooking loss at equilibrium varies with temperature. Figure 8.2 indicates that some species continue to lose liquor after temperature equilibrium is reached. The rate of loss of liquor is low at temperatures where cooking is just beginning; the loss by cod appears to begin at around 32°C though only after an initial delay (Jason, 1963). Partly dehydrated fish does not begin to lose liquor until higher temperatures are reached.

Surface Area
It might be expected that pieces of fish with a large cut surface would lose more liquor than whole fish. However, the results of McCance and Shipp (1933) do not support this theory. The average weight losses from fish cooked 'round' (gutted and headed but not filleted) were 16·1%, which was not significantly different from the average loss (20·4%) from fillets or cut pieces. On the other hand, steaming of whole herring at 82°C led to weight losses of less than half those of herring fillets (Deschacht and Vansevenant, 1968). When fish is broken up by mixing during heat treatment, higher weight losses have been observed than with whole fish or fillets (Ward *et al.*, 1975). For example, the loss from sand-eels cooked to 100°C can be 42% with a further 13% being squeezed out under very slight pressure. Pressing at up to 100 kg·cm^{-2} released 66% of the original weight of the fish. A loss of 66% is typical of good industrial practice in fish-meal manufacture (Sparre, 1965).

Species and Size
The data in Fig. 8.2, and many of the references given earlier, indicate differences, sometimes large, between species. One cannot exclude the possibility that part of these differences may be accounted for by

size differences. No controlled comparison of size of fish has been carried out.

Pressure

Despite the importance of cooking and pressing in fish-meal manufacture, there is only one recent study of the effects of pressure on liquor release (Ward *et al.*, 1975). In a typical experiment with sprats cooked to 100°C, the total liquor loss was 58·4% of the original weight. Of this loss, 46·2% was released readily on cooking, 28·4% on transferring to the press and applying only slight pressure, 21·9% on pressing at 50 kg·cm^{-2} and 3·4% at 100 kg·cm^{-2}. A not-really comparable measurement of the total loss from baked salmon steaks after pressing at 560 kg·cm^{-2} was 71% of the original uncooked weight (Charley, 1952).

pH

When fish were soaked in aqueous solutions of different pH before heating, the cooking loss at a pH about 7·3 was no more than one-half that at pH 4·0 (McCance and Shipp, 1933).

Spoilage

No systematic study has been carried out; in one investigation no consistent effects were noted (Ward *et al.*, 1975).

Added Salts

Again, the effect of added salts has not been systematically studied. Sodium chloride did not greatly affect cook-out of canned halibut (Tarr, 1941), sodium tripolyphosphate and sodium chloride together were shown to reduce weight loss in hot smoking (Barnett *et al.*, 1969), while sodium tripolyphosphate and sodium chloride individually reduced the total weight loss after cooking frozen chinook salmon (Boyd and Southcott, 1965).

Many other factors such as seasonal variation, individual variability, stage of rigor mortis reached and prior treatments such as freezing, irradiation and dehydration have been given little attention.

As far as composition of the cooking liquor is concerned, Table 8.1, drawn from data for cod steamed for 45 min (McCance and Shipp, 1933), shows that the cook liquor is mostly water (37% of the original amount of water) with small amounts of solids (10% of the original solids) and oil (28% of original). By contrast, Table 8.2 shows the

TABLE 8.1
COMPOSITION OF 100 g RAW COD AND THE CORRESPOND-
ING COOKED COD AND COOK LIQUOR

Component (g)	Raw cod	Cooked cod	Cook liquor
Water	81	51	30
Solids	18	16	2
Oil	1	1	0
Total weight	100	68	32

TABLE 8.2
COMPOSITION OF 100 g RAW HERRING, THE COOKED, PRESSED HERRING
AND THE TOTAL LIQUOR

Component (g)	Raw herring	Cooked, pressed herring	Total liquor
Water	70	17	53
Solids	18	14	4
Oil	12	1	11
Total weight	100	32	68

amount and composition of the liquor from cooking and pressing of herring in a commercial fish-meal process (Windsor, 1971). While much higher proportions of the original water and oil appear in the liquor (76% and 92%), so also does a higher percentage of the solids (22%).

8.2.4 Microscopic Changes

Only two publications have been found that deal with microscopic changes occurring solely as the result of heating. In the first (Charley and Goertz, 1958), the appearance in the optical microscope of salmon pieces baked to an internal temperature of 70°C was studied. Some disintegration of fibres was observed as well as an increase in their width and a disappearance of kinks and twists. The change in width is difficult to reconcile with the overall shrinkage of muscle that occurs on heating. In addition, fibrous connective tissue became granulated and jelly-like whilst a considerable dispersion of fat globules occurred within the tissue.

In the second study (Schaller and Powrie, 1972), the appearance in the scanning electron microscope of rainbow-trout muscle after heating at 60°C and 97°C was similar to that observed with beef and chicken. Apart from some disintegration occurring at the I band, much of the normal appearance of the myofibril was retained at 97°C. Trout appeared to be different in that gaps at the level of the H-zone occurred in addition to transverse fractures at the Z-disc observed in all species. Another common finding was the presence of coagulated granules of sarcoplasmic proteins between fibres. Heating to 60°C produced less visible damage though it was much more apparent in trout as compared to the other species. None of these observations were compared directly with sensory changes.

8.2.5 Proteins

8.2.5.1 *Proteins in Fish of Normal Moisture Content*
The amount of denaturation and coagulation which occurs when intact fish is heated at different temperatures and conditions has been measured via the amount of protein extractable by, or remaining soluble in, salt solution. In an early investigation (Lobanov and Bykova, 1938) fish (unspecified) was heated at different temperatures and the amount of protein remaining extractable in 10% neutral sodium chloride was measured. The development of inextractability commenced at 30–35°C, and was 40% and 90% complete at 40°C and 60–65°C, respectively. Similar findings were reported more recently for fish and cuttlefish (Burdina and Melnikova, 1974). When cod and hilsa are heated at a constant temperature of 30°C without allowing drying to occur, a considerable fall in the extractable myofibrillar proteins occurs over about 40 h (Howgate and Ahmed, 1972). The fall which was greater with cod was attributed to the fact that this species inhabits a colder water environment than hilsa; there is strong evidence on several proteins that those present in organisms subjected to lower environmental temperatures are less stable than those present in organisms subjected to higher temperatures. In the same period of heating, only about one-quarter of the sarcoplasmic proteins of cod and hilsa became inextractable which is in line with the general finding (Aman and Smirnova, 1972) that this group as a whole is more stable than the myofibrillar group. Similar relative stabilities of these two fractions were noted when carp and pike were cooked by boiling in water for 20 min or by baking in a microwave oven for 3 min (Aman and Smirnova, 1972). Either treatment rendered about one-half

of the myofibrillar fraction inextractable but had only a slight effect on the sarcoplasmic fraction. The fact that more myofibrillar protein was not rendered inextractable under these conditions is somewhat surprising.

If most of the sarcoplasmic proteins in fish muscle are removed by washing in water and the residue ground with salt and gently heated, the protein does not form an opaque coagulum but a firm, translucent gel. This phenomenon forms the basis for the traditional Japanese fish-jelly product known as Kamaboko. Over the past twenty years production of this and similar products has expanded enormously in Japan (Tanikawa, 1963, 1971). The reactions giving rise to gel formation have not been elucidated. In one investigation relevant here, the ground, extracted muscle of various species was heated to different temperatures and the gel strength measured (Ueda et al., 1968). A clearly defined maximum strength was found at 25–35°C depending upon species. In those species which gave good quality Kamaboko of high gel strength, the temperature at which maximum strength occurred was highest.

For some purposes it is useful to know the temperature to which cooked-fish products have been subjected. A test has been devised in which the cooked product is extracted with water at pH 4·5 and the extract gradually heated (Doesburg and Papendorf, 1969). The temperature at which coagulation occurs in the extract is related to that at which the product was cooked. For lean and fatty fish, the relationship for temperatures between 60 and 100°C is linear and curved, respectively.

8.2.5.2 Proteins in Suspensions and Solutions

In attempts to understand the general behaviour of fish proteins on heating, a number of investigators have studied muscle either suspended or partly dissolved in salt solutions, or solutions of protein fractions of the muscle. Mackerel, horse mackerel, tuna and, for comparison, rabbit muscle, were minced, placed in salt solutions, heated to different temperatures and the amount of soluble protein measured (Simidu and Takuma, 1951). The temperature at which insolubility started to develop was about 35°C and half the protein became insoluble at 40–45°C. The corresponding temperature to the latter for rabbit was about 52°C, confirming again the principle relating environmental temperature to stability noted above.

These experiments were extended to include yellowtail tuna,

croaker and lizard fish, with similar results, but in addition, the effect of pH was studied (Simidu and Simidu, 1960). On heating for a given time and temperature, the pH at which half the protein became insoluble varied with the species. For lizard fish and croaker the pH was about 5·5 and for mackerel and horse mackerel about 6·0.

It is noticeable from these experiments and others that about 10% of the total myofibrillar protein does not become insoluble after even quite prolonged heating at temperatures up to 100°C. The major component of this heat-stable fraction is tropomyosin (Odense *et al.*, 1969). If similar dispersions of lizard-fish proteins in salt solution are heated to different temperatures for the same time and their viscosity measured, the values plotted against temperature show a well-defined maximum (Shimizu *et al.*, 1962). The maximum occurs at about 40°C. Above this temperature the viscosity falls to a value much less than that of unheated samples.

With isolated fish actomyosins actually in solution rather different results were obtained in that no maximum was observed (Suyama, 1951; Ueda *et al.*, 1963, 1964). The temperature at which the first fall in viscosity occurs is about 30°C for several species but 45°C for rabbit and chicken actomyosins, again in line with the principle previously noted.

This predominantly Japanese work shows that there are small but consistent differences in the stability of the proteins of different fish species when measured by several criteria and these differences can sometimes be related to the different behaviour of the muscle when it is heat processed, as for example in Kamaboko manufacture. This finding is a further manifestation of subtle species differences in protein stability (Connell, 1964).

In a rather novel study it was found that in homogenates of Bombay duck (bummalo, *Harpodon nehereus*) dispersed in 5% sodium chloride at pH 7·5, heating for 10 min at 60°C rendered 1–2% of the myofibrillar protein insoluble whereas, after irradiation with 0·25 Mrad, heating under the same conditions rendered it 83% insoluble (Warrier *et al.*, 1973). Conceivably, this type of experiment could be exploited to throw light on the nature of the reactions involved in normal heat denaturation and coagulation.

Since the composition and behaviour of fish-muscle proteins are basically similar to those of meat proteins, it is to be expected that many of the findings pertaining to denaturation and crosslinking reactions will be common. A number of investigations, however, have been reported exclusively on fish, which supplement the information available on meat. Thus, the hydrogen-ion titration curve of cod myofibrils heated at 100°C for about 30 min has been compared to that of the unheated material (Connell and Howgate, 1964). A study of this curve can give information mainly on the numbers of charged groups and their intrinsic dissociation constants. It was found that only a slight change in the numbers of charged groups like carboxyl, lysyl, histidyl and tyrosyl occurred on heating. There was a shift in the pH value of the myofibrils of 0·2 units towards the alkaline side on heating and slight changes in dissociation constants of the carboxyl and (lysyl + tyrosyl) groups. In all, the findings provided no evidence for significant involvement of charged groups in covalent crosslinking resulting from heating. During this study rather similar observations were made on beef myofibrils in contrast to other work (Hamm and Deatherage, 1960; Bendall and Wismer-Pedersen, 1962) which reported large decreases in the numbers of charged groups. This difference probably arises from differences in the methods used to determine the groups; in one case a dye-binding method was employed and it is likely that steric inaccessibility of the bulky dye molecules in the coagulated protein mass has given rise to low values.

It was found that cooked lingcod, dispersed in 6M guanidine hydrochloride (Gu·HCl) at pH 10·5, formed a gel which could be dissolved by adding mercaptoethanol or sodium borohydride (Buttkus, 1974). This was taken to indicate the existence of intermolecular disulphide bonds in the heated material. Since unheated muscle dissolves completely in solutions of hydrogen-bond breaking solvents such as Gu·HCl (Connell, 1957), this presumably means that the disulphide bonds are formed on heating. Similar conclusions were reached from studies of heated beef (Hamm and Hofmann, 1965) and heated, dried cod (Connell, 1957, 1958).

In relation to reactions of sulphur amino acids, it was found that the total amounts of methionine and cysteine were not affected by heating at 115°C or 126°C but the 'available' amounts of these same amino acids were significantly reduced (Pieniezak and Rakowska, 1974).

8.2.5.3 *Proteins in Fish of Reduced Moisture Content*
The above discussion has dealt almost exclusively with protein reactions occurring in fish muscle possessing normal water contents. It is

also of interest to consider reactions occurring in dried fish containing up to 10–15% water. These reactions are of importance to the drying stage of fish-meal production and in the preparation and storage of dried fish products for human consumption.

Fish meals prepared by different manufacturing processes can vary a great deal in their protein nutritive value. Much of this variability is due to differences in the amount of so-called 'available' lysine (Ford, 1973). Meals which are known to have received more severe heat treatments, for example, are lower in available lysine. In addition, deficiencies in methionine and cysteine/cystine may arise. As a result of experiments on the controlled heating of carefully dried fish and fish meal it is becoming evident (Ford, 1973; Bjarnason and Carpenter, 1970) that the lysine is reacting with the amide groups of asparagine and glutamine to give new peptides which are either not hydrolysable or are sterically prevented from being hydrolysed by digestive proteases. The sulphur amino acids may also be involved in such peptide or crosslink formation. It has been found that the amino acid, lanthionine, is present in severely heated dried cod but not in unheated samples (Connell, 1958). Lanthionine contains a thioether link formed from disulphide bonds present in the original protein. Two other protein reactions, which may affect nutritive value, are known to occur when dried fish is heated; the conversion of methionine to methionine sulphoxide and Maillard reactions between sugars, particularly ribose and galactose, and protein amino groups (Ford, 1973; Jones, 1969). Finally, the presumptive formation of disulphide bonds from sulphydryl groups has already been mentioned (Connell, 1957, 1958).

In line with other observations on the relative stabilities of muscle proteins it was found that when freeze-dried beef and cod were heated under identical conditions the proteins of the latter became insoluble more rapidly (Connell, 1962). Also with cod, myosin became inextractable much more rapidly than the sarcoplasmic proteins. It is worth noting here that the apyrase enzyme of freeze-dried carp is much more stable than that of fish of normal water content heated under the same conditions (Nemitz and Partmann, 1959).

The way in which the conformation of either normal or dried-fish muscle proteins changes on heating is an unexplored field. Indeed, a full description involving the many proteins present is almost inconceivable. One small clue in this area is an unconfirmed report, using x-ray analysis, that heated, dried cod muscle showed evidence of the presence of β-folds in the protein whereas the unheated sample showed none (Connell, 1958).

8.2.5.4 *Hydrolysis*

When muscle is heated, the fraction of nitrogen which is not precipitated by trichloroacetic acid increases. This so-called extractable fraction consists of ammonia, amines, TMAO, amino acids, lower peptides and proteins not coagulable by the acid. The reaction has been studied in carp (Mudrak, 1953), cod and hilsa (Howgate and Ahmed, 1972), Caspian sprats (Abdel-Latif, 1969) and sheatfish (Saduakasov, 1972), but most extensively in herring (Hughes, 1961a). In the herring experiments, both excised muscle and eviscerated whole herring were heated at 116°C. Much of the increase in extractable nitrogen is caused by the degradation of collagen to gelatin, of a molecular weight not precipitable by the acid, and smaller peptides, but in addition a sizeable increase in ammonia derived from unknown sources occurs. A smaller contribution from unidentified nitrogenous compounds was also noted. Since the whole herring contained a higher proportion of collagen in the form of skin, the contribution from this protein was greater than in the muscle alone. Under normal conditions of heat processing, these experiments show that in herring, at least, increases of 5–20% in the extractable nitrogen fraction would occur. The effect of different methods of processing and of season on gelatin formation in herring has also been studied (Hughes, 1963a).

8.2.6 Lipids

No simple chemical hydrolysis of lipids occurs when fish tissue (muscle and liver) is heated at 100°C for periods up to 90 min (Olley and Lovern, 1960). On the other hand, heating cod for 30 min at the same temperature hardly affected phospholipase activity, which means that, in normally cooked fish, some enzymic hydrolysis of lipids in the stored material could occur.

Very little change in the detailed phospholipid composition of carp or pike was noted when they were cooked 'normally' for 20 min or in a microwave oven for 3 min (El-Bastavizi and Smirnova, 1972).

Heating undoubtedly results in oxidation of lipids in fish but few systematic studies of the reaction are recorded. A rapid increase of peroxide value occurs in hilsa heated for about 40 h at 30°C, without loss of moisture (Howgate and Ahmed, 1972). In the same vein, roasting dentex fish at 220–240°C for 40 min results in a significant diminution of polyunsaturated fatty acids, presumably through oxi-dative reactions (Quaglia *et al.*, 1974).

As described below, the concentrations of carbonyl compounds increase on heating fish. Undoubtedly many of these compounds arise from the formation and thermal decomposition of the oxidation products of lipids. It has been shown, for example, that steaming fish under oxygen results in a greatly increased production of carbonyl compounds compared to cooking under nitrogen (Hughes, 1963b). Model studies carried out with mixtures of methyl esters of fish fatty acids and serum albumin under simulated conditions of frying have shown that peroxides may react with free amino groups to form insoluble brown pigments (Pokorny *et al.*, 1973).

Rather curiously, and for reasons unknown, heating herring meal for short times at temperatures up to 125°C retards lipid oxidation during subsequent storage (Lea *et al.*, 1960; Myklestad *et al.*, 1972).

8.2.7 Low Molecular-Weight Compounds

Amines
The concentration of amines in heated fish is greatly affected by its previous history. During spoilage or frozen storage, TMAO, urea and other precursors present in fresh fish, break down to ammonia, MMA, DMA and TMA, all of which may be detected in quite large amounts after heating the stored material. The large production of ammonia, presumably from the thermal destruction of urea, is a handicap in the heat processing of elasmobranch flesh.

'Normal' cooking by boiling leads to some increase in ammonia and volatile amines as compared to the raw fish (De and Nazrul, 1966). Much increased concentrations of ammonia, DMA and TMA have been noted in herring heated for up to 5 h at 120°C (Hughes, 1959), although only small amounts of MMA and no higher amines were found (Hughes, 1958). The source of the ammonia under these condi-tions is possibly the breakdown of creatine, creatinine or histidine, with perhaps a contribution from the amide groups of peptides and proteins. The TMA clearly derives from TMAO since the concen-tration of this falls concomitantly at these elevated temperatures (Hughes, 1958, 1959; Ronold and Jakobsen, 1947). There is consider-able evidence that, under conditions akin to those obtained in canning or frying, TMAO in several species of fish and shellfish also decomposes into DMA and formaldehyde (Vaisey, 1956; Ota, 1958; Sundsvold *et al.*, 1971; Ito *et al.*, 1971; Tokunaga, 1975a). The formation of formaldehyde is of importance in that this substance is not normally permitted as an additive and its detection in canned fish products may, therefore, give rise to unwarranted accusations of malpractice. Reports that the reaction is accelerated by cysteine (Vaisey, 1956; Ota, 1958) have been denied (Sundsvold *et al.*, 1971; Tokunaga, 1975a), although iron and haemoglobin have been confirmed as catalysts (Ronold and Jakobsen, 1947; Vaisey, 1956; Sundsvold *et al.*, 1971; Tokunaga, 1975a).

Because TMA is formed during heating it cannot be used as a reliable measure of the degree of freshness of the raw material used for canning (Tokunaga, 1975b). It should be noted here that hypoxanthine is stable on canning, in herring at least, and is probably suitable as a measure of freshness (Hughes and Jones, 1966). Also, with albacore, bluefin and yellowfin tunas, a high correlation between the hypoxanthine contents of the raw and canned products has been found (Crawford, 1970). Higher amines are reported to be released during the canning of horse mackerel (Shimomura *et al.*, 1971).

α-Amino Acids

On steaming haddock for 30 min, as in 'normal' cooking, no experimentally significant change in the relative amounts of 'free' amino acids occurs although a very slight increase in total quantity, attributable to proteolysis, was observed (Hardy *et al.*, 1976). At higher temperatures of up to 140°C, however, it is reported that after 1 h a considerable loss occurs in the free amino acids of sprats, cysteine being affected most (Kushtalov *et al.*, 1971). Although some anomalies are present in this report it is claimed that under these conditions tryptophan, histidine, asparagine, lysine and methionine are little changed. On the other hand, the only amino acid shown to be affected by heating herring at 116°C for periods up to 5 h was histidine, for which a loss of 86% was recorded (Hughes, 1961a; Hughes, 1964b). Histidine may be lost in a variety of ways, the most probable of which is reaction with aldehydes.

These relatively small changes in amino acid concentrations on heating are very likely in themselves to have no significance as far as flavour is concerned because the absolute amounts lie below the threshold of sensory detection.

Creatine and Creatinine

Dark-fleshed species in particular contain high concentrations of creatine (but no creatinine). During heating of herring, for example at 115°C for 2–5 h, about one-quarter of the creatine is lost, most of which is converted into creatinine (Hughes, 1960b). Almost all the creatine is said to be converted into creatinine or destroyed during the heat sterilisation of mackerel paste (Nasedkina and Krasnitskaya, 1972).

Sugars

These compounds undergo reactions under even very mild conditions of heating. Thus, steaming for 10 min causes a halving of the reducing-sugar concentration in some freshwater fish (De and Haque, 1966).

Table 8.3 shows changes in some sugar components of haddock during steaming for 30 min (Hardy *et al.*, 1976). The phosphorylated sugars are particularly unstable under these conditions. The other changes cannot be adequately explained but the loss in total glucose may indicate reaction with amino acids although no visible browning occurs.

Under more severe conditions (120°C, 2–5 h), considerable destruction of sugar phosphates in sole, seabass and cod (Nagayama *et al.*, 1962) and of glucose and ribose in herring (Hughes, 1964b) was noted. Although addition of reducing sugars to white fish causes an increase in browning during severe heat treatment (Ono and Nagayama, 1959), it is claimed that there is no direct relationship between the reducing-sugar concentration and intensity of browning (Nagayama, 1960). There is good evidence that free ribose rather than combined ribose or free glucose is the sugar most likely to be involved in browning reactions in heated white fish (Tarr, 1954).

TABLE 8.3

CHANGES IN SUGAR COMPONENTS OF HADDOCK ON STEAMING FOR 30 MIN

Component (mg/100 g)	Raw	Cooked
Free ribose	25·5	34·2
Ribose phosphates	83·8	71·1
Free glucose	24·1	26·7
Glucose-6-phosphate	35·0	18·4

The reactions between sugars and protein amino acids are significant in reducing the nutritive value of strongly heated fish, particularly in the partially dried state; this topic will be dealt with in a later section on nutritive value (Section 8.2.8).

Nucleotides, Nucleosides and Purine Bases

In a study of haddock steamed for 30 min (Hardy *et al.*, 1976), no experimentally detectable, or very slight, changes in the total amounts of several of these constituents were observed. The constituents included nicotinamide adenosine dinucleotide (NAD), adenosine triphosphate (ATP), adenosine diphosphate (ADP), adenosine mono-phosphate (AMP), uracil, guanine and hypoxanthine. However, a fall in inosine monophosphate (IMP) and an increase in inosine concentrations were found, indicating that the relevant dephosphorylating enzyme is active under these conditions. During the roasting of hagfish, ATP, ADP and AMP are entirely destroyed but 80% of IMP remains intact (Kim and Lee, 1973). Apart from the destruction of ATP and ADP, the notable feature accompanying the drying of file fish at about 50°C for 11 h and yellowfin puffer at about 27°C for 30 h was a large increase in inosine content (Lee *et al.*, 1974). Canning of shrimps results in a loss of up to 40% of AMP, IMP, inosine, adenosine and hypoxanthine, largely as a result of thermal destruction (Suryanarayana Rao *et al.*, 1969). Cooking crab at 100°C largely degrades ATP and ADP to AMP, inosine and hypoxanthine with only a very small production of IMP (Groninger and Brandt, 1969). Somewhat similar results were obtained on canned clam, red crab and oyster (Hashida *et al.*, 1968). The importance of any of these changes with respect to flavour has not been fully established.

Carbonyl Compounds

Table 8.4 shows the large number of carbonyl compounds which have been noted in heated fish of normal moisture content. Most of these have been authenticated by the mass spectrometric method. Undoubtedly many arise from the oxidation and thermal decomposition of lipids but it is conceivable that some arise from reactions in the fish before the heating stage. Some of these compounds have very low thresholds of sensory detection and are likely therefore to play an important rôle in determining the overall aroma of cooked fish. As pointed out above, formaldehyde may arise from decomposition of TMAO.

TABLE 8.4
CARBONYL COMPOUNDS IN HEATED FISH

Compound	Species*†	Conditions of heating**
Formaldehyde	Fish[a]	1
	Salmon[b]	1
	Fish[c]	2
	Cod[d]	3
	Herring[e]	4
	Cod[f]	5
Acetaldehyde	Fish[c]	2
	Cod[d]	3
	Cod[f]	5
	Cod[g]	6
	RDF[h]	7
	Herring[e]	4
Propanal	Cod[f]	5
	Cod[g]	6
	Horse mackerel[i]	1
Butanal	Fish[c]	2
	Cod[g]	6
	RDF[h]	7
	Horse mackerel[i]	1
Isobutanal	Herring[e]	4
2-Methylbutanal	Herring[e]	4
	Cod[f]	5
	RDF[h]	7
3-Methylbutanal	Cod[f]	5
	RDF[h]	7
Isopentanal	Horse mackerel[i]	1
2-Methylpentanal	Cod[f]	5
Hexanal	Cod[f]	5
	RDF[h]	7
Heptanal	Cod[f]	5
Octanal	Cod[f]	5
	RDF[h]	7
	Horse mackerel[i]	1
Nonanal	Cod[f]	5
	RDF[h]	7
Decanal	RDF[h]	7
Tetradecanal	Cod[f]	5

TABLE 8.4 (*Contd.*)

Hexadecanal	Cod[f]	5
Octadecanal	Cod[f]	5
Propenal	Cod[f]	5
	Horse mackerel[i]	1
But-*trans*-2-enal	Cod[f]	5
	Horse mackerel[i]	1
Pent-*cis*-2-enal	Cod[f]	5
Hex-*trans*-2-enal	Cod[f]	5
Hex-*cis*-3-enal	Cod[f]	5
Hept-*trans*-2-enal	Cod[f]	5
Hept-*cis*-4-enal	Cod[f]	5
Hept-*trans*-4-enal	Cod[f]	5
Oct-*cis*-2-enal	Cod[f]	5
Oct-*trans*-2-enal	Cod[f]	5
Non-*trans*-2-enal	Cod[f]	5
Dec-*trans*-2-enal	Cod[f]	5
Hept-*trans*-2, *cis*-4-dienal	Cod[f]	5
Hept-*trans*-2, *trans*-4-dienal	Cod[f]	5
Non-*trans*-2, *trans*-6-dienal	Cod[f]	5
Dec-*trans*-2, *cis*-4-dienal	Cod[f]	5
Dec-*trans*-2, *trans*-4-dienal	Cod[f]	5
Furfural	Cod[f]	5
Benzaldehyde	Cod[f]	5
	RDF[h]	7
o-Tolualdehyde	Cod[f]	5
Terephthalaldehyde	Cod[f]	5
Phenylacetaldehyde	Cod[f]	5
Acetone	Herring[e]	4
	Cod[f]	5
	Cod[g]	6
	Horse mackerel[i]	1
	RDF[h]	7
Butan-2-one	Cod[f]	5
	RDF[h]	7

TABLE 8.4 (*Contd.*)

3-Hydroxybutan-2-one	Fish[c]	2
Pentan-2-one	Cod[f]	5
	RDF[h]	7
	Cod[g]	6
Pentan-3-one	RDF[h]	7
Hexan-2-one	Cod[f]	5
	RDF[h]	7
	Cod[g]	6
Hexan-3-one	Cod[f]	5
4-Methylpentan-2-one	RDF[h]	7
Heptan-2-one	Cod[f]	5
	RDF[h]	7
Heptan-3-one	Cod[f]	5
	RDF[h]	7
Octan-2-one	Cod[f]	5
	RDF[h]	7
Nonan-2-one	Cod[f]	5
	RDF[h]	7
Nonan-5-one	Cod[f]	5
	RDF[h]	7
Undecan-2-one	Cod[f]	5
Hex-3-ene-2-one	Cod[f]	5
Oct-3-ene-2-one	Cod[f]	5
Oct-1-ene-3-one	Cod[f]	5
Oct-3,5-diene-2-one	Cod[f]	5
Acetophenone	Cod[f]	5
Cyclohexanone	Cod[f]	5
5-Aminopentanal	Fish[j]	8

*Reference sources: [a]Biegler (1959); [b]Lunde and Mathieson (1934); [c]Ota (1958); [d]Groninger (1961); [e]Hughes (1961b); [f]McGill *et al.* (1977); [g]Wong *et al.* (1967); [h]Quist and von Sydow (1974); [i]Shimomura *et al.* (1971); [j]Obata and Yamanishi (1952).

**1, Canning; 2, cooking, 113°C; 3, steaming; 4, boiling, 5 h under nitrogen; 5, steaming, 30 min; 6, 35°C, 3 h; 7, 121°C, 40 min; 8, cooking.

†RDF, Reconstituted dried fish.

Information on the influence of time and temperature of processing
and of freshness on the development of carbonyls in herring is
available (Hughes, 1963b). Further work on the production of
carbonyl compounds under unusual conditions of heating or with
unusual samples has been carried out but it is not detailed here; it
covers fish heated with a variety of special sauces (Kasahara and
Nishibori, 1975) and cooked, irradiated clam (Gadbois *et al.*, 1967).

Sulphur Compounds
Some of the volatile sulphur compounds have very low sensory
thresholds and are thus potentially important for aroma but, in
addition, some of them can react with the iron in steel cans to
produce the canning defect known as 'can blackening' (Piggott and
Dollar, 1963; Thompson, 1963).

Table 8.5 lists the compounds so far positively identified in heated
fish of normal moisture content. No definitive studies of the chemical
or enzymic reactions which give rise to these compounds have been
reported, although it is supposed that the precursors are largely the
free sulphur-containing amino acids and possibly thiamine (Thompson, 1963; Hughes, 1964a; Schutte, 1974). There is a considerable
increase in the amount of these compounds with time and temperature of heating and the rate of increase depends upon species. On the
other hand, there is evidence that the concentration of volatile
sulphur compounds is less in the fish as a result of canning (McLay,
1967).

Miscellaneous Compounds
A variety of compounds has been reported in heated fish, including
hydrocarbons (McGill *et al.*, 1977; Wong *et al.*, 1967), furan and furan
derivatives (McGill *et al.*, 1977; Quist and von Sydow, 1974), pyrazines (McGill *et al.*, 1977), organic acids (McGill *et al.*, 1977; De and
Nazrul, 1966; Hughes, 1960a) and alcohols (McGill *et al.*, 1977; Quist
and von Sydow, 1974; Wong *et al.*, 1967). It seems likely that the
pyrazines and, at high concentrations, the organic acids, could
contribute significantly to flavour.

8.2.8   Nutritive Changes
Knowledge up to the early 1960s was comprehensively reviewed in a
number of publications covering proteins (Geiger and Borgstrom,
1962), vitamins (Higashi, 1962; Braekkan, 1962), canning (Bramsnaes,

TABLE 8.5
SULPHUR COMPOUNDS IN HEATED FISH

Compounds	Species*†	Conditions of heating**
Hydrogen sulphide	Crab[a]	1
	Cuttlefish[b]	2
	Bivalves[b]	2
	Salmon[c,d]	3
	Herring[e]	4
	Herring[f]	5
	Cod[g]	6
	Oyster[h]	7
	Cod[i]	8
	RDF[j]	9
Methyl mercaptan	Oyster[h]	7
	Herring[e]	4
	Herring[f]	5
	Mackerel[k]	3
	Cod[i]	8
	RDF[j]	9
Ethyl mercaptan	RDF[j]	9
2-Propyl mercaptan	RDF[j]	9
Dimethyl sulphide	Salmon[l]	3
	Herring[e]	4
	Herring[f]	5
	Oyster[h]	7
	Cod[g]	6
	Cod[i]	8
	Skipjack tuna[k]	3
	Sea bream[k]	3
	RDF[j]	9
Ethylene disulphide	RDF[j]	9
Methyl ethyl sulphide	RDF[j]	9
Propylene sulphide	RDF[j]	9
Methyl isopropyl sulphide	RDF[j]	9
Diethyl sulphide	RDF[j]	9
Methyl propyl sulphide	RDF[j]	9
Carbon disulphide	Cod[g]	6
	RDF[j]	9

TABLE 8.5 (*Contd.*)

Dimethyl disulphide	Cod[i]	8
	RDF[j]	9
Thiophene	RDF[j]	9
2-Methylthiophene	RDF[j]	9
3-Methylthiophene	RDF[j]	9
2-Ethylthiophene	RDF[j]	9
2,5-Dimethylthiophene	Cod[i]	8
Propylthiophene	Cod[i]	8
2,4-Dimethylthiazole	Cod[i]	8
4,5-Dimethylthiazole	Cod[i]	8
2,4,5-Trimethylthiazole	Cod[i]	8
2-Ethyl-4,5-dimethylthiazole	Cod[i]	8
2-Acetylthiazole	Cod[i]	8
5-Ethyl-2,4-dimethylthiazole	Cod[i]	8
3,5-Dimethyl-1,2,4-trithiolane[††]	RDF[j]	9
Ethylthiazoline[††]	Cod[i]	8
Sulphur dioxide	Flat fish[m]	10

*Reference sources: [a]Oya and Kawaguchi (1932); [b]Shimada (1933); [c]Tanikawa *et al.* (1956); [d]Tanikawa (1958); [e]Hughes (1964a); [f]McLay (1967); [g]Wong *et al.* (1967); [h]Yueh (1961); [i]McGill *et al.* (1977); [j]Quist and von Sydow (1974); [k]Ooyama (1973); [l]Motohiro (1962); [m]Gamble *et al.* (1975).
**1, 115°C, 2 h; 2, 80, 100, 120°C; 3, canning; 4, 100°C, 1 h; 5, 99°C, 20 min; 6, 35°C, 3 h; 7, boiling; 8, steaming, 30 min; 9, 121°C, 20 min; 10, 100°C, 10 min.
†Reconstituted dried fish.
††Tentative identification.

1962; Lassen, 1965a), drying, salting and smoking (Cutting, 1962) and general nutritive value (Tarr, 1962). Among the major findings was that normal heat treatment, up to that as severe as occurs in canning, does not affect the amino acids of several species of fish as determined after total acid hydrolysis. This is true of amino acids as heat sensitive as methionine. Also, such heat treatments do not reduce the biological value as measured by animal feeding tests. On the other hand, some types of fish-meal processes do lead to a loss of biological value as the result of chemical changes, particularly to lysine. Digestibility measured using enzymes *in vitro* was variously reported to slightly increase or slightly decrease as a result of heat treatments. Of the B vitamins, riboflavin, niacin, pantothenic acid, biotin, pyridoxine and B_{12} are retained to a considerable extent during cooking and canning; retinol, β-carotene and vitamin D are slightly reduced; thiamine is destroyed to varying degrees depending upon species and conditions of heat treatment.

Most work since then has served to fill in details. The main advance has been the deeper understanding referred to earlier (Ford, 1973; Bjarnason and Carpenter, 1970) of the reasons for the development of unavailability of lysine and other amino acids during severe heat treatment. It has been confirmed with carp that different normal cooking treatments do not affect the total amino acids (Aman, 1973). Similarly, canning does not affect the essential amino acids (Wierzchowski and Zyczynska, 1971). The effects of dry or moist heat up to 150°C on the amino acids and protein value of fish meal or protein concentrate have been studied (Dubrow and Stillings, 1970; Anon, 1975). Autoclaving is said to slightly reduce the relative nutritive value of cod protein (Kennedy and Ley, 1971). Canning sprats at 112 or 126°C had little effect on available lysine (Kolakowski *et al.*, 1973) and likewise, frying sardines for 6 min at 180°C had little effect on biological value or digestibility (Bender, 1972). On the other hand, losses of available lysine of up to 29% were observed when several fish were fried for 4 min at 180°C (Tooley and Lawrie, 1974). This was attributed to thermal damage and reactions with oxidised components of the oil.

Disagreements continue as to whether increasing the severity of heat treatment decreases or increases digestibility by enzymes *in vitro* (Krauze *et al.*, 1970; Ziecik and Fik, 1971; Choi *et al.*, 1974; Sheikh and Shah, 1974; Valyavskaya, 1969).

A loss of about 70% in pyridoxine and niacin is reported during the boiling of mussels for 10 min (Korobkina *et al.*, 1969) and in thiamine during the canning of fish (Burger and Walters, 1973). Considerably smaller losses occur in riboflavin, niacin and thiamine during the autoclaving or normal cooking of cod (Kennedy and Ley, 1971; Blegen and Wilsher, 1969). Among the B vitamins, pyridoxine suffers the greatest loss (about 50%) during boiling or baking of a variety of species (Miuccio *et al.*, 1974).

REFERENCES

Abdel-Latif, K. K. (1969) *Izv. Vyssh. Ucheb. Zaved. Pishch. Tekhnol.*, (3), 85.
Ackman, R. G. (1974) In: *Fishery Products*, ed. Kreuzer, R., p. 112. West Byfleet, England: Fishing News (Books) Ltd.
Aitken, A. & Campbell, D. (1969) Unpublished work. Torry Research Station, Aberdeen.
Aman, M. E. B. (1973) *Voprosy Pitaniya*, (1), 69.
Aman, M. E. B. & Smirnova, G. A. (1972) *Ryb. Khoz.*, (6), 71.
Andross, M. (1941) *Chem. & Ind.*, **19**, 176.
Annamma, T. T. & Rao, C. V. N. (1974) *Fishery Technol.*, **11**, 28.
Anon. (1975) *Expanding the Utilization of Marine Fishery Resources for Human Consumption.* FAO Fisheries Reports, No. 175.
Atwood, H. L. (1972) In: *The Structure and Function of Muscle*, ed. Bourne, G. H., 2nd edn. Vol. 1, p. 421. London & New York: Academic Press.
Babbitt, J. K. (1973) *J. Fd. Sci.*, **38**, 1101.
Baldwin, R. E., Strong, D. H. & Torrie, J. H. (1962) *Fd. Technol.*, **16**(7), 115.
Bannerman, A. M. (1975) *Torry Research Station Advisory Note No. 18.* Edinburgh: HMSO.
Barnett, H. J., Nelson, R. W. & Dassow, J. A. (1969) *Fishery Ind. Res.*, **5**(3), 103.
Bendall, J. R. & Wismer-Pedersen, J. (1962) *J. Fd. Sci.*, **27**, 144.
Bender, A. E. (1972) *PAG Bull.*, **2**(1), 10.
Biegler, P. (1959) *Fishwar. u. Feinkostindustr.*, **31**, 102.
Bjarnason, J. & Carpenter, K. J. (1970) *Brit. J. Nutr.*, **24**, 313.
Blegen, E. & Wilsher, B. (1969) *Tidsskrift för Hermetikindustri*, **55**, 253.
Boon, D. D. (1975) *J. Fd. Sci.*, **40**, 756.
Boyd, J. W. & Southcott, B. A. (1965) *J. Fish, Res. Bd. Can.*, **22**, 53.
Braekkan, O. R. (1962) In: *Fish in Nutrition*, eds. Heen, E. & Kreuzer, R., p. 141. London: Fishing News (Books) Ltd.
Bramsnaes, F. (1962) In: *Fish in Nutrition*, eds. Heen, E. & Kreuzer, R., p. 153. London: Fishing News (Books) Ltd.
Burdina, L. I. & Melnikova, O. M. (1974) *Ryb. Khoz.*, (10), 56.
Burger, I. H. & Walters, C. L. (1973) *Proc. Nutr. Soc.*, **32**, 1.
Buttkus, H. (1974) *J. Fd. Sci.*, **39**, 484.
Chappell, G. M. (1954) *Brit. J. Nutr.*, **8**, 325.
Charley, H. (1952) *Fd. Res.*, **17**, 136.
Charley, H. & Goertz, G. E. (1958) *Fd. Res.*, **23**, 17.
Charm, S. E. (1971) *The Fundamentals of Food Engineering*, 2nd edn. Westport, Conn.: Avi. Publ. Co.
Choi, H. M., Shin, K. S., Youn, J. E. & Lee, B. W. (1974) *Korean J. Fd. Sci. Technol.*, **6**, 70.
Connell, J. J. (1957) *J. Sci. Fd. Agric.*, **8**, 526.
Connell, J. J. (1958) In: *Fundamental Aspects of the Dehydration of Foodstuffs*, p. 167. London: Society of Chemical Industry.
Connell, J. J. (1962) In: *Freeze-drying of Foods*, ed. Fisher, F. R., p. 50. Washington D.C.: National Academy of Sciences.

Connell, J. J. (1964) In: *Proteins and their Reactions*, eds. Schultz, H. W. & Anglemier, A. F. p. 255. Westport, Conn.: Avi. Publ. Co.

Connell, J. J. & Howgate, P. F. (1964) *J. Fd. Sci.*, **29**, 717.

Connell, J. J. & Howgate, P. F. (1971) In: *Fish Inspection and Quality Control*, ed. Kreuzer, R., p. 155. London: Fishing News (Books) Ltd.

Cooper, D. le B. (1937) *J. Biol. Bd. Can.*, **3**, 100.

Crawford, L. (1970) *Bull. Jap. Soc. Sci. Fish.*, **36**, 1136.

Cutting, C. L. (1962) In: *Fish in Nutrition*, eds. Heen, E. & Kreuzer, R., p. 161. London: Fishing News (Books) Ltd.

Cutting, C. L., Reay, G. A. & Shewan, J. M. (1956) *Dehydration of Fish*. Food Investigation Special Report No. 62. London: HMSO.

De, H. N. & Haque, M. (1966) *Pak. J. Sci. Ind. Res.*, **9**, 133.

De, H. N. & Nazrul, H. (1966) *Sci. Res. (Dacca)*, **3**, 110.

Deschacht, W. & Vansevenant, A. (1968) *Mededelingen van de Rijksfaculteit Landbouwwetenschappen te Gent*, **33**, 1661.

Doesburg, J. J. & Papendorf, D. (1969) *J. Fd. Technol.*, **4**, 17.

Dollar, A. M., Goldner, A. & Olcott, H. S. (1967) *Fishery Ind. Res.*, **3**(4), 19.

Dubrow, D. L. & Stillings, B. R. (1970) *J. Fd. Sci.*, **35**, 677.

Dyer, W. J., Fraser, D. I., McIntosh, R. G. & Myer, M. (1964) *J. Fish. Res. Bd. Can.*, **21**, 577.

El-Bastavizi, A. M. & Smirnova, G. A. (1972) *Voprosy Pitaniya*, **31**(3), 90.

Forbes, J. C. (1927) *Contr. Can. Biol. Fisheries*, **3**, 469.

Ford, J. E. (1973) In: *Proteins in Human Nutrition*, eds. Porter, J. W. G. & Rolls, B. A., p. 515. London & New York: Academic Press.

Fujita, H. & Kishimoto, A. (1956) *Bull. Jap. Soc. Sci. Fish.*, **22**, 306.

Gadbois, D. F., Mendelsohn, J. M. & Ronsivalli, L. J. (1967) *J. Fd. Sci.*, **32**, 511.

Gamble, A., Hardy, R. & Keay, J. N. (1975) Unpublished work. Torry Research Station, Aberdeen.

Geiger, E. & Borgstrom, G. (1962) In: *Fish as Food*, ed. Borgstrom, G. Vol. 2, pp. 29,115. London & New York: Academic Press.

Groninger, H. S. (1961) *Fd. Technol.*, **15**, 10.

Groninger, H. S. & Brandt, K. R. (1969) *J. Milk Fd. Technol.*, **32**, 1.

Grosjean, O., Cobb, B. F., Mebine, B. & Brown, W. D. (1969) *J. Fd. Sci.*, **34**, 404.

Hamm, R. & Deatherage, F. E. (1960) *Fd. Res.*, **25**, 587.

Hamm, R. & Hofmann, K. (1965) *Nature*, **207**, 1269.

Hamm, W. S., Butler, C. & Heerdt, M. (1944) *Food Inds.*, (6), 75.

Hanover, L. M., Webb, N. B., Howell, A. J. & Thomas, F. B. (1973) *J. Milk Fd. Technol.*, **36**, 409.

Hanson, J. & Lowy, J. (1960) In: *The Structure and Function of Muscle*, ed. Bourne, G. H., 1st edn. vol. 1, p. 265. London & New York: Academic Press.

Hardy, R., McGill, A. S. & Thomson, A. B. (1976) Unpublished work. Torry Research Station, Aberdeen.

Hashida, W., Mouri, T. & Shiga, I. (1968) *Fd. Technol.*, **22**, 1436.

Higashi, H. (1962) In: *Fish in Nutrition*, eds. Heen, E. & Kreuzer, R., p. 125. London: Fishing News (Books) Ltd.

Howgate, P. F. & Ahmed, S. F. (1972) *J. Sci. Fd. Agric.*, **23**, 615.
Hughes, R. B. (1958) *Nature*, **181**, 1281.
Hughes, R. B. (1959) *J. Sci. Fd. Agric.*, **10**, 431.
Hughes, R. B. (1960a) *J. Sci. Fd. Agric.*, **11**, 47.
Hughes, R. B. (1960b) *J. Sci. Fd. Agric.*, **11**, 700.
Hughes, R. B. (1961a) *J. Sci. Fd. Agric.*, **12**, 475.
Hughes, R. B. (1961b) *J. Sci. Fd. Agric.*, **12**, 822.
Hughes, R. B. (1963a) *J. Sci. Fd. Agric.*, **14**, 432.
Hughes, R. B. (1963b) *J. Sci. Fd. Agric.*, **14**, 893.
Hughes, R. B. (1964a) *J. Sci. Fd. Agric.*, **15**, 290.
Hughes, R. B. (1964b) *J. Sci. Fd. Agric.*, **15**, 293.
Hughes, R. B. & Jones, N. R. (1966) *J. Sci. Fd. Agric.*, **17**, 434.
Ito, Y., Sakuto, H., Takada, H. & Tanimura, A. (1971) *Shokuhin Eiseigaku Zasshi.*, **12**, 404.
Jarenbäck, L. & Liljemark, A. (1975) *J. Fd. Technol.*, **10**, 229.
Jason, A. C. (1963) Unpublished work. Torry Research Station, Aberdeen.
Jones, N. R. (1967) In: *Chemistry and Physiology of Flavour*, eds. Schultz, H. W., Day, E. A. & Libby, L. M., p. 267. Westport, Conn.: Avi. Publ. Co.
Jones, N. R. (1969) In: *Proc. 1st Int. Congr. Fd. Sci. Technol.*, ed. Leitch, J. M. Vol. 1, p. 199. London: Gordon & Breach.
Kasahara, K. & Nishibori, K. (1975) *Bull. Jap. Soc. Sci. Fish.*, **41**, 43.
Kawakami, T. (1934) *Bull. Jap. Soc. Sci. Fish.*, **3**, 75.
Kennedy, T. S. & Ley, F. J. (1971) *J. Sci. Fd. Agric.*, **22**, 146.
Kim, Y. G. & Lee, E. H. (1973) *Korean J. Fd. Sci. Technol.*, **5**, 206.
Koizumi, C. & Matsuura, F. (1967) *Bull. Jap. Soc. Sci. Fish.*, **33**, 651.
Kolakowski, E., Fik, M. & Seidler, T. (1973) *Przemy. Spozy.*, **27**, 118.
Korobkina, G. S., Danilova, E. N. & Kalinina, N. N. (1969) *Voprosy Pitaniya*, **28**(5), 85.
Krauze, S., Oledzka, R. & Buczymska, Z. (1970) *Rocz. Panstw. Zakl. Hig.*, **21**(3), 287.
Kushtalov, G. N. & Saduakasov, T. S. (1971) *Ryb. Khoz.*, (12), 66.
Kushtalov, G. N., Korzhenko, V. P. & Hamady, K. (1971) *Ryb. Khoz.*, (5), 61.
Lamb, J. (1976) *Chem. & Ind.*, (24), 1046.
Lassen, S. (1965a) In: *The Technology of Fish Utilisation*, ed. Kreuzer, R., p. 235. London: Fishing News (Books) Ltd.
Lassen, S. (1965b) In: *Fish as Food*, ed. Borgstrom, G. Vol. 4, p. 207. London & New York: Academic Press.
Lea, C. H., Parr, L. J. & Carpenter, K. J. (1960) *Brit. J. Nutr.*, **14**, 91.
Lee, E. H., Chung, S. Y., Kim, Y. G., Yang, S. T. & Kim, S. H. (1974) *Korean J. Fd. Sci. Technol.*, **6**, 177.
Lobanov, D. I. & Bykova, S. V. (1938) *Voprosy Pitaniya*, **7**(2), 12.
Love, R. M. (1970) *Chemical Biology of Fishes*. London & New York: Academic Press.
Lunde, G. & Mathieson, E. (1934) *Ind. Eng. Chem.*, **26**, 974.
McCance, R. A. & Shipp, H. L. (1933) *The Chemistry of Flesh Foods and their Losses on Cooking*. MRC Special Report Series, No. 187. London: HMSO.

McCance, R. A. & Widdowson, E. M. (1960) *The Composition of Foods*, 3rd edn. MRC Special Report Series, No. 297. London: HMSO.

McGill, A. S., Hardy, R. & Gunstone, F. D. (1977) *J. Sci. Fd. Agric.*, **28**, 200.

McLay, R. (1967) *J. Sci. Fd. Agric.*, **18**, 605.

Meesemaecker, R. & Sohier, Y. (1959) *Fd. Mfr.*, **34**, 148, 193.

Migata, M. (1953) *Bull. Jap. Soc. Sci. Fish.*, **18**, 558.

Miuccio, C., Floridi, S., Schiesser, A., Fidanza, A., Fratoni, A., de Siena, E. & Polara, A. (1974) *Boll. Soc. Ital. Biol. Sper.*, **50**, 131.

Mohr, V. (1971) Ph.D. Thesis, University of Aberdeen.

Motohiro, T. (1962) *Mem. Fac. Fish. Hokkaido Univ.*, **10**, 1.

Mudrak, L. T. (1953) *Trudy Moskov. Tekh. Inst. Rybnoe Prom.*, **5**, 201.

Murray, J. & Burt, J. R. (1969) *Torry Research Station Advisory Note No. 38.* Edinburgh: HMSO.

Myklestad, O., Bjornstad, J. & Njaa, L. R. (1972) *Fiskeridirektoratets Skrifter Serie Teknol. Undersøkelser*, **5**, No. 10.

Nagayama, F. (1960) *Bull. Jap. Soc. Sci. Fish.*, **26**, 1026.

Nagayama, F., Hiraido, H. & Sano, K. (1962) *Bull. Jap. Soc. Sci. Fish.*, **28**, 1188.

Nandakumaren, M., Choudhuri, D. R. & Pillai, V. K. (1969) *Fishery Technol.*, **6**, 49.

Nasedkina, A. E. & Krasnitskaya, A. L. (1972) *Izvestia TINRO*, **83**, 39.

Nemitz, G. & Partmann, W. (1959) *Z. Lebensm. Unters.-Forsch.*, **109**, 121.

Obata, Y. & Yamanishi, T. (1952) *Bull. Jap. Soc. Sci. Fish.*, **17**, 326.

Odense, P. H., Lueng, T. C., Green, W. A. & Dingle, J. R. (1969) *Biochim. Biophys. Acta*, **188**, 124.

Olley, J. & Lovern, J. A. (1960) *J. Sci. Fd. Agric.*, **11**, 644.

Ono, T. & Nagayama, F. (1959) *Bull. Jap. Soc. Sci. Fish.*, **24**, 833.

Ooyama, S. (1973) *Kaseigaku Zasshi.*, **24**, 694.

Osada, H. (1974) *Proc. 4th Int. Congr. Fd. Sci. Technol.*, **1b**, 104.

Ota, F. (1958) *Bull. Jap. Soc. Sci. Fish.*, **24**, 338.

Oya, T. & Kawaguchi, T. (1932) *Bull. Jap. Soc. Sci. Fish.*, **1**, 7.

Parry, D. A. (1970) In: *Proteins as Human Foods*, ed. Lawrie, R. A., p. 365. London: Butterworths.

Patterson, S. & Goldspink, G. (1972) *Z. Zellforsch.*, **133**, 463.

Pieniezak, D. & Rakowska, M. (1974) *Proc. 4th Int. Congr. Fd. Sci. Technol.*, **7a**, 64.

Piggott, G. M. & Dollar, A. M. (1963) *Fd. Technol.*, **17**(4), 115.

Pokorny, J., El-Zeany, B. A. & Janicek, G. (1973) *Z. Lebensm. Unters.-Forsch.*, **151**, 31.

Quaglia, G. B., Viola, M. A., Fabriani, G. & Fidanza, A. (1974) *Abstr. IV. Int. Congr. Fd. Sci. Technol.*, Madrid, **1**, 682.

Quist, I. H. & von Sydow, E. C. F. (1974) *J. Agric. Fd. Chem.*, **22**, 1077.

Ronold, D. A. & Jakobsen, F. (1947) *J. Soc. Chem. Ind.*, **66**, 160.

Saduakasov, T. S. (1972) *Izvestiya Vysshikh Uchebnykh Zavedenii Pishchevaya Tekhnologiya*, (4), 99.

Schaller, D. R. & Powrie, W. D. (1972) *Can. Inst. Fd. Sci. Technol. J.*, **5**, 184.

Schutte, L. (1974) *CRC Crit. Rev. Fd. Technol.*, **4**, 457.

Sheikh, A. S. & Shah, F. H. (1974) *Pak. J. Sci. Ind. Res.*, **17**, 136.

Shimada, K. (1933) *Bull. Jap. Soc. Sci. Fish.*, **2**, 23.
Shimizu, Y., Hosokawa, Y. & Simidu, W. (1962) *Bull. Jap. Soc. Sci. Fish.*, **28**, 616.
Shimomura, M., Yashimatsu, F. & Matsumoto, F. (1971) *Kaseigaku Zasshi*, **22**, 106.
Sidwell, V. D., Foncannon, P. R., Moore, N. S. & Bonnet, J. C. (1974) *Mar. Fish. Rev.*, **36**(3), 21.
Simidu, U. & Simidu, W. (1960) *Bull. Jap. Soc. Sci. Fish.*, **26**, 1099.
Simidu, W. & Takeda, K. (1951) *Bull. Jap. Soc. Sci. Fish.*, **17**, 132.
Simidu, W. & Takuma, H. (1951) *Bull. Jap. Soc. Sci. Fish.*, **17**, 103.
Sparre, T. (1965) In: *Fish as Food*, ed. Borgstrom, G. Vol. 3, p. 411. London & New York: Academic Press.
Sundsvold, O. C., Uppstad, B., Ferguson, G. W., Feeley, D. & McLachlan, T. (1971) *J. Assoc. Publ. Anal.*, **9**, 86.
Suryanarayana Rao, S. V., Rangaswamy, J. R. & Lahiry, N. L. (1969) *J. Fish. Res. Bd. Can.*, **26**, 704.
Suyama, M. (1951) *Bull. Jap. Soc. Sci. Fish.*, **17**, 135.
Takahashi, T. (1965) In: *Fish as Food*, ed. Borgstrom, G. Vol. 4, p. 339. London & New York: Academic Press.
Tanaka, T. (1958) *Bull. Tokai Reg. Fish. Res. Lab.*, **20**, 81.
Tanikawa, E. (1958) *Mem. Fac. Fish. Hokkaido Univ.*, **6**, 102.
Tanikawa, E. (1963) *Advan. Fd. Res.*, **12**, 368.
Tanikawa, E. (1971) *Marine Products in Japan*. Tokyo: Koseisha-Koseikaku Co.
Tanikawa, E., Motohiro, T. & Shoji, S. (1956) *Bull. Fac. Fish. Hokkaido Univ.*, **6**, 317.
Tarladgis, B. G. (1962) *J. Sci. Fd. Agric.*, **13**, 481.
Tarr, H. L. A. (1941) *Fish. Res. Bd. Can. Prog. Rep. Pacific Stations*, No. 48, p. 19.
Tarr, H. L. A. (1954) *Fd. Technol.*, **8**, 15.
Tarr, H. L. A. (1962) In: *Fish as Food*, ed. Borgstrom, G. Vol. 2, p. 235. London & New York: Academic Press.
Thompson, M. H. (1963) *Fd. Technol.*, **17**(5), 157.
Tokunaga, T. (1975a) *Bull. Jap. Soc. Sci. Fish.*, **41**, 535.
Tokunaga, T. (1975b) *Bull. Jap. Soc. Sci. Fish.*, **41**, 547.
Tooley, P. J. & Lawrie, R. A. (1974) *J. Fd. Technol.*, **9**, 247.
Tsuyuki, H. (1974) In: *Chemical Zoology*, eds. Florkin, M. & Scheer, B. T. Vol. 8, p. 287. London & New York: Academic Press.
Tülsner, M. & Wagenknecht, W. (1976) *Fischerei Forsch.*, **14**(1), 57.
Ueda, T., Shimizu, Y. & Simidu, W. (1964) *Bull. Jap. Soc. Sci. Fish.*, **30**, 352.
Ueda, T., Shimizu, Y. & Simidu, W. (1968) *Bull. Jap. Soc. Sci. Fish.*, **34**, 357.
Ueda, T., Simidu, W. & Shimizu, Y. (1963) *Bull. Jap. Soc. Sci. Fish.*, **29**, 537.
Vaisey, E. B. (1956) *Can. J. Biochem. Physiol.*, **34**, 1085.
Valyavskaya, M. E. (1969) *Ryb. Khoz.*, **45**(7), 68.
Wagenknecht, W. & Tülsner, M. (1974) *Fischerei Forsch.* **12**(1), 69.
Ward, A., Wignall, J. & Windsor, M. L. (1977) *J. Sci. Fd. Agric.*, **28**, 941.
Warrier, S. B. K., Ninjoor, V., Sawant, P. L. & Kumata, U.S. (1973) *J. Fd. Technol.*, **8**, 283.

Wierzchowski, J. & Zyczynska, J. (1971) *Przemy. Spozy.*, **25**, 343.
Windsor, M. L. (1971) *Torry Research Station Advisory Note No.* 49. Edinburgh: HMSO.
Wong, N. P., Damico, J. N. & Salwin, H. (1967) *J. Assoc. Off. Agric. Chem.*, **50**, 8.
Yamanaka, H., Bito, M. & Yokoseki, M. (1973) *Bull. Jap. Soc. Sci. Fish.*, **39**, 1293, 1299.
Young, O. C. & Sidaway, E. P. (1943) *Fish. Res. Bd. Can. Prog. Rep. Pacific Stations*, No. 56, p. 7.
Yueh, M. H. (1961) *Dissert. Abstr.*, **22**, 730.
Ziecik, M. & Fik, M. (1971) *Zeszyty Nauk. Wyzsza Szkola Rolnicza Szczecinie*, 135.

CHAPTER 9

Fruits

S. D. HOLDSWORTH

Campden Food Preservation Research Association, Chipping Campden, UK

Fruits are subjected to heating during a number of different processes such as simple cooking, bottling, canning, jam, purée and juice manufacture, sun drying and dehydration. In general, because of their low pH values, preservation of fruits can be effected using relatively mild heating conditions. However, because of their fragile cells, sensitive aroma compounds and unstable pigments, heating may lead to profound changes of texture, flavour and colour.

On heating, changes of texture may occur owing to the loss of semipermeability of cell membranes, and solubilisation and breakdown of pectic substances in the cell walls and middle lamella. Aroma components may be lost by volatilisation, thermal degradation or reaction with other constituents, in some cases resulting in a loss of desirable flavour and, in others, the formation of undesirable flavours. Likewise, pigments may degrade resulting in a loss of colour intensity or new coloured compounds which can be either desirable or objectionable may form. Such changes are usually accelerated by increasing the time and temperature of heating but are also very dependent on the type of fruit, its maturity and condition, acid, sugar and moisture content as well as other influencing substances such as metal ions and oxygen.

In this chapter, the various fruits are discussed separately rather than on the basis of types of processing treatment, since each fruit may exhibit a quite different response to heating, although in many cases similar reactions do occur and some overlap is unavoidable. It has not been possible to cover all types of fruit in this review and so attention has been concentrated on those which were considered to be representative of the wide variety of fruits available.

TABLE 9.1
GENERAL SOURCES OF INFORMATION ON FRUIT

Subject	Reference
General botanical information and proximate composition	Winton & Winton (1935) Bender (1965) Duckworth (1966) Purseglove (1968) Harrison *et al.* (1969) Kefford & Chandler (1970) Hulme (1970, 1971) Brouk (1975) van Oss *et al.* (1975) McCance & Widdowson (1960)
Specific composition pH	Adam & Dickinson (1959)
Colour	Tankersley (1963) Anthistle & Dickinson (1959) Gallop (1965) Chichester (1972) Mathew & Parpia (1971) Borenstein & Bunnell (1966) Shrikhande (1976)
Texture and drained weights	van Buren (1970) Reeve (1970) Adam (1965) Mizrahi & Kopelman (1975)
Flavour and aroma	Salunkhe & Do (1977) Shankaranarayana *et al.* (1975) Joslyn & Goldstein (1964) Nursten & Williams (1967) Nursten (1970)
Micronutrients	Harris & Karmas (1975) McCance & Widdowson (1960)
Specific operations Drying	Labuza (1972) Salunkhe *et al.* (1973) Holdsworth (1971) Hinton & Holdsworth (1975)
Canning	Adams & Blundstone (1971) Blundstone *et al.* (1971) Hinton & Holdsworth (1975)

The subject matter of each section is arranged as indicated in Table 9.1, which also contains a list of useful references from which much of the general information was obtained. Information is also given on the chemical and physical effects of the various heating processes applied to fruits (discussed in alphabetical order), although in many instances this is very meagre. Some of this information is related to purely subjective considerations but where space permits and information is available, explanations for changes of texture, flavour and colour are outlined and references to more detailed studies are indicated. The effects of storage temperature on the deterioration of processed fruit products have been noted where investigations have been made over a wide range of temperatures. It will also be observed that, in some cases, the physical and chemical changes in heated fruit products are caused by other factors, such as diffusion and dehydration phenomena, as well as heat, and consequently the indirect effects of heating are also mentioned.

9.1 APPLE

9.1.1 Structure and Composition

The apple (*Pyrus malus*) consists essentially of fleshy receptacular tissue enclosed in protective tissue (skin). The inner components are the seeds, carpellary vascular bundles, endocarp, exocarp and mesocarp. However, only the fleshy tissue is of direct interest to the food processor. The main chemical constituents of the edible portion are: water, 84%; sugar, 9%; acids (mainly malic acid), 0·7%; pectin, 3%; protein, 0·3%; fat, 0·3%; micronutrients per 100 g: calcium, 5 mg; iron, 0·3 mg; vitamin A, 80 IU*; thiamine 0·03 mg; riboflavin, 0·02 mg; niacin, 0·2 mg; and ascorbic acid, 4 mg. The main aromatic constituents are the amyl esters of formic, caproic and caprylic acids and geraniol. Amongst the less common nitrogenous components, pipecolic acid, γ-methyl proline, γ-hydroxyproline, γ-methyl-hydroxyproline and homoserine have been reported. The principal amino acids present are aspartic acid, asparagine and glutamic acid with moderate amounts of serine, α-alanine, γ-aminobutyric acid, valine, the leucines, phenylalanine, piperidine-2-carboxylic acid and smaller amounts of β-alanine, arginine, histidine, tyrosine and tryptophan.

*1 IU vitamin A ≡ activity of 0·60 μg crystalline β-carotene.

During growth, the reducing sugars and sucrose increase continuously whilst the starch reaches a peak and then declines before harvesting. The concentration of phenolics and chlorogenic acid falls continuously during growth. The anthocyanin concentration in the skin of many varieties increases during maturation, the red colour being mainly due to the presence of cyanidin-3-galactoside. Ethylene and carbon dioxide are important metabolic products which are synthesised during the ripening process. Oxidising enzymes (polyphenolase, polyphenol oxidase, catechol oxidase) are also present in the flesh and these lead to the oxidation of chlorogenic acid and catechins. The darkening and browning of the tissue when exposed to air results from these interactions.

The texture of apples is determined by the interactions of the pectin with hemicellulose, cellulose, pentosans and hexosans. During the ripening process there is some breakdown of the protopectin resulting in softening of the tissue. Protopectin consists of polygalacturonic acid (pectin) crosslinked with metallic ions (Ca^{2+} or Mg^{2+}) with hydrogen bonding between the hydroxyl groups. For a more detailed description of the biochemistry of apples see Hulme and Rhodes (1971).

9.1.2 Effects of Heat

The major effect of heating on apple flesh is to cause breakdown of the structural integrity resulting in a 'mushy' texture, the extent of which depends very much on variety and growing conditions. Sterling (1955) demonstrated that cellular separation is caused by gelatinisation of the starch but rupture of cell walls did not occur. Gormley (1975) investigated the quality of apple slices, prepared from the 'Golden Delicious' variety, for use in pie making. They were not very suitable since they did not break down on heating and tended to develop a rubbery texture, although the addition of 2·5% malic acid solution before processing improved both texture and flavour.

The main factor which appears to affect the breakdown of apple flesh is pH (Doesburg, 1961). Plant tissue generally softens considerably in the pH range 4·5–7·0. This is caused by an increase in soluble pectic substances brought about by depolymerisation of insoluble protopectin and hydrolysis of hemicelluloses which are attached to the pectic substances by hydrogen bonding. Apples with a low acid content are not suitable for sauce manufacture since insufficient degradation occurs to produce the necessary reduction of cell elasticity and adhesion. Several workers (Reeve and Leinbach, 1953; Reeve, 1953; Kertesz *et al.*, 1959; Toldby and Wiley, 1962) have studied the factors which affect the breakdown of apples to give a good-quality sauce.

Whereas for sauce making breakdown is desirable, in the canning of apple slices a firm texture is required. Shallenberger *et al.* (1963) showed that the firmness was a function of both blanching temperature and harvest date. In general, raising the blanch temperature increased the firmness, probably due to pectin crosslinking. More detailed investigations of the changes in texture of processed apples have been reported by Fletcher (1970). Yankov (1973) determined the velocity constants for the degradation of protopectin in ten varieties of apple over the temperature range 75–110°C. The half-life times ranged from 825 min at 75°C to 1·1 min at 110°C.

One of the major problems encountered in apple processing is the occurrence of discolouration. The action of heat on some varieties causes pinkish discolouration which has been attributed to the decomposition of colourless leucoanthocyanins to red anthocyanins. Anthistle and Dickinson (1959) believe that the discolouration in severely processed canned apples may arise from polymerisation of leucoanthocyanins into brown 'phlobaphenes'. The blue–purple colours which appear in canned-apple products are caused by the formation of complexes between metal ions (Sn^{2+} and Fe^{3+}) and anthocyanins produced by the action of heat (Hughes *et al.*, 1974).

Discolouration of canned apple sauce may also be brought about by storage at relatively high temperatures owing to Maillard browning reactions between amino acids and reducing sugars (Luh and Kamber, 1963). Hydroxymethylfurfural is formed and, although its presence does not itself give any discolouration or off-flavour, high levels indicate that processing or storage temperatures have been excessive. A rapid lowering of consistency is also observed which may be attributed to the conversion of protopectin to water-soluble pectin.

The effects of thermal processing on the polyphenolic substances in apple juice have been studied by Skorikova and Lyashenko (1972). At temperatures above 85°C, thermal degradation occurred but at temperatures below 75°C enzymic oxidation took place, with a maximum rate at 45°C. Dimick *et al.* (1951) showed that polyphenol oxidase could be inactivated by heating apple purée for 9 s at 81°C.

List (1969) studied the influence of heat treatment on the nitrogenous constituents of apple juices and found that the concentration of free amino acids generally increased after heating. Some components, in particular γ-aminobutyric acid, ornithine, alanine and glutamic acid, decreased in concentration to an extent which depended on the variety of apple from which the juice was made.

Heating during the dehydration of apple slices causes several physical and chemical changes, viz. shrinkage, loss of nutrients, flavour and colour. The kinetics of water removal and optimisation of drying conditions to minimise browning have been investigated by a number of workers (Saravacos and Charm, 1962; Sykes and Kelly, 1969; Labuza and Simon, 1970). If the natural flavour is to be retained, it is important to avoid decomposition of fructose and loss of volatile acids and esters (Sazena et al., 1956). The darkening of apple slices during drying is related to the ascorbic acid content since enzymic browning will not proceed until all the ascorbic acid has been oxidised. Non-enzymic browning has been studied by Escher and Neukom (1971) as a means of optimising the drying conditions of apple purée. Drying to a final moisture content below 2% is necessary, resulting in poor dryer performance.

During drying it is observed that the acidity of apple tissue decreases owing to the hydrolysis of higher molecular-weight carbohydrates which cause corresponding increases in soluble solids and reducing sugars. Lee et al. (1967) compared the chemical and histological changes occurring during different drying techniques and found significant differences. The average cell-wall thickness was reduced from 1·01 μm for the fresh material to 0·58 μm for a conventionally dried product and 0·93 μm for a freeze-dried product. Ruchkovskii et al. (1975) have emphasised the need to minimise the accumulation of benzopyrene during dehydration by using suitable drying conditions.

Weight losses of apples when stewed, puréed and baked were found to be 6, 8 and 13%, respectively (Pequignot et al., 1975). Changes in the volatile components of apple products have been reported by several workers (Mattick et al., 1958; Nursten and Woolfe, 1972; Brule, 1973; Örsi and Erdös, 1973). The following compounds were formed during heating: furfural, acetyl-2-furan, methyl-2-furan, furfuryl alcohol, acetyl-2-pyrrole, vinyl-4-guaiacol, vinyl-4-phenol and n-octan-1,3-diol. The cooked flavour of the heated juice is considered to be due to n-octan-1,3-diol (Brule, 1973). The furan-type compounds are probably derived from the degradation of sugars and the flavonol glycosides give rise to pentoses and methyl pentoses which in turn would give furfural and 5-methyl-2-furfural. Nursten and Woolfe (1972) also found two aldehydes, *viz.* phenyl acetaldehyde, produced by the Strecker degradation of phenylalanine, and benzaldehyde, which probably originates from amygdalin in the pips. They also found damascenone and the two farnesenes, all of which may have been formed by degradation of precursors (Demole and Berthet, 1971). Another off-flavour component which is formed by the action of heat on apple sauce is *n*-caproic acid, although the source of this compound is not clear (Mattick *et al.*, 1958).

9.2 APRICOT

9.2.1 Structure and Composition
The apricot (*Prunus armeniaca*) is characterised by a pit or stone (highly lignified endocarp), fleshy pulp (mesocarp) and a thin skin (epicarp). The mesocarp consists of parenchyma cells and vascular bundles containing fibres. The cells are generally thick walled giving rise to their typical textural characteristics. The main components are: water, 87%; protein, 0·6%; fat, trace; carbohydrate, 7%; micro-nutrients per 100 g: iron, 0·2 mg; calcium, 17 mg; vitamin A, 2500 IU; thiamine, 0·04 mg; riboflavin, 0·05 mg; niacin, 0·6 mg; and ascorbic acid, 7 mg. The high level of carotenoid pigments, mainly β-carotene, is responsible for the intense orange colour (Curl, 1960). Citric acid is the principal acid present, the other main components being pectic substances and polyphenolic compounds (El-Sayed and Luh, 1965). The main volatile components of fresh apricot were identified by Tang and Jennings (1967) and a subsequent study was devoted to the identification of the lactonic compounds present (Tang and Jennings, 1968).

9.2.2 Effects of Heat
The softening of apricots is a particular problem in the canning industry and is due in part to the action of pectin esterase (PE) and polygalacturonase (PG) (Joux, 1957; Luh *et al.*, 1974). Protopectin is also degraded by heat (Souty and Perret, 1970) and high processing temperatures must be avoided, especially if the acidity of the fruit is high. Pectolytic enzymes derived from fungal infections may also be troublesome since they are relatively heat stable (Paroz *et al.*, 1973).

Thermal destruction of the carotenoid compounds in apricot has been extensively studied (Aczel, 1969, 1971, 1973, 1974; Dalal and Salunkhe, 1964). The rate of loss from canned samples is highly dependent on storage temperature as well as processing temperature. Browning of canned apricots is due partly to Maillard-type reactions involving acid–base catalysed thermal decomposition of reducing sugars as well as breakdown of the anthocyanins by hydrolytic opening of the pyrylium ring with the formation of brown polyphenolic compounds.

Dimick *et al.* (1951) investigated the thermal inactivation of polyphenol oxidase in various fruit purées. They showed that 15 s at 92°C or 60 s at 83°C was sufficient to destroy the enzyme in apricot purée.

Several factors govern the drained-weight behaviour of canned apricots, in particular the filled weight and maturity of the fruit (Luh *et al.*, 1959). Processing time and temperature also affect the rate of diffusion of soluble material and is probably related to protopectin breakdown.

An interesting problem may occur when heat treatment is insufficient to inactivate β-glucosidase contained in the stone. This results in the hydrolysis of amygdalin to produce hydrocyanic acid which may lead to an undesirable flavour in canned whole apricots and is a slight but potential hazard (Hershkovitz and Kanner, 1970; Stoewsand *et al.*, 1975). Intense blue discolourations are also experienced in canned whole apricots due to the complexing of cyanides with ferric ions.

Shelf-life of canned apricots is also affected by temperature. Vitamin C, in particular, is susceptible to rapid destruction at high storage temperatures (Brenner *et al.*, 1948).

Chemical changes occurring during the processing of sun-dried apricot juice have been studied by Salem and Hegazi (1973). Among the essential amino acids, only slight changes were found in the levels of valine, leucine and tyrosine while the concentrations of lysine, arginine and threonine were decreased. Phenylalanine and histidine were most affected, losses being about 40% and 80%, respectively. The decrease in the total amino acid concentration was thought to be due to loss of insoluble proteins which remain in the pomace, as well as to non-enzymic browning during sun drying. Comparative studies using hot-air drying, dehydro-freezing and freeze-drying have been carried out on apricots by Lee *et al.* (1966a). Freeze-drying resulted in the greatest retention of volatile reducing substances and volatile carbonyl compounds, whereas the air-dried samples retained the least. The parenchyma cells of the air-dried product were elongated and shrunk, and cavities had formed owing to release of intercellular gases. The cell walls were also substantially thinner and less continuous owing to dissolution of cell-wall components. Freeze-drying was shown to be the most satisfactory method of preservation since it produced the least thermal damage.

9.3 AVOCADO

9.3.1 Structure and Composition

The avocado or alligator pear (*Persea americana*) is a large berry consisting of a single carpel and seed. The fruit tissue (pericarp) is composed of a thick rind (exocarp), an edible portion (mesocarp) and a thin layer next to the seed coat (endocarp). The avocado has a composition rather uncharacteristic of a fruit and has a high nutritive value. Its composition is very variable but typical values are as follows: carbohydrate, 5%; protein, 2%; fat, 17–20% (but can vary from 4–32%); micronutrients per 100 g: iron, 1 mg; calcium, 15 mg; vitamin A, 200 IU; thiamine, 0·1 mg; riboflavin, 0·15 mg; niacin, 1·9 mg; pantothenic acid, 1 mg; pyridoxine, 0·45 mg; and ascorbic acid, 16 mg. The carbohydrates are atypical of fruits and the following have been identified: perseitol (D-glycero-D-galacto-heptitol), D-manno-heptulose, D-glycero-D-manno-octulose, D-erythro-D-galacto-octitol, D-talo-heptulose, D-glycero-D-galacto-heptose, D-glycero-L-galacto-octulose, D-erythro-L-gluco-nonulose and D-erythro-L-galacto-nonulose. The principal amino acids are asparagine, aspartic acid, glutamine and glutamic acid. The fat content is particularly high, especially the edible portion which is rich in oleic, palmitic, linoleic and palmitoleic triglycerides. Although the avocado is rather deficient in vitamins A and C, it is a rich source of the vitamin B group.

During the ripening process there is a rapid decrease in protopectin with a concomitant increase in water-soluble pectins and a softening of texture. The biochemical changes associated with ripening and growth have been discussed in an excellent review by Biale and Young (1971).

9.3.2 Effects of Heat

The occurrence of off-flavours and particularly the development of an objectionable bitter taste during heating are the main factors limiting the preservation of the avocado. If these problems could be overcome, the potential utilisation of avocado products would be greatly increased.

Immature avocado fruits also possess an unpleasant flavour. The main components in this case appear to be three long-chain C_{17} compounds, 4-keto-2-hydroxyl-1-acetate, a 1,2-dihydroxy-4-acetoxy compound and a 1,4-dihydroxy-2-acetoxy compound, each with a terminal acetylenic bond (Kashman, 1969).

The problem of off-flavour and bitterness induced by heat has received attention from several workers (Cruess *et al.*, 1951; Bates, 1970; Brown, 1972; Ben-Et *et al.*, 1973; Garcia *et al.*, 1975). Compounds reported to be involved include 1-acetoxy-2,4-dihydroxy-*n*-heptadeca-16-ene and 1,2,4-trihydroxy-*n*-heptadeca-16-ene (Ben-Et *et al.*, 1973). Garcia *et al.* (1975) investigated the effect of time and temperature of heating on the detection of off-flavour in avocado paste. The z-value obtained (24–26) was similar to typical z-values of spoilage organisms, which means that it would be difficult to design a heating process which would destroy these organisms without producing off-flavours.

9.4 BANANA

9.4.1 Structure and Composition

The banana is the fruit of the plant *Musa sapientum* which grows under tropical and sub-tropical conditions. The fully ripe fruit is elongated and red or yellow in colour. The skin (mesocarp) is thick and soft and covers the firm edible tissue. The main constituents are: water, 71%; protein, 1·1%; fat, trace; carbohydrate, 19·2%; micronutrients per 100 g: iron, 0·4 mg; calcium, 7 mg; vitamin A, 300 IU; thiamine 0·04 mg; riboflavin, 0·07 mg; niacin, 0·6 mg; and ascorbic acid, 10 mg. During the post-harvest ripening period, starch is hydrolysed and sugars accumulate. Normally, green fruit contains 1–2% sugars, mainly sucrose, glucose and fructose, and this increases to about 20% when the fruit is fully ripe. During the ripening phase, the flesh becomes softer owing to interconversion of pectic substances, pectin methyl esterase being the main enzyme system involved. The banana fruit contains at least 200 individual volatile compounds, the most important being isoamyl acetate, amyl acetate, amyl propionate and amyl butyrate (Hultin and Proctor, 1961). The precursors of these compounds are probably the leucines. When the surface of the banana or the macerate is exposed to the air for any length of time it rapidly darkens owing to oxidative reactions involving polyphenol oxidase and the conversion of tyrosine to dopamine, 2-(3,4-dihydroxyphenyl)ethylamine. Ascorbic acid is readily lost when the fruit is comminuted in air (Palmer, 1971).

9.4.2 Effects of Heat

Banana has a pH of about 4·5, which means that a long heat process is required to ensure commercial sterility. This would impair the flavour and lead to discolouration. Consequently, the product is usually acidified prior to canning. One of the most successful methods of processing the purée is to use a relatively high temperature and short time in conjunction with aseptic filling.

Two types of discolouration are found in processed banana products: the first is oxidative browning (see above) which may be eliminated by blanching (Guyer and Erickson, 1954); and the second is a pink discolouration owing to breakdown of leucoanthocyanins (Ranganna and Parpia, 1974a,b; Agarwal et al., 1963), which is less noticeable in banana purée if it is acidified to pH 4·2 before retorting (Guyer and Erikson, 1954).

The pink discolouration is primarily a function of the extent of heating, which determines the intensity of colour produced. The conversion of colourless leucoanthocyanins to coloured anthocyanins has been suggested to be an acid-catalysed dehydration to flavan-3-ene followed by oxidation. One of the problems encountered in studying the chromogen is that it is present in a water-soluble form immediately after processing but shortly afterwards becomes insoluble. Ranganna and Parpia (1974b) concluded that the phenomenon was primarily a polymerisation effect accelerated by heat and acid and not involving tin. The presence of tin, however, could result in the formation of an insoluble white precipitate which changes to red on heating. Other flavonoid components may cause yellow to brownish-red discolourations. A similar problem arises with canned apples and pears (loc. cit.).

9.5 BLACKCURRANT

9.5.1 Structure and Composition

The blackcurrant is the fruit of the bush *Ribes nigra*. It is a small berry which grows on short stems known as 'strigs'. The composition of the fruit is: water, 77%; protein, 0·9%; fat, trace; carbohydrate, 6·6%; micronutrients per 100 g: iron, 1·3 mg; calcium, 60 mg; vitamin A, 300 IU; thiamine, 0·03 mg; riboflavin, 0·06 mg; niacin, 0·25 mg; and ascorbic acid, 200 mg. The fruit is of special interest because of its high content of vitamin C and it is mainly processed as a juice concentrate.

9.5.2 Effects of Heat

Nursten and Williams (1969a,b) have identified about 150 individual compounds in a commercial blackcurrant concentrate and compared these with the components of the fresh fruit. 2-Methylbut-3-ene-2-ol, which has a pungent odour, and other C_5 alcohols were thought to be produced by thermal degradation of terpenes. Swedish workers (Andersson and von Sydow, 1964, 1966; von Sydow and Karlsson, 1971a,b; Karlsson-Ekström and von Sydow, 1973) have also studied the effects of heating on blackcurrant aroma. The main changes were the formation of furan derivatives and an increase in dimethylsulphide, ethanol, propanal, 2-methylpropanal and 2-methylbutanal. There was some rearrangement of the monoterpenes, and caryophythene, which is present in large amounts, decreased considerably on heating.

Blackcurrants are mainly utilised in the form of a pure or blended fruit juice and marketed as a rich source of vitamin C. Consequently, it is important that the content of the vitamin is maintained as high as possible. Some data indicating the chemical composition of raw berries and various types of juice are given by Charley (1970).

9.6   CHERRY

9.6.1   Structure and Composition

The cherry is a fruit of the *Prunus* species and two types are important—the sweet cherry (*Prunus arium*) and sour cherry (*Prunus cerasus*), consisting of two groups—dark fruit (morellos) and light fruit (amarelles). The fruit is small with a globular stone. The composition of the edible portion is: water, 71%; protein, 1·0%; fat, 0·4%; micronutrients per 100 g: iron, 0·4 mg; calcium, 16 mg; vitamin A, 570 IU; thiamine, 0·05 mg; riboflavin, 0·05 mg; niacin, 0·4 mg; and ascorbic acid, 7 mg. During the ripening period, acid content decreases and reducing sugars increase markedly. The most important constituents in relation to acceptability are the polyphenols and pectins (Romani and Jennings, 1971).

9.6.2 Effects of Heat

Heat affects the colour of processed cherries in two ways: it may actually degrade the pigments and it may also induce their migration from the dark skin into the flesh and syrup.

Chytra *et al.* (1962) have studied the effect of thermal processing on the stability of cherries and concluded that the main factor involved in degradation of the anthocyanins is oxygen, the reaction being accelerated by heat. Ruskov and Tanchev (1973) also studied anthocyanin degradation over a range of temperatures and pH values.

Anthocyanins are also degraded by enzyme constituents (Siegel *et al.*, 1971) and, consequently, a blanching treatment sufficient to destroy enzymes enhances the stability of these pigments. Fung and Yankov (1970) investigated the inactivation of polyphenol oxidases in canning. Dastur *et al.* (1968) determined the effectiveness of various heat-processing procedures using peroxidase and three yeast strains as indicators. Heating times required ranged from 1·4 min in the Steritort for water-packed cherries, to 3·4 min for syrup-packed cherries at 200°F in the still retort.

Ingalsbe *et al.* (1965) found that the absorbance of an alcoholic hydrochloric acid extract of cherry anthocyanins at 515 nm could be used as an index for predicting the depth of colour in processed products. These pigments are released on heating and migrate into the flesh and syrup resulting in a lighter coloured product than might be expected from the external appearance of the raw fruit. Ammerman (1957) showed that the colour loss was very dependent on processing temperature.

Dalal and Salunkhe (1964) studied the effects of storage temperatures up to 40°C and found that higher temperatures resulted in the most degradation of pigment, highest loss of pectin, and greatest gain in acidity and total and free reducing sugars. The loss in pectin was thought to be due to conversion of protopectin to water-soluble pectin, resulting in softening of the product.

The breakdown mechanism involved in the degradation of the pigments is not clearly understood. Hydrolytic fissure of the pyrylium ring with the formation of brown insoluble polyphenolic compounds is a possibility. However, oxidation reactions are most likely involved together with polymerisation and hydrolysis to give insoluble red–brown, as well as soluble brown, products.

Mahdi *et al.* (1959) showed that a major off-flavour component formed during heating and subsequent storage of canned cherries was pyrrolidone carboxylic acid. The amount of this compound produced was stoichiometrically related to the decrease in glutamine.

$$H_2C\text{------}CH_2 \qquad\qquad H_2C\text{------}CH_2$$
$$O{=}C \quad HCNH_2 \longrightarrow O{=}C \quad HC\text{---}COOH + NH_3$$
$$H_2N \quad\; COOH \qquad\qquad\quad N$$
$$\qquad\qquad\qquad\qquad\qquad\qquad H$$

glutamine   pyrrolidone carboxylic acid

The heating process may also firm the texture of canned cherries, which is particularly desirable if they are destined for pie-making. Pectin methylesterase causes demethylation of esterified carboxyl groups of the pectin (LaBelle and Moyer, 1960; LaBelle, 1971; van Buren, 1974). A small amount of demethylation which may occur prior to retorting can lead to increased firmness of the canned product, probably due to crosslinking of the partially demethylated molecules in the presence of naturally occurring calcium salts (Buch *et al.*, 1961).

Like other stone fruit, when inadequately heated, canned cherries develop hydrocyanic acid on storage owing to enzymatic degradation of amygdalin in the pits (Stoewsand and Anderson, 1973). The benzopyrene content of dried cherries has been studied by Ruchkovskii *et al.* (1975).

9.7 GRAPEFRUIT

9.7.1 Structure and Composition

The grapefruit is the fruit of the tree *Citrus maxima*. It is yellow in colour, similar to the lemon, and globular in shape. It consists of up to 14 carpel segments contained in a thick rind which is divided into two parts, the oil-bearing outer skin (flavedo), and the inner, spongy part (albedo). The approximate composition is: water, 91%; protein, 0·4%; fat, 0·1%; micronutrients per 100 g: calcium, 15 mg; iron, 0·3 mg; vitamin A, 10 IU; thiamine, 0·03 mg; riboflavin, 0·01 mg; niacin, 0·2 mg; and ascorbic acid, 28 mg. Some varieties are highly pigmented due to the presence of lycopene. The principal acidic component is citric acid but several other acids are also present, in particular malic, oxalic and malonic acids. The flavour of grapefruit juice is due principally to a sesquiterpene, nootkatone, although many other volatile compounds are present. The main terpene hydrocarbon found in the flavedo is (+)-limonene. A particularly important component is the bitter-tasting flavonoid naringin, which is a rhamnoglucoside of the aglycone, naringenin, where X is the neohesperidosyl group $(1 \rightarrow 2$-linked rhamnose and glucose molecules)

naringenin

Biochemical changes during growth and storage have been discussed at length by Ting and Attaway (1971). Kefford (1959) and Kefford and Chandler (1970) give more detailed information concerning the composition of grapefruit.

9.7.2 Effects of Heat

Most of the information concerning the effect of heat on grapefruit is derived from the experience of the canning industry, the main products being canned segments and juice (Blundstone *et al.*, 1971). The degree of bitterness depends very much on the amount of albedo or pith remaining on the segments and, during commercial juice production, it is often necessary to de-bitter using absorption techniques and enzymatic hydrolysis to naringin or prunin. The bitter principle often crystallises out from the segments and juice during cooling and storage of the canned products, resulting in either a cloudy liquor or the formation of large globular crystals.

The major quality characteristics of grapefruit segments are related to the drained weight and texture (Bakal and Mannheim, 1968; Ludin *et al.*, 1969; Levi *et al.*, 1969; Kopelmann, 1975). The disintegration of segments as a result of heating during the canning process has been discussed by Basker (1965, 1967). Addition of calcium chloride reduces the extent of distintegration but also lowers the drained weight of the product (Levi *et al.*, 1969).

An excellent account of the chemistry and technology of grapefruit juice has been given by Veldhuis (1971a). One of the main problems in the pasteurisation of the highly acid juice is that, unless the pectic enzymes are destroyed, the cloudy or milky appearance of the juice is lost. This is due to the action of pectin esterase converting the pectin into pectinic acid which precipitates leaving a clear supernatant liquid. Flash pasteurisation, using a relatively high-temperature–short-time process is now used extensively and this leads to an improvement in cloud stability compared to in-can sterilisation.

Kirchner *et al.* (1953) have studied the changes in the chemical constituents of grapefruit juice after processing and storage. Table 9.2 gives a summary of their results for the volatile water-soluble constituents of fresh, freshly canned and stored canned grapefruit juice, revealing that quite significant changes occur, particularly on storage. The two acids designated A and B were not identified although it was established that they were both unsaturated and had an empirical formula $C_6H_8O_2$. A similar investigation was carried out by Kirchner and Miller (1953) on the volatile oil constituents. The following compounds were found in all three juices: d-limonene, β-caryophyllene, α-caryophyllene, α-pinene, caryophyllene oxide, citral, carvone, linalool, carveol, α-terpineol, linalool monoxide and a number of unidentified but related compounds. The changes in the stored canned juice were qualitatively similar to those in the freshly canned juice but were generally greater in magnitude. The most significant changes

TABLE 9.2

VOLATILE WATER-SOLUBLE CONSTITUENTS OF GRAPEFRUIT JUICE. (FROM KIRCHNER *et al.*, 1953)

Constituent	Fresh juice (mg/kg)	Freshly canned juice (mg/kg)	Stored canned juice (mg/kg)
Acetaldehyde	1·45	0·33	0·60
Acetone	0	0	0·10
Furfural	0	trace	8·2
Ethanol	400	400	460
Methanol	0·2	0·2	23
Acetic acid	0	1·9	23·3
Acid A[a]	0	4·8	2·9
Acid B[a]	0	1·9	1·6

[a]Unidentified, but found to be unsaturated with an empirical formula of $C_6H_8O_2$.

were a decrease in limonene, probably giving linalool monoxide and
α-terpineol, and an increase in furfural arising from decomposition of
sugars. The sesquiterpene, β-caryophyllene, also decreased on
processing and was thought to break down to give a $C_{15}H_{26}O$ alcohol
and a $C_{15}H_{26}O$ ketone. These chemical changes must be in part
responsible for the cooked flavour which develops during processing
and the off-flavour which results from storage of the canned product.

Grapefruit juice only contains small quantities of carotenoids,
resulting in a pale yellow colour and thus, as with lemon juice (loc.
cit.), any occurrence of non-enzymic browning is particularly
objectionable.

9.8 GUAVA

9.8.1 Structure and Composition

The guava (*Psidium guajava*) is a tropical fruit grown mainly in
South Africa, India and Central and South America. It is a luscious
fruit eaten out of hand, preserved after the removal of the seeds and
also made into jelly. It has a thick rind with a central placenta
containing seeds. It varies considerably in size, shape and colour
(green, white, yellow or pink). The approximate composition is:
water, 80%; protein, 1%; fat, 0·4%; carbohydrate, 13%; micronutrients per 100 g: iron, 1 mg; vitamin A, 200 IU; thiamine, 0·05 mg;
riboflavin, 0·04 mg; niacin, 1·0 mg; and ascorbic acid, 200–300 mg. The
acids present are mainly citric and malic acids and the major carotenoids are α- and β-carotene. The content of vitamin C is probably
greater on average than blackcurrants and only the acerola (West
Indian cherry) is a richer source of this vitamin.

The major volatile constituents have been identified by Stevens *et
al.* (1970) and Torline and Ballschmieter (1973). The predominant
compounds were found to be *cis*-3-hexene-1-ol, hexanol and hexanal.
The most characteristic flavour compared was β-ionone.

9.8.2 Effects of Heat

Luh (1971) has described the technology of purée and nectar production. The pH varies from 3·0 to 3·5 and, therefore, only mild heat
processes are required for preservation. Flash pasteurisation has
proved to be a very effective technique and is less damaging to the
flavour compared to conventional batch processes. Muralikrishna *et
al.* (1968) have studied the physicochemical changes which accom-

pany thermal concentration of guava in a vacuum evaporator. They found that the vitamin C content measured as ascorbic acid mg/°Brix was constant throughout the process (see also Pruthi *et al.*, 1955). The loss of flavour was very marked at the higher degrees of concentration and it was found that the optimum concentration was 65–66°Brix. Sanchez Nieva *et al.* (1970) heated guava nectar base to various temperatures between 80 and 102°C and determined pH, total acidity, total and reducing sugars, vitamin C and colour. There was very little change in composition or quality although 2–12% of the vitamin C was destroyed. Ranganna (1974) has discussed the pink discolouration which occurs in the canned products.

9.9   JACK FRUIT

9.9.1   Structure and Composition
The Jack or Jak Fruit is a tropical fruit which grows from the large branches and trunk of the *Artocarpus integrifolia* tree. It is probably the largest of fruits grown (individual fruits may weigh as much as 15 kg) and most of the interest in its utilisation has originated from India. Both the pulp and seeds are eaten. The approximate composition of the pulp, according to Pruthi *et al.* (1955), is: total solids, 22·8%; reducing sugars, 6·1%; total sugars, 15·9%; carotene, 0·13 mg/100 g; protein, 0·44% micronutrients per 100 g: calcium, 35·1 mg; iron 1·01 mg; phosphorus, 14·8 mg; vitamin A, 400 IU; thiamine, 0·1 mg; niacin, 0·4 mg; and ascorbic acid, 10 mg. The main sugars are sucrose, glucose and fructose with some maltose (Bhatia *et al.*, 1955a).

9.9.2   Effects of Heat
The effects of processing operations on the nutritive value of canned Jack fruit have been studied by Pruthi *et al.* (1955). The retention of ascorbic acid, of which the fruit has very little, was found to be about 90%. Sugar content increased owing to diffusion from syrup to fruit. Physicochemical changes on canning result in considerable inversion of the sugars during subsequent storage at 37°C (Bhatia *et al.*, 1956).

The texture of canned Jack fruit is soft but firm. It is, however, dependent upon the maturity of the raw product and when thick, crisp flesh is canned there is a tendency for the product to be fibrous (Bhatia *et al.*, 1955b).

9.10 LEMON

9.10.1 Structure and Composition

The lemon is the fruit of the tree *Citrus limon*, also known by the varietal name *Citrus medica* var. *limonum*. It is a small fruit with a hard skin which is usually yellow in colour. Its structure is very similar to that of other citrus fruits except that it is elongated rather than spherical in shape. The approximate composition is: water, 85%; protein, 0·5%; fat, 0·3%; micronutrients per 100 g: calcium, 25 mg; iron, 0·4 mg; vitamin A, trace; thiamine, 0·02 mg; riboflavin, trace; niacin, 0·1 mg; and ascorbic acid, 31 mg. The peel is rich in terpenes, particularly limonene. Kefford (1959) and Kefford and Chandler (1970) give further details of the components of lemon.

9.10.2 Effects of Heat

Lemon is normally processed only as juice and not as segments (Swisher and Swisher, 1971). Problems of enzyme inactivation during pasteurisation are very similar to those encountered with grapefruit juice. In order to ensure stability of the cloud, it is necessary to heat the juice to between 69° and 74°C. Nowadays, flash pasteurisation at 77°C with a 30-s holding time is commonly used commercially. To prevent quality loss it is essential to cool the heated juice rapidly and for the same purpose it is also advisable to deaerate before heating.

A major problem with processed lemon juice, particularly since it has a very pale colour, is the development of browning during processing and especially during storage. Clegg (1964) and Clegg and Morton (1965) consider that the α,β-unsaturated carbonyls, formed by decomposition of ascorbic acid, react with amino acids to produce the brown colour. The physicochemical changes in lemon concentrate have also been studied by Pruthi (1959a) who observed a progressive darkening during processing as well as a decrease in pH from 2·43 to 1·87.

9.11 MANGO

9.11.1 Structure and Composition

The mango is the fruit of the *Mangifera indica* tree which is grown widely on the Indian sub-continent and in other tropical countries. The fruit is similar in shape to a large plum, containing a stone (endocarp) surrounded by the fruit flesh (mesocarp) which is firm and sweet. It varies in size from 6 to 12 cm in diameter. The approximate composition is: water, 83%; carbohydrate, 14%; vitamin A, 1000–8000 IU/100 g and ascorbic acid, 30 mg/100 g. The main acid constituent is citric acid although glycolic, oxalic, malic and tartaric acids are also present. The amino acids which have been identified are aspartic acid, glutamic acid, alanine, glycine, serine and α-aminobutyric acid. Further details on the composition of the mango are given by Hulme (1971b).

9.11.2 Effects of Heat

Mango slices, pulp and nectar are canned or bottled. The main difficulty when canning slices is to prevent softening, which can be achieved to some extent by adding firming agents such as calcium chloride and calcium lactate (Ahmad and Rahman, 1968a,b). The effects of various heat treatments and packaging conditions on sliced mangoes in syrup have been examined by de Martin et al. (1971/1972, 1973) who found wide differences in texture and colour depending on the process employed. Depending on variety, the pH may vary from about 3·4 to 4·7 and a pasteurisation process in boiling water is normally sufficient to achieve microbiological stability. Siddappa and Bhatia (1956a,b) found that processing did not greatly affect the β-carotene or ascorbic acid content of canned slices, although the ascorbic acid was destroyed rapidly on storage. Dehydro-canning has been shown to be an effective method of improving the textural properties of canned mango (Mathur et al., 1973).

Karim and Riaz-Ur-Rehman (1970a,b) have studied the effect of heat processing on the quality of canned mango pulp. Acidity (as citric acid) increased from 0·959–0·985% in the fresh fruit to 1·209–1·254% after canning, and ascorbic acid decreased from 22–24 mg/100 g to 12–14 mg/100 g after storage for 195 days. Pectin fractions were also determined (in terms of percent anhydrogalacturonic acid) and it was found that the water-soluble and ammonium oxalate-soluble fractions both increased during heat processing and storage, the increase being greatest in the pulp which was pre-heated and then processed for 15 min at 100°C. Total pectin and alkali-soluble pectin both decreased after canning and storage. Ranganna and Siddappa (1961) have pointed out that colour deterioration of canned mango pulp may be caused by cis–trans isomerisation of carotenoids.

Siddappa et al. (1965) have determined the effect of drying method

TABLE 9.3
EFFECT OF DRYING METHOD ON RETENTION OF SOME MANGO CONSTI-
TUENTS. (FROM SIDDAPPA *et al.*, 1965)

Drying method	Retention (%)					
	ascorbic acid		β-carotene		total carotenoids	
	canned pulp	sulphited pulp	canned pulp	sulphited pulp	canned pulp	sulphited pulp
Freeze-drying	88·20	96·56	94·97	96·56	102·10	103·70
Spray-drying	77·05	63·54	103·40	98·26	101·90	105·40
Drum-drying	86·44	–	96·92	–	97·95	–

on the retention of ascorbic acid, β-carotene and total carotenoids of canned and sulphited pulp. Their results are summarised in Table 9.3. Only ascorbic acid suffered an appreciable loss, the lowest retention being recorded for the spray-dried material. Further details of the chemistry and technology of mango processing may be obtained from Leverington (1957), Jain (1961) and Brekke *et al.* (1968a).

9.12 MELON

9.12.1 Structure and Composition

The two main genera of melons which are eaten as dessert fruit are muskmelon (*Cucumis*) and watermelon (*Citrullus*). They may vary in shape from spherical to oblong or oblate, the edible flesh being derived from the pericarp. The flesh varies in colour from green to yellow or even red and the approximate composition is: water, 90%; protein, 1%; fat, 0·1%; total sugars, 7%; micronutrients per 100 g: calcium, 10 mg; iron, 0·4 mg; potassium, 330 mg; sodium, 20 mg; vitamin A, 4200 IU; thiamine, 0·06 mg; riboflavin, 0·02 mg; niacin, 0·9 mg; and ascorbic acid, 25 mg. The predominant pigment giving rise to the colour of the orange-fleshed muskmelon is β-carotene and the red colour of other varieties is due to lycopene. The chemical and physical aspects of muskmelon in relation to texture have been studied by Dinus and Mackey (1974). Results indicated that the texture is determined largely by the type and amount of cell-wall constituents. Some of the volatile components have been identified by

Kemp (1972). A series of alcohols and aldehydes, each containing nine carbon atoms, appears to be characteristic of this fruit. Further information on the composition and characteristics of muskmelon are given by Bindra (1973).

9.12.2 Effects of Heat

Muskmelon may be processed as slices or cubes in syrup. The product is much softer than the raw fruit and flavour is often impaired. Cutin and Samish (1958) studied the composition of a number of varieties of melon before and after canning. The pH of the fruit varied from 4·4 to 4·8 and an acidified syrup was used to allow the application of a milder heat treatment. The ascorbic acid content was reduced from 16–29 mg/100 g to 12–20 mg/100 g by processing. Siddappa and Bhatia (1958) have also studied the canning of musk-melon together with other fruits. More detailed information on the effects of canning Indian varieties has been given by Rao et al. (1968). The main difficulty was in obtaining a product of acceptable texture and only one variety of the nine tested was suitable.

9.13 ORANGE

9.13.1 Structure and Composition

The orange is the fruit of the tree *Citrus sinensis*. The edible portion is referred to as the endocarp and consists of a series of segments, carpels or loculs which contain the thin-walled juice vesicles. Surrounding the endocarp is the peel, which comprises 20–50% of the weight of the fruit and consists of the flavedo and albedo. The flavedo, or outer peel, is a layer of tissue underlying the epidermis and contains the chromoplasts and oil sacs. The albedo, or inner peel, is a layer of spongy white tissue which is connected to the core and supplies the water and nutrients from the tree which are necessary for fruit growth and development.

The approximate composition of the edible portion is: water, 86%; protein 0·6%; fat, 0·1%; micronutrients per 100 g: calcium, 24 mg; iron, 0·3 mg; vitamin A, 120 IU; thiamine, 0·06 mg; riboflavin, 0·02 mg; niacin, 0·1 mg; and ascorbic acid, 36 mg. The detailed chemistry and composition of citrus fruits has been reviewed by Kefford (1959) and Kefford and Chandler (1970). The pH of the orange is around 3·5, which is higher than lemon and grapefruit, and consequently more acceptable to the palate. The main enzyme system is a methyl esterase which hydrolyses polygalacturonic acid poly-methyl esters. The principal pigments which develop on ripening are carotenoids, mainly xanthophyll 5,6- and 5,8-epoxides. Blood oranges are coloured by the presence of cyanidin-3-glucoside and delphinidin-3-glucoside. The major volatile components of whole oranges are d-limonene, β-myrcene, α-pinene, acetaldehyde, octanal, ethanol and ethyl acetate.

9.13.2 Effects of Heat

The preservation of orange products is mainly carried out by canning the segments (mandarin), canning, bottling or freezing the juice or comminuted fruit, and by drying the juice to give a powder. The main objectives in all juice-preservation methods is to obtain a stable product which is a rich source of vitamin C and has a full orange flavour.

Heat treatment of orange juice is essential in order to inhibit the enzyme pectin esterase and prevent precipitation of the cloud. The cooked flavour of heat-treated orange juice, as well as other fruit juices and products, is probably due to losses of volatiles, thus exposing masked flavours, rather than chemical changes (Pollard and Timberlake, 1971).

Despite the fact that huge quantities of orange juice are processed, relatively little attention has been given to the effects of heat on chemical changes. Blundstone et al. (1971) have reviewed the available literature on the chemistry of canned citrus products. The main deteriorative effects of high temperature are those encountered during storage, although the chemical changes have not been considered in detail. Losses of vitamin C on processing have been attributed to oxidation and anaerobic destruction which are influenced by pH and the level of oxygen in the headspace. Immediately after processing, however, retention of vitamin C is generally at least 90% and it is only during storage that marked changes take place, particularly at higher temperatures. Maleki and Sarkissian (1967) have measured changes in the composition of canned orange juice during storage. Non-enzymic browning reactions are also accelerated by high storage temperatures.

Veldhuis (1971b) has given an excellent account of the technology involved in the processing of orange and tangerine juices. A product which crystallised in the juice evaporators was found to be the flavonone glycoside, hesperidin. This compound may also cause cloudiness leading to white crystalline deposits in some canned orange products and can be prevented by the addition of hesperidinase (Shimoda *et al.*, 1968).

Many attempts have been made in the past to produce a stable orange powder. Apart from its hygroscopic character, the main problem encountered is non-enzymic browning, particularly during storage, and the off-flavour associated with this phenomenon. Berry and Tatum (1965) studied the formation of 5-hydroxymethylfurfural in stored foam-mat dried orange powder and orange concentrate. Acid degradation of sugars was considered to be one of the main routes for the formation of these compounds. Shaw *et al.* (1970) and Tatum *et al.* (1967) identified eighteen components which contribute to the off-flavour of stored orange powder. These are shown in Table 9.4. In later work, compound 18, which is referred to by its empirical formula in Table 9.4, is reported to be 2,3-dihydro-3,5-dihydroxy-6-methyl-4H-pyran-4-one (Shaw *et al.*, 1977). These workers also estimated the taste thresholds of these compounds and compared them

TABLE 9.4

SOME COMPOUNDS IDENTIFIED IN STORED ORANGE POWDER. (FROM SHAW *et al.*, 1970)

Compound	Flavour contribution
1. N-Ethylpyrrole-2-carboxaldehyde	burned
2. Methylcyclopentenolone	burned
3. 5-Methyl-2-furfural	burned
4. 4-Hydroxy-2,3,5-hexanetrione	bitter
5. 3-Hydroxy-2-pyrone	burned
6. Furfuryl alcohol	sour
7. Tiglic acid	burned
8. Furfural	burned
9. Benzoic acid	burned
10. Acetic acid	sour
11. Levulinic acid	burned
12. 2-Methyl-2-carboxaldehyde	burned
13. 2-Acetylfuran	burned
14. 2-Acetylpyrrole	burned
15. 2-Hydroxyacetylfuran	–
16. 5-Hydroxymethylfurfural	–
17. γ-Butyrolactone	–
18. $C_6H_8O_4$ (empirical formula)[a]	bitter

[a]Reported by Shaw *et al.* (1977) to be 2,3-dihydro-3,5-dihydroxy-6-methyl-4H-pyran-4-one.

with the actual amounts present in instant orange-juice products. Most of the significant work relating to the browning of orange-juice systems is also summarised in this paper.

Siddappa *et al.* (1956) have followed the changes in ascorbic acid content of orange juice during concentration and drying. The retention of vitamin C was between 85 and 90% during concentration to 72° Brix but losses were very rapid on storage at 24–30°C. Vacuum shelf-drying resulted in a loss of 31·3–57·4% but complete destruction was found when air-drying was employed.

9.14 PAPAYA

9.14.1 Structure and Composition

The papaya or pawpaw is the fruit of the tree *Carica papaya*. It has a structure similar to that of the melon and is a green or yellow colour on the outside with a golden-yellow or orange-coloured pulp. The general composition is: water, 89%; carbohydrate, 9%; protein, 0·5%; micronutrients per 100 g; calcium, 0·01 mg; iron, 4 mg; vitamin A, 2500 IU; and ascorbic acid, 80 mg. It is an important source of the enzyme papain, which is used as a meat tenderiser, and is also rich in pectin. The major carotenoid pigments are zeaxanthin, cryptoxanthin and β-carotene (Yamamoto, 1964).

9.14.2 Effects of Heat

The technology of manufacture of papaya products is well established and a large number of products have been reported (Anon, 1963; Stafford *et al.*, 1966; Brekke *et al.*, 1968b).

Enzyme inactivation by heating is necessary to prevent off-flavour development (Chan *et al.*, 1972) as well as gelation (Aung and Ross, 1965). Unfortunately, only a limited heat treatment is possible because of the delicate flavour and it appears that it is even difficult to satisfactorily destroy all the pectin esterase by heat processing the acid purée in containers using rotation (Aung and Ross, 1965). Off-flavours are due to components of the skin or pips, probably benzyl isothiocyanate and hydrogen sulphide produced by enzymatic hydrolysis of benzyl glucosinolate by myrosinase (Tang, 1970a,b).

Siddappa and Bhatia (1956a) studied the effect of canning on the β-carotene content of papaya and found that, after storage at 25–30°C for 12 months, the retention was 52%. Later work by Chan (1975) showed changes in the carotenoid composition of processed purée although the nutritional significance of these changes was not known. Only a small loss of ascorbic acid accompanied purée manufacture.

9.15 PASSION-FRUIT (GRANADILLA)

9.15.1 Structure and Composition

The passion-fruit (*Passiflora* spp.) is a native of Brazil, but is now grown widely throughout the tropical and sub-tropical areas of the world. The main varieties are *P. edulis* (purple passion-fruit), *P. edulis* var. *flavicarpa* (yellow passion-fruit) and *P. laurifolia* and *P. quadiagulasis*, which are the largest of the genus but have a less distinctive flavour. The passion-fruit is a medium-sized oval fruit between 2–3 inches long. A brittle shell encloses a juicy yellow pulp which contains the seeds.

The approximate composition of the passion-fruit is: water, 73%; carbohydrate, 16%; protein, 1·2%; fat, trace; micronutrients per 100 g: calcium, 16 mg; iron, 1·1 mg; vitamin A, 200 IU; and vitamin C, 20 mg. Luh (1971) gives details of the composition of Indian, Hawaiian and Australian varieties. The distinctive orange–yellow colour is due to a mixture of carotenoid pigments including phytofluene, α-carotene, β-carotene and ζ-(zeta)-carotene (Pruthi and Lal, 1958). Aroma components are numerous, the main constituents being ethyl butanoate, ethyl hexanate, a 'tetramethyl benzpyran' compound, ethyl acetate, heptan-2-one and hexyl acetate (Parliament, 1972; Marray *et al.*, 1973). Pruthi (1963) has reviewed the physiology, chemistry and technology of passion-fruit.

9.15.2 Effects of Heat

Passion-fruit is mainly processed as either the juice or pulp but the distinctive aroma and flavour are very sensitive to heat treatment (Huet, 1973; Murray, 1972; Murray *et al.*, 1972; Parliament, 1972). High-temperature–short-time processes are generally favoured and spin processing is recommended (Pruthi, 1959a,b; Seale and Sherman, 1960). Only small losses of ascorbic acid (2–3·5%) were noted during processing and similar losses of carotene were found during pasteurisation. However, considerable losses were found on storage, the extent being very dependent on storage time and temperature. Aung and Ross (1965) studied the thermal destruction of catalase in passion-fruit juice and demonstrated that pasteurisation at 80°C for just over two minutes was sufficient to inactivate the enzyme.

Passion-fruit juice has a high content of starch which gelatinises, resulting in a very viscous syrup. This causes heat transfer problems in heat exchangers and, consequently, spin pasteurisation has been developed as an in-can technique (Pruthi, 1963).

9.16 PEACH

9.16.1 Structure and Composition

The peach is the fruit of the tree *Prunus persica*. The main varieties are classed commercially as freestone or clingstone according to whether their flesh colour is white or yellow. The fruit is velvety on the outside, white to deep yellow, often with a deep red colour and has white to yellow flesh with a central stone. The general composition is: water, 78·5%; acids, 0·57%; reducing sugars, 3·4% sucrose, 5·6%; protein, 0·6%; micronutrients per 100 g: calcium, 5 mg; iron, 0·4 mg; thiamine, 0·02 mg; riboflavin, 0·05 mg; niacin, 1·0 mg; and ascorbic acid, 10 mg. The pH of the fruit varies from 3·68 to 4·07. The important flavour constituents are the γ-octalactones, deca- and dodeca-lactones (Molina *et al.*, 1973), as well as many other compounds including linalool, acetic acid, isovaleric acid, caprylic acid, acetaldehyde, furfural, isoamyl acetate and hexyl acetate (Luh, 1971).

9.16.2 Effects of Heat

The main method of preserving peaches is by canning, although they are also dried to a large extent.

Discolouration of canned freestone peaches is often a problem (Luh *et al.*, 1965; Luh and Kanujoso, 1966; Seelenberger and Luh, 1971; Chung and Luh, 1972). Peaches with a high concentration of red pigment at the pit cavity tend to discolour on the surface. Immediately after canning, the syrup colour changes to pink or violet owing to the dissolution of cyanidin-3-monoglucoside (Hsia *et al.*, 1965a,b) and formation of complexes with stannous ions. During storage the pigment tends to turn brown.

Clingstone peaches are susceptible to enzymic browning owing to polyphenoloxidase activity (Luh *et al.*, 1967; Luh and Phithakpol, 1972). It is considered that the enzyme is activated by pitting, lye peeling and canning operations resulting in the oxidation of catechol derivatives to *o*-quinones and their subsequent polymerisation to brown-coloured pigments. The main substrates for enzymic browning found to be present were chlorogenic acid, caffeic acid, p-coumaryl quinic acid, catechins and leucoanthocyanins. The use of ascorbic acid for preventing this type of discolouration has been reported by Reyes and Luh (1962) and Takahana and Ogura (1967). Li et al. (1972) found some relationship between sensory ratings for colour and flavour of canned freestone peaches and three groups of tannin substances (total phenols, leucoanthocyanins and flavonols), the correlation with colour being the strongest. Dimick et al. (1951) studied the influence of time, temperature and pH on the inactivation of polyphenoloxidase in peach purée. Heating for 9 s at 92°C was sufficient to inactivate the enzyme.

The effect of canning on the carotenoid constituents of peaches has been studied by Mitchell et al. (1948), Panalaks and Murray (1970) and Aczel (1970, 1971). The major carotenoids identified and analysed before and after canning were neo-β-carotene B, neo-β-carotene U and all-trans-β-carotene, all of which were lost to some extent during canning. On the basis of crude carotene, Mitchell et al. (1948) found that the average loss (for 11 varieties) was 52% (1944 crop) and 54% (1945 crop) and Panalaks and Murray (1970) found a 68% loss for commercial samples which had received an unspecified process. The most detailed information on this subject has been given by Aczel (1969, 1970, 1971) and some of his data are shown in Table 9.5. Much of the colour loss in canned peaches and apricots may be due to isomerisation of intensely coloured 5,6-epoxides to less highly coloured 5,8-epoxides (Borenstein and Bunnell, 1966).

Destruction of ascorbic acid in peaches has been studied by Mitchell et al. (1948) and Souty (1972). The average loss on canning (18 min at 100°C) was about 7·5% with considerable variation between varieties.

The general quality aspects of canned peaches, as affected by maturity and processing time, have been investigated by Owens et al. (1973). These workers used an FMC Steritort and processed at 104°C and 5 rpm for 3, 5, 7, 9 and 11 min, quality evaluation being carried out after 4 weeks' storage. The texture, measured as the force required to shear the peach halves, was found to be 33·5, 23, 17, 15 and 12 kg, respectively, for the process times given. Further results are given in Table 9.6.

The effect of heat on the texture of peaches has also been studied by Postlmayr et al. (1956), Karadzhov (1969) and Souty and Perret (1970). The protopectin content was found to decrease during the cooking period, some being converted to water-soluble pectin, parti-

TABLE 9.5

EFFECT OF PROCESSING AND STORAGE ON CAROTENOID RETENTION IN PEACHES (FROM ACZEL, 1969)

Carotenoid (mg/100 g)	Raw peach	Bottled and pasteurised[a]	Duration of storage at 37°C (days)			
			7	17	21	30
Total carotenoid	2·12	2·00	1·94	1·97	1·90	1·90
β-Carotene	0·48	0·40	0·38	0·36	0·30	0·30

[a] 25 min at 96–98°C.

TABLE 9.6

EFFECT OF MATURITY OF PEACHES ON QUALITY FACTORS (FROM OWENS ET AL., 1973)

Maturity	pH	Soluble solids (%)	Average shear force (kg)	Acceptable processing time (min)
Immature	3·7	4·7	16·0	7
Medium ripe	3·8	5·2	23·5	9
Ripe	4·0	7·2	21·0	5

cularly during the latter stages of heating. According to Adams and Blundstone (1971), the ripe clingstone peach is firm owing to the retention of protopectin in thick cell walls and the formation of water-soluble pectin during heating has little effect on its texture. In the freestone peach, however, much of the protopectin is converted to water-soluble pectin during ripening and is contained in a thin cell wall. Any further degradation of protopectin will significantly change its textural properties and the stage of maturity is therefore very critical in canning this variety. Changes in the drained weight of canned peaches have been discussed by Leonard et al. (1958) and Antreotti et al. (1971).

Other quality factors of processed peaches, such as colour and flavour, have been examined (Leonard et al., 1961; Boggess, 1974). For immature fruit, heat sterilisation leads to a considerable improvement of colour by destroying chlorophyll, but in mature fruit there is only slight improvement since little chlorophyll is present. Samples of higher Brix : acid ratio had a superior flavour when canned. Pink discolouration of canned peaches is not normally a problem providing the product is cooled rapidly after processing (Mahadeviah, 1966). Volatile flavour components are very easily lost on canning, particularly acetaldehyde and methyl octanoate (Li, 1966).

The effect of different methods of dehydration on the quality and composition of dried peaches has received some attention. Lee et al. (1966b) showed that hot-air drying, freeze-drying and sun-drying all slightly reduced acidity and increased total and reducing sugars. Volatile loss was as much as 60% using sun-drying or hot-air drying but only 10% using freeze-drying. Korobkina and Kurtov (1970) compared changes in ascorbic acid and carotene content and polyphenol oxidase activity for sun-dried peaches. It is generally known that sun-drying of fruit such as peaches results in a product of superior quality compared to that produced by dehydration. According to McBean et al. (1971), part of the difference is due to the higher retention of chlorophyll or its conversion to brown pheophytin during dehydration, whereas in sun-drying the chlorophyll appears to degrade to colourless products.

9.17   PEAR

9.17.1   Structure and Composition

The pear is the fruit of the tree *Pyrus communis*. It is a pome fruit, similar in internal structure to the apple, but having a different shape, being narrow at the stem end. The general composition is: water, 83%; protein, 0·4%; fat, 0·3%; micronutrients per 100 g: calcium, 11 mg; iron, 0·2 mg; vitamin A, 20 IU; thiamine, 0·02 mg; riboflavin, 0·03 mg; niacin, 0·1 mg and ascorbic acid, 3 mg. The pH of pears varies considerably from 3·62 to 4.33. The volatile components of pears have been listed by Luh (1971); decadienoate esters are of particular importance, e.g. methyl *trans*-2-*cis*-4-decadienoate as well as hexyl acetate (see also, Creveling and Jennings, 1970). The main enzyme system is polyphenol oxidase which gives rise to brown discolouration products but pectin esterase which affects the texture is also present. Malic and citric acids are the main acids.

9.17.2 Effects of Heat

Luh *et al.* (1955) have studied the formation of volatile reducing substances in canned 'Bartlett' pears in relation to the maturity of the fruit. Changes in the drained weight have been correlated by Antreotti (1971) with maturity and syrup strength and changes in weight have also been investigated for various cooking processes by Pequignot *et al.* (1975).

Polyphenol oxidase in pears is responsible for the oxidation of *ortho*- but not *meta*- or *para*-dihydroxy phenolic compounds. The main substrates which cause brown pigment formation in pears are catechol, chlorogenic acid, caffeic acid, *d*-catechol and protocatechinic acid (Luh and Kamber, 1963; Tate *et al.*, 1964). Luh and Sioud (1966) have studied the polyphenolic browning effects in pear purée canned aseptically. Leucoanthocyanins, (+)-catechin, (−)-epicatechin, chlorogenic acids, *p*-coumaryl quinic acids and caffeic acid were all identified. Polyphenol oxidase may be inactivated by heating the purée for 9 s at 91°C or 120 s at 84°C (Dimick *et al.*, 1951; Skorikova and Lyashenko, 1972). Another form of discolouration which is equally undesirable in heat-processed purées and canned pears, is a pink discolouration which is encouraged by long processing or cooling times. This has been investigated by many workers (Joslyn, 1941; Joslyn and Peterson, 1956; Luh *et al.*, 1960; van der Merwe, 1963; Khan and Khan, 1965; Nortje, 1966; and Chandler and Clegg, 1970a,b,c). In this phenomenon, the rôle of leucoanthocyanins is important and Chandler and Clegg (1970a) indicate that the coloured component is an insoluble anthocyanin–tin complex. Ranganna and Parpia (1974b) consider that processing causes polymerisation of the leucoanthocyanins, the extent depending on the duration of heating and the concentration of acid. The reaction appears to involve conversion to a phlobaphene-like polymer with conjugated quinonoid rings and xanthyllium nuclei. It has been reported that the pink discolouration can be reduced by the addition of sequestrants such as the disodium salt of ethylenediaminetetraacetic acid, citrate or phosphate (Furia, 1968). It would appear that two different reactions may contribute to this 'pinking' phenomenon, only one of them involving tin.

The consistency of pear purées and nectars is related to the pectin and cellulose contents. The effect of temperature on the flow properties of pear purée has been investigated by Harper and Lebermann (1965). Dame et al. (1956) have studied the influence of maturity on the pectin content of canned 'Bartlett' pears.

The problems of drying pears have been discussed by McBean (1969). Enzymic browning occurs during preparation and the rehydrated product is soft in texture.

9.18 PINEAPPLE

9.18.1 Structure and Composition

The pineapple is the fruit of the tropical plant *Ananas sativus*. It is a composite fruit made up of smaller fruits, known as fruitlets, arranged around a central core. The flesh colour varies from deep yellow to white. The general composition is: water, 84%; protein, 0·3%; fat, 0·1%; micronutrients per 100 g: calcium, 12 mg; iron, 0·3 mg; vitamin A, 50 IU; thiamine, 0·08 mg; riboflavin, 0·02 mg; niacin, 0·1 mg; and ascorbic acid, 26 mg. The main carbohydrates are sucrose, fructose and glucose. The main amino acids are asparagine, alanine, glutamine and serine in decreasing order of concentration. Pineapple contains four important enzyme systems: peroxidase, indol-3yl-acetic acid oxidase, phosphatase and bromelin (Dull, 1971).

9.18.2 Effects of Heat

Considerable attention has been given to the aroma and flavour constituents of pineapple (Flath and Forrey, 1970; Näf-Müller and Willhalm, 1971; Dupaigne, 1972). Reviews have been published by Silverstein (1971) and Mehrlich and Felton (1971). One of the major components with an intense odour of 'burnt pineapple' was found to be 2,5-dimethyl-4-hydroxy-2,3-dihydro-3-furanone. A number of compounds have been identified in the headspace of canned pineapple products, some of which are thermal breakdown products, including acetic acid, 5-hydroxymethylfurfural, furfural, formaldehyde, acetaldehyde and acetone (Gawler, 1962; Howard and Hoffman, 1967). The furfural compounds result from sugar–acid interactions.

The retention of vitamin C in canned pineapple products has been studied by several workers, but the results are rather contradictory. Moschette *et al.* (1947) reported losses of 5–15% after 12 months' storage at 10–26·5°C but Dhopeshwarkar and Magar (1950) found a loss of 83% after 4 months' storage at 28–30°C. Lal and Pruthi (1955) found retentions of 72–89% after 4–12 months at 24–30°C. Further data on vitamin C retention in canned pineapple products are given by Darrock and Gortner (1965).

Two processes for pasteurisation of sliced pineapple in syrup were developed by Kato *et al.* (1975). These included a conventional process involving exhausting, seaming and heat treatment in water at 100°C for 20 min and a rotary process (100 rpm) for 4 min in steam. The rotary process gave products of superior organoleptic properties.

Canned pineapple is usually a deep yellow colour owing to complexing of carotenoids with tin. The presence of sulphite, however, causes blackening of the product by the formation of stannous sulphide (Oda and Okada, 1966). The carotenoids of pineapple contain a high proportion of epoxide groups which readily isomerise to the furanoid forms in acid conditions, with a corresponding spectral shift (Singleton *et al.*, 1961).

9.19 PLUM

9.19.1 Structure and Composition

The plum is a fruit of the *Prunus* species. It consists of a thin skin (epicarp) enclosing the edible flesh (mesocarp) which contains the stone (endocarp). The mesocarp consists of large parenchyma cells together with smaller cells and vascular bundles. The approximate composition is: water, 84%; protein, 0·8%; fat, 0·2%; micronutrients per 100 g: calcium, 16 mg; iron, 0·5 mg; vitamin A, 330 IU; thiamine, 0·06 mg; niacin, 0·5 mg and ascorbic acid, 5 mg. Its soluble solids content is 11–14% and contains about 1% malic acid (Dickinson and Gawler, 1954, 1956; Rees, 1958; Romani and Jennings, 1971).

9.19.2 Effects of Heat

The volatile components of the plum (*Prunus salicina* var. *santa rosa*) have been studied by Forrey and Flath (1974) who identified 53 compounds. Acetate esters predominate with appreciable quantities of the higher γ-lactones as well. Most of the components, with the exception of ethyl anisate, are fairly common fruit volatiles.

Aczel (1970) has investigated changes in the carotenoid content of plums after sterilisation and storage. Some of the results are shown in Table 9.7.

TABLE 9.7

CHANGES IN THE CAROTENOID CONTENT OF PLUMS AFTER
STERILISATION AND STORAGE

Carotenoid (mg/100 g)	Fresh	After canning	After storage[a]
Total carotenoids	1·51	1·40	0·92
β-Carotene	0·57	0·49	0·28

[a]Canned product stored for 30 days.

Ingalsbe *et al.* (1965) have studied the relationship between anthocyanin pigments in the fresh purple plum and its canned product, as well as similar studies on cherries (loc. cit.). The heat stability of polyphenol oxidase in three varieties of plum has been determined by Fung and Yankov (1970). Parkinson and Barker (1957) showed that relatively little chlorogenic acid was lost on storage of re-canned and bottled plum syrup stored at room temperature or 37°C. They did, however, record a continual formation of hydroxymethylfurfural produced by degradation of sugars in the acid environment. Anthistle and Dickinson (1959) found a significant reduction in the amount of chrysanthemin in bottled 'Victoria' plums which they attributed to the effects of heating. The effect of insufficient heating and failure to inactivate the β-glucosidase of plum stones have been studied by Dickinson (1957, 1958), Haisman and Knight (1967) and Haisman (1968). The result is the production of hydrocyanic acid during storage of the canned product.

Another defect, of a seasonal nature, is the formation of stone gum in canned plums. The exact cause and steps required to prevent this occurrence have not yet been determined.

Markh and Skorikova (1959) have studied the biochemical changes which take place during the drying of plums, in particular the polyphenol oxidase-catalysed pigment formation. The benzopyrene content of plums dried in hot air depends on drying conditions and has been found to range from 0·07 to 1·10 mg per 100 g (Ruchkovskii et al., 1975).

9.20 RASPBERRY

9.20.1 Structure and Composition
The raspberry is the fruit of the bush *Rubus idaeus*. It is a soft, small aggregate fruit with a central receptacle plug surrounded by drupelets. The usual colour is red although black and yellow varieties are known. The general composition is: water, 83%; protein, 1·3%; fat, trace; micronutrients per 100 g: calcium, 40 mg; iron, 0·9 mg; vitamin A, 130 IU; thiamine, 0·02 mg; riboflavin, 0·07 mg; niacin, 0·3 mg; and ascorbic acid, 24 mg. The pectin content is about 0·4% and total sugars amount to 4%. The pH varies between 3·41 and 3·95 (Green, 1971).

9.20.2 Effects of Heat
Krupcik and Braunova (1973) have studied the changes in the main aroma constituents of raspberries on heat processing to give compotes, jams and syrups. The major difference between the fresh and processed materials was the increase in ethanol content which was twice as great in the jam and twenty times as great in the syrups, as compared to the fresh fruit. The main component of raspberry flavour is 1-(p-hydroxyphenyl)-3-butanone (Schinz and Seidel, 1961).

Heat also degrades the anthocyanin pigments, mainly cyanidin derivatives, and several workers have studied the kinetics of the breakdown (Daravingas and Cain, 1966; Popov et al., 1969; Tanchev, 1972a; Ruskov and Tanchev, 1973). Anthistle and Dickinson (1959) have reported on the chrysanthemin content of canned raspberries on storage.

An interesting investigation of the effects of processing on raspberries has been carried out by Board et al. (1966). In this work a comparison was made between a stationary and a spin-cook process.

With the spin-cook process the drained weight increased with increased rate of rotation. The flavour and colour were similar to the product of the stationary process but there were more broken berries. These results are consistent with the work of Reeve (1965) who showed that raspberries were more fragile when heated. He also differentiated between 'crumbliness' (fragmentation) and 'mushiness' in canned raspberries. Crumbliness arises from excessive drupelet abortion that weakens coherence between normally developed drupelets of the fruit. Mushiness is due to fragility of the pulp tissue. Apparently, the susceptibility of certain varieties to mushiness is not related to pectin esterase activity (Leinbach et al., 1951).

9.21 STRAWBERRY

9.21.1 Structure and Composition

The strawberry is the fruit of the plant genus *Fragaria*. It is a composite fruit with an edible pulpy receptacle surmounted by seeds. The colour varies from pink to intense dark red (*e.g.*, *Fragaria* var. *senga sengana*). The approximate composition is: water, 89%; protein, 0·8%; fat, 0·5%; micronutrients per 100 g: calcium, 26 mg; iron, 0·8 mg; vitamin A, 50 IU; thiamine, 0·03 mg; riboflavin, 0·06 mg; niacin, 0·3 mg; and ascorbic acid, 58 mg. The total solids amount to 10·2% of which 7·8% are soluble and 2·4% insoluble. Some other components Green, 1971) are pectin, 0·54%, reducing sugars, 4·31% and sucrose, 0·87%. The sugar : acid ratio is 5·3 and the pH is 3·16–3·76. The principal anthocyanin is pelargonidin-3-glucoside.

9.21.2 Effects of Heat

The aroma constituents of strawberries have been studied by Winter *et al.* (1962), Teranishi *et al.* (1963) and McFadden *et al.* (1965), who identified over 150 volatile compounds. These works did not, however, elucidate the source of strawberry aroma. Sloan *et al.* (1969) made a further study of the flavour changes resulting from heat processing strawberry purée for 30 min at 120°C. Two significant compounds which were produced during the heating were dimethyl sulphide and isobutyraldehyde from the Strecker degradation of valine. Other compounds were furan and the furan derivatives, 2-furfuraldehyde, 2-acetylfuran and ethyl furoate, probably derived from sugar degradation. More recent work by Krupcik and Braunova (1973) has indicated the changes in the main aroma constituents on processing of strawberries.

Apart from the loss of flavour on heating strawberries, the colour also deteriorates and there is a need to add artificial colour. The degradation of anthocyanins in heated strawberry products has been studied by numerous workers (Tanchev, 1971, 1972a; Ruskov and Tanchev, 1973; Adams, 1972; Adams and Ongley, 1972). Adams and Ongley (1973a,b) have studied the degradation of pelargonidin-3-glucoside and showed that most of the degradation takes place during the storage of the canned product, and is rapid at high temperatures. Although the mechanism of degradation has yet to be established, it has been suggested that the breakdown of pure pelargonidin-3-glucoside in solution is due to the hydrolytic opening of the pyrylium ring with the formation of a sugar-substituted chalcone. Further degradation of this ketone leads to the insoluble brown pigment which is observed as the final discolouration. Adams (1972) gives an excellent literature review of this topic as well as experimental evidence for the mechanism of anthocyanin degradation.

Loss of texture on processing strawberries is well known and very little improvement has ever been achieved in the canning process. Board *et al.* (1966) studied the effect of spin-cook processing on strawberry texture and other quality attributes and found that spin-cook or rotary-cook processes improved the integrity, shape and texture but not the flavour or colour. Bradley (1966) also studied the effect of processing on canned strawberries and observed that the drained weight was higher using spin cooking than for a rotary cook. This indicates that the duration of the heating period has a pronounced effect on cellular structure and consequent diffusion processes.

Sistrunk and Cash (1970) have studied the changes in colour and polysaccharides of strawberry purée. They observed an increase in water-soluble pectin, hemicellulose and cellulose during holding at 50°C for 24 h and that the amount of these constituents was greater at pH 3·0 than either 3·4 or 3·8. Schaller *et al.* (1970) studied the effect of heating and pectolytic degradation on the rheological characteristics of strawberry purée.

9.22 TOMATO

9.22.1 Structure and Composition
The tomato is the fruit of the plant *Lycopersicon esculentum* which is a member of the potato family, Solanaceae. The fruit is essentially a swollen ovule, the seeds being contained in the parenchyma, held by

the outer and inner walls of the pericarp. The general composition is: water, 93%; protein, 1·1%; fat, 0·3%; micronutrients per 100 g: calcium, 11 mg; iron, 0·6 mg; vitamin A, 700 IU; thiamine, 0·06 mg; riboflavin, 0·04 mg; niacin, 0·5 mg; and ascorbic acid, 23 mg. The soluble carbohydrates are almost all reducing sugars and the predominant acids are citric followed by malic. Glutamic acid is the main amino acid, rarely found in other fruits. Methionine and S-methylmethionine are also present. The pigments which develop on ripening are the yellow pigments, β-carotene and xanthophylls, and at a later stage the red pigment, lycopene. Further details of the composition are given by Hobson and Davies (1971) and a bibliographical guide to post-harvest handling and physiology is given by Kader and Morris (1974).

9.22.2 Effects of Heat

The aroma components of tomato have been extensively studied (Pyne and Wick, 1965; Schormüller and Grosch, 1964; Buttery and Seifert, 1968; Kazeniae and Hall, 1970; Stevens, 1970; Buttery et al., 1969, 1971; Nelson and Hoff, 1969; Viani et al., 1969; Stone, 1971; Seck and Crouzet, 1973). The main volatile constituents are n-hexanal, 2- and 3-methyl-1-butanol, cis-3-hexene-1-ol and several rather unusual compounds such as: 2,6-dimethylundeca-2,6-diene-10-one; 2,6,10-trimethylpentadeca-2,6,10-triene-14-one; 6,10,14-trimethylpentadeca-5,9,13-triene-2-one; 2,3-butanedione; 2,3-pentanedione; cinnamaldehyde, glyoxal and pyruvaldehyde. The effect of processing on tomato volatiles has been investigated by Badenhop (1966), Miers (1966), Johnson et al. (1968), Guadagni and Miers (1969) and Nelson and Hoff (1969). The main components of the aroma of heated tomato products are dimethylsulphide and linalool. Several other compounds are present in increased concentrations.

Rice and Pederson (1954), Villarreal et al. (1960) and Bradley (1960) have studied the development of pyrrolidone carboxylic acid in processed tomato products. It is probably formed by the action of heat on glutamine and asparagine. Mahdi et al. (1959, 1961) showed that the amount of the acid increases with storage time and reported that it contributed to the processing off-flavour.

El Miladi et al. (1969) investigated the effects of heat processing on the starch, proteins, amino acids and organic acids of tomato juice. The losses of starch and sugars resulting from processing were 40% and 19·4%, respectively. The hydrolysis of starch gives rise to glucose and other sugar/acid degradation products such as hydroxymethylfurfural. Denaturation of the protein resulted in an increase of free amino acids. The greatest increases were observed with glutamic acid, aspartic acid, alanine and threonine. Glutamine and asparagine were probably lost owing to the formation of pyrrolidone carboxylic acid. The ratio of citric acid:pyrrolidone carboxylic acid:malic acid was found to be $15.5:0.4:1.0$ before processing compared to $11.0:2.6:1.0$ after processing.

The kinetics of the thermal degradation of methyl methionine sulphonium salt, a product of which is dimethylsulphide, have been determined by Williams and Nelson (1974). The reaction exhibited first-order kinetics with an activation energy of about $28\,kcal\cdot mol^{-1}$, the reaction rate doubling for a 5–6°C temperature increase.

Hamdy (1961) showed that, on processing fresh tomato juice, both pyruvic acid and dihydroxytartaric acid were destroyed whilst α-ketoglutonic acid and glutamic acid increased.

Dekazos (1972) has studied the development of callose, an amorphous polymer of glucose residues in β-1,3 linkages, as a result of mechanical bruising and thermal treatment. Callose is thought to be an important contributor to the texture and viscosity of processed tomato products.

Pectic enzymes must be inactivated in the early stages of tomato purée manufacture, otherwise a low-viscosity product is obtained. Luh and Daoud (1971) investigated the effect of break temperature and holding time on the chemical and physical properties of canned tomato pulp and on the activity of polygalacturonase (PG) and pectin esterase (PE). The bulk viscosity was found to be higher as the break temperature increased, owing to the rapid inactivation of the enzyme systems. The critical conditions for inactivation of the enzymes were found to be 15 s at 82°C for PE and 15 s at 104°C for PG. Inactivation of PE is most critical since it produces pectic acid, the substrate for PG. (See also Kattan, 1956; Moyer *et al.*, 1959; and Miers *et al.*, 1970.)

Panalaks and Murray (1970) showed that canning tomatoes resulted in a considerable increase in the concentration of neo-β-carotene B ($4\times$), neo-β-carotene U ($2.5\times$) and *all-trans-β*-carotene ($1.2\times$). (See also Nakagawa *et al.*, 1971.) The use of unripe tomatoes in preserves may lead to a brown or reddish-brown discolouration owing to the conversion of chlorophyll to pheophytin during heating (Adams and Blundstone, 1971).

Canning whole tomatoes presents a number of problems, the most important of which concerns the severity of the process. The pH of tomatoes varies from 3·6 to 4·8 and consequently, at the higher pH, acidification must be used if a satisfactory botulinum cook is to be achieved under relatively mild processing conditions. Powers (1976) has produced a critical and comprehensive review of this subject. The effect of heat processing on acidified canned tomatoes has been investigated by Schoenemann and Lopez (1973) with special reference to enzyme inactivation.

Wholeness retention in canned tomatoes has been studied by Mohr and Adair (1974) and the effects of different heat treatments by Bellucci et al. (1971) and Leonard et al. (1975). The latter workers compared two processes, viz. 40·8 min heat at 101·7°C with a 10·8-min cool, and a 12-min Steriflamme process with 10-min cool. The Steriflamme process gave a better texture and greater retention of ascorbic acid.

The effect of heat on tomato concentrate, pulp and paste during continuous pasteurisation and sterilisation has been investigated by several workers. Leonard et al. (1964) compared the effects of HTST processing with those of conventionally canned products. Thiamine retention was high using either process although there was a progressive loss on storage. Pyridoxine retention was also high. Excessive heating may cause a brown discolouration owing to oxidation of lycopene (Adams and Blundstone, 1971).

Nutting et al. (1955), Ammerman (1957), Luh et al. (1958, 1964) and Noble and Gill (1973) have studied the effect of temperature in the range 6–55°C on the storage stability of canned tomato paste. The main changes were a darkening of the serum, probably owing to Maillard-type reactions, and degradation of ascorbic acid. Rivas and Luh (1968) examined the polyphenolic compounds in canned tomato paste and found two chlorogenic acid isomers, caffeic acid and two of its derivatives, ferulic acid, rutin and naringenin. The chlorogenic acids and other polyphenols are substrates for enzymatic oxidation by polyphenol oxidase.

Olaru and Economu (1970) have studied the effect of non-enzymic browning on the quality of canned tomato paste as well as peeled tomatoes stored at 20, 30 and 55°C. Both products remained unchanged during storage for 1 year at 20°C, but there were incipient changes to the paste after 7 months and the peeled tomatoes after 12 months when stored at 30°C, although both samples were edible. Storage at the highest temperature resulted in both products being unacceptable after 10–30 days.

REFERENCES AND BIBLIOGRAPHY

Aczel, A. (1969) *Konzerv-es Paprikaipar*, No. 3, 60.
Aczel, A. (1970) *Elelmiszervizsgalti Közlemenyok*, **16**(4/5), 317.
Aczel, A. (1971) *Ind. Obst u. Gemüse*, **56**(16), 465.
Aczel, A. (1973) *Lebensm.-Wiss. u. Technol.*, **6**, 36.
Aczel, A. (1974) *Ind. Obst u. Gemüse*, **59**, 491.
Adam, W. B. (1965) *J. Assoc. Publ. Analysts*, **3**, 36.
Adam, W. B. & Dickinson, D. (1959) *The pH Values of Canned Fruit and Vegetables*, Sci. Bull. No. 3. Chipping Campden, Glos.: CFPRA.
Adams, J. B. (1972) *Changes in the Polyphenols of Red Fruits during Heat Processing—the Kinetics and Mechanism of Anthocyanin Degradation*, Tech. Bull. No. 22. Chipping Campden, Glos.: CFPRA.
Adams, J. B. & Blundstone, H. A. W. (1971) In: *The Biochemistry of Fruits and their Products*. ed. Hulme, A. C. Vol. 2, p. 507. London & New York: Academic Press.
Adams, J. B. & Ongley, M. H. (1972) *Changes in the Polyphenols of Red Fruits during Heating—the Degradation of Anthocyanins in Canned Fruits*, Tech. Bull. No. 23. Chipping Campden, Glos.: CFPRA.
Adams, J. B. & Ongley, M. H. (1973a) *J. Fd. Technol.*, **8**, 139.
Adams, J. B. & Ongley, M. H. (1973b) *J. Fd. Technol.*, **8**, 305.
Agarwal, P. C., Prabhakar, J. V., Ranganna, S. & Bhatnagar, H. C. (1963) *Fd. Sci.* (Mysore), **12**, 200.
Ahmad, M. & Rahman, R. (1968a) *Pak. J. Sci. Res.*, **20**(3), 77.
Ahmad, M. & Rahman, R. (1968b) *Pak. J. Sci. Res.*, **20**(4), 140.
Ammerman, G. R. (1957) *Dissert. Abstr.*, **17**, 1435.
Andersson, J. & von Sydow, E. (1964) *Acta Chem. Scand.*, **18**, 1105.
Andersson, J. & von Sydow, E. (1966) *Acta Chem. Scand.*, **20**, 522, 529.
Anon, (1963) *Papaya*. Industrial monograph No. 2. Mysore, India: CFTRI.
Anthistle, M. J. & Dickinson, D. (1959) *Natural Colouring Matters in Canned Fruits*. Research leaflet No. 4. Chipping Campden, Glos.: CFPRA.
Antreotti, R., Tamasicchio, M. & Castelyetri, F. (1971) *Industria Conserve*, **46**(1), 32.
Aung, T. & Ross, E. (1965) *J. Fd. Sci.*, **30**, 144.
Badenhop, A. F. (1966) *Dissert. Abstr. B.*, **27**, 1970.
Bakal, A. & Mannheim, H. C. (1968) *Israel J. Technol.*, **6**, 269.
Basker, H. B. (1965) *Israel J. Technol.*, **3**, 160.
Basker, H. B. (1967) *Israel J. Technol.*, **5**, 221.
Bates, R. P. (1970) *J. Fd. Sci.*, **35**, 478.
Bellucci, G., Leoni, C. & Aldini, R. (1971) *Industria Conserve*, **46**, 108.
Bender, A. E. (1965) *Dictionary of Nutrition and Food Technology*. London: Butterworths.
Ben-Et, G., Dolev, A. & Tatarsky, D. (1973) *J. Fd. Sci.*, **38**, 546.
Berry, R. E. & Tatum, J. H. (1965) *J. Agric. Fd. Chem.*, **12**, 588.
Bhatia, B. S., Siddappa, G. S. & Lal, G. (1955a) *Indian J. Agric. Sci.*, **25**(4), 303.

Bhatia, B. S., Siddappa, G. S. & Lal, G. (1955b) *Indian Fd. Packer*, 9(9), 7.
Bhatia, B. S., Siddappa, G. S. & Lal, G. (1956) *J. Sci. Ind. Res.*, 15c(4), 91.
Biale, J. B. & Young, R. E. (1971) In: *The Biochemistry of Fruits and their Products*. ed. Hulme, A. C. Vol. 2, p. 1. London & New York: Academic Press.
Bindra, U. (1973) *Indian Fd. Packer*, 27(2), 41.
Blundstone, H. A. W., Woodman, J. S. & Adams, J. B. (1971) In: *The Biochemistry of Fruits and their Products*, ed. Hulme, A. C. Vol. 2, p. 543. London & New York: Academic Press.
Board, P. W., Gallop, R. A. & Sykes, S. M. (1966) *Fd. Technol.*, 20, 1203, 1210.
Boggess, T. S. (1974) *Georgia Agric. Exptl. Stn. Res. Rept. No.* 185, Georgia, USA.
Borenstein, B. & Bunnell, R. H. (1966) *Advan. Fd. Res.*, 15, 195.
Bradley, B. F. (1966) *J. Sci. Fd. Agric.*, 17, 226.
Bradley, D. B. (1960) *J. Agric. Fd. Chem.*, 8, 232.
Brekke, J., Cavaletto, C. & Stafford, A. L. (1968a) *Mango Purée Processing*. Tech. Prog. Rept. No. 167. University of Hawaii: Hawaii Agric. Exptl. Stn.
Brekke, J., Chan, H. T., Jr. & Cavaletto, C. G. (1968b) *Papaya Purée and Nectar*. Res. Bull. No. 170. University of Hawaii: Hawaii Agric. Exptl. Stn.
Brenner, S., Wodicka, V. D. & Dunlop, S. G. (1948) *Fd. Technol.*, 2, 207.
Brouk, B. (1975) *Plants Consumed by Man*. London & New York: Academic Press.
Brown, R. I. (1972) *J. Agric. Fd. Chem.*, 20, 753.
Brule, G. (1973) *Annalyes de Technologie Agricole*, 22, 45.
Buch, M. L., Satori, K. G. & Hills, C. H. (1961) *Fd. Technol.*, 15, 526.
Buttery, R. G. & Seifert, R. M. (1968) *J. Agric. Fd. Chem.*, 16, 1053.
Buttery, R. G., Seifert, R. M. & Ling, L. C. (1969) *Chem. & Ind.*, 238.
Buttery, R. G., Seifert, R. M., Guadagni, D. G. & Ling, L. C. (1971) *J. Agric. Fd. Chem.*, 19, 524.
Carroll, E. A., Guyer, R. B., Bissett, O. W. & Veldhuis, M. K. (1957) *Fd. Technol.*, 11, 516.
Chan, H. T., Jr. (1975) *J. Fd. Sci.*, 40, 701.
Chan, H. T., Jr., Flath, R. A., Forrey, R. R., Cavaletto, C. G. & Nakayama, T. O. M. (1972) Abstracts of papers, *Am. Chem. Soc.*, 164, AGFD: 64.
Chandler, B. V. & Clegg, K. M. (1970a) *J. Sci. Fd. Agric.*, 21, 315.
Chandler, B. V. & Clegg, K. M. (1970b) *J. Sci. Fd. Agric.*, 21, 319.
Chandler, B. V. & Clegg, K. M. (1970c) *J. Sci. Fd. Agric.*, 21, 323.
Charley, V. L. S. (1970) In: *Fruit and Vegetable Juice Processing Technology*, eds. Tressler, D. K. & Joslyn, M. A., 2nd edn., p. 284. Westport, Conn.: Avi. Publ. Co. Inc.
Chichester, C. O. (1972) *The Chemistry of Plant Pigments*, Suppl. 3. *Advances in Food Research*. London & New York: Academic Press.
Chung, J. I. & Luh, B. S. (1972) *Confructa*, 17, 8.
Chytra, M., Curda, D. & Kyzlink, V. (1962) *Sborn. Praz. Vys. Skol. Chem. Technol. Potravin Technol.*, p. 57.
Clegg, K. M. (1964) *J. Sci. Fd. Agric.*, 15, 878.
Clegg, K. M. & Morton, A. D. (1965) *J. Sci. Fd. Agric.*, 16, 191.
Creveling, R. K. & Jennings, W. G. (1970) *J. Agric. Fd. Chem.*, 18, 19.

Cruess, W. V., Gibson, A. & Brekke, J. (1951) *Canner*, **112**(2), 11; **112**(3), 14.
Curl, A. L. (1960) *Fd. Res.*, **25**, 190.
Cutin, J. & Samish, Z. (1958) *KTAVIM* (Records of the Agric. Res. Stn.) (*Israel*), **8**(3/4), 33.
Czerkaskyj, A. (1970) *J. Fd. Sci.*, **35**, 608.
Dalal, K. B. & Salunkhe, D. K. (1964) *Fd. Technol.*, **18**(8), 88.
Dame, C., Jr., Leonard, S. J., Luh, B. S. & Marsh, G. L. (1956) *Fd. Technol.*, **10**, 28.
Daravingas, G. V. & Cain, R. F. (1966) *J. Fd. Sci.*, **30**, 400.
Darrock, J. G. & Gortner, W. A. (1965) *J. Agric. Fd. Chem.*, **13**, 27.
Dastur, K., Weckel, K. G. & von Elbe, J. (1968) *Fd. Technol.*, **22**, 1176.
Dekazos, E. D. (1972) *J. Fd. Sci.*, **37**, 562.
de Martin, Z., Geromel, E. J., Bleinroth, E. W., Angelucci, E. & Pupo, L. M. (1971/72) *Coletanea do Instituto de Technologia de Alimentos*, **4**, 127.
de Martin, Z., Geromel, E. J., Bleinroth, E. W., Angelucci, E., Pupo, L. M., Garrutti, R. S., Tosello, Y., de Castro, I. J. & de Barros, A. B. M. (1973) *Coletanea do Instituto de Tecnologia de Alimentos*, **8**(2), 65.
Demole, E. & Berthet, D. (1971) *Helv. Chim. Acta*, **54**, 681.
Dhopeshwarkar, G. A. & Magar, N. G. (1950) *Curr. Sci.*, **19**, 288.
Dickinson, D. (1957) *J. Sci. Fd. Agric.*, **8**, 721.
Dickinson, D. (1958) Tech. Memorandum No. 23. Chipping Campden, Glos.: CFPRA.
Dickinson, D. & Gawler, J. H. (1954) *J. Sci. Fd. Agric.*, **5**, 525.
Dickinson, D. & Gawler, J. H. (1956) *J. Sci. Fd. Agric.*, **7**, 699.
Dimick, K. P., Ponting, J. D. & Makower, B. (1951) *Fd. Technol.*, **5**, 237.
Dinus, L. A. & Mackey, A. C. (1974) *J. Text. Studies*, **5**, 41.
Doesburg, J. J. (1961) *Qual. Plant Mater. Veg.*, **8**, 115.
Duckworth, R. B. (1966) *Fruit and Vegetables*. Oxford & London: Pergamon Press.
Dull, G. G. (1971) In: *The Biochemistry of Fruits and their Products*. ed. Hulme, A. C. Vol. 2, p. 303. London & New York: Academic Press.
Dupaigne, P. (1972) *Rivista Italiana Essenze, Perfumi, Piante Officinali Aromi Sapari, Cosmetici*, **54**, 559.
Dushchenko, V. P. & Ganya, G. P. (1972) *Konservnaya i Ovoshchesushil'naya Promyshlennost*, **27**(3), 33.
El Miladi, S. S., Gould, W. A. & Clements, R. L. (1969) *Fd. Technol.*, **23**, 691.
El-Sayed, A. S. & Luh, B. S. (1965) *J. Fd. Sci.*, **30**, 1016.
Escher, F. & Neukom, H. (1971) *Lebensm.-Wiss u. Technol.*, **4**, 145.
Flath, R. A. & Forrey, R. R. (1970) *J. Agric. Fd. Chem.*, **18**, 306.
Fletcher, S. W. (1970) Ph.D. Dissertation, University of Massachusetts, Amherst.
Forrey, R. R. & Flath, R. A. (1974) *J. Agric. Fd. Chem.*, **22**, 496.
Fung, D. T. & Yankov, S. (1970) *Nauchni Trudove, Vissh. Institut po Khranitelna i elua i Vkusova Promyshlennost*, **17**, 297.
Furia, T. E. (1968) In: *Handbook of Food Additives*, ed. Furia, T. E., p. 289. Cleveland, Ohio: The Chemical Rubber Co.
Gallop, R. A. (1965) *Variety, Composition and Colour in Canned Fruits*. Sci. Bull. No. 5. Chipping Campden, Glos.: CFPRA.
Garcia, R., Andrade, J. & Rolz, C. (1975) *J. Fd. Sci.*, **40**, 200.

Gawler, J. H. (1962) *J. Sci. Fd. Agric.*, **13**, 57.

Gormley, T. R. (1975) *Lebensm.-Wiss u. Technol.*, **8**, 168.

Green, A. (1971) In: *The Biochemistry of Fruits and their Products*, ed. Hulme, A. C. Vol. 2, p. 375. London & New York: Academic Press.

Guadagni, D. G. & Miers, J. C. (1969) *Fd. Technol.*, **23**, 375.

Guyer, R. B. & Erickson, F. B. (1954) *Fd. Technol.*, **8**, 165.

Haisman, D. R. (1968) *Victoria Plums*, Tech. Bulls. Nos. 5, 14, 15. Chipping Campden, Glos.: CFPRA.

Haisman, D. R. & Knight, D. J. (1967) *J. Fd. Technol.*, **2**, 241.

Hamdy, N. M. (1961) *Dissert. Abstr.*, **21**, 2097.

Harper, J. C. & Lebermann, K. W. (1965) *Proc. 1st Int. Congr. Fd. Sci. Technol.*, **1**, 710. London & New York: Gordon & Breach.

Harris, R. S. & Karmas, E. (1975) *Nutritional Evaluation of Food Processing*, 2nd edn., Westport, Conn.: Avi. Publ. Co. Inc.

Harrison, S. G., Masefield, G. B. & Wallis, M. (1969) *The Oxford Book of Food Plants*. London: Oxford University Press.

Hershkovitz, E. & Kanner, J. (1970) *J. Fd. Technol.*, **5**, 197.

Hinton, H. R. & Holdsworth, S. D. (1975) *Materials and Technology*. Vol. 7, p. 711. London & Amsterdam: J. H. de Bussy Longman.

Hobson, G. E. & Davies, J. N. (1971) In: *The Biochemistry of Fruits and their Products*, ed. Hulme, A. C. Vol. 2, p. 437. London & New York: Academic Press.

Holdsworth, S. D. (1971) *J. Fd. Technol.*, **6**, 331.

Howard, G. E. & Hoffman, A. (1967) *J. Sci. Fd. Agric.*, **18**, 106.

Hsia, C. L., Luh, B. S. & Chichester, C. O. (1965a) *Proc. 1st Int. Congr. Fd. Sci. Technol.*, **1**, 429. London & New York: Gordon & Breach.

Hsia, C. L., Luh, B. S. & Chichester, C. O. (1965b) *J. Fd. Sci.*, **30**, 5.

Huet, R. (1973) *Fruits*, **28**, 397.

Hughes, J. T., Markham, K. R. & Page, G. G. (1974) *Fd. Technol. New Zealand*, **9**, 15.

Hulme, A. C. (ed.) (1970) *The Biochemistry of Fruits and their Products*. Vol. 1. London & New York: Academic Press.

Hulme, A. C. (ed.) (1971a) *The Biochemistry of Fruits and their Products*. Vol. 2. London & New York: Academic Press.

Hulme, A. C. (1971b) In: *The Biochemistry of Fruits and their Products*, ed. Hulme, A. C. Vol. 2, p. 233. London & New York: Academic Press.

Hulme, A. C. & Rhodes, M. J. C. (1971) In: *The Biochemistry of Fruits and their Products*, ed. Hulme, A. C. Vol. 2, p. 333. London & New York: Academic Press.

Hultin, H. O. & Proctor, B. E. (1961) *Fd. Technol.*, **15**, 440.

Ingalsbe, D. W., Carter, G. H. & Neubert, A. M. (1965) *J. Agric. Fd. Chem.*, **13**, 580.

Jain, N. L. (1961) *Rev. Fd. Technol. (Mysore)*, **3**, 131.

Johnson, J. H., Gould, W. A., Badenhop, A. F. & Johnson, R. M., Jr. (1968) *J. Agric. Fd. Chem.*, **16**, 255.

Joslyn, M. A. (1941) *Ind. Eng. Chem.*, **33**, 308.

Joslyn, M. A. & Goldstein, J. L. (1964) *Advan. Fd. Res.*, **13**, 179.

Joslyn, M. A. & Peterson, H. (1956) *Nature*, **178**, 318.

Joux, J. L. (1957) *C.R. Acad. Agric. Fr.*, **43**, 506.

Kader, A. A. & Morris, L. L. (1974) *Post-Harvest Handling and Physiology of Tomatoes*. Vegetable Crops Series 162. Davis, California: Dept. Veg. Crops., University of California.

Karadzhov, I. (1969) *Nauchni Trudove, Nauchnoizsledovatelski Institut po Konservnaya Promyshlennost, Plovdiv*, **6**, 165.

Karim, M. A. & Riaz-Ur-Rehman. (1970a) *Pak. J. Sci. Res.*, **22**(1/2), 44.

Karim, M. A. & Riaz-Ur-Rehman. (1970b) *Pak. J. Sci. Res.*, **22**(1/2), 51.

Karlsson-Ekström, G. & von Sydow, E. (1973) *Lebensm.-Wiss u. Technol.*, **6**, 86.

Kashman, Y. (1969) *Israel J. Chem.*, **7**, 173.

Kato, K., de Martin, Z. J., Zucchini, A., da Silva, S. D., Miya, E. E. & Yogomizo, Y. (1975) *Coletanea do Instituto de Tecnologia de Alimentos*, **6**, 513.

Kattan, A. A., Ogle, W. L. & Kramer, A. (1956) *Proc. Am. Soc. Hort. Sci.*, **68**, 470.

Kazeniae, S. J. & Hall, R. M. (1970) *J. Fd. Sci.*, **35**, 519.

Kefford, J. F. (1959) *Advan. Fd. Res.*, **9**, 285.

Kefford, J. F. & Chandler, B. V. (1970) *The Chemical Constituents of Citrus Fruits*, Suppl. No. 2. *Advances in Food Research*. London & New York: Academic Press.

Kemp, T. R. (1972) *J. Agric. Fd. Chem.*, **20**, 196.

Kertesz, Z. I., Eucare, M. & Fox, G. (1959) *Fd. Res.*, **24**, 14.

Khan, S. A. & Khan, S. (1965) *W. Pak. J. Agric. Res.*, **3**, 48.

Kirchner, J. G. & Miller, J. M. (1953) *J. Agric. Fd. Chem.*, **1**, 512.

Kirchner, J. G., Miller, J. M., Rice, R. G., Keller, G. I. & Fox, M. M. (1953) *J. Agric. Fd. Chem.*, **1**, 510.

Kopelman, I. J., Mizrahi, S. & Kochba, M. (1975) *J. Fd. Sci.*, **40**, 695.

Korobkina, Z. & Kurtov, I. A. (1970) *Konservnaya i Ovoshchesushil'naya Promyshlennost*, (1), 29.

Krupcik, J. & Braunova, Z. (1973) *Conf. Proc. Aromatickych Iatkach v Pozivatinach*, Bratislava, Czechoslovakia, p. 100.

LaBelle, R. L. (1971) *J. Fd. Sci.*, **36**, 323.

LaBelle, R. L. & Moyer, J. C. (1960) *Fd. Technol.*, **14**, 347.

Labuza, T. P. (1972) *CRC Crit. Rev. Fd. Technol.*, **3**, 217.

Labuza, T. P. & Simon, I. B. (1970) *Fd. Technol.*, **24**, 712.

Lal, G. & Pruthi, J. S. (1955) *Indian J. Hort.*, **12**, 137.

Lee, C. Y., Salunkhe, D. K. & Nury, F. S. (1966a) *J. Sci. Fd. Agric.*, **17**, 393.

Lee, C. Y., Salunkhe, D. K., Watters, G. G. & Nury, F. S. (1966b) *Fd. Technol.*, **20**, 845.

Lee, C. Y., Salunkhe, D. K. & Nury, F. S. (1967) *J. Sci. Fd. Agric.*, **18**, 89.

Leinbach, L. R., Seegmiller, C. G. & Wilbur, J. S. (1951) *Fd. Technol.*, **5**, 51.

Leonard, S. J., Luh, B. S. & Mrak, E. M. (1958) *Fd. Technol.*, **12**, 80.

Leonard, S. J., Luh, B. S., Chichester, C. O. & Simone, M. (1961) *Fd. Technol.*, **15**, 492.

Leonard, S. J., Luh, B. S., Simone, M. & Everson, C. (1964) *Fd. Technol.*, **18**(1), 81, 84, 87.

Leonard, S. J., Marsh, G. L., Merson, R. L., York, G. K., Buhlert, J. E., Heil, J. R. & Wolcott, T. (1975) *J. Fd. Sci.*, **40**, 254.

Leverington, R. E. (1957) *Fd. Technol. Australia*, **9**, 205.

Levi, A., Samish, Z., Ludin, A. & Hershkowitz, E. (1969) *J. Fd. Technol.*, **4**, 179.

Li, K. C. (1966) Quoted by Adams, J. B. & Blundstone, H. A. W. (1971) In: *The Biochemistry of Fruits and their Products*, ed. Hulme, A. C. Vol. 2. London & New York: Academic Press.

Li, K. C., Boggess, T. S., Jr. & Heaton, E. K. (1972) *J. Fd. Sci.*, **37**, 177.

List, D. (1969) *Ind. Obst u. Gemüse*, **54**, 191, 253.

Ludin, A., Samish, Z., Levi, A. & Hershkowitz, E. (1969) *J. Fd. Technol.*, **4**, 171.

Luh, B. S. (1971) In: *Fruit and Vegetable Processing Technology*, eds. Tressler, D. K. & Joslyn, M. A., p. 302. Westport, Conn.: Avi. Publ. Co. Inc.

Luh, B. S., Chichester, C. O. & Leonard, S. J. (1965) *Proc. 1st Int. Congr. Fd. Sci. Technol.*, **1**, 401. London & New York: Gordon & Breach.

Luh, B. S., Chichester, C. O., Co, H. & Leonard, S. J. (1964) *Fd. Technol.*, **18**, 561.

Luh, B. S. & Daoud, H. N. (1971) *J. Fd. Sci.*, **36**, 1039.

Luh, B. S., Hsu, E. T. & Stachowicz, K. (1967) *J. Fd. Sci.*, **32**, 251.

Luh, B. S. & Kamber, P. J. (1963) *Fd. Technol.*, **17**(1), 105.

Luh, B. S. & Kanujoso, B. W. T. (1966) *Fruchtsaft Ind.*, **5**, 196.

Luh, B. S., Leonard, S. J. & Marsh, G. L. (1958) *Fd. Technol.*, **12**, 380.

Luh, B. S., Leonard, S. J. & Mrak, E. M. (1959) *Fd. Technol.*, **13**, 253.

Luh, B. S., Leonard, S. J. & Patel, D. S. (1960) *Fd. Technol.*, **14**, 53.

Luh, B. S., Leonard, S. J., Patel, D. S. & Claybol, L. L. (1955) *Fd. Technol.*, **15**, 639.

Luh, B. S., Peupier, L. Y. & Liu, Y. K. (1974) *California Agriculture*, **28**(7), 4.

Luh, B. S. & Phithakpol, B. (1972) *J. Fd. Sci.*, **37**, 264.

Luh, B. S. & Sioud, F. B. (1966) *Fd. Technol.*, **20**, 1591.

Mahadeviah, M. (1966) *Indian Fd. Packer*, **20**(1), 5.

Mahdi, A. A., Rice, A. C. & Weckel, K. G. (1959) *J. Agric. Fd. Chem.*, **7**, 712.

Mahdi, A. A., Rice, A. C. & Weckel, K. G. (1961) *J. Agric. Fd. Chem.*, **9**, 143.

Maleki, M. & Sarkissian, S. (1967) *J. Sci. Fd. Agric.*, **18**, 501.

Markakis, P. (1973) *CRC Crit. Rev. Fd. Technol.*, **4**, 437.

Markh, A. T. & Skorikova, Y. G. (1959) *Trudy Odesskk. Tekhnol. Inst. Prom.*, **9**, 39.

Mathew, A. G. & Parpia, H. A. B. (1971) *Advan. Fd. Res.*, **19**, 75.

Mathur, V. K., Siddaiah, C. H., Bhatia, B. S. & Nath, H. (1973) *Indian Fd. Packer*, **27**, 15.

Mattick, L. R., Moyer, J. C. & Shallenberger, R. S. (1958) *Fd. Technol.*, **12**, 613.

McBean, D. McG. (1969) *CSIRO Fd. Pres. Quart.*, **29**(3), 49.

McBean, D. McG., Joslyn, M.A. & Nury, F.S. (1971) In: *The Biochemistry of Fruits and their Products*. ed. Hulme, A. C., Vol. 2, p. 633. London & New York: Academic Press.

McCance, R. A. & Widdowson, E. M. (1960) *The Composition of Foods.* MRC Special Report Series No. 297. London: HMSO.

McFadden, W. H., Teranishi, J., Corse, J., Black, G. R. & Mon, T. R. (1965) *J. Chromatogr.*, **18**, 10.

Mehrlich, F. P. & Felton, G. E. (1971) In: *Fruit and Vegetable Juice Processing Technology*, ed. Tressler, D. K. & Joslyn M. A., 2nd edn., p. 155. Westport, Conn.: Avi. Publ. Co. Inc.

Miers, J. C. (1966) *J. Agric. Fd. Chem.*, **14**, 419.

Miers, J. C., Sanshuck, D. W., Nutting, M. D. & Wagner, J. R. (1970) *Fd. Technol.*, **24**, 1399.

Mitchell, J. H., van Blaricom, L. O. & Roderick, D. B. (1948) *Bull. No.* 372. Clemson, S. Carolina: S. Carolina Agric. Exptl. Stn.

Mizrahi, S. & Berk, Z. (1970) *J. Sci. Fd. Agric.*, **21**, 250.

Mizrahi, S. & Firstenberg, R. (1975) *J. Fd. Technol.*, **10**, 557.

Mizrahi, S. & Kopelman, J. J. (1975) *Confructa*, **20**, 5.

Mohr, W. P. & Adair, R. G. (1974) *Can. Inst. Fd. Sci. Technol. J.*, **7**, 274.

Molina, P. J., Soler, A. & Cambronero, J. (1973) *Annales de Bromatologia*, **25**, 403.

Moore, E. L., Rouse, A. H. & Atkins, C. D. (1956) *Proc. Florida State Hort. Soc.*, **69**, 176.

Moore, E. L., Rouse, A. H. & Atkins, C. D. (1962) *Fd. Technol.*, **16**(12), 91.

Moschette, D. S., Hinman, W. F. & Halliday, E. G. (1947) *Ind. Eng. Chem.*, **39**, 994.

Moyer, J. C., Robinson, W. B., Ransford, J. R., LaBelle, R. L. & Hand, D. B. (1959) *Fd. Technol.*, **13**, 270.

Muralikrishna, M., Nanjundaswamy, A. M. & Siddappa, G. S. (1968) *Indian Fd. Packer*, **22**(1), 5.

Murray, K. E. (1972) Abstracts of papers, *Am. Chem. Soc.*, **164**, AGFD: 74.

Murray, K. E., Shipton, J. E. & Whitfield, F. B. (1972) *Australian J. Chem.*, **25**, 1921.

Murray, K. E., Shipton, J. E. & Whitfield, F. B. (1973) *Fd. Technol. Australia*, **25**, 446.

Näf-Müller, R. & Willhalm, B. (1971) *Helv. Chim. Acta*, **54**, 1880.

Nakagawa, H., Kushida, T., Ogura, N. & Takehana, H. (1971) *J. Fd. Sci. Technol. (Japan)*, **18**, 259.

Nelson, P. E. & Hoff, J. E. (1969) *J. Fd. Sci.*, **34**, 53.

Noble, A. C. & Gill, T. (1973) Abstracts of papers, *Am. Chem. Soc.* **166**, AGFD: 129.

Nortje, B. K. (1966) *S. Afr. J. Agric. Sci.*, **9**, 681.

Nursten, H. E. (1970) In: *The Biochemistry of Fruits and their Products.* ed. Hulme, A. C. Vol. 1, p. 239. London & New York: Academic Press.

Nursten, H. E. & Williams, A. A. (1967) *Chem. & Ind.*, 486.

Nursten, H. E. & Williams, A. A. (1969a) *J. Sci. Fd. Agric.*, **20**, 91.

Nursten, H. E. & Williams, A. A. (1969b) *J. Sci. Fd. Agric.*, **20**, 613.

Nursten, H. E. & Woolfe, M. L. (1972) *J. Sci. Fd. Agric.*, **23**, 803.

Nutting, M. D., Harris, J. G., Feustel, I. C. & Olcott, H. S. (1955) *Fd. Technol.*, **9**, 466.

Oda, K. & Okada, T. (1966) *Rept. Toyo J. Coll. Inst. Fd. Technol.*, (1964–1965) Ser. **7**, 49.

Olaru, M. & Economu, V. (1970) *Industria Alimentara*, **21**(5), 241.

Örsi, F. & Erdös, Z. (1973) *Conf. Proc. Aromatickych Iatkach v Pozivatinach* Bratislava, Czechoslovakia, p. 22.

Owens, C. R., Drake, S. R., Ammerman, G. R. & Dull, G. (1973) *Hort. Sci.*, **8**, 123.

Palmer, J. G. (1971) In: *The Biochemistry of Fruits and their Products*, ed. Hulme, A. C. Vol. 2, p. 65. London & New York: Academic Press.

Panalaks, T. & Murray, T. K. (1970) *Can. Inst. Fd. Sci. Technol. J.*, **3**, 145.

Parkinson, T. L. & Barker, C. J. (1957) *J. Sci. Fd. Agric.*, **8**, 639.

Parliament, T. H. (1972) *J. Agric. Fd. Chem.*, **20**, 1043.

Paroz, P., Seale, P. E. & Harper, K. A. (1973) *Fd. Technol. Australia*, **25**(3), 130.

Pequignot, G., Vinit, F., Chabert, C., Bodard, M. & Perles, S. (1975) *Annales de la Nutrition et d'Alimentation*, **29**, 439.

Pollard, A. & Timberlake, C. F. (1971) In: *The Biochemistry of Fruits and their Products*, ed. Hulme, A. C. Vol. 2, p. 573. London & New York: Academic Press.

Popov, K., Kolev, D. & Vladimirov, G. (1969) *Nauchni Trudove, Nauchnoizsledovatelski Institut po Konservnaya Promyshlennost, Plovdiv*, **6**, 65.

Postlmayr, H. L., Luh, B. S. & Leonard, S. J. (1956) *Fd. Technol.*, **10**, 618.

Powers, J. J. (1976) *CRC Crit. Rev. Fd. Sci. Nutr.*, **7**, 371.

Pruthi, J. S. (1959a) *Food Sci. (Mysore)*, **8**, 396.

Pruthi, J. S. (1959b) *Indian Fd. Packer*, July, 7.

Pruthi, J. S. (1963) *Advan. Fd. Res.*, **12**, 203.

Pruthi, J. S., Lal, G., Dhopeshwarkar, G. A. & Magar, N. (1955) *J. Indian Chem. Soc. (Ind. News Edn.)*, **18**, 236.

Pruthi, J. S. & Lal, G. (1958) *Fd. Res.*, **23**, 505.

Pruthi, J. S. & Lal, G. (1959) *J. Sci. Fd. Agric.*, **10**, 188.

Purseglove, J. W. (1968) *Tropical Crops: Dicotyledons*. Vols. 1 & 2. London: Longmans.

Pyne, A. W. & Wick, E. L. (1965) *J. Fd. Sci.*, **30**, 192.

Ranganna, S. (1974) *Indian Fd. Packer*, **28**, 5.

Ranganna, S. & Parpia, H. A. B. (1974a) *Lebensm.-Wiss u. Technol.*, **7**, 101.

Ranganna, S. & Parpia, H. A. B. (1974b) *Lebensm.-Wiss u. Technol.*, **7**, 111.

Ranganna, S. & Siddappa, G. S. (1961) *Fd. Technol.*, **15**, 204.

Rao, P. V. S., Prasad, P. S. R. K. & Rao, G. N. (1968) *Indian Fd. Packer*, **22**(3), 18.

Rees, D. I. (1958) *J. Sci. Fd. Agric.*, **9**, 404.

Reeve, R. M. (1953) *Fd. Res.*, **18**, 604.

Reeve, R. M. (1965) *Fd. Technol.*, **19**, 78.

Reeve, R. M. (1970) *J. Text. Studies*, **1**, 247.

Reeve, R. M. & Leinbach, L. R. (1953) *Fd. Res.*, **18**, 592.

Reyes, P. & Luh, B. S. (1962) *Fd. Technol.*, **14**, 570.

Rice, A. C. & Pederson, C. S. (1954) *Fd. Res.*, **19**, 106.

Rivas, N. & Luh, B. S. (1968) *J. Fd. Sci.*, **33**, 358.

Romani, R. J. & Jennings, W. G. (1971) In: *The Biochemistry of Fruits and their Products*, ed. Hulme, A. C. Vol. 2, p. 411. London & New York: Academic Press.

Rouse, A. H., Atkins, C. D. & Moore, E. L. (1956) *Proc. Florida, State Hort. Soc.*, **69**, 145.

Ruchkovskii, B. S., Fiktin, L. A. & Palyura, A. N. (1975) *Voprosy Pitaniya*, No. 4, 78.

Ruskov, P. & Tanchev, S. S. (1973) *Prikladnaya Biokhimiya i Mikrobiologiya*, **9**, 907.

Salem, S. A. & Hegazi, S. M. (1973) *J. Sci. Fd. Agric.*, **24**, 123.

Salunkhe, D. K., Do, J. Y. & Bolin, H. R. (1973) *CRC Crit. Rev. Fd. Technol.*, **4**, 153.

Salunkhe, D. K. & Do, J. Y. (1977) *CRC Crit. Rev. Fd. Sci. Nutr.*, **8**, 161.

Sanchez Nieva, F. Hernandez, I. & Bueso de Vinas, G. (1970) *J. Agric. University Puerto Rico*, **54**, 211.

Saravacos, G. D. & Charm, S. E. (1962) *Fd. Technol.*, **16**, 78, 91.

Sazena, S. K., Parekh, C. M. & Lal, G. (1956) *The Bull. CFTRI (Mysore)*, **5**, 241.

Schaller, A., Leuprecht, H. & Theodorinis, N. (1970) *Confructa*, **15**, 72.

Schinz, H. & Seidel, C. F. (1961) *Helv. Chim. Acta*, **44**, 278.

Schoenemann, D. R. & Lopez, A. (1973) *J. Fd. Sci.*, **38**, 195.

Schormüller, J. & Grosch, W. (1964) *Z. Lebensm. Unters.-Forsch.*, **126**, 38.

Seale, P. E. & Sherman, G. D. (1960) *Commercial Passion-Fruit Processing in Hawaii*, Hawaii Agric. Exptl. Stn., circular No. 58.

Seck, S. & Crouzet, J. (1973) *Phytochem.*, **12**, 2925.

Seelenberger, P. & Luh, B. S. (1971) *Confructa*, **16**(3/4), 145.

Shallenberger, R. S., Moyer, J. C., LaBelle, R. L., Robinson, W. B. & Hand, D. B. (1963) *Fd. Technol.*, **17**, 102.

Shankaranarayana, M. L., Abraham, K. O., Raghavan, B. & Natarajan, C. D. (1975) *CRC Crit. Rev. Fd. Sci. Nutr.*, **6**, 271.

Shankaranarayana, M. L., Raghavan, B., Abraham, K. O. & Natarajan, C. D. (1973) *CRC Crit. Rev. Fd. Technol.*, **4**, 395.

Shaw, P. E., Tatum, J. H., Kew, T. J. & Berry, R. E. (1970) *Conf. Proc. Citrus Chemistry and Utilization, Winter Haven, Florida*, USDA ARS 72–79, p. 21.

Shaw, P. E., Tatum, J. H. & Berry, R. E. (1977) In: *Developments in Food Carbohydrate—I*, eds. Birch, G. G. & Shallenberger, R. S., p. 91. London: Applied Sci. Publ.

Shimoda, Y., Oku, M., Mori, D. & Sawayama, Z. (1968) *Rept. Tokyo Inst. Fd. Technol. (Japan)*, **8**, 130.

Shrikhande, A. J. (1976) *CRC Crit. Rev. Fd. Sci. Nutr.*, **7**, 193.

Siddappa, G. S., Bhatia, B. S. & Lal, G. (1956) *Indian J. Sci. Ind. Res.*, **15c**, 28.

Siddappa, G. S. & Bhatia, B. S. (1956a) *Indian J. Sci. Ind. Res.* **15c**, 118.

Siddappa, G. S. & Bhatia, B. S. (1956b) *The Bull. CFTRI (Mysore)*, **5**, 236.

Siddappa, G. S. & Bhatia, B. S. (1958) *Fd. Sci. (Mysore)*, **7**(5), 114.

Siddappa, G. S., Krishnamurthy, G. V., Nanjundaswamy, A. M. & Setty, L. (1965) *Proc. 1st Int. Congr. Fd. Sci. Technol.*, ed. Leitch, J. M., **4**, 702. London & New York: Gordon & Breach.

Siegel, A., Markakis, P. & Bedford, C. L. (1971) *J. Fd. Sci.*, **36**, 962.
Silverstein, R. M. (1971) In: *The Biochemistry of Fruits and their Products*, ed. Hulme, A. C. Vol. 2, p. 325. London & New York: Academic Press.
Singleton, V. L., Willis, A. G. & Young, H. Y. (1961) *J. Fd. Sci.*, **26**, 49.
Sistrunk, W. A. & Cash, J. N. (1970) *Fd. Technol.*, **24**, 473.
Skorikova, G. & Lyashenko, E. P. (1972) *Izvestiya Vysshikh Uchebnykh Zavedenii Pishchevaya Tekhnologiya*, No. 3, 80.
Sloan, J. L., Bills, D. & Libbey, L. M. (1969) *J. Agric. Fd. Chem.*, **17**, 1370.
Souty, M. (1972) *Qual. Plant Mater. Veg.*, **21**, 223.
Souty, M. & Andre, P. (1975) *Annales de Technologie Agricole*, **24**, 217.
Souty, M. & Perret, A. (1970) *Annales de Technologie Agricole*, **19**, 41.
Stafford, A. E., Cavaletto, C. G. & Brekke, J. E. (1966) *Papaya Processing*. Tech. Prog. Rept. No. 157. University of Hawaii: Hawaii Agric. Exptl. Stn.
Sterling, C. (1955) *Fd. Res.*, **20**, 474.
Stevens, K. L., Brekke, J. E. & Stern, D. J. (1970) *J. Agric. Fd. Chem.*, **18**, 598.
Stevens, M. A. (1970) *J. Am. Soc. Hort. Sci.*, **95**, 461.
Stoewsand, G. S. & Anderson, J. L. (1973) *J. Fd. Sci.*, **38**, 1256.
Stoewsand, G. S., Anderson, J. L. & Lamb, R. C. (1975) *J. Fd. Sci.*, **40**, 1107.
Stone, E. J., Hall, R. M. & Kazenak, S. J. (1971) Abstracts of papers, *Am. Chem. Soc.*, **162**, AGFD: 31.
Swisher, H. E. & Swisher, L. H. (1971) In: *Fruit and Vegetable Juice Processing Technology*. ed. Tressler, D. K. & Joslyn, M. A., p. 125. Westport, Conn.: Avi. Publ. Co. Inc.
Sykes, S. M. & Kelly, F. H. C. (1969) *J. Sci. Fd. Agric.*, **20**, 654.
Takahana, H. & Ogura, N. (1967) *Chiba Univ. Hort. Sci. Rept. No.* 15, p. 39.
Tanchev, S. S. (1971) *Nauchni Trudove, Vissh. Institut po Khranitelna i elua i Vkusova Promyshlennost*, **18**, 383.
Tanchev, S. S. (1972a) *Z. Lebensm. Unters.-Forsch.*, **150**, 28.
Tanchev, S. S. (1972b) *Ind. Obst u. Gemüse*, **57**, 315.
Tang, C. S. (1970a) Abstracts of papers, *Am. Chem. Soc.*, **160**, AGFD: 92.
Tang, C. S. (1970b) *Phytochemistry*, **10**, 117.
Tang, C. S. & Jennings, W. G. (1967) *J. Agric. Fd. Chem.*, **15**, 24.
Tang, C. S. & Jennings, W. G. (1968) *J. Agric. Fd. Chem.*, **16**, 252.
Tankersley, E. W. (1953) *Colour and Colour Changes in Food, Especially Fruit*. Bibliographic Series No. 2. Chicago, Illinois: Quartermaster Food and Container Institute.
Tate, J. N., Luh, B. S. & York, G. K. (1964) *J. Fd. Sci.*, **29**, 829.
Tatum, J. H., Shaw, P. E. & Berry, R. E. (1967) *J. Agric. Fd. Chem.*, **15**, 773.
Teranishi, R., Corse, J. W., McFadden, W. H., Black, D. R. & Morgan, A. I., Jr. (1963) *J. Fd. Sci.*, **28**, 478.
Ting, S. V. & Attaway, J. A. (1971) In: *The Biochemistry of Fruits and their Products*, ed. Hulme, A. C. Vol. 2, p. 107. London & New York: Academic Press.
Toldby, V. & Wiley, R. C. (1962) *Proc. Am. Soc. Hort. Sci.*, **81**, 78.
Torline, P. & Ballschmieter, H. M. B. (1973) *Lebensm. -Wiss u. Technol.*, **6**, 32.
van Buren, J. P. (1970) *CRC Crit. Rev. Fd. Technol.*, **1**, 5.
van Buren, J. P. (1974) *J. Fd. Sci.*, **39**, 1203.

van der Merwe, H. B. (1963) *Fd. Inds. S. Africa*, **61**, 56.

van Oss, J. F., Codo, L. W., Dijkhoff, K., Fearon, J. H., Roebersen, H. G. & Stanford, E. G. (eds.) (1975) *Materials and Technology. Vol. 7: Vegetable Food Products.* London & Amsterdam: J. H. de Bussy, Longman.

Veldhuis, M. K. (1971a) In : *Fruit and Vegetable Juice Processing Technology,* ed. Tressler, D. K. & Joslyn, M. A., 2nd edn., p. 92. Westport, Conn.: Avi. Publ. Co. Inc.

Veldhuis, M. K. (1971b) In: *Fruit and Vegetable Juice Processing Technology,* ed. Tressler, D. K. & Joslyn, M. A. 2nd edn., p. 31. Westport, Conn.: Avi. Publ. Co. Inc.

Viani, R., Bricout, J., Marion, J. P., Muggler-Chavan, F., Reymond, D. & Egli, R. H. (1969) *Helv. Chim. Acta*, **52**, 887.

Villarreal, F., Luh, B. S. & Leonard, S. J. (1960) *Fd. Technol.*, **14**, 176.

von Sydow, E. & Karlsson, G. (1971a) *Lebensm.-Wiss u. Technol.*, **4**, 54.

von Sydow, E. & Karlsson, G. (1971b) *Lebensm.-Wiss u. Technol.*, **4**, 152.

Williams, M. P. & Nelson, P. E. (1974) *J. Fd. Sci.*, **39**, 457.

Winter, M., Palluy, E., Hinder, M. & Willhalm, B. (1962) *Helv. Chim. Acta*, **45**, 2186.

Winton, A. L. & Winton, K. B. (1935) *The Structure and Composition of Foods. Vol. 2: Vegetables, Legumes, Fruits.* New York: John Wiley.

Yamamoto, H. Y. (1964) *Nature*, **201**, 1049.

Yankov, S. I. (1973) *Nauchni Trudove, Vissh. Institut po Khranitelna i elua i Vkusova Promyshlennost*, **20**, 29.

Yufera, E. P., Mosse, J. K. & Iranzo, J. R. (1961) In: *New Results in Science and Technology of Fruit Juices.* Vol. III, p. 17. Zurich: International Federation Fruit Juice Producers, Julius-Verlag.

CHAPTER 10

Vegetables

S. D. HOLDSWORTH

Campden Food Preservation Research Association, Chipping Campden, UK

Vegetables, unlike the majority of fruits, are primarily eaten in the cooked form and are also widely processed by various techniques including canning, freezing and dehydration. Despite the fact that most vegetables are heat treated in some way, the amount of information in terms of detailed chemical and physical changes is relatively meagre. Where this information is available, it has been quoted more extensively, but in many cases where a change has been observed without explanation of the underlying mechanism, only brief mention has been made.

Many of the observed effects of processing are not due to heat alone and many investigations, especially those involving additives, are carried out to annul the effects of heat. However, where heat has been involved, either directly or indirectly, a note has been made to assist research workers. The effect of storage temperature on the deterioration of processed vegetables has only been mentioned where detailed work has been reported.

It will be noted that in many operations, such as canning and dehydration, the vegetable receives not only the heat treatment of the process but also a blanching treatment. This is rather different to the case of most fruits where pre-process blanching is usually not required.

The structure of each section of this chapter consists basically of a brief description of the vegetable concerned (in alphabetical order), as well as its approximate composition, followed by a discussion of the effects of heat on the volatile components, flavour, chemical composition, colour and texture. A list of references from which

TABLE 10.1
GENERAL SOURCES OF INFORMATION ON VEGETABLES

Subject	Reference
General botanical information and proximate composition	Winton & Winton (1935)
	Bender (1965)
	Duckworth (1966)
	Purseglove (1968)
	Harrison *et al.* (1969)
	Brouk (1975)
	van Oss *et al.* (1975)
	Watt *et al.* (1963)
Specific composition	
pH	Adam & Dickinson (1959)
Colour	
browning reactions	Mathew & Parpia (1971)
caroteniods	Borenstein & Bunnell (1966)
anthocyanins	Shrikhande (1976)
general	Chichester (1972)
	Herrmann (1976)
Texture	Doesburg (1961, 1965)
	van Buren (1970)
	Reeve (1970)
	Mohsenin (1970)
	Cultrera & Giannone (1965)
drained weights	Adam (1965)
Flavour and aroma	Bernhard (1966)
	Salunkhe & Do (1977)
	Neukom (1967)
	Shankaranarayana *et al.* (1973)
	Johnson *et al.* (1971)
Micronutrients	Harris & Karmas (1975)
Processing	Luh & Woodroof (1975)
	Labuza (1972)
	Salunkhe *et al.* (1973)
	Holdsworth (1971)
	Hinton & Holdsworth (1975)

much of the more general information has been obtained is given in Table 10.1.

10.1 ASPARAGUS

10.1.1 Structure and Composition

The plant *Asparagus officinalis* is a member of the Liliaceae family and is leafless but has stems. The part which is eaten is the young shoot. It is normally green in colour and must be blanched by mounding soil over the crowns before growth starts. The approximate composition is: protein, 1·4%; fat, 0·1%; micronutrients per 100 g: calcium, 14 mg; iron, 0·6 mg; vitamin A, 670 IU*; thiamine, 0·11 mg; riboflavin, 0·13 mg; niacin, 0·9 mg; and ascorbic acid, 22 mg. The pH of the canned product is in the range 5·5–6·0 whereas that of the raw product is 6·2–6·7 (Eheart and Gott, 1965). The main flavonols are quercetin and raempferol (Wöldecke and Herrmann, 1974a).

10.1.2 Effects of Heat

It has frequently been observed (de Eds and Couch, 1948; Stevenson, 1950; Dame, 1957) that processing asparagus causes the formation of a yellow precipitate which has been identified as the flavonoid glycoside, rutin (quercetin-3-rutinoside). The dark discolouration, which often develops in canned asparagus after the can has been opened, is due to an interaction between iron, oxygen and rutin. Davis *et al.* (1961) believe the reaction involves oxidation of ferrous ions to ferric ions which then react with rutin to produce the discolouration. They concluded that if the tin:iron ratio is greater than 15:1 the stannous ion reduces and holds the iron in the ferrous state, thus diminishing its ability to react with rutin. Addition of citric acid was also found to inhibit darkening. Hernandez and Vosti (1963) and Lueck (1970) have studied the formation of iron complexes with tin in the presence of asparagus as well as in model systems.

The effect of processing on the chemical composition of asparagus was further investigated by Dame *et al.* (1957) who showed that steam blanching caused little change in rutin and ascorbic acid but water blanching (100°C, 3 min) caused a 24% loss of ascorbic acid and 22% loss of rutin. Other workers have studied nutrient retention during cooking and canning (Gleim *et al.*, 1944; Hinman *et al.*, 1944; Lamb *et*

*1 IU vitamin A ≡ activity of 0·60 µg crystalline β-carotene.

al., 1947; Wagner *et al.*, 1947). The vitamins retained after processing varied between 83–93% for ascorbic acid, 70–84% for thiamine and 89–99% for riboflavin. Wagner *et al.* (1947) showed that there was a greater retention of ascorbic acid (94%), thiamine (99%) and riboflavin (90%) for a 15-min process at 120°C than for a 25-min process at 115·6°C which gave retentions of 83, 84 and 89%, respectively, although the major losses of nutrients occurred during blanching. Cruess and Sugihara (1949) found that the oxidising enzymes present in asparagus were catalase and peroxidase.

Mouri *et al.* (1968a) have investigated the changes in nucleic acids during boiling of asparagus. Nucleotides were formed by autolytic reactions involving adenosine triphosphate and adenosine diphosphate.

Ralls (1959) investigated the formation of acetoin (3-hydroxy-2-butanone) in canned asparagus. It was considered that, during the initial heating period, pyruvic acid is converted to acetoin, the reaction being catalysed by thiamine. The concentration of acetoin was found to increase with time, reaching a maximum of about 340 p.p.m. after 15 min and then decreasing with further heating. The cause of the decrease was thought to be due to the destruction of thiamine. The rôle of acetoin as a flavour component may be due to the ease with which it autooxidises to biacetyl.

The effect of heat on the texture of asparagus has been studied by several workers (Barbiroli *et al.*, 1972; Berwell *et al.*, 1973; Monzini *et al.*, 1974; Motohiro *et al.*, 1973; Motohiro and Inoue, 1973). The effect of blanching and canning has received particular attention from the last-mentioned workers who measured shear value, springiness and hardness of raw, blanched, and canned asparagus. Blanching was shown to increase the springiness and shear value but decreased the hardness, and the values of all these factors were reduced appreciably by retorting. The cells of the asparagus stalks were found to be deformed severely by the heating process.

In an interesting study by Freytag and Ney (1968) the rate of dimethylsulphide formation was compared during cooking and during the boiling of a solution of S-methylmethionine sulphonium salt. They concluded that a possible degradation route for methionine was the formation of S-methylmethionine sulphonium salt and subsequent thermal breakdown to dimethylsulphide and acrolein.

A number of other compounds have been identified in asparagus, including acetaldehyde, vanillin, a methyl ketone, ammonia, primary amines, a thiol ester and β,β-dimercaptoisobutyric acid (Jansen, 1949; Hall *et al.*, 1950; Gutterman and Lovejoy, 1951; Lovejoy, 1952).

10.2 BEETROOT

10.2.1 Structure and Composition

The garden, table or common red beet is the root of the plant *Beta vulgaris*. Some other species are mangel-wurzels, sugar beets (grown especially for the sugar content) and chard. The shape of beets varies from an elongated conical shape to flat-topped globular. The cross-section of red beet shows alternating light and dark concentric rings. The light rings consist of zones of bundles each consisting of phloem, cambium and xylem elements. Separating the light rings are darker zones which are rich in deep-red cell sap. The colour varies from deep red to yellow or white. The composition of garden beet is approximately: water, 83%; protein, 1·8%; carbohydrate (mainly sucrose), 10%; micronutrients per 100 g: iron, 0·7 mg; calcium, 30 mg; vitamin A, 20 IU; thiamine, 0·03 mg; riboflavin, 0·04 mg; niacin, 0·06 mg; and ascorbic acid, 10 mg. The pH is between 5·2 and 5·5.

10.2.2 Effects of Heat

Colour is one of the more important quality attributes of canned beetroot and, consequently, a knowledge of the behaviour of the pigments on heating is important. The main red and yellow pigments of garden or table beets are the betacyanins and betaxanthins. The major betacyanin present in beets is betanin (Wyler and Dreiding, 1957; Schmidt and Schoeuleben, 1957; Peterson and Joslyn, 1960; Wyler *et al.*, 1963). von Elbe *et al.* (1972) have carried out a quantitative study of the betacyanins in table beet and reported the presence of isobetanin (5-O-betaglucoside of betanin), isobetanidin (5-O-betaglucoside of betanidin), prebetanidin (sulphate monoester of betanin) and isoprebetanin (sulphate monoester of isobetanin). Lusas (1959, 1960) studied changes in colour of beet juice on canning and found a strong correlation between optical density of the raw juice and colour of the canned product. Shannon (1972) has carried out extensive work on changes of soluble solids, red-pigment content and firmness of several cultivars. Clark and Moyer (1955) and Boscan (1962) have studied the surface darkening of beets resulting from oxidation of phenolic components, owing to both autooxidation and

betanin and isobetanin

enzymic oxidation by beet phenolase. Vilece *et al.* (1955) found that even sterilised beet purée turned brown near the surface owing to residual oxygen in the headspace of the container. More recent work concerning the effect of heat treatments on the pigments of beetroot has been reported by Aurstad and Dahle (1973). Both tin and iron may react with beet pigments to produce blackening (Pyysalo and Kuusi, 1973) and it is usual to avoid handling or cutting beetroot with any metal other than stainless steel (Huffman, 1963).

Several flavour changes result from heating beet purée. Pyrrolidone carboxylic acid is formed by decomposition of glutamine (Shallenberger *et al.*, 1959; Lee *et al.*, 1971) and acetoin is a product of the degradation of pyruvic acid (Ralls, 1959). One of the main volatile flavour constituents which has been isolated is geosmin (*trans*-1,10-dimethyl-trans-9-decalol), probably derived from Actinomycetes organisms (Murray *et al.*, 1975; Acree *et al.*, 1976).

The effect of heat on the texture of beet dice and slices has been studied by Patton *et al.* (1943), Chwiej and Kurlowicz (1972), Shannon and Bourne (1971) and Konishi *et al.* (1975). The texture of cooked and canned beetroot is very important in the assessment of its quality and it is usual to pre-cook prior to canning. For small roots, 2–4-cm diameter, about 15 min in boiling water is required and about 20 min for large roots, 4–6-cm diameter.

The effect of heating on the ascorbic acid retention of beet (variety 'Ruby Queen') has been reported by Lee *et al.* (1976). The average ascorbic acid content of the raw beet was 9·28 mg/100 g and this was reduced to about half (4·70 mg/100 g) after soaking in 12% sodium hydroxide at 88°C for 10 min. Retorting the cans for 13 min at 125°C further reduced ascorbic acid content to 2·15 mg/100 g. Ives *et al.* (1945) have studied the retention of B-group vitamins in canned beets.

Relatively little information is available concerning the dehydration of beet and the chemical and physical changes which take place during the drying cycle. Ede and Hales (1948) have studied the kinetics of air drying. Cording *et al.* (1963) have used explosive puffing to produce dried beet dice and Weichel (1966) has employed a spray dryer to produce powder for use as a food colour.

10.3 BROCCOLI OR CALABRESE

10.3.1 Structure and Composition
Broccoli is the flower of the plant *Brassica oleracea* (Italian group). It is commonly known as white- and purple-sprouting broccoli depending on the variety. The florets grow on a stalk with leaves and all parts are eaten when young. The approximate composition is: water, 89·1%; protein, 3·6%; fat, 0·3%; carbohydrate, 5·9%; micronutrients per 100 g: calcium, 103 mg; phosphorus, 78 mg; iron, 1·1 mg; vitamin A, 2500 IU (flower clusters); thiamine, 0·10 mg; riboflavin, 0·23 mg; and ascorbic acid, 113 mg. The pH of the canned product is about 5·6.

10.3.2 Effects of Heat
The main method of processing is by quick-freezing which involves blanching, although a small amount is canned. The fresh vegetable is eaten after boiling.

The main volatile components contributing to aroma and flavour are: dimethylsulphide and trimethylsulphide, 2,4,5-trithiahexane, 4-methylthiobutyl- and 2-phenylethyl isothiocyanates, 4-methylthio-butylcyanide, 2-phenylethylcyanide and a number of aliphatic and aromatic aldehydes including nonanal and phenylacetaldehyde (Buttery *et al.*, 1976).

The effect of heat on the retention of ascorbic acid has been widely studied (Paul and Ferley, 1954; Martin *et al.*, 1960; Eheart and Gott, 1965; Jara, 1974; Rognerud, 1972; Odland and Eheart, 1975). Cooking for 20 min in boiling water reduced the ascorbic acid content from 30·8 to 22·7 mg/100 g and microwave cooking for 15 min resulted in a similar loss (Martin *et al.*, 1960). A range of heating techniques has been used by Eheart and Gott (1965) to study the effect of heat on chlorophyll, ascorbic acid content and pH of broccoli. These techniques included stir-fry, microwave cooking, boiling in water with a 4:1 ratio or 0·5:1 ratio of water to broccoli. The stir-fry method was the best for retention of nutrients and boiling using the larger ratio of water to product was found to be beneficial to all attributes except ascorbic acid retention. Rognerud (1972) obtained similar results regarding the loss of ascorbic acid but found that the best method of processing was steam cooking closely followed by pressure cooking. Odland and Eheart (1975) compared various methods of blanching broccoli and found that the use of ammonium bicarbonate in conjunction with steam blanching resulted in an excellent product, which was as green as water-blanched broccoli and had a nutrient retention as high as that obtained using conventional steam blanching. It was thought that the volatile acids which tend to accelerate chlorophyll degradation are neutralised by the presence of ammonia. The effect of blanching time on the enzymic production of ethyl alcohol has been studied by Buck and Joslyn (1953) who showed that for blanching times less than 3 min, off-flavours developed, accompanied by a significant increase in ethyl alcohol. Yields and solids losses during steam blanching and cooling have been reported by Bomben *et al.* (1975).

Changes in the lipid components of broccoli brought about by various heat treatments have been investigated by Dahlke (1966). The effects were most pronounced on the lipids of the neutral fraction whereas the free fatty acids and phospholipid fraction suffered little change.

Kylen *et al.* (1961) and Schrumpf and Charley (1975) have studied the effects of microwave heating on the quality attributes of broccoli (see also Eheart and Gott, 1965). Microwave heating tends to dehydrate the tissue and increase the crystallinity of the carbohydrate gels of the cell walls. The effects are very complex and, with broccoli, the outer layers tend to become tough and the inner core becomes rather soft. Schrumpf and Charley (1975) found that the weight loss of the cooked vegetable was 26·8% using microwave heating for 5 min but only 11·0% after boiling in water for 12 min.

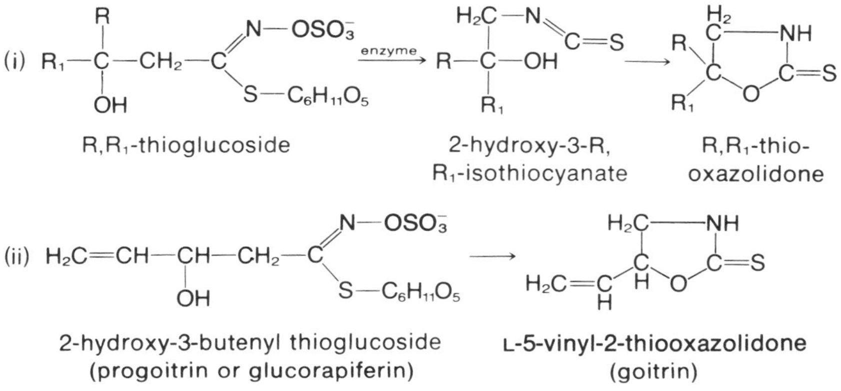

FIG. 10.1   Decomposition of thioglucosides.

Kozlowsa (1971) has studied the destruction of thioglucoside derivatives, *i.e.* isothiocyanates, thiocyanates and L-5-vinyl-2-thiooxazolidone (goitrin), losses amounting to 30–50% when broccoli was boiled. The thiooxazolidones are formed by decomposition of thioglucosides and the cyclisation of isothiocyanates, as shown in Fig. 10.1.

10.4   BRUSSELS SPROUTS

10.4.1   Structure and Composition

Brussels sprouts are the leaf buds of the plant *Brassica oleracea gemmifera*. The heads resemble small cabbages and grow out from the vertical stalk. The general composition is: water, 85·2%; protein, 4·9%; fat, 0·4%; carbohydrate, 8·3%; micronutrients per 100 g: calcium, 36 mg; phosphorus, 80 mg; iron, 1·5 mg; vitamin A, 550 IU; thiamine, 0·1 mg; riboflavin, 0·16 mg; and ascorbic acid, 102 mg.

10.4.2   Effects of Heat

Self *et al.* (1963) have studied the low-boiling volatiles of cooked Brussels sprouts and suggested that those which are commonly found in other vegetables arise from the decomposition and degradation of metabolites, such as proteins and amino acids, which are normally present in all biological material. The main components produced after boiling for 30 min are given in diminishing order of concentration as follows: methanethiol, dimethylsulphide, methanol, hydrogen sulphide, acetaldehyde, propionaldehyde, acetone, ethanethiol and 2-methylpropanal.

More recently, MacLeod and MacLeod (1970a) have made an exhaustive analysis of flavour volatiles and identified further components including diethyl ketone, diacetyl, allyl cyanide, allyl isothiocyanate and *cis*-pent-3-ene-1-ol. Allyl isothiocyanate is produced by the enzymic action of myrosinase on sinigrin, a thioglucoside, and allyl cyanide is produced by thermal degradation (Fig. 10.2). Consequently the frozen product, which has been blanched to inhibit enzyme action, shows an increase in the allyl cyanide and decrease in allyl isothiocyanate content. Kozlowsa (1971) found that thioglucosides in Brussels sprouts amounted to 16·2 mg/100 g and that vinyl thiooxazolidone was also present.

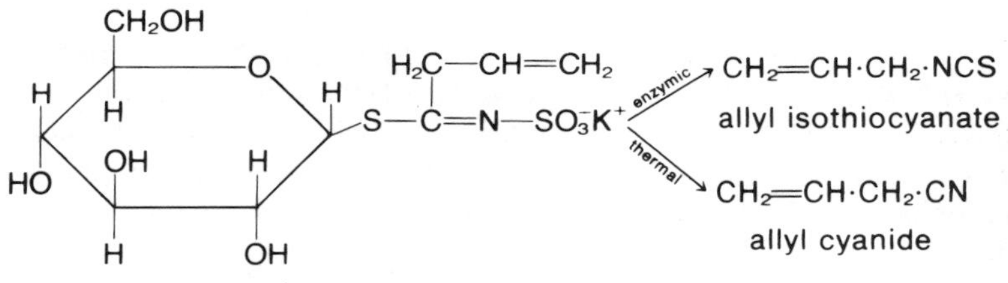

Sinigrin–potassium myronate

FIG. 10.2   Breakdown of sinigrin.

Swirski *et al.* (1969) found that, on heating Brussels sprouts, a water-soluble green pigment was formed. This was shown to be a complex mixture containing a water-soluble protein moiety, copper and zinc ions, and chlorophylls and their derivatives. The phenomenon does not appear to have received further attention.

Brussels sprouts are rarely canned, probably because of the rather objectionable sulphide smell produced by the decomposition of sulphur-containing proteins. The effect of blanching and sterilisation on the quality of canned sprouts has been studied by Steinbuch (1969, 1970) who found they were susceptible to oxidation if the headspace was too great, resulting in off-flavours. The best conditions for preventing the formation of bitter flavours were found to be a long, low-temperature blanch (70°C, 15 min) followed by a short sterilisation at 125°C with rotation.

Much work has been carried out on the blanching of sprouts for freezing (Lindquist *et al.*, 1951; Masure, 1953; Sykes and Tinsley, 1955; Böttcher, 1962; Sweeney and Martin, 1961; Dietrich and Neumann, 1965; Dietrich *et al.*, 1970; Bomben *et al.*, 1973, 1975). The major requirement is to give the minimum blanch which will result in adequate retention of colour and flavour. Failure to inactivate enzymes completely results in a pink discolouration and off-flavour and, since blanching time is dependent on size of material, small sprouts are preferred for freezing. Dietrich and Neumann (1965) found that water blanching inactivated enzymes more rapidly than steam blanching and produced less chlorophyll degradation. For large sprouts, a pre-blanch tempering in water was beneficial and reduced the conversion of chlorophyll to pheophytin. However, steam blanching gave the greatest retention of ascorbic acid (see also Adam and Horner, 1941; Adam and Stanworth, 1941). Dietrich *et al.* (1970) showed that less chlorophyll degradation was produced by water blanching than by microwave or steam blanching or by combinations of these methods. Individual quick blanching (IQB), a modified method of steam blanching, results in lesss leaching of solids than other methods (Bomben *et al.*, 1973).

10.5 CABBAGE

10.5.1 Structure and Composition

Cabbage is the leaves of the plant *Brassica oleracea capitata*. The colour varies from intense red to green or almost white. The fresh leaves are usually boiled and eaten rather than being processed, although dehydration has been used to some extent. The average composition is: water, 92·4%; protein, 1·3%; fat, 0·2%; carbohydrate, 5·4%; micronutrients per 100 g: calcium, 49 mg; iron, 0·4 mg; phosphorus, 29 mg; vitamin A, 130 IU; thiamine, 0·05 mg; riboflavin, 0·05 mg and ascorbic acid, 47 mg.

10.5.2 Effects of Heat

The volatiles of cabbage have been extensively studied (see excellent reviews by Johnson *et al.*, 1971 and Salunkhe and Do, 1977). The major components are:

(a) Sulphides and mercaptans, including hydrogen sulphide, alkyl mono-, di- and trisulphides, and alkyl thiols;
(b) alcohols, mainly methanol, ethanol and hex-*cis*,3-enol;

(c) isothiocyanates including methyl-, allyl-, but-3-enyl- and 3-methylthiopropyl derivatives;

(d) cyanides (allyl cyanide); and

(e) aldehydes and ketones (Jensen *et al.*, 1953; Hewitt *et al.*, 1956; Dateo *et al.*, 1957; Clapp *et al.*, 1959; Bailey *et al.*, 1961; MacLeod and MacLeod, 1968, 1970a,b,c). More recently, Murray and Whitfield (1975) have identified 3-isopropyl-2-methoxypyrazine and Buttery *et al.* (1976) have identified other volatile compounds including 3-methylthiopropyl cyanide, 4-methylthiobutyl cyanide 2-phenylethyl cyanide, 2-phenylethyl isothiocyanate and 2,4,5-trithiahexane. The development of isothiocyanates from thioglucosides has already been mentioned with regard to Brussels sprouts (loc. cit.) (see also Kozlowsa, 1971).

The effect of cooking on cabbage has been studied by Dateo *et al.* (1957) and MacLeod and MacLeod (1970a,c). Saturated aldehydes are formed by Strecker degradation of the corresponding amino acid, dimethylsulphide and dipropylsulphide, particularly after long periods of cooking. Allyl isothiocyanate and allyl cyanide behave in a similar manner as described for Brussels sprouts (loc. cit.) *i.e.* the amount formed increases to a maximum and then falls as cooking is continued. MacLeod and MacLeod (1970c) suggest this is due to the exhaustion of sinigrin rather than the destruction of the enzyme myrosinase. Microwave irradiation was also studied and it was found to have a different effect from boiling. The amount of *trans*-pent-ene-1-al formed was much greater and the maximum concentrations of allyl isothiocyanate and allyl cyanide were reached much more rapidly using microwave heating.

Maruyama (1970) has identified dimethyltrisulphide, formed by decomposition of S-methyl-1-cysteine, as a major contributor to the aroma profile. Virtanen (1967) has studied the mustard oil glucosides of cabbage, in particular the indole thioglucoside, glucobrassicin. The enzymatic degradation is shown in Fig. 10.3.

The effect of dehydration on the flavour volatiles of cabbage has been studied by Bailey *et al.* (1961) and MacLeod and MacLeod (1970b). The major component remaining after dehydration is dimethylsulphide. Allyl cyanide was greatly increased but allyl isothiocyanate was almost completely lost. However, if myrosinase is added to the product before reconstitution, the characteristic flavour

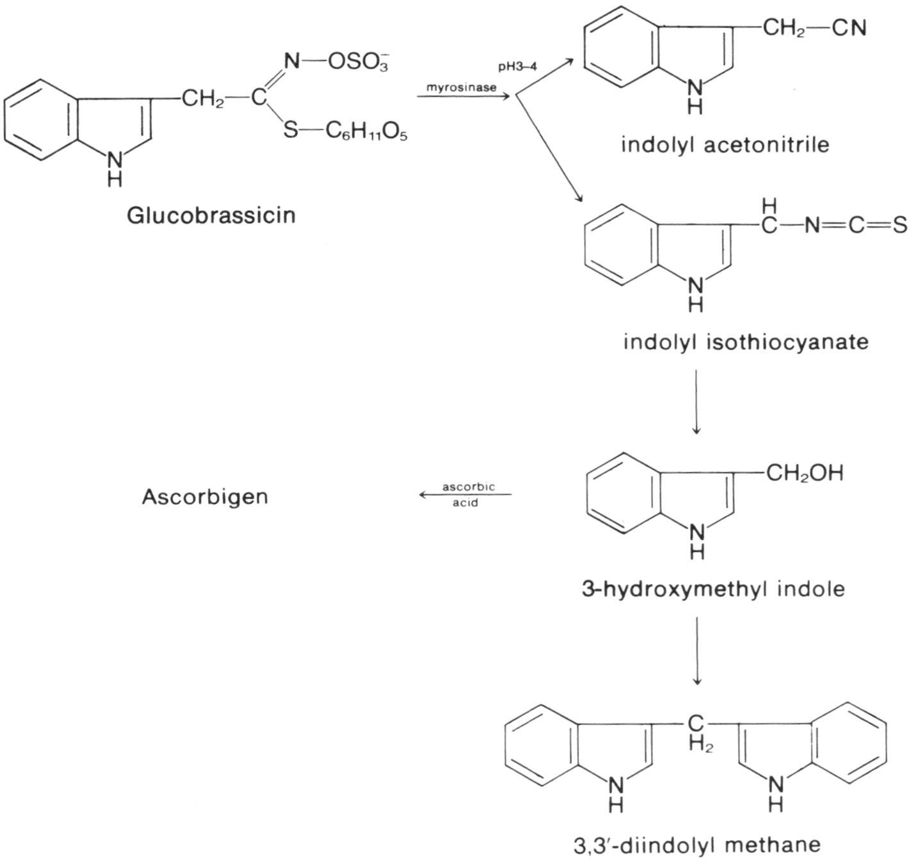

FIG. 10.3 Enzymatic degradation of glucobrassicin.

is regenerated to a large extent (Bailey *et al.*, 1961; Schwimmer, 1963). This implies that, although the glucosinolate is not destroyed by processing, myrosinase is inactivated. Dehydrated samples also contained far less saturated alcohols than fresh cabbage and, although the total aldehyde contents were similar, increases of formaldehyde and acetaldehyde occurred during drying. A number of compounds were also produced which were not present in the raw cabbage, including diethyl ether, *trans*-2-butanenitrile and acrylonitrile.

Hrdlicka and Kyzlink (1969) investigated changes in the volatile amines of canned cabbage subjected to a range of sterilising treatments. The production of volatile amines was maximum at 110°C but decreased as the temperature was raised further. The main amines present were methyl-, propyl-, ethyl-, isoamyl- and hexyl-amines; 1,4-diaminobutane; 1,5-diaminopentane; N,N'-di-1,4-diaminobutane; N-di-1,4-diaminobutane and dimethylamine.

A pink discolouration in dried cabbage has been observed by Ranganna and coworkers (1967, 1968, 1974a,b). This is considered to be due to the non-enzymic interaction of the products of ascorbic acid and amino acid degradation. The amino acids are thought to form aldehydes via the Strecker degradation and then react with dehydro-ascorbic acid and 2,3-diketogulonic acid. The discolouration is intensified by blanching, which causes the rapid oxidation of ascorbic acid. Low temperatures, such as those encountered in freeze-drying, reduce the rate of oxidation resulting in a pink discolouration whereas air-dried material was brown. Mahadeviah *et al.* (1965) also reported a pink discolouration in canned cabbage.

Steam blanching prior to dehydration of cabbage increased the yield by an average of 13·5% compared to water blanching and reduced the loss of ascorbic acid from 28·5% to 22·7% (Gooding, 1956). The water-blanched product was also more susceptible to browning during drying.

The effects of cooking on ascorbic acid destruction in cabbage have been studied by Kumar and Chandrasekhana (1973) and Herrmann (1974). Changes in weight of fresh and dried vegetables, including cabbage, have been reported by Pequignot *et al.* (1975).

10.6   CARROT

10.6.1   Structure and Composition

The carrot is the root of *Daucus carota*. It is usually orange-coloured but some varieties are deeper red and others are white or yellow. Structurally, the carrot is a tapering root which, in transverse section, is circular, having rings darker in colour on the outside (cortex), lighter orange towards the centre (outer phloem) and a greenish-yellow section at the core (inner phloem). The intense colouration is due to the presence of carotenoid pigments. The approximate composition is: water, 88·2%; protein, 1·1%; fat, 0·2%; carbohy-drates, 9·7%; micronutrients per 100 g: calcium, 37 mg; phosphorus, 36 mg; iron, 0·7 mg; vitamin A, 11 000 IU; thiamine, 0·05 mg; riboflavin,

0·05 mg and ascorbic acid, 6 mg. The pH of canned carrots varies from 5·1 to 5·9 and the effect of processing temperature on this parameter has been reported by Bibeau *et al.* (1974) and Adam and Dickinson (1959).

10.6.2 Effects of Heat

The volatiles in carrot root have been extensively studied (Self *et al.*, 1963; Hrdlicka *et al.*, 1967a; Buttery *et al.*, 1968; Heatherbell, 1970; Heatherbell and Wrolstad, 1971a,b; Heatherbell *et al.*, 1971; Alabran and Mabrouk, 1973; Murray and Whitfield, 1975; Cronin and Stanton, 1976). A large number of components were identified by Johnson *et al.* (1971) including a number of terpenes and their derivatives. 2-Methoxy-3-*sec*-butylpyrazine was found to be a major contributor to carrot aroma (Cronin and Stanton, 1976) and important compounds isolated by Heatherbell (1970), Heatherbell and Wrolstad (1971a,b) and Heatherbell *et al.* (1971) were acetaldehyde, sabinene, myrcene and terpinolene. In the cooked product, Self *et al.* (1963) found that acetaldehyde and dimethylsulphide were present in greatest amounts followed by methane and methanethiol.

Heatherbell and Wrolstad (1971b) studied the effects of canning and freeze-drying on carrot volatiles. Canning resulted in a large increase in the amount of methanol present and a significant increase in the amounts of acetaldehyde, propanol and acetone, as well as ethanethiol and dimethylsulphide, which were not present in the raw material. In the case of the higher boiling volatiles there was a decrease in most components in the canned product compared with raw carrot, the only exceptions being increases in *p*-cymene, octanal, 2-decenal and α-*p*-dimethylstyrene. The presence of sulphur compounds in the canned product is probably due to the thermal degradation of S-methylmethionine sulphonium salt. The freeze-drying process resulted in a substantial loss of volatile compounds and a consequent loss of flavour.

The sugars and amino acids present in carrot, which may interact during processing, have been studied by Alabran and Mabrouk (1973) and the effect of drying on the amino acids has been reported by Paukova (1975). Shallenberger *et al.* (1960) investigated the cause of bitterness in canned carrots and concluded that a terpene or sesquiterpene was responsible.

Several workers have reported the effects of processing on the carotenoid content of carrots (Lamb *et al.*, 1947; Weckel *et al.*, 1962;

Della Monica and McDowell, 1965; Heutschel and Overbeck, 1971; Pazrincevic-Trajkovic and Baras, 1970; Baloch *et al.*, 1977). The main effect is oxidation, which is accelerated by high temperature. Panalaks and Murray (1970) found that the amount of carotene extracted was increased by processing since cell rupture allowed more efficient extraction to take place.

The effect of heat on thiamine retention in carrots has been reported by Ingalls *et al.* (1950) and by Feliciotti and Esselen (1957) who determined kinetic parameters for the degradation.

The general effects of dehydration have been studied qualitatively and quantitatively by several workers (Gooding and Tucker, 1955; Gooding *et al.*, 1960; Palmer *et al.*, 1965; Farine *et al.*, 1965). The explosion puffing technique has been employed by Brolchain (1973) and by Cording *et al.* (1963) who give data regarding the effect of temperature and pressure on the porous characteristics of the product. The reconstitution properties of carrots dried by different techniques have been discussed by Haas *et al.* (1974). The most recent work on dehydration of carrot has been carried out by Baloch *et al.* (1977) who investigated the effect of processing variables on the quality of the dried product. Cooking in boiling water resulted in a gradual loss of carotenoids (8·2% after 15 min) and considerable leaching of soluble solids. These workers also showed that the storage life of the dried product was dependent upon the treatments received prior to drying. Increased leaching of soluble solids tended to result in more carotenoid destruction and less non-enzymic browning. The changes in structure brought about by processing have been investigated by Pendlington and Ward (1965), Sterling and Shimazu (1961), Rahman *et al.* (1971), Barbiroli *et al.* (1972) and Monzini *et al.* (1974). Changes in the crystallinity of cellulose brought about by heating are responsible for alteration of the texture, especially the softening which occurs during cooking. The texture of carrots cooked by microwave energy has been studied by Schrumpf and Charley (1975) who showed that the weight loss as a percentage of fresh weight was 34·2% using this method compared to 15·7% using a conventional cooking method. Microwave cooking also causes some dehydration of tissue, increasing the crystallinity of the carbohydrate gels of the cell wall, resulting in increased toughness.

The effect of blanching on carrots has also been studied by Adam and Stanworth (1941), Gooding (1956), Sistrunk (1969), Mohammad and Ehteschamuddin (1973) and Bomben *et al.* (1975).

Carrot purée has been processed in continuous heat exchangers and aseptically canned, which has enabled the effect of heating up to 150°C to be studied (Luh *et al.*, 1969). These workers showed that the aseptically canned product was superior to the retorted product in colour, texture and flavour. Greater amounts of 2-pyrrolidone-5-carboxylic acid and galacturonic acids were also present in the retorted product. More recently, Bibeau *et al.* (1974) and Bibeau and Clydesdale (1975) have suggested that the glutamine concentration in the raw material could be used as an indicator of processing quality. Glutamine is converted by cyclisation into 2-pyrrolidone-5-carboxylic acid which is thought to be responsible for off-flavour development.

Carrot juice is difficult to process because the application of heat causes coagulation and precipitation of the pigments, which is probably associated with protein denaturation (Stephens *et al.*, 1971). HTST processing has been employed as a means of stabilising the juice (Bates and Koburger, 1974). It was found that heating the juice to 100°C prior to HTST heating for 15 s at 143°C reduced the amount of coagulum.

10.7 CAULIFLOWER

10.7.1 Structure and Composition
The cauliflower is the white edible flower of *Brassica oleracea botrytis*. It is similar to broccoli except that the flower head is very much larger. The colour varies from white to yellow green. The average composition is: water, 91%; protein, 2·7%; fat, 0·2%; carbohydrate, 5·2%; micronutrients per 100 g: calcium, 25 mg; phosphorus, 56 mg; iron, 1·1 mg; vitamin A, 60 IU; thiamine, 0·11 mg; riboflavin, 0·10 mg; and ascorbic acid, 78 mg. The pH of the canned product varies between 5·7 and 6·1.

10.7.2 Effects of Heat
Cauliflower is mainly cooked and eaten fresh although the florets are preserved by freezing and, to a lesser extent, by canning. It is also pickled in various forms.

The volatile components of cooked cauliflower have been studied by Self *et al.* (1963) who found large amounts of methanethiol, dimethylsulphide and hydrogen sulphide, with similar amounts of acetaldehyde, propionaldehyde, acetone, ethanethiol and *n*-propanethiol. Hrdlicka *et al.* (1969) investigated the formation of volatile carbonyl compounds and found that methyl glyoxal, furfural, hydroxymethylfurfural and hexenal were produced during heating. Further work by MacLeod and MacLeod (1970a) has revealed many more components including allyl cyanide and allyl isothiocyanate, which are decomposition products of sinigrin (see Brussels sprouts). The ratio of cyanide to isothiocyanate is quite different to that found in cabbage, the small amount of isothiocyanate implying a lack of enzyme to facilitate the reaction. Buttery *et al.* (1976), using fresh cauliflowers, found octanol, nonanal, 3-methylthiopropyl cyanide, 4-methylthiobutyl cyanide, 2-phenylethyl cyanide and 2-phenylethyl isothiocyanate, as well as other compounds in smaller quantities. Maruyama (1970) has identified dimethyltrisulphide as a major aroma component and suggested that this is formed by decomposition of S-methyl-1-cysteine.

Heat causes discolouration of cauliflower florets during processing. The usual discolouration is pink, which is the result of a combination of leucoanthocyanin formation and metal–flavonol interactions. Other discolourations are brown, black and green–black, and these probably occur when the latter reaction predominates. The main polyphenols present in cauliflower are kaempferol and quercetin (Chandler, 1964; Setty and Ranganna, 1972; Holfelder and Eid, 1973). Non-enzymic browning reactions were also found to cause pink discolourations in cooked cauliflower (Strachan and Nonnecke, 1961).

The main enzyme systems in cauliflower are peroxidase, ascorbic acid oxidase and catalase (Rosoff and Cruess, 1949). It is necessary to destroy all three to retain quality in frozen florets.

Blanching of cauliflower has been extensively studied, especially with regard to ascorbic acid retention (Malakar, 1963), textural changes (Hoogzand and Doesburg, 1961; Mohammad and Ehteschamuddin, 1973; Monzini *et al.*, 1974), and loss of soluble solids (Bomben *et al.*, 1975). Other workers have studied the effect of cooking, including boiling water and high-speed steam cooking, on changes in weight (Pequignot *et al.*, 1975) and ascorbic acid content (Gibson and MacDonald, 1976; Herrmann *et al.*, 1974).

10.8   CELERY

10.8.1   Structure and Composition
Celery belongs to the parsley family and is known botanically as *Apium graveolens*. The edible portion consists of the stalks or

petioles, which grow in bundles. The stalks are channelled inside, taper towards the leaf at the top, and contain fibrous strands on the outside. The colour varies from white to green depending on the variety. The approximate composition is: water, 94·1%; protein, 0·9%; fat, 0·1%; carbohydrates, 3·9%; micronutrients per 100 g: calcium, 39 mg; phosphorus, 28 mg; iron, 0·3 mg; vitamin A, 240 IU; thiamine, 0·03 mg; riboflavin, 0·03 mg; and ascorbic acid, 6 mg. The pH of canned celery varies from 5·3 to 6·0.

10.8.2 Effects of Heat

Johnson *et al.* (1971), in an excellent review of the volatile components of celery, have summarised the work of many investigators. The volatile components in the stalk, as opposed to the seed oil have been studied by Gold and Wilson (1961, 1963a,b) who identified several phthalides: 3-isobutylidene-3a,4-dihydrophthalide; 3-isovalidene-3a,4-dihydrophthalide; 3-isobutylidenephthalide and 3-isovalidenephthalide. These compounds, together with 2,3-butane-dione and *cis*-3-hexene-1-yl pyruvate, were considered to be chiefly responsible for the characteristic flavour. Further work by Wilson (1969a,b; 1970) has revealed a range of hydrocarbons, alcohols and carbonyls in celery purée. Changes in carbonyl volatile compounds during processing have been studied by Hrdlicka *et al.* (1967b) and the relationshop between the bitter flavour and dihydrophthalides has received attention from Pan (1960, 1961). Self *et al.* (1963) identified hydrogen sulphide propanol, dimethylsulphide and methanol in cooled celery.

Mihalyi and Vamos-Vigyazo (1975) have examined the distribution of peroxidase in celery and studied the heat inactivation of this enzyme.

Air-drying of celery (Gold, 1962; Neubert *et al.*, 1966, 1968) produces a rather unsatisfactory product with poor flavour, tough fibre and low coefficient of rehydration. Wilson (1965) showed that by heating celery under pressure and explosively puffing, a product with improved quality characteristics was obtained. Sullivan and Cording (1969) further investigated the explosive-puff drying of celery. In their process, the superheated water within the tissue is flashed off, leaving a porous structure which facilitates reconstitution.

Relatively little work has been reported on the blanching and canning of celery. Vulsteke (1969) was unable to correlate a black discolouration, which appeared after heating, with either variety or location. This may, however, be due to a failure to sufficiently inactivate oxidising enzymes in the thick part of celery heart, resulting in the oxidation of phenolic compounds.

10.9 LEEK

10.9.1 Structure and Composition
The leek is a member of the lily family and is known botanically as *Allium porrum*. The edible portion is the cylindrical formation of leaves which grows into the bulb. Leek may be eaten raw but it is usually boiled and served as a plate vegetable. It is also used to flavour stews and soups. The approximate composition is: water, 85·4%; protein, 2·2%; fat, 0·3%; carbohydrate, 11·2%; micronutrients per 100 g: calcium, 52 mg; phosphorus, 50 mg; iron, 1·1 mg; vitamin A, 40 IU; thiamine, 0·1 mg; riboflavin, 0·06 mg; and ascorbic acid, 17 mg.

10.9.2 Effects of Heat
The volatile compounds of leek have been investigated by a number of workers including Yoshimura (1953), Self *et al.* (1963), Saghir *et al.* (1964) and Schreyen *et al.* (1976). The main components identified in the cooked product included formaldehyde, propanal, acetone, methanethiol, ethanethiol, propanethiol, hydrogen sulphide and dimethylsulphide. Other compounds isolated from the fresh product included dimethyl-, methylpropyl-, methyl-2-propenyl- and dipropyl thiosulphinates as well as methylpropyl-, methyl-2-propenyl-, propyl-2-propenyl and di-2-propenyl disulphides. The lachrymatory principle of onion-type plants is thiopropanal sulphoxide, which decomposes on heating to *n*-propanal and 2-methylpent-2-enal, both of these compounds being detected in leek by Schreyen *et al.* (1976). These workers identified 67 volatile compounds in cooked leek. The alkanals and furan derivatives found were considered to be formed by Maillard reactions between amino acids and reducing sugars. The effect of heat on sugars is probably responsible for the formation of furan-3-one derivatives. The formation of a large quantity of 3,4-dimethylthiophene and its isomers was considered to result from the decomposition of the alkenyl disulphides accompanied by the evolution of hydrogen sulphide (Boelens and Brandsma, 1972). The components which are believed to contribute to specific leek flavour are propanethiol, allyl methyldisulphide, methylpropyldisulphide, dipropyldisulphide and methylpropyltrisulphide.

Relatively little work has been published on the non-volatile components of leek. Quantitative analyses of quercetin and kaempferol in different cultivars have been reported by Starke and Herrmann (1967a).

Changes in weight of fresh and dried leeks during cooking have been investigated by Pequignot *et al.* (1975) and Herrmann *et al.* (1974) have reported on the loss of vitamin C during the holding period for hot vegetables, including leeks.

10.10 MUSHROOM

10.10.1 Structure and Composition
The mushroom which is commonly eaten and processed is a cultivated gill fungus, *Psalliota bispora* (also known as *Agaricus bispora*). The earliest stage of growth is characterised by a button-like form in which the spherical pileus is joined to a pillar-like stipe by the velum. The latter is broken during the expansion of the pileus and the typical umbrella-like form is developed. The pileus flattens during the final stage of growth when the diameter reaches up to 10 cm and the stipe is about 7 cm long. The average composition of mushrooms is: water, 90·4%; protein, 2%; fat, 0·3%; carbohydrate, 4·4%; micronutrients per 100 g: calcium, 6 mg; phosphorus, 116 mg; iron, 0·8 mg; vitamin A, trace; thiamine, 0·1 mg; riboflavin, 0·46 mg; and ascorbic acid, 3 mg. The pH of canned mushrooms is 5·8–6·4 (Hashimoto *et al.*, 1968).

10.10.2 Effects of Heat
The main volatile components of mushroom have been identified by Cronin and Ward (1971) as 3-methylbutanal, butanol, 3-methylbutanol, pentanol, 3-octanone, oct-1-ene-3-one, hexanol, 3-octanol, furfural, oct-1-ene-3-ol, benzaldehyde, phenylacetaldehyde, α-terpineol and benzyl alcohol. Picardi and Issenberg (1973) considered that oct-1-ene-3-one played an important part in the flavour of cooked mushrooms and Wascowicz (1974) found that, of all the volatile compounds in fresh mushrooms, only oct-1-ene-3-ol had a strong fungal-type odour. Pyysalo (1975, 1976) has also carried out extensive work on mushroom volatiles and found other compounds of interest such as acetaldehyde, pentenal, hexanal, N-methyl-N-formyl-hydrazones and γ- and δ-lactones. The nitrogenous flavour components of dehydrated mushroom have been examined by Craske

and Reuter (1965) who found that steam distillation produced off-flavours and concluded that true mushroom flavour was non-volatile.

Hashimoto *et al.* (1968) examined the organic acids of raw and canned mushrooms and found there was a significant decrease during processing. Malic acid was present in the greatest amount but there were also significant quantities of fumaric and pyroglutamic acids.

Mouri *et al.* (1968b) and Hashida *et al.* (1968) studied the 5'-nucleotides in mushrooms and changes brought about by heating. It was concluded that, during mild heating, adenosine-5'-monophosphate and uridine-5'-monophosphate were formed from nucleoside polyphosphates by the enzymic action of phosphomonoesterase. Further work on the effects of different methods of drying on the free amino acids and amines in mushrooms has been reported by Dudareva (1974).

The effect of blanching and drying on the riboflavin content of mushrooms has been studied by Mlodecki *et al.* (1973a,b). Maximum retention was obtained by using a pre-drying temperature of 50–70°C. Zhuk and Rod'Kina (1975) found that the thiamine content (0·24 mg/100 g dry weight) of fresh mushrooms (*Xeracomus*) was reduced by about 10% after washing, by a further 15% after blanching for 2 min at 95°C and by a further 25% after sterilisation at 130°C for 5 min.

Losses of dry matter during the blanching of mushrooms (*Lactarius rufus*) have been measured by Kurkela and Holström (1976). They found that a 6-min blanch in boiling water was necessary to inactivate polyphenol oxidase, losses amounting to 10% dry matter using a water : product ratio of 5 : 1 and 20–30% using a ratio of 10 : 1. Similar work has been carried out by Mehlitz and Geerds (1968) and Maggioni and Renosto (1970). Shrinkage of mushrooms also causes problems in canning (Steinbuch, 1974) and dehydration (McArdle and Curwen, 1962; Chen and Chen, 1974).

Air-drying of mushrooms has been investigated by Komanowsky *et al.* (1970). Excessive blanching was found to produce very dark products, presumably owing to the loss of soluble compounds which inhibit non-enzymic browning. An improvement was achieved by a mild sulphite treatment. Non-enzymic browning of processed mushrooms has also been studied by Voinovitch *et al.* (1949), Voinovitch (1951), Goodman (1957), Hughes (1959) and Kuhn and Beelman (1971). Luh and Eidels (1969a,b) have studied the chemical changes in freeze-dried mushrooms stored at various temperatures.

An HTST process, involving flame cooking, has been developed for mushrooms and is reported to give an exceptionally good product (Bradley, 1970; Beauvais, 1964; Lawler, 1967).

10.11 ONION

10.11.1 Structure and Composition

Onion is a bulb-type plant known botanically as *Allium cepa*. The flesh is usually white, although some varieties are brownish or purple. When cut or bruised, the characteristic pungent aroma, which contains a lachrymatory substance, is released. The approximate composition is: water, 89·1%; protein, 1·5%; fat, 0.1%; carbohydrate, 8·7%; micronutrients per 100 g: calcium, 27 mg; phosphorus, 36 mg; iron, 0·5 mg; vitamin A, 40 IU; thiamine, 0·03 mg; riboflavin, 0·4 mg; and ascorbic acid, 10 mg.

10.11.2 Effects of Heat

The main method of processing onions is by dehydration and it is important that the dried product has a high pungency. Consequently, the effect of heating on the volatile compounds is of major concern. A considerable amount of work has been carried out on onion volatiles and this has been summarised by Johnson *et al.* (1971) and Whitaker (1976). The lachrymatory factor in onions is formed by the action of the enzyme allinase on S-(1-propenyl)-cysteine sulphoxide which breaks down to thiopropanal sulphoxide (Brodnitz and Pascale, 1971; Virtanen and Matikkala, 1961; Virtanen and Spare, 1961; Wilkens, 1962; Müller and Virtanen, 1966; Schwimmer, 1968). The reaction is believed to take place as

$$CH_3 \cdot CH{=}CH{-}\overset{\overset{\displaystyle O}{\|}}{S}{-}CH_2{-}CH(NH_2)COOH \xrightarrow{\text{allinase}} CH_3 \cdot CH{=}CH{=}S{=}O$$

S-(1-propenyl)-cysteine sulphoxide   thiopropanol sulphoxide

A large number of organic sulphides, disulphides and trisulphides have been identified in onion (Boelens and Brandsma, 1972; Boelens *et al.*, 1970, 1971). The action of heat on the unsaturated disulphides results in the formation of dimethyl thiophene and saturated disulphides plus minor amounts of unsaturated monosulphides and saturated trisulphides, as shown in Fig. 10.4 (Boelens *et al.*, 1971).

The decomposition of the S-alkycysteine derivatives has also been shown to give rise to sulphoxides. Freeman and Whenham (1975) surveyed 27 *Allium* species in terms of S-alk(ene)yl-L-cysteine sulphoxides present as flavour precursors. The species could be classified as containing S-1-propenyl-, S-2-propenyl- or S-methyl-L-cysteine sulphoxides. Onions fell in the first category. The same authors (Freeman and Whenham, 1975) studied the effect of pickling, canning, boiling, dehydration and frying on the flavour volatiles of onion. Extremely high losses were reported using all techniques and only the freeze-dried sample had the original characteristic flavour of freshly cut onion. Schwimmer *et al.* (1964) considered that the poor flavour potential of dehydrated onion was due to loss of substrate rather than enzyme destruction. Bernhard (1968, 1969) compared the disulphides present in fresh and reconstituted dehydrated onion and found losses of dimethyl- (89%), methyl-*n*-propyl- (98%), methylallyl- (97%), di-*n*-propyl- (99·8%) and *n*-propylallyl- (99·4%) disulphides. The main degradation reactions of S-alkyl-L-cysteine sulphoxide are shown in Fig. 10.5. The alkyl groups which are predominant in the case of onion are 1-propyl, 1-propenyl and methyl groups. Further work on the relationship between flavour of canned onions and chemical composition has been reported by Chua *et al.* (1968).

Several workers have studied the pink discolouration which appears in dehydrated and heat processed onions and purée (Lukes, 1959; Yamaguchi *et al.*, 1965; Joslyn and Peterson, 1958, 1960). Shannon *et al.* (1967) postulated that a colour developer is formed by the action of allinase, presumably on S-1-propenylcysteine. This then reacts with free amino acids to produce a pigment precursor which

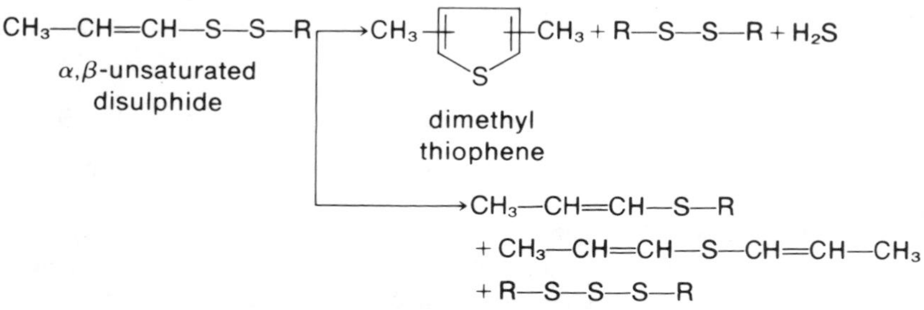

$$CH_3—CH=CH—S—S—R \longrightarrow CH_3 \text{---} \text{[dimethyl thiophene ring]} \text{---} CH_3 + R—S—S—R + H_2S$$

α,β-unsaturated
disulphide

dimethyl
thiophene

$$\longrightarrow CH_3—CH=CH—S—R$$
$$+ CH_3—CH=CH—S—CH=CH—CH_3$$
$$+ R—S—S—S—R$$

FIG. 10.4 Thermal breakdown of unsaturated disulphides.

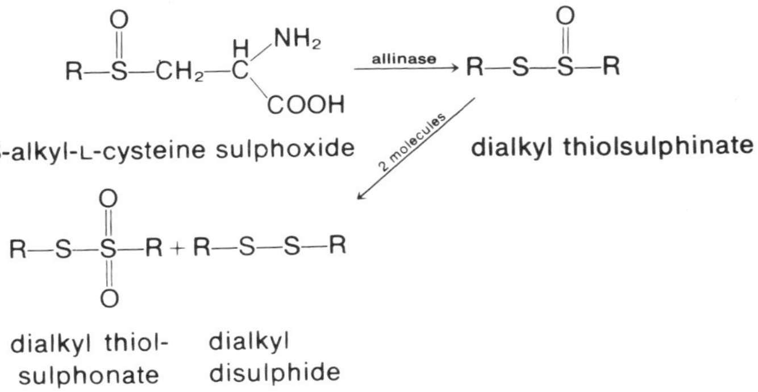

FIG. 10.5 Degradation of S-alkyl-L-cysteine sulphoxide.

further reacts with carbonyl compounds to produce the pink discolouration.

Other onion components which have received attention are flavonols (Starke and Herrmann, 1976b). The epidermis of onion contains glucosides of quercetin while the dry outer skins contain quercetin mainly in the free state. The possible presence of 3-alkyl-2-methoxypyrazines has also been investigated (Murray and Whitfield, 1975).

Various workers have studied the organoleptic quality of dehydrated onion. Maleki (1965) investigated the pungency of onion in relation to the type of heat treatment applied before drying. He concluded that heating at 140°F for 12 min yielded a product of satisfactory pungency, colour and microbiological quality. Ignall (1960) compared the equivalent weight of dehydrated sliced onion to the original fresh material. Shimazu et al. (1965) investigated the effect of different methods of drying on the rehydration characteristics. The freeze-dried product rehydrated much more rapidly than any of the air-dried products, probably because the freezing process does not cause shrinkage and further drying produces larger internal voids.

10.12 PEPPERS

10.12.1 Structure and Composition

Peppers belong to the family of Solanacae and are known botanically as *Capsicum annuum*. They are also known as paprika, chilli or pimiento. The two main varieties are coloured either red or green. The structure is rather like that of a tomato, the seeds being on the walls of false, incomplete septa which are ingrowths of the thick pericarp. However, the seed-box cavity, formed between the septa and the pericarp, does not contain fluid. The berries are approximately isodiametrical and about 6 cm in cross-section, although they tend to elongate slightly. The approximate composition is: water, 88·8%; protein, 1·3%; fat, 0·2%; carbohydrate, 9·1%; micronutrients per 100 g: calcium, 10 mg; phosphorus, 25 mg; iron, 0·7 mg; vitamin A, 770 IU; thiamine, 0·09 mg; riboflavin, 0·06 mg; and ascorbic acid, 235 mg. The main flavonoids are quercetin and luteolin (Wöldecke and Herrmann, 1974b).

10.12.2 Effects of Heat

The major volatile constituents of peppers are 2-methoxy-3-isobutyl-pyrazine, trans-β-ocimene, limonene, methyl salicylate, linalool, nona-trans,cis-2,6-dienal and deca-trans,trans-2,4-dienol (Buttery et al., 1969a,b). An extremely potent odour is associated with 2-methoxy-3-isobutylpyrazine. The 'hot' taste of the chilli and tabasco type of peppers is due to the presence of capsaicin, N-(4-hydroxy-3-methoxybenzyl)-8-methyl-nona-trans,6-enamide (Nelson and Dawson, 1923).

Jankov (1970) has studied the physical changes, including gas content, volume retention and gross density increase, which occurred when sliced green peppers were blanched by various methods. The gas content was found to decrease from 14·0 to 3·3 vol.% during steam blanching and weight loss for all treatments was about 4–5%. Lee et al. (1974) found that steam heating resulted in greater chlorophyll destruction than either hot-air or microwave heating.

Park (1975) measured changes in carotenoids, capsaicin and ascorbic acid on sun-drying and oven-drying. Carotenoids and capsaicin increased during sun-drying but ascorbic acid decreased by 76% using this method and by 89% using an oven. Park and Lee (1975) also measured changes of free amino acids and sugars. Amino acid content remained unchanged after sun-drying but decreased considerably after oven-drying. The higher temperatures of the latter method accelerated reaction between amino acids and sugars which caused the product to appear dark red. Haas et al. (1974) reported the effects of degree of drying on the rehydration characteristics of several vegetables including peppers.

10.13 POTATO

10.13.1 Structure and Composition

Potato is the tuber of the *Solanum tuberosum* plant. The skin or periderm is whitish, yellow-brown or reddish, and encloses the cortex layer, with the pith dividing the inner phloem into segments. The size of potato tubers depends upon variety and maturity. If they are exposed to light during growth, they develop a green colour owing to chlorophyll formation. This is also accompanied by the accumulation of glycoalkaloids, solanine in particular (see the review by Jadhav and Salunkhe, 1975). The average composition of potatoes is: water, 79·8%; protein, 2·1%; fat, 0·1%; carbohydrate, 17·1%; micronutrients per 100 g: calcium, 7 mg; phosphorus, 53 mg; iron, 0·6 mg; vitamin A, trace; thiamine, 0·1 mg; riboflavin, 0·04 mg; and ascorbic acid, 20 mg. The pH of the potato tuber is between 5·6 and 6·2. A detailed account of the distribution and composition of the dry matter in potato tuber has been given by Burton (1966). The main pigments in potatoes are the carotenoids, especially in the yellow-flesh varieties. The skin of pigmented varieties contains anthocyanins.

10.13.2 Effects of Heat

The effects of heat have been more widely studied in potatoes than in any other vegetable product, owing to their importance in Western diets.

The volatile components of fresh potato have been investigated by Kröner and Wegner (1942), Wegner (1949), Self and Swain (1963), Swain and Self (1964), Schormuller and Weder (1966) and Self (1967). The main compounds identified were: hydrocarbons including naphthalene, methylnaphthalene, biphenyl, limonene, mesitylene, dimethylbenzene; alcohols including pentanol, hexanol, 2-methylbutanol, 1-octene-3-ol, *trans*-2-octenol, geraniol, linalool, nerol, α-terpineol; carbonyls including alkyl aldehydes and ketones, benzaldehyde, furfural and methional; organic acids, esters, ethers and sulphur- and nitrogen-containing compounds (see Johnson *et al.*, 1971).

Buttery *et al.* (1970) characterised the higher boiling constituents of potato using steam distillation at atmospheric pressure. The oil obtained, the major component being 2-pentylfuran, had an aroma similar to cooked potato whereas the oil obtained by steam distillation under vacuum had an aroma similar to raw potato. The earthy aroma of potatoes is considered to be due to 2-methoxy-3-isopropylpyrazine (Buttery and Ling, 1973).

The flavour of cooked and processed potato products is quite different from that of the raw material owing to the formation of various compounds, some containing sulphur (Self et al., 1963a,b; Gumbmann and Burr, 1964). Johnson et al. (1971) have suggested that possible flavour precursors are the organic and amino acids. Buri et al. (1970) examined the rôle of free amino acids and nucleotides in the flavour of cooked potato and Buttery and Ling (1974) identified various thiazoles, in particular 2,4,5-trimethyl-, 2-isopropyl-4,5-dimethyl-, 2-isopropyl-4-methyl-5 ethyl-, 2-isobutyl-4,5-dimethyl- and 2-acetylthiazole. The most extensive study of cooked potato flavour has been carried out by Nursten and Sheen (1974) who isolated 35 components and discussed the nature of the characteristic flavour which they considered was due to a pyrazine-type compound. Potato chips have also received attention from Deck and Chang (1975), Mookherjee et al. (1965), Buttery et al. (1971), Buttery and Ling (1972) and Buttery (1973). The main compounds identified were monocarbonyls, although several were unusual aldol-type condensation products (Buttery, 1973). Baked potatoes have been studied by Buttery et al. (1973) and Pareles and Chang (1974) who concluded that the baked flavour was due to a combination of 2-isobutyl-3-methyl-, 2,3-diethyl-5-methyl- and 3,5-diethyl-2-methyl- pyrazines. Considerable work has been carried out on the flavour of dehydrated products for development of instant mashed potato but little has been published. Sapers (1970) and Sapers et al. (1970, 1971) investigated the cause of off-flavour in explosion-puffed potato and concluded that 2-methylpropanal, 2-methylbutanal and 3-methylbutanal were mainly responsible, with a contribution from pyrazine derivatives. Off-flavour development as a consequence of non-enzymic browning has also been studied by Cording and Sullivan (1973) and Sullivan et al. (1974).

The effects of heat on other components in processed potato products have also received attention. Numa (1971, 1972) and Numa and Nomura (1969) considered that the increased indophenol value of boiled potatoes was caused by degradation products of ascorbic acid, such as diketogulonic acid. Changes in the ascorbic acid content of processed potatoes have been measured by Peppler and Feldheim (1964), Domah et al. (1974), Witkowski and Paradowski (1975), Jadhav et al. (1975) and Gibson and MacDonald (1976). The earlier work is summarised by Burton (1966) with regard to conventional cooking procedures. Changes in the free and bound amino acids brought about by various processing methods have been investigated by Jaswal (1973). Katsai and Kochetova (1974) studied the physicochemical changes occurring at the surface of potatoes during steam peeling. Microscopic observations showed that the surface-layer cells became rounded, intracellular spaces increased, cell walls were damaged and starch grains were released and partly gelatinised. Polyphenol oxidase action took place at the interface between the damaged and undamaged cells resulting in the appearance of the characteristic dark ring, particularly in the presence of air. Cunningham and Zaehringer (1972) found that, in addition to variety and maturity, the quality of baked potatoes is influenced by the temperature and time of baking and holding time. Data for weight changes during dehydration of potatoes have been given by Pequignot et al. (1975).

A major discolouration, referred to as non-enzymic blackening, often occurs shortly after potatoes have been cooked. This phenomenon has been the subject of considerable investigation (Wager, 1955; Bate-Smith et al., 1958; Heisler et al., 1962, 1963, 1964; Hughes, 1962; Hughes et al., 1962; Weeratne et al., 1964; Vertregt, 1968; Talley, 1969; Hughes and Evans, 1969). It appears to be caused by complex formation between iron and chlorogenic acid, accompanied by oxidation, the complexes being the monophenolate (green) around pH 5·5, and around pH 6·5 the diphenolate (grey–blue) and triphenolate (brown). The tendency for different varieties to blacken is proportional to their chlorogenic acid content although citric acid, owing to its chelating ability, can inhibit blackening to some extent.

The losses of soluble material during blanching prior to freezing, frying or dehydration have been widely investigated (Adam and Horner, 1941; Adam and Stanworth, 1941; Gooding, 1956 (dehydrated); McWeeny et al., 1964 (dehydrated); Collins and McCarty, 1969; Brown and Morales, 1970 (frozen French fries); Mohammad and Ehteschamuddin, 1973 (dehydrated); Mitchell and Rutledge, 1973 (potato crisps); Thorman et al., 1977). Collins and McCarty (1969) showed that microwave blanching was more effective than boiling water. For potatoes, with a mean radius of 2·27 cm, the optimum conditions for inactivating peroxidase were 13 min in boiling water or 4·7 min using microwave heating, and for polyphenol oxidase, 6–7·5 min and 3–3·5 min, respectively.

The most important quality characteristic of cooked potato is its texture, which has been studied extensively. The behaviour of potato on heating is complex and depends on a number of factors including variety, maturity, agronomic effects, as well as processing conditions. On boiling in water, the starch gelatinises around 60–70°C and cell walls become weakened by the degradation and removal of pectic substances. Stickiness may occur owing to starch-granule rupture and complete disintegration may take place as a result of the weakening of intercellular adhesion caused by pectin degradation. The texture of cooked potatoes with respect to 'mealiness' and 'sloughing' has been reviewed by Warren and Woodman (1974). They consider that mealiness is the subjective perception of the flow characteristics of cooked-potato tissue and is controlled primarily by the solids content of the tuber, whereas sloughing is related to intercellular adhesion. Bettelheim and Sterling (1955) established a correlation between mealiness and starch or dry-matter content.

Sloughing is observed during the boiling of potatoes (Davis, 1966) and in canned potatoes (Sterling and Bettelheim, 1955; Bettelheim and Sterling, 1955; Weckel et al., 1959; Zaehringer and Cunningham, 1971; Warren et al., 1975). It may be prevented by a mild heat treatment at 50–70°C before boiling, which was though to induce some starch retrogradation (Potter et al., 1959; Reeve, 1972). Bartolome and Hoff (1972), however, considered that heating above 50°C leads to a loss of integrity of the cellular membrane, allowing intercellular electrolytes to activate pectin methylesterase. This enzyme increases the number of free carboxyl groups in the cell-wall pectin which are available to form bridges with calcium and magnesium, resulting in greater resistance of the tissue to thermal disruption. Intercellular adhesion has been studied in relation to cell size (Linehan et al., 1968) and chemical composition (Linehan and Hughes, 1969a–d). Further work has been carried out by Hughes et al. (1975a,b,c) with regard to the release of pectic substances during cooking, cell size and the effect of ions and pH. Increased cooking times or the presence of potassium chloride in the cooking water reduced the compressive strength of the tissue and increased the amount of pectic material released. Calcium chloride had the reverse effect. Eipeson and Paulus (1973) studied the changes in chemical composition of potatoes during canning. Dry matter was reduced to 80–90% of the original value and the quantity of starch leached out was proportional to the severity of processing. HTST processes were found to reduce such losses.

10.14 SPINACH

10.14.1 Structure and Composition

Spinach is the leaf of the plant *Spinacia oleracea*. The leaves are either boiled and eaten as such, or made into purée in which form they may also be canned or frozen. The approximate composition is: water, 90·7%; protein, 3·2%; fat, 0·3%; carbohydrate, 3·6%; micronutrients per 100 g: calcium, 93 mg; phosphorus, 38 mg; iron, 2·2 mg; vitamin A, 8100 IU; thiamine, 0·07 mg; riboflavin, 0·14 mg; and ascorbic acid, 28 mg. The pH of the canned purée varies between 5·4 and 6·0. The main organic acid present is oxalic acid in the form of calcium oxalate and, since this is insoluble, much of the calcium is nutritionally unavailable.

10.14.2 Effects of Heat

Ralls (1959) has studied the thiamine-catalysed production of acetoin and biacetyl from pyruvic acid formed during heat processing of canned spinach and Murray and Whitfield (1975) have identified some 3-alkyl-2-methoxypyrazines.

The stability of chlorophyll has been examined by several workers (Tan and Francis, 1962; Gupte and Francis, 1964; Gupte *et al.*, 1964; Kahn and Bannister, 1965; Clydesdale, 1966; Fleischman, 1969; La-Jollo, 1971; Loef, 1974). The object of most of this work was to prevent the breakdown of chlorophyll to pheophytin during processing. HTST processes were found to give better chlorophyll retention than conventional processes. One of the major factors which accelerates chlorophyll breakdown is the reduction of pH brought about by processing. Lin *et al.* (1970, 1971) studied the organic acid profiles of thermally processed spinach purée and found the most notable changes were the increase of acetic and pyrrolidone carboxylic acids and decrease of fumaric acid. These changes were less marked using an HTST process. During storage it was found that pyruvic, glutamic, oxaloacetic and malonic acids were also produced, which contributed to the change of pH. The kinetics of the thermal degradation of chlorophyll were investigated by Gupte *et al.* (1964) who showed that the activation energies for the breakdown of chlorophyll a and chlorophyll b were 143 and 35 kcal·mol^{-1}, respectively. Chlorophyll degradation in freeze-dried spinach has also been studied as a function of water activity (LaJollo, 1971).

The kinetics of thiamine degradation in canned spinach purée have been determined by Feliciotti and Esselen (1957). More detailed information on the loss of nutrients and other components as a result of processing have been reported by Heutschel and Overbeck (1971), Marchesini *et al.* (1974), Astler-Dumas (1975), Heintze *et al.* (1975), Paulus *et al.* (1975a,b), Zohm *et al.* (1975) and Fricker *et al.* (1975).

Inactivation of enzymes by blanching has been widely studied. The kinetics of the thermal destruction of peroxidase have been investigated by Resende *et al.* (1969a,b) up to 176°C, and by Delincee and Schäfer (1975) and Duden *et al.* (1975) up to 100°C. The stability of spinach catalase has been studied by Sapers and Nickerson (1962) at relatively low temperatures (55–65°C).

The effect of blanching on mineral and oxalate contents of spinach has been reported by Kramer and Smith (1947), Schaller (1962), Bengtsson (1969) and Kovari (1972). Richter and Handke (1973) showed that blanching reduces the total and soluble oxalic acid content of spinach both by leaching and conversion of soluble oxalates into insoluble calcium oxalates. Techniques for reducing the loss of solubles during blanching have been discussed by Ralls *et al.* (1973) with particular reference to in-plant hot-gas blanching. The effect of blanching on the quality of canned spinach has been studied by Sistrunk and Osborne (1972) and on the quality of dehydrated products by Mohammad and Ehteschamuddin (1973).

10.15 SWEETCORN

10.15.1 Structure and Composition

Sweetcorn is a cereal, known botanically as *Zea mays* var. *saccharata*, but is consumed and processed in a similar manner to vegetables. It consists of a cob (spadix) enveloped in leaves with the edible grains (niblets) arranged on the outside. It is eaten fresh after boiling and preserved by canning 'on the cob' or as niblets, freezing or drying. The approximate composition of the niblets is: water, 72·7%; protein, 3·5%; fat, 1%; carbohydrate, 22·1%; micronutrients per 100 g: calcium, 3 mg; phosphorus, 111 mg; iron, 0·7 mg; vitamin A, 400 IU; thiamine, 0·15 mg; riboflavin, 0·12 mg; and ascorbic acid, 12 mg.

10.15.2 Effects of Heat

The raw product does not contain dimethylsulphide although it is formed when sweetcorn is heated (Self *et al.*, 1963; Casey *et al.*, 1963). Experimental work has shown the amount of dimethylsulphide does not increase in proportion to processing time and it is considered that the heat-labile precursor, S-methylmethionine sulphonium salt, becomes depleted (Bills and Keenan, 1968; Keenan and Lindsay, 1968). The higher boiling volatiles of canned sweetcorn have been studied by Libbey *et al.* (1974) who found several compounds which they thought contributed to flavour, *viz.* diacetyl, 2,5-dimethylpyrazine and 2,6-dimethylpyrazine. The pyrazines are probably formed by heat-induced reactions between cysteine and glucose. The presence of 3-alkyl-2-methoxypyrazines was investigated by Murray and Whitfield (1975). The main low boiling aroma constituents of heat-processed sweetcorn were found to be hydrogen sulphide, methanethiol, acetaldehyde, ethanol, ethanethiol and dimethylsulphide (Flora, 1974; Flora and Wiley, 1974). Changes in the nutritive value of sweetcorn owing to processing have been studied by Lamb *et al.* (1947), Ingalls *et al.* (1950), Ammerman and Lee (1972) and Gauhar (1973). Changes in the contents of nucleic acids and related compounds have been reported by Mouri *et al.* (1968a).

Kinetic studies on the heat inactivation of peroxidase in sweetcorn have been carried out by Vetter *et al.* (1959), Yamamoto *et al.* (1962) and Chenchin and Yamamoto (1973), at temperatures up to 150°C. Daoud *et al.* (1970) processed sweetcorn purée in a continuous sterilisation system for 24 s at 140°C and compared the aseptically canned purée with that processed conventionally (42 min at 115·6°C). The aseptically canned product was lower in titratable acidity and ammonium nitrogen, but higher in thiamine, amino nitrogen and pH than the retorted product. Aseptic processing also resulted in a product of superior organoleptic quality.

10.16   SWEET POTATO

10.16.1   Structure and Composition

The sweet potato, known botanically as *Ipomoea batatas*, is a root tuber which is elongated compared to the potato. The colour of the skin is usually slightly red or purple, but it may be white, yellow, orange, red or brown, depending on the cultivar. The cultivars are also subdivided according to their texture after cooking, *i.e.* whether they are soft ('Jersey' types) or firm ('Puerto Rico' types). The approximate composition is: water, 70·6%; protein, 1·7%; fat, 0·4%; carbohydrate, 26·3%; micronutrients per 100 g: calcium, 32 mg; phosphorus, 47 mg; iron, 0·7 mg; vitamin A, 8800 IU; thiamine, 0·1 mg; riboflavin, 0·06 mg; and ascorbic acid, 21 mg. The sweetness is due to the high level of sugars.

10.16.2 Effects of Heat
Jenkins and Gieger (1957) studied the effect of heat on the sugar content of sweet potatoes during baking. Non-reducing sugars were found to increase in concentration more rapidly than reducing sugars. Deobald *et al.* (1969) found that the concentrations of glucose and sucrose remained fairly constant but maltose was formed during heating (see also Sistrunk *et al.*, 1954; Lambon, 1958; Hoover and Kushman, 1966; Hoover and Harman, 1967). Maltose is produced by the enzymic action of α-amylase on starch at temperatures close to that of gelatinisation.

The effects of processing on various components of canned sweet potato were studied by Arthur and McLemore (1955, 1957), who found that the carotenoids were fairly stable but considerable degradation of vitamin C occurred. Panalaks and Murray (1970) also investigated the fate of carotenoids during cooking, canning and dehydration. Lee (1974) studied the isomerisation of carotene in sweet potatoes canned under various conditions. Ammerman and Lee (1972) studied the texture of sweet potatoes processed in a rotary retort and McConnell and Gottschall (1957) investigated the break-down of sweet potatoes during processing. Arthur and McLemore (1956) suggested that the *in vivo* discolouration of sweet-potato tissue occurs when the rate of oxidation of chlorogenic acid is increased or the available quantity of reduced ascorbic acid is decreased.

REFERENCES AND BIBLIOGRAPHY

Acree, T. E., Lee, C. V., Butts, R. M. & Barnard, J. (1976) *J. Agric. Fd. Chem.*, **24**, 430.
Adam, W. B. (1965) *J. Assoc. Publ. Analysts*, **3**, 36.
Adam, W. B. & Dickinson, D. (1959) *The pH Values of Canned Fruit and Vegetables*, Sci. Bull. No. 3. Chipping Campden, Glos.: CFPRA.

Adam, W. B. & Horner, G. (1941) Annual Report Research Station, Chipping Campden, Glos., p. 21.

Adam, W. B. & Stanworth, J. (1941) Annual Report Research Station, Chipping Campden, Glos., p. 32.

Alabran, D. M. & Mabrouk, A. F. (1973) *J. Agric. Fd. Chem.*, **21**, 205.

Ammerman, G. R. & Lee, V. C. (1972) *Mississippi Farm Res.*, **35**(4), 6.

Arthur, J. C., Jr. & McLemore, T. A. (1955) *J. Agric. Fd. Chem.*, **3**, 782.

Arthur, J. C., Jr. & McLemore, T. A. (1956) *J. Agric. Fd. Chem.*, **4**, 553.

Arthur, J. C., Jr. & McLemore, T. A. (1957) *J. Agric. Fd. Chem.*, **5**, 863.

Astler-Dumas, M. (1975) *Annales de la Nutrition et de l'Alimentation*, **29**(3), 239.

Aurstad, K. & Dahle, H. K. (1973) *Z. Lebensm. Unters.-Forsch.*, **151**(3), 171.

Bailey, S. C., Bazinet, M. L., Driscoll, J. L. & McCarthy, A. I. (1961) *J. Fd. Sci.*, **26**, 163.

Baloch, A. K., Buckle, K. A. & Edwards, R. A. (1977) *J. Fd. Technol.*, **12**, 285, 295.

Barbiroli, G., Garutti, M. A. & Mazzaracchio, P. (1972) *Rassegna Chimica*, **24**(6), 361.

Bartolome, L. G. & Hoff, J. E. (1972) *J. Agric. Fd. Chem.*, **20**, 266.

Bate-Smith, E. C., Hughes, J. C. & Swain, T. (1958) *Chem. & Ind.*, 627.

Bates, R. P. & Koburger, J. A. (1974) *Proc. Florida State Hort. Soc.*, **87**, 245.

Beauvais, M. (1964) *Revue de la Conserve*, **19** (October), 95.

Bender, A. E. (1965) *Dictionary of Nutrition and Food Technology*. London: Butterworths.

Bengtsson, B. L. (1969) *J. Fd. Technol.*, **4**, 141.

Bernhard, R. A. (1966) *Advances in Chemistry*, Series No. 56, p. 131. American Chemical Society.

Bernhard, R. A. (1968) *J. Fd. Sci.*, **33**, 298.

Bernhard, R. A. (1969) *Qual. Plant Mater. Veg.*, **18**, 72.

Berwell, A. M., Calvo, C., Curan, L. & Primo, E. (1973) *Revista de Agroquimica y Tecnologia de Alimentos*, **13**, 463.

Bettelheim, F. A. & Sterling, C. (1955) *Fd. Res.*, **20**, 71, 118.

Bibeau, T. C. & Clydesdale, F. M. (1975) *J. Milk Fd. Technol.*, **38**, 518.

Bibeau, T. C., Clydesdale, F. M. & Sawyer, F. M. (1974) *J. Fd. Sci.*, **39**, 365.

Bills, D. D. & Keenan, T. W. (1968) *J. Agric. Fd. Chem.*, **16**, 643.

Boelens, H. & Brandsma, L. (1972) *Recl. Trav. Chim. Pays-Bas*, **91**, 141.

Boelens, H., de Valois, P. J., Wobben, H. J. & van der Gen, A. (1970) Abstracts of papers, *Am. Chem. Soc.*, **160**, AGFD: 52.

Boelens, H., de Valois, P. J., Wobben, H. J. & van der Gen, A. (1971) *J. Agric. Fd. Chem.*, **19**, 984.

Bomben, J. L., Dietrich, W. C., Farkas, D. F., Hudson, J. S., de Marchena, E. S. & Sanshuck, D. W. (1973) *J. Fd. Sci.*, **38**, 590.

Bomben, J. L., Dietrich, W. C., Hudson, J. S., Hamilton, H. K. & Farkas, D. F. (1975) *J. Fd. Sci.*, **40**, 660.

Borenstein, B. & Bunnell, R. H. (1966) *Advan. Fd. Res.*, **15**, 195.

Boscan, L. (1962) *J. Fd. Sci.*, **27**, 574.

Böttcher, H. (1962) *Nahrung*, **6**, 446.

Bradley, J. J. (1970) M.S. Thesis, Pennsylvania State University.

Brodnitz, M. H. & Pascale, J. V. (1971) *J. Agric. Fd. Chem.*, **19**, 269.
Brolchain, P. O. (1973) *Process Biochem.*, **8**(8), 26.
Brouk, B. (1975) *Plants Consumed by Man*. London & New York: Academic Press.
Brown, M. S. & Morales, J. A. W. (1970) *Am. Potato J.*, **47**, 321.
Buck, P. A. & Joslyn, M. A. (1953) *J. Agric. Fd. Chem.*, **1**, 309.
Buri, R., Signer, V. & Solms, J. (1970) *Lebensm.-Wiss u. Technol.*, **3**, 63.
Burton, W. G. (1966) *The Potato*, 2nd edn. Wageningen, Holland: H. Veenman & Zonen NV.
Buttery, R. G. (1973) *J. Agric. Fd. Chem.*, **21**, 31.
Buttery, R. G., Guadagni, D. G. & Ling, L. C. (1973) *J. Sci. Fd. Agric.*, **24**, 1125.
Buttery, R. G., Guadagni, D. G., Ling, L. C., Seifert, R. M. & Lipton, W. (1976) *J. Agric. Fd. Chem.*, **24**, 829.
Buttery, R. G. & Ling, L. C. (1972) *J. Agric. Fd. Chem.*, **20**, 698.
Buttery, R. G. & Ling, L. C. (1973) *J. Agric. Fd. Chem.*, **21**, 745.
Buttery, R. G. & Ling, L. C. (1974) *J. Agric. Fd. Chem.*, **22**, 912.
Buttery, R. G., Seifert, R. M., Guadagni, D. G., Black, D. R. & Ling, L. C. (1968) *J. Agric. Fd. Chem.*, **16**, 1009.
Buttery, R. G., Seifert, R. M., Guadagni, D. G. & Ling, L. C. (1971) *J. Agric. Fd. Chem.*, **19**, 969.
Buttery, R. G., Seifert, R. M., Guadagni, D. G. & Ling, L. C. (1969a) *J. Agric. Fd. Chem.*, **17**, 1322.
Buttery, R. G., Seifert, R. M., Lundin, R. E., Guadagni, D. G. & Ling, L. C. (1969b) *Chem. & Ind.*, 490.
Buttery, R. G., Seifert, R. M. & Ling, L. C. (1970) *J. Agric. Fd. Chem.*, **18**, 538.
Casey, J. E., Self, R. & Swain, T. (1963) *Nature*, **200**, 885.
Chandler, B. V. (1964) *CSIRO Fd. Pres. Quart.*, **24**, 11.
Chen, H. C. & Chen, C. S. (1974) *J. Agric. Eng. Res.*, **19**(1), 97.
Chenchin, E. E. & Yamamoto, H. Y. (1973) *J. Fd. Sci.*, **38**, 40.
Chichester, C. O. (1972) *The Chemistry of Plant Pigments*, Suppl. 3. *Advances in Food Research*. London & New York: Academic Press.
Chua, G. K., Lacroix, L. J., Levy, R. & Unrau, A. M. (1968) *Proc. Am. Soc. Hort. Sci.*, **93**, 817.
Chwiej, M. & Kurlowicz, M. (1972) *Roczniki Technologii i Chemii Zywnosci*, **22**(3/4), 289.
Clapp, R. C., Long, R. Jr., Dateo, G. P., Bissett, F. M. & Hasselstrom, T. (1959) *J. Am. Chem. Soc.*, **81**, 6278.
Clark, W. L. & Moyer, J. C. (1955) *Fd. Technol.*, **9**, 308.
Clydesdale, F. M. (1966) *Dissert. Abstr. B.*, **27**, 1180.
Collins, J. L. & McCarty, I. E. (1969) *Fd. Technol.*, **23**, 337.
Cording, J., Jr. & Sullivan, J. F. (1973) *Fd. Eng.*, **45**(10), 95.
Cording, J., Jr., Eskew, R. K., Sullivan, J. F. & Eisenhardt, N. H. (1963) *Fd. Eng.*, **35**(6), 52.
Craske, J. D. & Reuter, F. H. (1965) *J. Sci. Fd. Agric.*, **16**, 243.
Cronin, D. A. & Stanton, P. (1976) *J. Sci. Fd. Agric.*, **27**, 145.
Cronin, D. A. & Ward, M. K. (1971) *J. Sci. Fd. Agric.*, **22**, 477.

Cruess, W. V. & Sugihara, J. (1949) *Fd. Technol.*, **3**, 370.
Cultrera, R. & Giannone, L. (1965) *The Effect of Heat Treatment on the Structure of Plant Tissues*, Dechema Monograph, **56**, 173.
Cunningham, H. H. & Zaehringer, M. V. (1972) *Am. Potato J.*, **49**(7), 271.
Dahlke, L. C. (1966) *Dissert. Abstr. B.*, **27**, 1530.
Dame, C., Jr. (1957) *Fd. Res.*, **22**, 658.
Dame, C., Jr., Chichester, C. O. & Marsh, G. L. (1957) *Fd. Res.*, **22**, 673.
Daoud, H. N., Luh, B. S. & Seehafer, M. E. (1970) *Confructa*, **15**, 4.
Dateo, G. P., Clapp, R. C., Mackay, D. A. M., Hewitt, E. I. & Hasselstrom, T. (1957) *Fd. Res.*, **22**, 440.
Davis, R. B., Guyer, R. B., Daly, J. J. & Johnson, H. T. (1961) *Fd. Technol.*, **15**, 212.
Davis, W. C. (1966) *Dissert. Abstr. B.*, **27**, 73.
Deck, R. E. & Chang, S. S. (1975) *Chem. & Ind.*, (30), 1343.
de Eds, F. & Couch, F. (1948) *Fd. Res.*, **13**, 378.
Delincee, H. & Schäfer, W. (1975) *Lebensm.-Wiss u. Technol.*, **8**, 217.
Della Monica, E. S. & McDowell, S. E. (1965) *Fd. Technol.*, **19**(10), 141.
Deobald, H. J., Hasling, V. C., Catalano, E. A. & McLemore, T. A. (1969) *Fd. Technol.*, **23**, 826.
Dietrich, W. C., Huxsoll, C. C. & Guadagni, D. G. (1970) *Fd. Technol.*, **24**, 613.
Dietrich, W. C. & Neumann, H. J. (1965) *Fd. Technol.*, **19**, 1174.
Doesburg, J. J. (1961) *Qual. Plant Mater. Veg.*, **8**, 115.
Doesburg, J. J. (1965) *Pectic Substances in Fresh and Preserved Fruits and Vegetables*, No. 25, 152 pp. Wageningen, Delft: Inst. Res. Storage, Processing of Hort. Produce.
Domah, A. A. M. B., Davidek, J. & Velisek, J. (1974) *Z. Lebensm. Unters. -Forsch.*, **154**, 270.
Duckworth, R. B. (1966) *Fruit and Vegetables*. Oxford & London: Pergamon Press.
Dudareva, N. T. (1974) *Prikladnaya Biokhimiya i Mikrobiologiya.*, **10**, 326.
Duden, R., Fricker, A., Heintze, K., Paulus, K. & Zohm, H. (1975) *Lebensm.-Wiss u. Technol.*, **8**, 147.
Ede, A. J. & Hales, K. C. (1948) *The Physics of Drying in Heated Air with Particular Reference to Fruit and Vegetables*. Food Investigation Special Report No. 53, DSIR. London: HMSO.
Eheart, M. S. & Gott, C. (1965) *Fd. Technol.*, **19**, 867.
Eipeson, W. E. & Paulus, K. (1973) *Potato Res.*, **16**, 270.
Farine, G., Wuhrmann, J. J., Patron, A. & Vurtaz, L. (1965) *Proc. 1st Int. Congr. Fd. Sci. Technol.*, **3**, 603. London: Gordon & Breach.
Feliciotti, E. & Esselen, W. B. (1957) *Fd. Technol.*, **11**, 77.
Fleischman, D. L. (1969) Ph.D. Dissertation, University of Massachusetts, Amherst.
Flora, L. P. (1974) Ph.D. Dissertation, University of Maryland.
Flora, L. P. & Wiley, R. C. (1974) *J. Fd. Sci.*, **39**, 770.
Freeman, G. G. & Whenham, R. J. (1974) *J. Sci. Fd. Agric.*, **25**, 499.
Freeman, G. G. & Whenham, R. J. (1975) *J. Sci. Fd. Agric.*, **26**, 1869.

Freytag, W. & Ney, K. N. (1968) *Z. Lebensm. Unters. -Forsch.*, **3**, 293.

Fricker, A., Duden, R., Heintze, K., Paulus, K. & Zohm, H. (1975) *Lebensm.-Wiss u. Technol.*, **8**, 172.

Gauhar, A. (1973) *Pak. J. Sci. Res.*, **25**(1/2), 197.

Gibson, R. S. & MacDonald, I. (1976) *HCIMA Review.*, **2**(1), 41.

Gleim, E. G., Tressler, D. K. & Fenton, F. (1944) *Fd. Res.*, **9**, 471.

Gold, H. V. (1962) *Proc. Florida State Hort. Soc.*, **75**, 336.

Gold, H. J. & Wilson, C. W. (1961) *Proc. Florida State Hort. Soc.*, **74**, 291.

Gold, H. J. & Wilson, C. W. (1963a) *J. Fd. Sci.*, **28**, 484.

Gold, H. J. & Wilson, C. W. (1963b) *J. Org. Chem.*, **28**, 985.

Gooding, E. G. B. (1956) *Fd. Mfr.*, **31**, 369.

Gooding, E. G. B. & Tucker, C. G. (1955) *Fd. Mfr.*, **30**, 447.

Gooding, E. G. B., Tucker, C. G. & MacDougall, D. B. (1960) *Fd. Mfr.*, **35**, 249.

Goodman, R. N. (1957) *Agric. Exptl. Stn. Bull. No.* 688, University of Missouri.

Gumbmann, M. R. & Burr, H. K. (1964) *J. Agric. Fd. Chem.*, **12**, 404.

Gupte, S. M., El-Bisi, H. M. & Francis, F. J. (1964) *J. Fd. Sci.*, **29**, 379.

Gupte, S. M. & Francis, F. J. (1964) *Fd. Technol.*, **18**(10), 141.

Gutterman, G. M. & Lovejoy, R. D. (1951) *J. Assoc. Offic. Agric. Chem.*, **34**, 231.

Haas, G. J., Prescott, H. E., Jr. & Cante, C. J. (1974) *J. Fd. Sci.*, **39**, 681.

Hall, C. B., Marshall, A. & Hartman, J. (1950) *Proc. Am. Soc. Hort. Sci.*, **56**, 315.

Harris, R. S. & Karmas, E. (1975) *Nutritional Evaluation of Food Processing*, 2nd edn. Westport, Conn.: Avi. Publ. Co. Inc.

Harrison, S. G., Masefield, G. B. & Wallis, M. (1969) *The Oxford Book of Food Plants.* London: Oxford University Press.

Hashida, W., Mouri, T. & Shiga, I. (1968) *Rept. Toyo Jr. Coll. Inst. Fd. Technol.*, 1966–67, Ser. 8, 281.

Hashimoto, K., Isobe, N. & Takahashi, Z. (1968) *Rept. Toyo Jr. Coll. Inst. Fd. Technol.*, 1966–67, Ser. 8, 369.

Heatherbell, D. A. (1970) Ph.D. Dissertation, Oregon State University.

Heatherbell, D. A. & Wrolstad, R. E. (1971a) *J. Agric. Fd. Chem.*, **19**, 281.

Heatherbell, D. A. & Wrolstad, R. E. (1971b) *J. Fd. Sci.*, **36**, 225.

Heatherbell, D. A., Wrolstad, R. E. & Libbey, L. M. (1971) *J. Fd. Sci.*, **36**, 219.

Heintze, K., Duden, R., Fricker, A., Paulus, K. & Zohm, H. (1975) *Lebensm.-Wiss u. Technol.*, **8**, 17.

Heisler, E. G., Siliciliano, J. & Treadway, R. H. (1962) *Fd. Technol.*, **16**(6), 120.

Heisler, E. G., Siliciliano, J., Treadway, R. H. & Woodward, C. F. (1963) *J. Fd. Sci.*, **28**, 453.

Heisler, E. G., Siliciliano, J., Woodward, C. F. & Porter, W. L. (1964) *J. Fd. Sci.*, **29**, 555.

Hernandez, H. H. & Vosti, D. C. (1963) *Fd. Technol.*, **17**, 95.

Herrmann, K. (1976) *Deut. Lebensm. -Rundschau*, **72**(3), 90.

Herrmann, K., Nebe, G. & Suter, G. (1974) *Ernährung*, **21**(4), 104.

Heutschel, H. & Overbeck, G. (1971) *Qual. Plant Mater. Veg.*, **21**(1/2), 73.
Hewitt, E. J., Mackay, D. A. M., Konignbacker, K. & Hasselstrom, T. (1956) *Fd. Technol.*, **10**, 487.
Hinman, W. F., Brush, M. K. & Halliday, E. G. (1944) *J. Am. Dietet. Assoc.*, **20**, 752.
Hinton, H. R. & Holdsworth, S. D. (1975) *Materials and Technology*. Vol. 7, p. 711. London & Amsterdam: J. H. de Bussy, Longman.
Holdsworth, S. D. (1971) *J. Fd. Technol.*, **6**, 331.
Holfelder, E. & Eid, K. (1973) *Ind. Obst u. Gemüse*, **58**(6), 15.
Hoogzand, C. & Doesburg, J. J. (1961) *Fd. Technol.*, **15**, 160.
Hoover, M. W. & Harman, S. J. (1967) *Fd. Technol.*, **21**, 1529.
Hoover, M. W. & Kushman, L. J. (1966) *Am. Soc. Hort. Sci.*, **88**, 501.
Hrdlicka, J., Curda, D. & Pavelka, J. (1967a) *Sb. Vys. Chem.-Technol., Praze, Potraviny*, **15**, 55.
Hrdlicka, J., Curda, D. & Pavelka, J. (1967b) *Sb. Vys. Chem.-Technol., Praze, Potraviny*, **14**, 45.
Hrdlicka, J. & Kyzlink, V. (1969) *Sb. Vys. Sk. Chem. -Technol., Praze, Potraviny*, **24**, 47.
Hrdlicka, J., Vit, V. & Janicek, G. (1969) *Sb. Vys. Sk. Chem. -Technol., Praze, Potraviny*, **26**, 37.
Huffman, W. A. H. (1963) *Rept.* 902, p. 14. Welaco, Texas: US Fruit & Veg. Prod. Lab.
Hughes, D. H. (1959) *Mushroom Sci.*, **4**, 447.
Hughes, J. C. (1962) *J. Natl. Inst. Agric. Botany*, **9**, 235.
Hughes, J. C., Ayers, J. E. & Swain, T. (1962) *J. Sci. Fd. Agric.*, **13**, 224, 229.
Hughes, J. C. & Evans, J. L. (1969) *Europ. Potato J.*, **12**, 26.
Hughes, J. C., Faulks, R. M. & Grant, A. (1975a) *Potato Res.*, **18**, 495.
Hughes, J. C., Faulks, R. M. & Grant, A. (1975b) *J. Sci. Fd. Agric.*, **26**, 731.
Hughes, J. C., Faulks, R. M. & Grant, A. (1975c) *J. Sci. Fd. Agric.*, **26**, 739.
Ignall, H. R. (1960) *Fd. Technol.*, **14**, 601.
Ingalls, R., Brewer, W. D., Tobey, H. L., Plummer, M., Bennett, B. B. & Ohlson, M. A. (1950) *Fd. Technol.*, **4**, 258.
Ives, M., Zepplin, M., Ames, S. R., Strong, F. M. & Elvehjem, C. A. (1945) *J. Am. Dietet. Assoc.*, **21**, 357.
Jadhav, S., Steele, L. & Hadziyev, D. (1975) *Lebensm.-Wiss u. Technol.*, **8**, 225.
Jadhav, S. J. & Salunkhe, D. K. (1975) *Advan. Fd. Res.*, **21**, 308.
Jankov, S. I. (1970) *Confructa*, **15**(2), 88.
Jansen, E. F. (1949) *J. Biol. Chem.*, **176**, 651.
Jara, D. G. (1974) Ph.D. Dissertation, University of Massachusetts, Amherst.
Jaswal, A. S. (1973) *Am. Potato J.*, **50**(3), 86.
Jenkins, W. F. & Gieger, M. (1957) *Fd. Res.*, **22**, 420.
Jensen, K. A., Conti, J. & Kjaer, A. (1953) *Acta Chem. Scand.*, **7**, 1267.
Johnson, A. E., Nursten, H. E. & Williams, A. A. (1971) *Chem. & Ind.*, (43), 556, 1212.
Joslyn, M. A. & Peterson, R. A. (1958) *J. Agric. Fd. Chem.*, **6**, 754.
Joslyn, M. A. & Peterson, R. A. (1960) *J. Agric. Fd. Chem.*, **8**, 72.
Kahn, J. S. & Bannister, T. T. (1965) *Photochem. Photobiol.*, **4**, 27.

Katsai, B. E. & Kochetova, L. T. (1974) *Konservnaya i Ovoshchesushil'naya Promyshlennost*, No. 2, 22.

Keenan, T. W. & Lindsay, R. C. (1968) *J. Dairy Sci.*, **51**, 112.

Komanowsky, M., Talley, F. B. & Eskew, R. K. (1970) *Fd. Technol.*, **24**, 1020.

Konishi, E., Fuchigami, M. & Okamoto, K. I. (1975) *J. Jap. Soc. Fd. Nutr.*, **38**(1), 44.

Kovari, I. (1972) *Hütöipar*, **19**(1), 25.

Kozlowsa, H. (1971) *Zeszty Nautowe Wyzszej Szkoly Polniczej w Olsztynie*, Suppl. E3.

Kramer, A. & Smith, M. H. (1947) *Ind. Eng. Chem.*, **39**, 1007.

Kröner, W. & Wegner, H. (1942) *Naturwiss.*, **30**, 586.

Kuhn, G. D. & Beelman, R. (1971) *Pennsylvania Packer*, April–May–June, p. 7.

Kumar, V. V. S. & Chandrasekhana, N. (1973) *J. Fd. Sci. Technol. (India)*, **10**(1), 42.

Kurkela, R. & Holström, B. (1976) *Nahrung*, **20**(1), 7.

Kylen, A. M., Charles, V. R., McGrath, B. H., Schleter, J. M., West, L. C. & van Duyne, F. O. (1961) *J. Am. Dietet. Assoc.*, **39**, 321.

Labuza, T. P. (1972) *CRC Crit. Rev. Fd. Technol.*, **3**, 217.

LaJollo, F. (1971) *J. Fd. Sci.*, **36**, 850.

Lamb, F. C., Pressley, A. & Zuch, T. (1947) *Fd. Res.*, **12**, 273.

Lambon, M. G. (1958) *Fd. Technol.*, **12**, 150.

Lawler, F. K. (1967) *Fd. Eng.*, February, 65.

Lee, C. Y., Shallenberger, R. S. & Acree, T. E. (1971) *J. Fd. Sci.*, **36**, 1078.

Lee, C. Y., Downing, D. L., Iredale, H. D. & Chapman, J. A. (1976) *Fd. Chem.*, **1**, 15.

Lee, K. L., Park, J. R. & Lee, S. W. (1974) *J. Korean Soc. Fd. Nutr.*, **3**(1), 13.

Lee, W. G. (1974) Ph.D. Dissertation, Mississippi State University.

Libbey, L. M., Morgan, M. E., Hansen, L. A. & Scanlan, R. A. (1974) Abstracts of papers, *Am. Chem. Soc.*, **168**, AGFD: 4.

Lin, Y. D., Clydesdale, F. M. & Francis, F. J. (1970) *J. Fd. Sci.*, **35**, 641.

Lin, Y. D., Clydesdale, F. M. & Francis, F. J. (1971) *J. Fd. Sci.*, **36**, 240.

Lindquist, F. E., Dietrich, W. C., Masure, M. P. & Boggs, M. M. (1951) *Fd. Technol.*, **5**, 198.

Linehan, D. J. & Hughes, J. C. (1969a) *J. Sci. Fd. Agric.*, **20**, 110.

Linehan, D. J. & Hughes, J. C. (1969b) *J. Sci. Fd. Agric.*, **20**, 113.

Linehan, D. J. & Hughes, J. C. (1969c) *J. Sci. Fd. Agric.*, **20**, 119.

Linehan, D. J. & Hughes, J. C. (1969d) *Europ. Potato J.*, **12**, 41.

Linehan, D. J., Stooke, C. E. & Hughes, J. C. (1968) *Europ. Potato J.*, **11**, 221.

Loef, D. W. (1974) *Confructa*, **19**(3/4), 120.

Lovejoy, R. D. (1952) *J. Assoc. Offic. Agric. Chem.*, **35**, 179.

Lueck, R. H. (1970) *J. Agric. Fd. Chem.*, **18**, 607.

Luh, B. S., Antonakos, J. & Daoud, H. N. (1969) *Fd. Technol.*, **23**, 377.

Luh, B. S. & Eidels, L. (1969a) *Fruchsaft-Industrie*, **14**(2), 58.

Luh, B. S. & Eidels, L. (1969b) *Confructa*, **14**, 8.

Luh, B. S. & Woodroof, J. G. (1975) *Commercial Vegetable Processing*. Westport, Conn.: Avi. Publ. Co. Inc.

Lukes, T. M. (1959) *Fd. Technol.*, **13**, 391.

Lusas, E. W. (1959) *Dissert. Abstr.*, **19**, 1707.

Lusas, E. W., Rice, A. C. & Weckel, K. G. (1960) *Res. Bull.* 218. Madison: University of Wisconsin.

McArdle, F. J. & Curwen, D. (1962) *Mushroom Sci.*, **5**, 447.

McConnell, E. R. & Gottschall, P. B. (1957) *Fd. Technol.*, **11**, 209.

MacLeod, A. J. & MacLeod, G. (1968) *J. Sci. Fd. Agric.*, **19**, 273.

MacLeod, A. J. & MacLeod, G. (1970a) *J. Fd. Sci.*, **35**, 734.

MacLeod, A. J. & MacLeod, G. (1970b) *J. Fd. Sci.*, **35**, 739.

MacLeod, A. J. & MacLeod, G. (1970c) *J. Fd. Sci.*, **35**, 744.

McWeeny, D. J., Moody, J. P. & Burton, H. S. (1964) *J. Sci. Fd. Agric.*, **15**, 253.

Maggioni, A. & Renosto, F. (1970) *Industria Conserve*, **45**, 311.

Mahadeviah, M., Ranganna, S., Sastry, L. V. L., Bhatnagar, H. C., Siddappa, G. S., Sathyavathi, V. K., Shah, G. R., Mookerjee, D. K. & Prabhakar, J. V., (1965) *J. Fd. Sci. Technol. (India)*, **2**, 10.

Malakar, M. C. (1963) *Nature*, **198**, 994.

Maleki, M. (1965) *Dissert. Abstr.*, **25**, 6523.

Marchesini, A., Montuori, F., Muffato, D. & Maestri, D. (1974) *J. Fd. Sci.*, **39**, 568.

Martin, M. E., Sweeney, J. P., Gilpin, G. L. & Chapman, V. J. (1960) *J. Agric. Fd. Chem.*, **8**, 387.

Maruyama, F. T. (1970) *J. Fd. Sci.*, **35**, 540.

Masure, M. P. (1953) *Fd. Technol.*, **7**, 363.

Mathew, A. G. & Parpia, H. A. B. (1971) *Advan. Fd. Res.*, **19**, 75.

Mehlitz, A. & Geerds, G. (1968) *Deut. Lebensm.-Rundschau*, **64**, 140.

Mihalyi, K. & Vamos-Vigyazo, L. (1975) *Acta Alimentaria Academiae Scientiarum Hungaricae*, **4**(3), 291.

Mitchell, R. S. & Rutledge, P. J. (1973) *J. Fd. Technol.*, **8**, 133.

Mlodecki, H., Wieckowska, E. & Jasinska-Sobocinska, A. (1973a) *Bromatologia i Chemia Toksylcologiczna*, **6**, 261.

Mlodecki, H., Wieckowska, E. & Kuleta-Tomasik, J. (1973b) *Bromatologia i Chemia Toksylcologiczna*, **6**, 29.

Mohammad, N. & Ehteschamuddin, A. F. M. (1973) *Pak. J. Sci. Res.*, **25**(1/2), 157.

Mohsenin, N. N. (1970) *Physical Properties of Plant and Animal Material*. Vol. 1. New York & London: Gordon & Breach.

Monzini, A., Crivelli, G., Buonocore, C. & Bassi, M. (1974) *Annali dell'Igtituto Sperimentale per la Valorizzazione Tecnologica dei Prodotti Agricoli*, **5**, 73.

Mookherjee, B. D., Deck, R. E. & Chang, S. S. (1965) *J. Agric. Fd. Chem.*, **13**, 131.

Motohiro, T. & Inoue, N. (1973) *J. Fd. Sci. Technol. (Japan)*, **20**, 1.

Motohiro, T., Numakura, T., Iseya, Z. & Sugiura, S. (1973) *J. Fd. Sci. Technol. (Japan)*, **20**, 5.

Mouri, T., Hashida, W. & Shiga, I. (1968a) *Rept. Toyo Jr. Coll. Inst. Fd. Technol.*, 1966–67, Ser. 8, 206.

Mouri, T., Hashida, W. & Shiga, I. (1968b) *Rept. Toyo Jr. Coll. Inst. Fd. Technol.*, 1966–67, Ser. 8, 231.

Müller, A. L. & Virtanen, A. I. (1966) *Acta Chem. Scand.*, **20**, 1163.
Murray, K. E., Bannister, P. A. & Buttery, R. G. (1975) *Chem. & Ind.*, 973.
Murray, K. E. & Whitfield, F. B. (1975) *J. Sci. Fd. Agric.*, **26**, 973.
Nelson, G. E. K. & Dawson, L. E. (1923) *J. Am. Chem. Soc.*, **45**, 2179.
Neubert, A. M., Wilson, C. W. & Miller, W. H. (1966) *Proc. Florida State Hort. Soc.*, **79**, 243.
Neubert, A. M., Wilson, C. W. & Miller, W. H. (1968) *Fd. Technol.*, **22**, 1297.
Neukom, H. (1967) Fortbildungskurs agriculturchens Inst. Eidgerioss Tech. Hoschsch. Zurich, 1967. *Symposia on Aroma and Flavour Substances in Foodstuffs*, Foster-Verlag AG, 288 pp.
Numa, S. (1971) *J. Agric. Chem. Soc. (Japan)*, **45**, 216.
Numa, S. (1972) *Agric. Biol. Chem.*, **36**, 1603.
Numa, S. & Nomura, D. (1969) *J. Agric. Chem. Soc. (Japan)*, **43**, 837.
Nursten, H. E. & Sheen, M. R. (1974) *J. Sci. Fd. Agric.*, **25**, 643.
Odland, D. & Eheart, M. S. (1975) *J. Fd. Sci.*, **40**, 1004.
Palmer, D. H., Taylor, A. W. & Withers, M. K. (1965) *Proc. 1st Int. Congr. Fd. Sci. Technol.*, **4**, 37. London: Gordon & Breach.
Pan, H. (1960) *Proc. Florida State Hort. Soc.*, **73**, 223.
Pan, H. (1961) *J. Fd. Sci.*, **26**, 337.
Panalaks, T. & Murray, T. K. (1970) *Can. Inst. Fd. Sci. Technol. J.*, **3**, 145.
Pareles, S. R. & Chang, S. S. (1974) *J. Agric. Fd. Chem.*, **22**, 339.
Park, C. R. (1975) *Korean J. Nutr.*, **8**(4), 167.
Park, C. R. & Lee, K. J. (1975) *Korean J. Nutr.*, **8**(4), 173.
Patton, M. G., Gorrel, F. L. & Brown, H. D. (1943) *Proc. Am. Soc. Hort. Sci.*, **43**, 225.
Paukova, E. N. (1975) *Izvestiya Vysshikh Uchebnykh Zavedenii Pishchevaya Tekhnologiya*, No. 6, 59.
Paul, P. & Ferley, M. (1954) *Fd. Res.*, **19**, 272.
Paulus, K., Duden, R., Fricker, A., Heintze, K. & Zohm, H. (1975a) *Lebensm.-Wiss. u. Technol.*, **8**, 11.
Paulus, K., Fricker, A., Duden, R., Heintze, K. & Zohm, H. (1975b) *Lebensm.-Wiss. u. Technol.*, **8**, 7.
Pazrincevic-Trajkovic, J. & Baras, J. (1970) *Hrana i Ishrana*, **11**(7/8), 325.
Pendlington, S. & Ward, J. P. (1965) *Proc. 1st Inst. Congr. Fd. Sci. Technol.*, **4**, 55. London: Gordon & Breach.
Peppler, E. & Feldheim, W. (1964) *Nahrung*, **8**, 597.
Pequignot, G., Vinit, F., Chabert, C., Bodard, M. & Perles, S. (1975) *Annales de la Nutrition et de l'Alimentation*, **29**(5), 439.
Peterson, R. G. & Joslyn, M. A. (1960) *Fd. Res.*, **25**, 429.
Picardi, S. M. & Issenberg, P. (1973) *J. Agric. Fd. Chem.*, **21**(6), 959.
Potter, A. L., Neel, E. M., Reeve, R. M. & Hendel, C. E. (1959) *Am. Potato J.*, **36**, 444.
Purseglove, J. W. (1968) *Tropical Crops: Dicotyledons*. Vols. 1 & 2. London: Longmans.
Pyysalo, H. (1975) Publication No. 13, Technical Research Centre of Finland, Materials and Processing Technology.
Pyysalo, H. (1976) *Acta Chem. Scand.*, **B30**(3), 235.

Pyysalo, H. & Kuusi, T. (1973) Z. Lebensm. Unters.-Forsch., 153, 224.
Rahman, A. R., Henning, W. L. & Westcott, D. E. (1971) J. Fd. Sci., 36, 500.
Ralls, J. W. (1959) J. Agric. Fd. Chem., 7, 505.
Ralls, J. W., Maagdenberg, H. J., Yacoub, N. L., Homnick, D., Zinnecker, M. & Mercer, W. A. (1973) J. Fd. Sci., 38, 192.
Ranganna, S. & Govindarajan, V. S. (1967) J. Fd. Sci. Technol. (India), 3, 155.
Ranganna, S. & Setty, S. R. L. (1968) J. Agric. Fd. Chem., 16, 529.
Ranganna, S. & Setty, L. (1974a) J. Agric. Fd. Chem., 22, 719.
Ranganna, S. & Setty, L. (1974b) J. Agric. Fd. Chem., 22, 1139.
Reeve, R. M. (1970) J. Text. Studies, 1, 247.
Reeve, R. M. (1972) J. Agric. Fd. Chem., 20, 1282.
Resende, R., Francis, F. J. & Stumbo, C. R. (1969a) Fd. Technol., 23, 63.
Resende, R., Stumbo, C. R. & Francis, F. J. (1969b) Fd. Technol., 23, 325.
Richter, E. & Handke, S. (1973) Z. Lebensm. Unters.-Forsch., 153, 31.
Rognerud, G. (1972) Tidsskrift för Hermetikindustrie, 58(5), 130.
Rosoff, H. D. & Cruess, W. V. (1949) Fd. Res., 14, 283.
Saghir, A. R., Mann, L. G., Bernhard, R. A. & Jacobsen, J. V. (1964) Proc. Am. Soc. Hort. Sci., 84, 386.
Salunkhe, D. K., Do, J. Y. & Bolin, H. R. (1973) CRC Crit. Rev. Fd. Technol., 4(2), 153.
Salunkhe, D. K. & Do, J. Y. (1977) CRC Crit. Rev. Fd. Sci. Nutr., 8, 161.
Sapers, G. M. (1970) J. Fd. Sci., 35, 731.
Sapers, G. M. & Nickerson, J. T. R. (1962) J. Fd. Sci., 27, 277, 282, 287.
Sapers, G. M., Osman, S. F., Dooley, C. J. & Panasiuk, O. (1971) J. Fd. Sci., 36, 93.
Sapers, G. M., Sullivan, J. F. & Talley, F. B. (1970) J. Fd. Sci., 35, 728.
Schaller, A. (1962) Die Kälte, 15, 187.
Schmidt, O. T. & Schoeuleben, W. (1957) Z. Naturforsch., 12b, 262.
Schormuller, J. & Weder, J. (1966) Z. Lebensm. Unters.-Forsch., 130, 158, 213.
Schreyen, L., Dirinck, P., Wassenhove, F. & Schamp, N. (1976) J. Agric. Fd. Chem., 24, 336.
Schrumpf, E. & Charley, H. (1975) J. Fd. Sci., 40, 1025.
Schwimmer, S. (1963) J. Fd. Sci., 28, 460.
Schwimmer, S. (1968) Phytochemistry, 7, 401.
Schwimmer, S., Vendstrom, D. W. & Guadagni, D. G. (1964) Fd. Technol., 18(8), 121.
Self, R. (1967) In: Chemistry and Physiology of Flavours, eds. Schultz, H. W., Day, E. A. & Libby, L. M., p. 362. Westport, Conn.: Avi. Publ. Co. Inc.
Self, R. & Swain, T. (1963) Proc. Nutr. Soc., 22, 176.
Self, R., Casey, J. C. & Swain, T. (1963a) Chem. & Ind., 863.
Self, R., Rolley, H. L. J. & Joyce, A. E. (1963b) J. Sci. Fd. Agric., 14, 8.
Setty, G. R. & Ranganna, S. (1972) Indian Fd. Packer, 26(6), 5.
Shallenberger, R. S., Atkin, J. D. & Moyer, J. C. (1960) Fd. Res., 25, 419.
Shallenberger, R. S., Pallsen, H. R. & Moyer, J. C. (1959) Fd. Technol., 13, 92.
Shankaranarayana, M. L., Raghavan, B., Abraham, K. O. & Natarajan, C. P. (1973) CRC Crit. Rev. Fd. Technol., 4, 395.
Shannon, S. (1972) J. Am. Soc. Hort. Sci., 97, 223.

Shannon, S. & Bourne, M. C. (1971) *J. Text. Studies*, **2**, 230.
Shannon, S., Yamaguchi, M. & Howard, F. D. (1967) *J. Agric. Fd. Chem.*, **15**, 417, 423.
Shimazu, F. S., Sterling, C. & York, G. K. (1965) *J. Fd. Sci.*, **30**, 742.
Shrikhande, A. J. (1976) *CRC Crit. Rev. Fd. Sci. Nutr.*, **7**, 193.
Sistrunk, W. A. (1969) *Arkansas Farm Res.*, **18**(6), 7.
Sistrunk, W. A. & Osborne, H. L. (1972) *Arkansas Farm Res.*, **21**(4), 11.
Sistrunk, W. A., Miller, J. C. & Jones, L. G. (1954) *Fd. Technol.*, **8**, 223.
Starke, H. & Herrmann, K. (1976a) *Z. Lebensm. Unters.-Forsch.*, **161**, 25.
Starke, H. & Herrmann, K. (1976b) *Z. Lebensm. Unters.-Forsch*, **161**, 137.
Steinbuch, E. (1969) *Sprenger Inst. Ann. Rept.* (1969), 50.
Steinbuch, E. (1970) *Sprenger Inst. Ann. Rept.* (1970), 39.
Steinbuch, E. (1974) *4th Int. Congr. Fd. Sci. Technol. Abstr.*, **5a**, 82.
Stephens, T. S., Saladana, G., Brown, H. E. & Griffiths, F. P. (1971) *J. Fd. Sci.*, **36**, 36.
Sterling, C. & Bettelheim, F. A. (1955) *Fd. Res.*, **20**, 130.
Sterling, G. & Shimazu, F. (1961) *J. Fd. Sci.*, **26**, 479.
Stevenson, A. E. (1950) *Fd. Res.*, **15**, 150.
Strachan, G. & Nonnecke, I. L. (1961) *Can. J. Plant Sci.*, **41**, 377.
Sullivan, J. F. & Cording, J., Jr. (1969) *Fd. Eng.*, **41**(7), 90.
Sullivan, J. F., Konstance, R. P., Calhoun, M. J., Talley, F. B., Cording, J., Jr. & Panasiuk, O. (1974) *J. Fd. Sci.*, **39**, 58.
Swain, T. & Self, R. (1964) *Europ. Potato J.*, **7**, 228.
Sweeney, J. P. & Martin, M. E. (1961) *Fd. Technol.*, **15**, 263.
Swirski, M. A., Allouf, R., Guimard, A. & Cheptel, H. (1969) *J. Agric. Fd. Chem.*, **17**, 799.
Sykes, S. M. & Tinsley, I. J. (1955) *CSIRO Fd. Pres. Quart.*, **15**(4), 69.
Talley, E. A. (1969) *Am. Potato J.*, **46**, 302.
Tan, C. T. & Francis, F. J. (1962) *J. Fd. Sci.*, **27**, 232.
Thorman, M., Wolf, W., Speiss, W. E. L., Gierschner, K., Baumann, G. & Jung, G. (1977) *Lebensm.-Wiss. u. Technol.*, **10**, 28.
van Buren, J. (1970) *CRC Crit. Rev. Fd. Technol.*, **1**(1), 5.
van Oss, J. F., Codd, L. W., Dijkhoff, K., Fearon, J. H., Roebersen, H. G. & Stanford, E. G. (eds.) (1975) *Materials and Technology. Vol. 7: Vegetable Food Products.* London & Amsterdam: J. H. de Bussey, Longman.
Vertregt, N. (1968) *Europ. Potato J.*, **11**, 226.
Vetter, J. L., Nelson, A. J. & Steinberg, M. P. (1959) *Fd. Technol.*, **13**, 410.
Vilece, R. J., Fagerson, I. S. & Esselen, W. B., Jr. (1955) *J. Agric. Fd. Chem.*, **3**, 433.
Virtanen, A. I. (1967) *Bibl. 'Nutritio et Dieta'*, **9**, 1.
Virtanen, A. I. & Matikkala, E. J. (1961) *Suomen Kemistitehti*, **B34**, 84.
Virtanen, A. I. & Spare, C. G. (1961) *Suomen Kemistitehti*, **B34**, 72.
Voinovitch, I. (1951) *Bull. Soc. Chim. Biol.*, **33**, 1414.
Voinovitch, I., Cheftel, H., Durocher, J. & Kahane, E. (1949) *Compt. Rend.*, **228**, 1823.
von Elbe, J. H., Sy, S. H., Maing, I.-Y. & Gabelman, W. H. (1972) *J. Fd. Sci.*, **37**, 932.

Vulsteke, G. (1969) *Qual. Plant Mater. Veg.*, **17**, 286.

Wager, H. G. (1955) *Fd. Mfr.*, **30**, 499.

Wagner, J. R., Strong, F. M. & Elvehjem, C. A. (1947) *Ind. Eng. Chem.*, **39**, 985.

Warren, D. S. & Woodman, J. S. (1974) *J. Sci. Fd. Agric.*, **25**, 129.

Warren, D. S., Gray, D. & Woodman, J. S. (1975) *J. Sci. Fd. Agric.*, **26**, 1689.

Wascowicz, E. (1974) *Bulletin de l'Academie Polanaise des Sciences, Sciences Biologiques*, **22**, 143.

Watt, B. K., Merrill, A. L., Pecot, R. K., Adams, C. F., Orr, M. L. & Miller, D. F. (1963) *Composition of Foods—(raw, processed and prepared)*, Agricultural Handbook No. 8. Washington D.C.: USDA.

Weckel, K. G., Scharschmidt, R. K. & Rieman, G. H. (1959) *Fd. Technol.*, **13**, 456.

Weckel, K. G., Santos, B., Hernan, E., Laferriere, L. & Gabelman, W. H. (1962) *Fd. Technol.*, **16**(8), 91.

Weeratne, P., Miller, E. V. & Murphy, H. J. (1964) *Am. Potato J.*, **41**, 39.

Wegner, H. (1949) *Z. Lebensm. Unters.-Forsch.*, **89**, 140.

Weichel, H. H. (1966) *Deut. Lebensm.-Rundschau*, **62**, 53.

Whitaker, J. R. (1976) *Advan. Fd. Res.*, **22**, 73.

Wilkens, W. F. (1962) *Dissert. Abstr.*, **22**, 3978.

Wilson, C. W. (1965) *Fd. Technol.*, **19**(8), 98.

Wilson, C. W. (1969a) *J. Fd. Sci.*, **34**, 521.

Wilson, C. W. (1969b) *J. Fd. Sci.*, **34**, 535.

Wilson, C. W. (1970) *J. Fd. Sci.*, **35**, 766.

Winton, A. L. & Winton, K. B. (1935) *The Structure and Composition of Foods. Vol. II: Vegetables, Legumes, Fruits.* New York: John Wiley.

Witkowski, C. & Paradowski, A. (1975) *Przemysl Fermentacyjny i Rolny*, **19**(6), 7.

Wöldecke, M. & Herrmann, K. (1974a) *Z. Lebensm. Unter.-Forsch.*, **155**, 151.

Wöldecke, M. & Herrmann, K. (1974b) *Z. Lebensm. Unters-Forsch.*, **155**, 216.

Wyler, H. & Dreiding, A. S. (1957) *Helv. Chim. Acta*, **40**, 191.

Wyler, H., Mabry, T. I. & Dreiding, A. S. (1963) *Helv. Chim. Acta.* **46**, 1745.

Yamagushi, M., Shannon, S., Howard, F. D. & Joslyn, M. A. (1965) *Proc. Am. Soc. Hort. Sci.*, **86**, 475.

Yamamoto, H. V., Steinberg, M. P. & Nelson, A. I. (1962) *J. Fd. Sci.*, **27**, 113.

Yoshimura, M. (1953) *Vitamins, Kyoto*, **14**, 633.

Zaehringer, M. V. & Cunningham, H. H. (1971) *Am. Potato J.*, **48**, 385.

Zhuk, Yu. T. & Rod'kina, N. A. (1975) *Konservnaya i Ovoshchesushil'naya Promyshlennost*, No. 12, 21.

Zohm, H., Duden, H., Fricker, A., Heintze, K. & Paulus, K. (1975) *Lebensm.-Wiss. u. Technol.*, **8**, 151.

CHAPTER 11

Milk and Dairy Products

R. L. J. LYSTER

National Institute for Research in Dairying, Reading, UK

Milk from domestic cattle is one of man's oldest foods and over the centuries the technology of its production and use to make cream, butter and cheese has been developed to a high degree. Particularly striking improvements have been made in the last 70 years.

11.1 STRUCTURE AND COMPOSITION OF MILK

Although milk has a deceptively simple appearance, its structure is complex. Fresh milk contains about 87% water in which are dissolved various salts, carbohydrates and proteins, and in which are dispersed two separate colloidal systems. One of these is the fat globules with their surrounding membranes, and the other is the casein micelles which contain an intimate mixture of protein molecules and insoluble salts, chiefly calcium phosphate. Both these colloid systems are stable to heat, but one is susceptible to mechanical agitation (as in butter making) and the other to enzymatic action (as in renneting for cheese making). Because of this double colloidal system, milk is probably capable of giving more different end products than any other single foodstuff. Recently, much commercial effort has been expended in creating new products and in seeking new outlets for old ones. However, most milk in the UK is still sold for liquid consumption (60%) or made into cheese (15%) or butter (10%) (Federation UK Milk Marketing Boards, 1976).

The composition of cows' milk is given in Table 11.1, in which the figures were chosen to represent an average for bulk milk; variations in composition occur as a result of time of year, method of feeding,

TABLE 11.1
THE MAJOR CONSTITUENTS OF COWS' MILK

Component	Composition (g/100 g)	
Water	87·6	
Lactose	4·7	
Fat	3·8	
Protein	3·3	
casein		2·6
whey protein		0·7
Salts	0·7	
calcium		0·12
phosphate		0·30

breed of cow, and many other factors. When milk is collected from animals other than the cow, the composition is markedly different; although the use of other milch animals such as the goat, sheep, buffalo, horse and camel is common in various parts of the world, most dairy research has concentrated on cows' milk, to which this article will be confined; nor will reference be made to human milk and the effects of heat on it.

The major components of the two colloidal phases of milk and the aqueous phase in which they are suspended, are shown in Table 11.2; again, these values were chosen as approximately representative of typical values. More extensive lists of milk constituents may be found elsewhere (Mulder and Walstra, 1974; Webb et al., 1974).

The tables show some of the intrinsic constituents of milk; because of its origin, milk also contains at least three other extrinsic components, namely dirt, bacteria and leucocytes. The amounts present vary greatly, depending on the level of farm hygiene. The larger dirt particles are usually removed by filtration; the smaller particles and the leucocytes may be removed by centrifugation. The presence of bacteria (and other microorganisms) is the principal reason for subjecting milk to heat treatment.

11.2 HEAT TREATMENT OF MILK

Because of its low viscosity, milk may be heated in either a continuous-flow system or a batch process. In either case, the treatment may be described by specifying the length of time spent by the milk at its

TABLE 11.2

COMPOSITION % OF MILK COLLOIDS AND THE
AQUEOUS PHASE

Fat
(a) Globules (diameter $0.1-10\mu$m)
    triglyceride   99.5
    diglyceride, fatty
      acid, vitamins, *etc.*   0.5

(b) Membrane (thickness $0.01\ \mu$m)
    protein (incl. enzymes)   49
    phospholipid   28
    glycerides   14
    other lipids   8

Casein micelles (diameter $0.01-0.5\ \mu$m)

Casein	93	
α_{s1}-casein		43
β-casein		27
κ-casein		14
other caseins		9
Ash	7	
calcium		2.7
phosphate		3.6

Aqueous phase

Lactose	4.7	
Whey proteins	0.7	
β-lactoglobulin		0.31
α-lactalbumin		0.16
serum albumin		0.03
immunoglobulins		0.07
others		0.07
Salts	0.7	
calcium		0.05
magnesium		0.01
phosphate		0.10
citrate		0.20
sodium		0.05
potassium		0.14
chloride		0.12

maximum temperature, adjusted if necessary for the time spent at elevated temperatures during heating and cooling. This simplification ignores the non-uniform distribution of residence times and temperatures that characterise real processes, but provides a useful approximation (Burton, 1958).

Some of the heat treatments that may be applied to milk are shown in Fig. 11.1, where maximum temperature (on a scale linear with respect to the reciprocal of the absolute temperature) is plotted against the logarithm of the time; this choice of scales allows various areas of the graph to be delimited by straight lines. Any real heat treatment can be approximated by a point somewhere on the graph. Thus, the minimum heat treatment for pasteurisation is defined legally at points A and B (The Milk (Special Designation) Regulations, 1963) and any point on the line joining A and B represents a heat treatment that can be assumed to have an equal effect. Any point above that line represents a more severe heat treatment, with the most severe being represented by points at the upper right-hand corner of the graph; such treatments may lead to excessive amounts of browning and also to colloidal instability.

The main purpose of heating milk is not only to kill pathogenic microorganisms, as in the pasteurisation treatments, but to improve the quality of milk with respect to non-pathogenic bacteria. For short-term storage, pasteurisation offers a sufficient improvement in quality but for long-term stability, a sterile product is essential. The

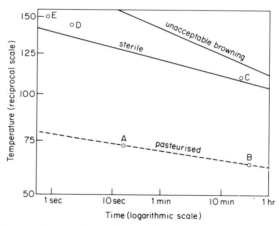

FIG. 11.1 Some time–temperature combinations applied to milk. The broken line marked 'pasteurised' is drawn through the points A (72°C/15 s) and B (64°C/30 min), two legally defined pasteurising treatments. The positions of the other lines are only approximate: point C (110°C/20 min) is for in-bottle sterilisation; point D (142°C/2 s) is for a UHT-sterile extended-life process; point E (150°C/0·8 s) is for a new French process (ATAD).

heat treatments needed to kill all bacteria and their spores in a reasonable volume of milk can be represented by points lying above the line marked 'sterile' on the graph. Three points are shown, each representing a heat treatment intended to give a sterile milk. Point C is for an in-bottle sterilisation process; point D is for an ultra-high temperature (UHT) process for extended-life milk (Burton, 1969) and point E is for a recent French process (ATAD) designed for the same purpose (Ged and Alais, 1976). Both points B and C represent processes of the batch type; the newer, more sophisticated methods tend to use as short a time and as high a temperature as possible. The reason for this is that the rate of chemical reactions (such as the Maillard reaction) usually has a smaller temperature dependence than the rate of destruction of bacterial spores, so that the lines on a graph such as Fig. 11.1, that define acceptable extents of reaction, have different slopes. Qualitatively, the effect of using high-temperature–short-time treatments is to minimise chemical changes for a given sporicidal or bactericidal effect (Burton, 1969), as can be seen from Fig. 11.1. Although qualitatively correct, the simplified approach expressed by use of such a graph should be used with caution if quantitative estimates are required.

11.3 EFFECTS OF HEATING ON MILK CONSTITUENTS

11.3.1 Proteins

The proteins of milk, like proteins from any source, may change their conformation or state of aggregation under the influence of heat, which may also produce changes in their covalent structures. Applied to enzymes and other globular proteins, such changes result in denaturation, with loss of enzyme activity and dramatic changes in solubility. However, the major proteins of milk, the caseins, are not globular proteins of this kind; in their natural state they are already in a partially disordered and extended conformation. Unlike a typical globular protein, each molecule is not present in a single preponderant conformation.

11.3.1.1 Caseins

As indicated in Table 11.2, the caseins are subdivided into three major components, α_{S1}-, β- and κ-casein. The amino acid sequences of each of these proteins are known (Whitney *et al.*, 1976) and have a high proportion of hydrophobic residues, giving these proteins a strong tendency to form aggregates. κ-Casein is especially important, since it acts as a protective colloid against flocculation by calcium ions, until attacked by rennet or other proteolytic enzymes. In the casein micelle, the caseins are firmly aggregated except at low temperatures; below 10°C especially, β-casein tends to dissolve out of the micelles into free solution in the whey. The micelles themselves have an open porous structure into which large molecules such as enzymes can diffuse (Ribadeau-Dumas and Garnier, 1970). In electron-microscope studies, they appear as rounded structures resembling balls of cotton-wool, possibly assembled from granular subunits; a typical micelle with a diameter of 0·1 μm might contain several hundred such subunits. Each of these subunits is believed to have 10–12 individual casein molecules and it is thought that κ-casein is evenly distributed throughout these subunits and the micelle (Bloomfield and Mead, 1975). Each micelle carries a net negative charge whose magnitude varies under different conditions; it gives rise to a zeta potential of about -20 mV at 25°C (Green and Crutchfield, 1971). The primary reaction in the clotting of milk by rennet or other proteolytic enzymes is cleavage of the polypeptide chain of κ-casein between phenyl-alanine-105 and methionine-106 (Green, 1977), resulting in the release from the micelle of the soluble macropeptide which consists of 64 mainly hydrophilic residues. Since the macropeptide carries many anionic groups, and leaves in the micelle *para-κ*-casein with a net positive charge, the zeta potential of the micelle drops to about -11 mV as a result of rennet activity. This initial step can be isolated from the subsequent coagulation step by keeping the temperature below about 10°C; this inhibits proteolysis much less than coagulation. When milk clots, it does so partly as a result of the decrease in the zeta potential which is responsible for a repulsive force between the micelles; other processes thought to be involved are the formation of salt bridges and hydrophobic bonds between coalescing micelles, probably involving calcium ions.

Because the caseins in their normal state partly resemble denatured proteins, the effect of heat on them is not easily detected by the usual physical methods. However, important changes do occur since, if excessive temperatures are used to pasteurise milk for cheese mak-ing, coagulation is slow and the curds are weak. It is still not possible to account completely for these changes at the molecular level; it is known that the rate of release of macropeptide from κ-casein in over-heated milk is not much slower than from normal milk, but there is some evidence that less peptide is released. It is also known that the sulphydryl (–SH) group of κ-casein can react with β-lactoglobulin when the two pure proteins are heated together on their own; whether quite the same reaction occurs in heated milk, however, is not entirely clear. The peptide bond cleaved by rennet is a labile one and this fact suggests that at least this part of the κ-casein molecule is stabilised in a special conformation which may be lost on heating. How these changes affect coagulation time and curd strength is not clear; other components also interact, especially the milk salts, since the coagulation time of heated milk can be reduced by dialysis against unheated milk (Kannan and Jenness, 1961).

More severe heating can lead to changes in covalent structure, such as the loss of phosphate groups from the phosphoserine of casein; in 20 min at 140°C, about one-half the casein phosphate is hydrolysed (Belec and Jenness, 1962). Partial cleavage of the rennet-sensitive peptide bond in κ-casein also occurs during such severe heating.

11.3.1.2   Whey Proteins

The whey proteins of milk are so called because they are not retained in the curd after clotting; they are in true solution in the aqueous phase and stand in strong contrast to the caseins in that they are compact globular proteins with a unique native conformation. The first effect of heat is to relax the constraints of this configuration and to allow access to a range of more disordered conformations, the change being easily observed by physical methods.

β-Lactoglobulin

As can be seen from Table 11.2, the most abundant whey protein is β-lactoglobulin. At room temperature it is a dimer of two identical subunits, each of which has a molecular weight of 18 400 and contains two disulphide bridges and one –SH group, normally unreactive. The complete amino acid sequence is known (Whitney et al., 1976) but there is some uncertainty about the position of one of the disulphide bonds in the native protein. The three-dimensional structure has not been determined and no enzymatic function is known for this protein. β-Lactoglobulin has been the object of many physicochemical studies (McKenzie, 1971) since it can easily be isolated in a very pure state; as a result, much is known of its aggregation at temperatures below 40°C. On raising the temperature above 40°C, the dimers dissociate to form monomers, without any significant change in conformation.

Between 50°C and 75°C, a large conformation change occurs which is accompanied by unmasking of the –SH group. This change in reactivity is of great importance in milk, since it allows the –SH group to react with disulphide bonds on other protein molecules; these disulphide-interchange reactions can produce significant changes in many of the properties of milk. Below about 65–70°C, the conformation changes are reversible on cooling, but at higher temperatures the denaturation is less easily reversed (Rüegg et al., 1975). In milk, the kinetics of the irreversible denaturation of β-lactoglobulin follow second-order rate equations and show a rather sharp change in activation energy at about 90°C; below this temperature the apparent activation energy is about 280 kJ·mole^{-1}, but above it, it is about 55 kJ·mole^{-1} (Lyster, 1970). From this it is clear that irreversible denaturation is a complex reaction and almost certainly consists of at least two consecutive reactions with different temperature dependencies. This is supported by measurements of the rate of denaturation in the presence of p-chloromercuribenzoate (PCMB), a reagent that combines firmly with the –SH group of β-lactoglobulin. At temperatures above 90°C, the apparent rate of denaturation is slowed down dramatically in the presence of PCMB, strongly suggesting that disulphide interchange catalysed by –SH groups is the rate-determining reaction in this temperature range. At temperatures below 90°C, the effect of PCMB is much smaller and is negligible at temperatures below 78°C, but the details of the reaction at these temperatures are still obscure.

Another consequence of this complicated temperature dependence is that the rate of denaturation at high temperatures is comparatively slow; even at 135°C, the denaturation half-time is 3·5 s. As a result, it is possible to use the extent of denaturation of β-lactoglobulin in milk processed in UHT plants to assess the relative severity of such heat treatments (Lyster et al., 1971).

α-Lactalbumin

After β-lactoglobulin, the next most abundant whey protein is α-lactalbumin (McKenzie, 1971; Whitney et al., 1976); its molecular weight is 14 176 and there are four disulphide bridges. The amino acid sequence and the positions of the disulphides are known, and the three-dimensional structure is very similar to that of lysozyme, an enzyme whose amino acid sequence shares many features in common with that of α-lactalbumin. The structural similarity to lysozyme is related to the enzymatic function of α-lactalbumin;

although not an enzyme itself, it forms part of the enzyme, lactose synthetase, in the mammary gland. This enzyme consists of two components, called the A and B proteins. The B protein is α-lactalbumin and the A protein is a galactosyl transferase capable, in the absence of α-lactalbumin, of transferring galactose residues from uridine diphosphate-galactose to N-acetylglucosamine. α-Lactalbumin binds to, and modifies, the activity of the A protein so that glucose becomes the preferred acceptor for galactose, giving lactose.

The properties of α-lactalbumin are in marked contrast to those of β-lactoglobulin. There is little or no tendency to aggregate to oligomeric forms at room temperature, while on heating a conformation change is observable at temperatures about 5°C lower than is the case with β-lactoglobulin (Rüegg et al., 1977). However, the conformation change is reversible to a greater extent, so that in terms of irreversible denaturation by heat, α-lactalbumin is considerably more stable than β-lactoglobulin. Studies on the pure protein have shown that the reason for this behaviour is the presence of the four disulphide bridges (Lyster, unpublished data); so long as these bonds are intact, the molecule can revert on cooling to its native configuration. This ability is lost if one of the disulphide bonds is broken, presumably because this allows the extent of disorder in the unfolded protein to increase. Hence, at temperatures above 70°C, any reaction involving the disulphide bonds leads to irreversible denaturation: for example, –SH groups react to give disulphide to a linear polymer, a normal addition polymerisation for not changed by this reaction, denaturation is effectively catalysed by –SH groups. This reaction is similar to the –SH catalysed polymerisation of the cyclic monomers of tri-, tetra- or penta-methylene disulphide to a linear polymer, a normal addition polymerisation for which the usual type of chain-reaction mechanism is well established. In heated milk, the –SH groups are supplied by β-lactoglobulin and the product of the reaction is a mixed disulphide of the denatured forms of the two proteins (and any other proteins with accessible disulphide bonds). As would be expected, the addition of PCMB to milk before heating slows down the rate of denaturation of α-lactalbumin considerably, especially at temperatures below 125°C. In the absence of –SH groups, there is a slow attack by the hydroxyl (OH⁻) ion on the disulphide bonds of α-lactalbumin, even at pH 7. The reaction products of this β-elimination are dehydroalanine and cysteine persulphide, leading to the formation of H_2S and other breakdown products of cystine. Since persulphide and H_2S can attack disulphide bonds in other native α-lactalbumin molecules in much the same way that –SH groups do, the rate of denaturation slowly accelerates, as in the initial phases of many chain-reaction mechanisms. At high temperatures, attack by OH^- ions becomes increasingly significant compared to the disulphide interchange reactions and this may account for the decreasing effect of PCMB at high temperatures. Thus, although the α-lactalbumin molecule certainly owes much of its heat stability to its disulphide bonds, it may also be viewed as a cyclic monomer awaiting a suitable reagent to allow it to rearrange its structure and denature irreversibly.

Immunoglobulins

The immunoglobulins in cows' milk vary in concentration, being especially high in colostrum—the secretion of the mammary gland—during the first few days of lactation; their presence in colostrum is of great value to the neonatal calf in resisting infection and controlling the gut flora. They are uniquely heterogeneous among milk proteins because they are synthesised by large numbers of cells or cell clones that each produce a different amino acid sequence. Three major types are present: IgG, IgA and IgM. They are also heterogeneous with respect to their heat stability and are partly denatured by pasteurisation; hence, they are rather less stable than the other major whey proteins. Although they contain numerous disulphide bonds and no –SH groups, their rate of denaturation is not affected by reagents that attack disulphide bonds. One of the activities associated with the immunoglobulins of milk is the agglutination of fat globules in cold milk (Mulder and Walstra, 1974); the resulting floccules of globules rise towards the surface under the force of gravity much more rapidly than a single globule would, and thus immunoglobulins are responsible for the high rate of creaming in cold milk; the ability to flocculate is lost on denaturation. Apart from this, their presence in milk for human consumption has little significance except for their nutritional value as proteins; even in cheese made from unpasteurised milk, the immunoglobulins do not seem to play any rôle in controlling the development of the required bacterial flora.

Serum albumin

Bovine serum albumin is always present in bulk milk, but may be absent from milk of a single healthy cow; it is not synthesised in the mammary gland but is transferred intact from the blood stream. The concentration varies but is particularly high (up to 0·2%) if the udder is infected; it is rather less stable than β-lactoglobulin to heat denaturation.

Minor milk proteins

Amongst the minor proteins of milk, the enzymes form a special group and have been much studied. Over 50 enzymes are now known to be present (Shahani, 1966; Got, 1971) but most of these are of little importance to milk as a foodstuff and will not be described here.

Alkaline phosphatase (EC 3.1.3.1) is present in the mammary glands of cows and in milk is associated with the fat-globule membrane. Its significance lies not in the nature of its enzyme activity but in its heat stability, which is just slightly greater than that of the bacillus responsible for tuberculosis, at one time the most important milk-borne disease. Its stability to heating has resulted in the very widespread adoption of legal tests for proper pasteurisation based on tests for residual alkaline phosphatase activity: as little as 0·2% of the original activity can easily be detected by a simple routine test. Any sample of supposedly pasteurised milk giving a positive result in the phosphatase test is presumed to have been heated insufficiently or to have become contaminated with raw milk. However, if heating was to temperatures greater than about 82°C, a positive result can occur owing to reactivation of the enzyme during storage after heating. No satisfactory way of distinguishing a false positive of this kind has been found; the reactivated enzyme seems to be indistinguishable from the native form.

Another enzyme that has been used for testing for proper pasteurisation is *lactoperoxidase* (EC 1.11.1.7); it is rather more stable to heat than alkaline phosphatase but reactivation has also been known to occur.

Milk always shows some proteolytic activity arising from proteases which may have several different origins. There is evidence that the serum enzyme *plasmin* and its precursor *plasminogen* are present in milk (Kaminogawa *et al.*, 1972); leucocytes are another source of proteases; and, perhaps most important, many microorganisms produce a protease. In milk stored cold before processing, as is now the usual practice, it is possible for growth of psychrophilic organisms, especially pseudomonads, to occur. The proteases formed by these organisms are rather stable to heat and are only partly denatured by quite severe UHT treatments (Alichanidis and Andrews,

1977). As a result, significant proteolytic activity is evident in the treated milk; this leads to the formation of a weak protein gel in the carton on prolonged storage. On the other hand, the natural proteolytic enzymes of milk, whether serum or leucocyte in origin, are much less stable to heat and, although not denatured by ordinary pasteurisation, are destroyed by heating to 80°C for 10 min.

Milk also contains a lipase which can be activated by vigorous agitation (Mulder and Walstra, 1974); if allowed to act for long enough on milk or any product containing milk fat, a rancid flavour develops. Usually this is not desirable but in some cheese varieties, partial lipolysis is essential for the proper development of flavour during ripening. However, milk lipase is almost completely denatured by pasteurisation and, in most cheeses, lipolysis occurs as a result of the microorganisms present.

Milk heat treatments

No other component of milk is modified by heat as dramatically as are the whey proteins; consequently it is common practice to use the extent of their denaturation in classifying the heat treatments of milk. Of these, pasteurisation is the most important; in Britain (Federation UK Milk Marketing Boards, 1976), 85% of the milk sold for liquid consumption is heated in a way that conforms to the legal definition of pasteurisation (The Milk (Special Designation) Regulations, 1963), which includes passing the test for alkaline phosphatase described above. Another legal test, for in-bottle sterilisation, requires that virtually total denaturation of whey proteins takes place (The Milk (Special Designation) Regulations, 1963). In this test, ammonium sulphate (to 20%) is added and some of the clear filtrate heated; development of any turbidity reveals the presence of undenatured whey protein in the milk. These legal tests thus use protein denaturation to classify a sample of milk as acceptable or unacceptable; a more extended classification is possible if quantitative measurements are made. A useful method of this sort is that defined by the American Dry Milk Institute (1971); the whey proteins soluble in reconstituted milk saturated with sodium chloride are measured and the amount found is used to classify the sample as having received a high, medium or low heat treatment. The method is widely used and is not restricted to the skim-milk powders for which it was originally designed; with suitable modifications, even whey powders can be assessed (Wyeth, 1972). For comparing different UHT heat treatments, the extent of denaturation of β-lactoglobulin has similarly been proposed as a suitable yardstick (Lyster *et al.*, 1971).

11.3.2 Lipids

The fat globules of milk form an oil-in-water emulsion with each globule being at least partly coated with a membrane, most of whose material is derived from the walls of the secretory cells of the mammary gland (Mulder and Walstra, 1974). After being extruded from these cells, the fat globules tend to lose their original membranes which partly dissolve in the aqueous phase. Since milk fat is mostly triglyceride in composition, physical properties such as melting-point range (0–40°C) depend on the chain length of the fatty acids present and the ratio of unsaturated to saturated fatty acids; these can vary considerably depending on the diet of the cow. Some properties of milk fat, such as the whipping ability of cream, depend more on the presence or state of the highly surface-active phospholipids which are present in the fat-globule membrane.

The dispersion of the fat is increased by homogenisation or reduced by churning, and both these processes require careful temperature control. In homogenisation, the fat globules (which must be in the liquid state) are disrupted by very large shearing forces to form smaller ones, changing the distribution of globule sizes from a broad curve with a maximum at $3–4-\mu$m diameter to a narrow peak at about $0·3\,\mu$m. As a consequence, the surface area is increased by a factor of 6–10 and the new surface may be occupied either by spreading of the original membrane material or by surface-active components such as casein or denatured whey protein; the latter is normally present because milk is usually homogenised at 70–80°C, which also ensures that the fat is liquid. On the other hand, for the churning of cream to butter, the fat must be partly solid; the temperature is kept at 15–20°C in churning by traditional methods which involve low shearing forces and the incorporation of air bubbles on whose surface clumps of globules form, followed by phase inversion to a water-in-oil and air-in-oil emulsion. During churning, much of the fat-globule membrane material, especially phospholipid and protein, is transferred to the aqueous phase; however, simply cooling milk produces a similar effect, but to a lesser extent, and advantage can be taken of this in choosing the temperature of various stages of the sequence of operations involved in butter making. One of the chief considerations is to minimise the rate of formation of the off-flavours arising from the oxidation of unsaturated fatty acids in butter fat; since the composition of membrane phospholipid is high in unsaturated fatty acid, this fraction is particularly susceptible to oxidation. Other flavour changes are associated with the release of H_2S from the membrane protein on heating which seems to occur faster from the fat globule than it does from the whey proteins.

11.3.3 Salts

The milk salts can be divided into those that form complexes which are affected by heat and those that do not; the latter include the simple ions of sodium, potassium, chloride and sulphate. The ions affected by heating include those of calcium, magnesium, citrate and phosphate, which are present in both the dissolved and solid states. The dissolved part consists of the free ions and various complexes such as calcium citrate. The solid phase is part of the casein micelle and is therefore in a highly dispersed form. The exact nature of the solid phase is still unclear, but the main component is calcium phosphate, probably mainly microcrystalline hydroxyapatite, but perhaps partly amorphous, with magnesium and citrate ions absorbed or incorporated in some way (Lyster, 1976). It would be expected that this solid phase in the micelle would be in equilibrium with the ions dissolved in the aqueous phase, but calculations suggest that milk is supersaturated with respect to hydroxyapatite, and calcium phosphates are notoriously slow to equilibrate. The dissolved complexes of calcium are relatively weak and any rise in temperature tends to break them down to their constituent ions. However, the reverse is true for solid calcium phosphates; all forms of calcium phosphate have a lower solubility at higher temperatures, and this is especially true of the more basic forms. There will, therefore, be three main effects of heating on the equilibrium distribution of calcium salts: first, to dissociate some of the soluble calcium complexes; second, to precipitate more solid calcium phosphate; and third, to tend to shift the composition of the solid phase towards a more basic calcium phosphate. The extent of such changes can be measured; for example, in one study, 16% of the soluble calcium appeared in the colloidal phase after heating the milk to 85°C for 30 min (Kannan and Jenness, 1961). Whether the new solid calcium phosphate builds up on that already present on the casein micelles, or whether it forms a new colloidal phase with denatured whey protein (as it does in heated cheese whey) is not known.

The milk salts also control the milk pH, which drops when the milk is heated. This drop is larger than that expected from consideration of the major buffering ions present, and is due to the release of protons from phosphate ions when calcium phosphate comes out of solution;

however, this may be offset by loss of carbon dioxide from open systems. Severe heat treatments may lead to the formation of acidic compounds from lactose.

Because of the lower solubilities of calcium phosphates at higher temperatures, a heated metal surface in contact with milk tends to acquire a deposit of solid calcium phosphate. In one UHT plant, β-$Ca_3(PO_4)_2$ was found on the heat-exchanger plates in contact with milk at temperatures between 90°C and 135°C (Lyster, 1965); under certain conditions, the formation of these deposits limited the useful length of each processing run because of their effect on the rate of heat transfer.

11.3.4 Sugars

Lactose is 4-o-β-D-galactopyranosyl-D-glucopyranose or Gal-p-β(1 → 4) Glc, and is synthesised in the mammary gland from blood glucose, part of which is converted to galactose (Webb et al., 1974). Small amounts of other disaccharides may be present in cows' milk, but in trace amounts only. Lactose exists in solution in two forms, each with its own characteristic optical rotation; the forms are designated α and β, the α form being that with the greater dextrorotation. At equilibrium at 20°C there is 1·68 times as much β form as α, but this ratio drops slightly at higher temperatures. Supersaturated solutions yield crystals of α-lactose monohydrate at any temperature below 93·5°C; above this point, anhydrous β-lactose forms. The two isomers differ in solubility and sweetness as well as optical rotation; the conversion of a fresh solution of either form to the equilibrium mixture is known as mutarotation. Lactose is one of the less sweet-tasting sugars; fructose is about 4 times sweeter than the equilibrium mixture of α- and β-lactose. If milk is dried too quickly for lactose crystals to form, as in milk powder manufacture, it forms an amorphous mixture of the α- and β-isomers. In this state, lactose is very hygroscopic; advantage is taken of this in the instantising process, in which a controlled amount of moisture is added at elevated temperatures, giving some crystallisation before re-drying. This results in a free-flowing powder that disperses almost instantly when it is added to water to form reconstituted milk. The rate of crystallisation of lactose is affected by many factors including temperature; in several products, such as ice-cream and sweetened condensed milk, it is important for the lactose crystals to be smaller than the minimum size that would impart a 'sandy' texture to the taste of the product.

This can be achieved by heavy seeding with microcrystals and careful control of the processing conditions. Lactose is a reducing sugar and on heating shows the expected tendency to enter into the Maillard reaction with the amino groups of proteins, especially the major milk protein, casein. The reaction may continue during subsequent storage at lower temperatures and lactuloselysine, probably formed by the Amadori rearrangement of lactosyllysine, has been isolated from the casein of stored UHT milk (Möller et al., 1977). Concomitant changes in the molecular-weight distribution of the casein suggested that further reactions involving crosslinking of different casein molecules were taking place during storage and that these could lead to gel formation.

11.3.5 Vitamins

Both fat-soluble and water-soluble vitamins are present in milk. The former are little affected by heating and only four of the water-soluble vitamins are affected (International Dairy Federation, 1972): these are ascorbic acid, thiamine, vitamin B_{12} and folic acid. The losses of these vitamins are shown in Table 11.3 for various heat treatments. Vitamin C is perhaps the most sensitive to heat, since it is partly present as dehydroascorbic acid which is rapidly lost on heating; the rest is present as ascorbic acid and is quite stable. Vitamin B_6 is slowly lost on storage of sterile milk but this does not seem to be related to heating.

TABLE 11.3

PERCENTAGE LOSSES EXPECTED OF VITAMINS AFFECTED BY HEATING OF MILK

Vitamin	Pasteurisation	In-bottle sterilisation	UHT sterilisation
Thiamine	5	20	10
Vitamin C	10	40	10
Folic acid	0	40	15
Vitamin B_{12}	0	60	5

11.4   EFFECTS OF HEATING ON FUNCTIONAL PROPERTIES

11.4.1 Flavour

Several functional properties of milk are affected by heating. The taste of raw milk fresh from the cow often has a flavour reminiscent of the smell of a cow-shed. Mild heat treatment, such as pasteurisation, removes this to give the normal bland flavour associated with liquid milk. One of the problems in developing the UHT-sterile processes for liquid milk was to retain this bland flavour in spite of the much more severe heat treatment needed to produce a sterile product (International Dairy Federation, 1972). More severe heat treatment, such as in-bottle sterilisation, can give rise to a cooked flavour associated with browning reactions and reminding some tasters of rice pudding. Prolonged heating, especially of sweetened condensed milk, produces caramelisation with its typical caramel flavour.

11.4.2   Colour

The milky whiteness of milk arises from light scattering by the casein micelles and, to a lesser extent, by the fat globules. The reflectance at different wavelengths in the visible range, however, is not uniform because of the presence of various coloured components in milk. The most important of these are the greenish-yellow of riboflavin in the aqueous phase, and the yellow of carotene in the fat phase; the actual amounts of both these compounds vary seasonally, depending on the composition of the cow's feed. There is also the tendency for the casein micelles to scatter blue light more strongly than red, from the normal wavelength dependence of light scattering. On heating milk, the apparent whiteness at first intensifies (Burton, 1955); this is probably caused by the increase in scattering as the whey proteins denature, but it may be partly due to changes in size or refractive index of the casein micelles. On further heating, the Maillard reaction leads to the casein micelles acquiring a brown tint which reduces reflectance at the blue end of the visible spectrum and eventually gives the milk a brown appearance. On the other hand, the colour of cream is much less affected by heat.

11.4.3   Viscosity

Several of the physical properties of milk, such as density and viscosity, are affected by heat, but they differ little from those of water appropriately modified to allow for the presence of other milk constituents. Temperature changes have more complicated effects on some milk products; even the viscosity of cream is a complicated function of the fat content, temperature and shear rate, especially for heavy creams at moderate temperatures (Mulder and Walstra, 1974). Butter, too, shows changes in consistency with temperature and time of storage, arising from the slow rate of crystallisation of milk fat. The details of these changes are well understood in physicochemical terms, having been studied intensively for many years because of the economic importance of butter. Much less is known of the processes involved in the behaviour of cheese when heated to the temperature at which it softens or melts.

11.5 QUALITY OF MILK

The quality of milk, that is, its fitness for any of its many uses, depends not only on the heat treatment it receives but also on its composition. With regard to the major components of milk (fat, protein, lactose, salts and water), the composition, though appearing constant to the consumer, in fact varies owing to a number of factors; the most significant of these are breed of cow, season and feed (Webb et al., 1974). For example, fat content may be 3·6% in milk from Friesian cows, or 5·0% in milk from Guernseys. In the latter case, the fat would probably have a stronger yellow colour from carotene, since this breed, and the other Channel Island breeds, transmit to the milk a larger fraction of the dietary carotene. Some special products are, or were, associated with particular breeds of cow, such as double Gloucester cheese. Seasonal variations in composition are relatively less; for herds excluding Channel Island, the extremes of fat content range from about 3·5% in May to about 4% in November (Federation UK Marketing Boards, 1976). This seasonal effect arises from two different causes: first, because calving is not spread uniformly throughout the months of the year, changes in composition owing to stage of lactation are not completely averaged out in bulk milk; and second, seasonal changes in feeding methods also affect milk composition. For example, most cows in Britain graze in the open from April to October, and milk taken at this time seems to give higher quality cheeses (Chapman and Burnett, 1972). As would be expected, the cost of making products such as cheese or butter depends partly on the yield from a given volume of milk; since the yield of product generally varies directly with the composition of the original milk, the quality of the latter affects the economic value of the product.

Apart from such variations in the main constituents of milk, the quality of milk may also be affected by relatively small amounts of some materials which may appear in milk by various routes. For example, milk can acquire from strongly flavoured feeds, taints which do not disappear during pasteurisation. Other compounds of importance (Cowie and Swinburne, 1977) are pesticides, herbicides and fungicides and their metabolites; heavy metals; other elements (iodine, etc.), especially their radioactive isotopes; various toxic substances of plant or fungal origin, such as aflatoxin; and finally, hormones. When such compounds have been detected in milk they are usually present at very low concentrations. Assessing the hazard from their ingestion in milk is extremely difficult for many reasons, nor is it usual to test milk routinely for these substances, presumably because the cow can be relied on to act as a filter to any acutely toxic substance. Little is known of the effect of heat on most of these substances, but many would be expected to be quite stable.

The quality of milk will also depend on hygiene in the milking parlour; insufficient cleaning of the udder before milking leads to heavy bacterial contamination and the presence of visible dirt in the milk. In extreme cases, flavour changes may result, but in general, milk seems to be rather resistant to spoiling in this way. Another source of variation in composition is the health of the cows producing it; mastitis, an inflammation of the udder caused by bacterial infection, is still a common disease, and leads to a drop in fat, casein and lactose content in milk and an increase in serum albumin, immunoglobulin and chloride content. These changes lead to a deterioration in suitability for cheese making. If the infected cow is treated with antibiotics, its milk is liable to contain residues which are capable of inhibiting the growth of cheese starter organisms; as a result, milk for cheese making is often tested routinely for antibiotics before use. Mastitis is also accompanied by a large increase in leucocyte content of milk as part of the mammary gland's natural response to infection; on disruption, these cells release proteolytic and other enzymes from their lysosomes.

Only a small part of the very large amount of detailed research that has been carried out on the physics and chemistry of milk and its products has been covered in this chapter. If further information is required, it may be found either in the references given above or in other papers cited therein.

REFERENCES AND BIBLIOGRAPHY

Alichanidis, E. & Andrews, A. T. (1977) *Biochim. Biophys. Acta*, **485**, 424.
American Dry Milk Institute (1971) Bull. No. 916. *Standards for Grades of Dry Milks including Methods of Analysis*. Chicago.
Belec, J. & Jenness, R. (1962) *J. Dairy Sci.*, **45**, 20.
Bloomfield, V. A. & Mead, R. J. (1975) *J. Dairy Sci.*, **58**, 592.
Burton, H. (1955) *J. Dairy Res.*, **22**, 74.
Burton, H. (1958) *J. Dairy Res.*, **25**, 324.
Burton, H. (1969) *Dairy Sci. Abstr.*, **31**, 287.
Chapman, H. R. & Burnett, J. (1972) *Dairy Inds.*, **37**, 207.
Cowie, A. T. & Swinburne, J. K. (1977) *Dairy Sci. Abstr.*, **39**, 391.
Federation UK Milk Marketing Boards (1976) *UK Dairy Facts and Figures*. Thames Ditton.
Ged, J. & Alais, C. (1976) *Le Lait*, **56**, 407.
Got, R. (1971) *Ann. Nutr. Aliment.*, **25**, A291.
Green, M. L. (1977) *J. Dairy Res.*, **44**, 159.
Green, M. L. & Crutchfield, G. (1971) *J. Dairy Res.*, **38**, 151.
International Dairy Federation (1972) *IDF Monograph on UHT Milk*. Brussels.
Kaminogawa, S., Mizobuchi, H. & Yamauchi, K. (1972) *Agric. Biol. Chem.*, **36**, 2163.
Kannan, A. & Jenness, R. (1961) *J. Dairy Sci.*, **44**, 808.
Lyster, R. L. J. (1965) *J. Dairy Res.*, **32**, 203.
Lyster, R. L. J. (1970) *J. Dairy Res.*, **37**, 233.
Lyster, R. L. J. (1972) *J. Dairy Res.*, **39**, 279.
Lyster, R. L. J. (1976) *Biochem. Soc. Trans.*, **4**, 735.
Lyster, R. L. J., Wyeth, T. C., Perkin, A. G. & Burton, H. (1971) *J. Dairy Res.*, **38**, 403.
McKenzie, H. A. (ed.) (1971) *Milk Proteins: Chemistry and Molecular Biology*. Vols. 1 & 2. New York: Academic Press.
Möller, A. B., Andrews, A. T. & Cheeseman, G. C. (1977) *J. Dairy Res.*, **44**, 267.
Mulder, H. & Walstra, P. (1974) *The Milk Fat Globule: Emulsion Science as Applied to Milk Products and Comparable Foods*. Farnham Royal, Bucks.: Commonwealth Agricultural Bureaux.
Ribadeau-Dumas, B. & Garnier, J. (1970) *J. Dairy Res.*, **37**, 269.
Rüegg, M., Moor, U. & Blanc, B. (1975) *Biochim. Biophys. Acta*, **400**, 334.
Rüegg, M., Moor, U., Lukesch, A. & Blanc, B. (1977) In: *Applications of Calorimetry in Life Sciences*, eds. Lamprecht, I. & Schaarschmidt, B., p. 59. Berlin: de Gruyter.
Shahani, K. M. (1966) *J. Dairy Sci.*, **49**, 907.
The Milk (Special Designation) Regulations (1963) (Statutory Instruments, 1963, No. 1571). London: HMSO.
Webb, B. H., Johnson, A. H. & Alford, J. A. (eds.) (1974) *Fundamentals of Dairy Chemistry*, 2nd edn. Westport, Conn.: Avi Publ. Co.
Whitney, R. McL., Brunner, J. R., Ebner, K. E., Farrell, H. M., Josephson, R. V., Morr, C. V. & Swaisgood, H. E. (1976) *J. Dairy Sci.*, **59**, 785.
Wyeth, T. C. (1972) *J. Soc. Dairy Technol.*, **25**, 136.

CHAPTER 12

Cereals, Roots, and Other Starch-Based Products

C. T. Greenwood and D. N. Munro

Cadbury Schweppes Ltd., London, UK

A prime requirement for the human diet is a source of energy. Although energy can be derived from fat and protein, it is easily and most cheaply obtained from the carbohydrate component. As has been described in Chapter 2, the chemical classification 'carbohydrate' covers a multitude of substances from simple sugars to the polymeric starch and cellulose. Pectins, gums and alginates are other examples of carbohydrates which are widely used in the food industries throughout the world for their own specialised properties, such as their ability to act as stabilisers, thickeners, gelling agents and humectants, *etc.*

This chapter deals with the most commonly available starch-containing materials, their use, and the effect of heat upon them. Such foodstuffs include certain abundant cereals—rice, maize, wheat—and the root vegetable, the potato. In order to make the starch digestible, these foodstuffs need to be heated. Raw starch is not easily metabolised, and can indeed cause physiological disorders when eaten (Birch, 1977). Hence, even in the most primitive human communities, the starchy material was usually harvested, ground, heated with water, and consumed as a gruel or porridge.

Heat treatment also enables desirable texture and taste to be developed. For example, the modern loaf of bread has an evenly aerated, non-sticky texture and a pleasant crust flavour, according to the use of an appropriate heat process.

A very extensive technology has been built up over time concerning the heating of starch-rich materials, although cooking practice has been largely empirical by nature. As our knowledge of food science has advanced, however, the newly-acquired skills have been applied to such cooking operations. Much of the present-day heat processing is based on a sound scientific understanding of the nature of the materials, and of the physical, chemical, and biological changes they undergo on heating.

12.1   NATURE OF THE MATERIALS

12.1.1   Rice

Rice as a dietary source of energy and starch is of great importance in the Eastern hemisphere and in developing countries, but is of lesser importance in the Western world. Rice occurs as a grain, *Oryza sativa*, whose main structural features are shown in Fig. 12.1.

The grain of rice consists of the endosperm, the main starchy portion, and the embryo or germ, which are separated by the scutellum. This is all contained within a hull or husk, which comprises an outer pericarp, testa, and aleurone layer. The starch granules themselves are tightly bound to the endosperm protein.

Typical analytical figures for the grain are

Starch	Protein	Moisture	Fat	Fibre	Ash
~65%	~8%	~11%	~2%	~9%	~1%

In contrast to other cereals, rice is generally consumed as a whole grain and not as a milled flour. Its processing, therefore, is relatively simple—the grain is usually cleaned and dehusked, then scoured and polished. Prior to consumption, the grains are heat-treated with water or steam, although in the case of parboiled rice previous soaking,

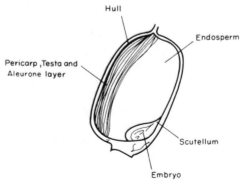

FIG. 12.1   The structure of the rice grain (*Oryza sativa*).

heating and drying steps have been carried out on the unhusked material.

12.1.1.1 *Rice Starch*

All commercial rice starch is manufactured by some variation of an alkaline-steeping process, as this treatment is necessary to loosen the firmly embedded granules from the protein matrix (Hogan, 1967). Agitation in water allows separation of the granules which are then washed and dried. No attempt is made to neutralise the final starch slurry, and hence the pH of the starch is generally around 8.

The rice starch granules are the smallest of the starches of commerce, and they vary in size from 3 to 8 μm (Schoch, 1967). Their shape is polygonal and, because of the small size, birefringence is not distinct. The gelatinisation temperature range of 68–78°C is somewhat higher than other common starches, and hence a higher cooking temperature is required to effect a viscous paste. Except for this feature, the viscosity behaviour as shown in the Brabender amylograph (see Chapter 2, Section 2.6.1.2) is typical of most cereal starches. The pasting curve (see Fig. 12.2) shows a moderate peak

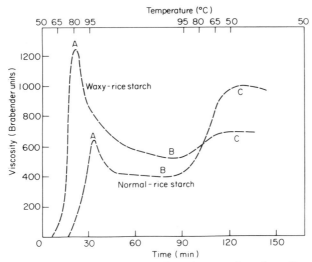

FIG. 12.2   The behaviour of the paste viscosity as a function of temperature and time in the Brabender amylograph for normal-rice starch and waxy-rice starch.

viscosity (point A) corresponding to the maximum volume occupied by the swollen granules, followed by a moderate decrease in viscosity during prolonged cooking owing to limited fragmentation and solubilisation of the relatively stable swollen granules (point B), and a high setback on cooling (point C), owing to retrogradation.

Rice starch has uses as a 'custard' or pudding starch because of the bland flavour of its pastes. A waxy or 'glutinous' variety of rice is also found in the Orient. The pasting properties of this starch—like waxy maize—show (see Fig. 12.2) a high peak viscosity, extensive breakdown during cooking, and very little setback on cooling. The starch paste is, however, very stable under conditions of repeated freezing and thawing. This starch can be used as a thickener for frozen fruit-pie fillings.

12.1.2   Wheat

Wheat, as a source of starch, is of great importance in the Western world. It occurs as a grain, *Triticum vulgare*, whose structure is shown in Fig. 12.3.

The grain of wheat consists of the endosperm, both inner and outer, and the embryo (shoot and root), which are separated by the scutellum. This assembly is contained within an outer fibrous covering, comprising the pericarp, both inner and outer, and the testa, which is hard and indigestible. An inner lining, the aleurone layer, contains a higher proportion of protein than carbohydrate. The endosperm is the starch-rich portion of the grain and comprises over 80% of the grain. The starch granules are firmly embedded in proteinaceous material.

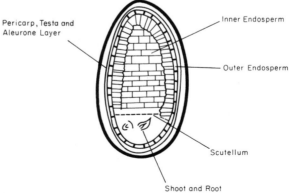

FIG. 12.3   The structure of the wheat grain (*Triticum vulgare*).

Typical analytical figures for the grain are:

Starch	Protein	Water	Fat	Fibre	Ash
66–72%	8–15%	10–14%	1–2%	1·5–2·5%	0·4–1·0%

12.1.2.1 Wheat Starch

In commercial processes, wheat starch is the byproduct of a process primarily designed to yield the maximum amount of baking-quality gluten from wheat flour (Anderson, 1967; Dahlberg, 1978).

Wheat starch has two distinct populations of granules, differing both in size and shape. Large starch granules, ranging in size from 15 to 35 μm comprise some 95% by weight and about 10% by number of the total starch, and are predominantly lenticular in shape. These granules form the major portion of prime commercial wheat starch, and are known as A-type granules. The smaller granules, known as B-type, range in size from 1 to 10 μm and are predominantly spherical. Both populations of granules are optically anisotropic and exhibit typical birefringence patterns.

With a gelatinisation temperature range of 56–62°C, the pasting behaviour of wheat starch is similar to that of normal maize starch (see Section 12.1.3.1). The starch polymer molecules are tightly bound within the granule and swelling is limited when the paste is heated. On cooling, the starch rapidly forms a rigid gel, with the opacity characteristic of large molecular aggregates.

The pasting behaviour of wheat starch is affected by two factors arising from the method of manufacture. First, the dry-milling process inflicts considerable physical damage on the starch granules, especially in the case of 'hard' wheat. This damage increases the swelling power and water absorption of the starch, and tends to decrease the maximum hot-paste viscosity. Secondly, by avoiding denaturation of the protein by chemical or heat treatment, some active amylolytic enzymes remain bound to the granule surface and their action tends to decrease the paste viscosity and final gel strength.

Wheat starch can be used as an alternative to maize starch in most food applications.

12.1.3 Maize

Maize, as a source of starch, is of great importance in various parts of the world, notably in the USA, India, and the developing nations. Dent corn (Zea mays indentata) is one principal maize grain whose structure is shown in Fig. 12.4.

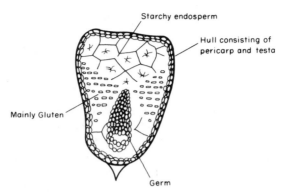

Starchy endosperm

Hull consisting of
pericarp and testa

Mainly Gluten

Germ

FIG. 12.4   The structure of the maize grain (*Zea mays indentata*).

The maize grain is somewhat larger than those of other cereals. It possesses a broad apex and a narrow base. The starchy endosperm, germ, and large scutellum, are contained within a hull, comprising pericarp, and testa. The starchy endosperm is of two types, the 'soft' endosperm, which consists mainly of starch granules, and the 'horny' endosperm, which is mainly comprised of gluten. The starch granules are tightly embedded in the protein matrix.

Typical analytical figures for the maize grain are:

Starch	Protein	Moisture	Fat	Fibre	Ash	Water solubles
60–72%	9–10%	12–15%	3–5%	2%	~1%	~2%

Maize is widely used in the food industry directly as 'grits' and flakes, which are prepared by cleaning, conditioning, milling, degerminating and separating the grain. These are essentially dry processes.

12.1.3.1   *Maize Starch*

Commercially, maize starch is isolated by an entirely wet process (Watson, 1967). The final wet product is either dried or transferred directly to a plant for conversion to glucose syrup or dextrose (see Chapter 2, section 2.3.6).

The three maize genotypes from which starch is isolated commercially are:

    (i) 'normal' or 'dent maize' which produces starch with an amylose content of *ca.* 28%;

    (ii) 'waxy maize' yielding starch with *ca.* 1% amylose; and

(iii) 'amylomaize' from which starch with an apparent amylose content in excess of 50% is separated.

The granules of the starches from normal and waxy maize range in size from 5 to 25 μm, and have a characteristic, angular appearance. They differ microscopically only in their iodine-staining properties; normal maize starch stains blue–black, whilst waxy maize starch appears deep red.

Amylomaize starches have quite different granular appearances, depending on the apparent amylose content. Starches with apparent amylose contents of 55% and 70% have many elongated and curiously shaped granules, ranging in size from a few micrometres to 100 μm in length.

Maize starches exhibit varying degrees of birefringence, and in amylomaize starches, the birefringence is weak and often localised.

The normal and waxy maize starches gelatinise in the range 62–72°C, whilst amylomaize gelatinises at temperatures in excess of 75°C, and some granules retain their birefringence even at 100°C.

The differences in properties of the starches of normal, waxy and amylomaizes are due to variations in the nature of the starch components and in the strength of the molecular associations within the starch granules. Intermolecular bonds largely govern the swelling behaviour of the starch and control its subsequent behaviour when subjected to controlled heating and subsequent cooling. As the apparent amylose content of the maize starches increases from below 1% to over 50%, the total intermolecular bonding is strengthened within the granule. Whether this is due to an increase in the number of bonds, or to an increase in individual bond strength, is not known, but this phenomenon is not simply a function of amylose content.

Typical pasting curves for waxy, normal and amylomaize starches in the Brabender amylograph are shown in Fig. 12.5. As waxy maize starch has a less closely bound structure than normal maize starch, it swells more readily thereby imparting a very much higher paste viscosity (point A) at similar starch concentrations. At the other extreme, amylomaize starch has such a tightly bound structure that little swelling occurs, and no effective increase in paste viscosity is produced even on prolonged heating. Since waxy maize starch swells to a much greater extent than normal maize starch, the pastes are much more fragile and less resistant to breakdown under applied shear (point B).

On cooling, the amylose molecules of normal maize starch retro-

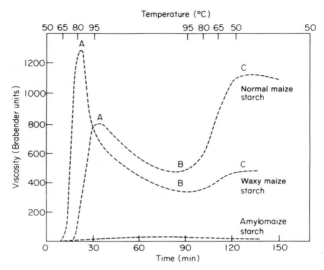

FIG. 12.5 The behaviour of the paste viscosity as a function of temperature and time in the Brabender amylograph for normal maize starch, waxy maize starch, and amylomaize starch.

grade and form sufficient intermolecular bonds to give the rigid three-dimensional structure of a gel. In contrast, the branched molecules of waxy maize do not associate to the same degree, and the paste still retains its viscous fluid form on cooling, with little setback (point C).

Normal maize starch is the main food starch, and when the native starch characteristics are not suitable for the particular use required, both chemical and physical modifications can be carried out to improve its response to certain processing conditions.

The food industry finds a considerable application for waxy maize starch because of its ability to form stable, translucent pastes. These may act as a carrier for flavour as well as providing a medium with suitable rheological characteristics, for use in such products as pie fillings.

Amylomaize starch is the result of an intensive plant-breeding programme to produce a starch with an amylose content of at least 80%. At this level of amylose, the starch would have desirable properties for film making. An amylose film is strong, impermeable to oxygen and, of course, edible. This latter characteristic makes amylose ideally suited for use in food containers, for example, sausage-skins and dehydrated-soup packets. However, amylomaize starch has not yet been found to yield commercially suitable films since, with an increase in apparent amylose content there is also an increasing difficulty in solubilising the starches and a progressive tendency towards retrogadation at elevated temperatures.

Amylomaize starch has been put to a limited use, so far, in the manufacture of fruit gums, where the ability of this starch to retrograde quickly at elevated temperatures is an advantage.

12.1.4 Potato

The potato, as a source of starch, is of great importance throughout the Northern hemisphere and also in South America and China. Its tuber, *Solanum tuberosum*, has the structure depicted in Fig. 12.6. The potato tuber consists of cells of water and starch, which are encapsulated in a tender cellular structure, the whole being encased in a thin, easily-removed skin of fibrous material.

Typical analytical figures for the tuber are:

Starch	Protein	Water	Fat	Fibre	Ash
15–20%	2–3%	75–80%	~0·1%	0·5–1·0%	1·0–1·5%

In comparison with the cereals, moisture content of the potato is very high, and starch content correspondingly lower. The starch, however, is more loosely bound, and hence easier to extract. For normal consumption, the potato is simply peeled, washed, cut, and cooked by methods such as boiling, frying, or roasting. It is also converted on a large scale into crisps (the American equivalent is 'chips') or dehydrated potato.

12.1.4.1 *Potato Starch*

Industrially, potato starch is isolated from the tuber by an entirely

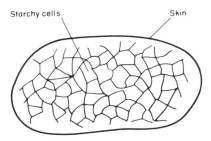

FIG. 12.6 The structure of the potato tuber (*Solanum tuberosum*).

wet process (Treadway, 1967). The product may be dried; or transferred directly to a plant for conversion to dextrose or glucose syrup (see Chapter 2, section 2.3.6).

Granules of potato starch have a broad size distribution, ranging typically from 10 to 100 μm. The size and properties of the granule are closely related to the tuber size. Starches isolated from small potatoes have properties which differ significantly from those isolated from very large tubers and, in consequence, potato starch prepared from cull potatoes is likely to be more variable in its properties than starch prepared from top-grade tubers of uniform size. Potato-starch granules are predominantly ellipsoidal with a marked hilum, although the smallest starch granules may be perfectly spherical; a pronounced ring structure is often evident, and the granules are strongly birefringent.

Potato starch (in common with other tuber starches) has quite different properties from cereal starches. Molecular association within the granule is relatively weak, and thus on heating the starch in water, gelation and subsequent pasting occur more readily.

Potato starch gelatinises in the temperature range of 56–67°C, some 5–6°C below that of normal maize starch. After gelation, the granules swell rapidly, with a concurrent release of some granular material. The greatly swollen granules interact to a considerable extent, and produce a very high peak viscosity in the Brabender amylograph (see Fig. 12.7, point A). The paste at this point is fragile, as the granular structure has been extensively weakened by the high degree of swelling. Thus, application of continued shear or high-temperature cooking results in a collapse of granular structure and a sharp fall in the paste viscosity (point B). The weak associative forces between potato-starch molecules are such that, on cooling the paste, fewer and smaller aggregates of retrograded material are formed than in the case of maize or wheat starch (point C). The resulting gel has less structural rigidity, and a characteristic translucency because the aggregates scatter little light.

The reason for the relatively weak intermolecular bonding in tuber starches is unknown, but probably reflects the nature of the branched component of the starch and its inability to participate in strongly bonded structures.

The industrial uses of potato starch are similar to those of maize starch and are mainly governed by economic factors. In countries such as Poland or the Netherlands, which produce large amounts of

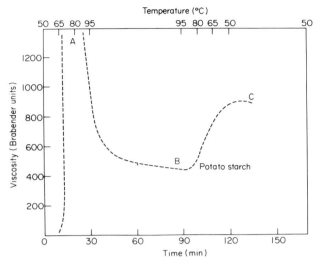

FIG. 12.7   The behaviour of the paste viscosity as a function of temperature and time in the Brabender amylograph for potato starch.

home-grown tubers, potato starch can compete effectively with imported maize starch.

Modification of potato starch, by physical and chemical means, provides as wide a range of products as is available for normal maize starch.

Potato starch has the highest hot-paste viscosity of the commercially available starches, and is an effective thickening agent. A common use of potato starch in foodstuffs is to improve the consistency of products such as soups or gravies. Whilst quite acceptable in European markets, potato-starch pastes have textural properties which are found undesirable by consumers in the United States. Granular interaction in the paste provides considerable resistance to deformation, and on pouring or gently stirring, the pastes exhibit a characteristic elasticity accompanied by a somewhat glutinous texture.

12.1.5   Other Commercial Food Starches

12.1.5.1   *Tapioca Starch*
Tapioca starch is isolated from the tuberous roots of the manioc plant

(*Manihot utilissima* or *Manihot palmata*), which is known in the English-speaking world as *cassava*. The approximate composition of cassava is:

Starch	Protein	Water	Fat	Fibre	Ash
20–30%	2–3%	75–80%	0·1%	1%	1–1·5%

The starch granules occur within the tuber cells which are similar in structure to those of the potato. They range in size from 5 to 35 μm, and are strongly birefringent.

The methods of commercial isolation of tapioca starch are similar to those used for potato starch.

The starch from cassava resembles potato starch in its swelling and gelatinisation properties. The food industry takes advantage, in its uses of tapioca starch, of the high paste clarity and resistance to retrogradation of the unmodified starch pastes and gels. For many food applications, however, tapioca starch is used in the form of chemically modified products, or partially gelatinised small pellets or 'pearls'. The latter products have less stringy paste properties and are useful for fruit-pie fillings.

12.1.5.2 *Arrowroot Starch*
This starch is isolated by pulping and sieving the root of the tropical plant, *Maranta arundinacea*. Arrowroot starch has specialised uses in the food industry, particularly in items formulated for children and invalids, such as arrowroot biscuits.

12.1.5.3 *Sorghum Starch*
Milo is the popular name for grain sorghum (*Sorghum vulgare*), from which sorghum starch is isolated.

Typical analytical figures for the grain are:

Starch	Protein	Moisture	Fat	Fibre	Ash	Water solubles
68%	10%	12%	3%	3%	2%	2%

Grain sorghum has, on average, a lower fat content and a higher content of starch and protein than normal maize. Although the grain is much smaller than that of maize, it is broadly similar in its morphology, and may be processed to yield starch by wet-milling, with only minor modifications to the procedure used for maize (Watson, 1967).

Waxy and normal varieties of sorghum starch, with below 1% and *ca.* 28% amylose, respectively, are produced commercially. Their microscopic appearance and granular swelling characteristics are almost identical to those of their maize counterparts and consequently sorghum starches may be used interchangeably with the corresponding maize starch. Both form viscous, relatively short, opaque gels, and are consequently used as thickening agents for sauces, gravies, puddings and pie fillings. Sorghum starches are not suitable for use in frozen products because they exhibit a pronounced tendency to retrograde under such conditions.

In the United States, sorghum starch is used to prevent caking in baking powder and powdered sugar, and for moulding gum-drops, *etc.* Salad dressing may contain starch paste as well as egg protein to emulsify the oil, and a mixture of maize and tapioca starch will result in the desired texture and stability.

12.1.5.4   *Sago Starch*
Sago is the name given to the starches obtained from the pith of certain palm trees, principally *Metroxylon sagu*, from which the large (20–60 μm) starch granules can be isolated in a relatively pure form.

Sago starch has uses, based on the high strengths of its gels, in confectionery items.

12.2   PHYSICAL CHANGES ON HEATING

In Chapter 2, the chemical nature of carbohydrates was discussed, and the polyhydroxyl nature of the fundamental sugar molecules and their inter- and intramolecular hydrogen bonding described. In the cooking process (with heat and water) the hydrogen-bond networks are altered and reformed. In the case of starch-containing materials, the starch granules swell and eventually burst, releasing their polysaccharide components. This '*gelatinisation*' phenomenon is of very great importance, for it is this change which is the essence of the conversion of raw starch to metabolisable carbohydrate, *i.e.* the cooking process.

Solubility change is another phenomenon occurring during heating of carbohydrates. Smaller carbohydrate molecules, such as sugars, are much more water soluble than the larger molecules, such as starch, but heat treatment of starch can give rise to degraded starch products whose solubility in water is much greater whilst still possessing some of the useful properties of their starch precursor.

The starch granule is not chemically homogeneous, and can be separated into at least two distinct fractions: *amylose* and *amylopectin* (see Chapter 2, section 2.5.2). On cooking rice, for example, these two components are released, and the type of rice and the precise conditions of the cooking process determines the ratio of the two, and hence the 'stickiness' of the cooked rice grains.

12.3 CHEMICAL CHANGES ON HEATING

Chemical changes to sugars brought about by heating are described in Chapter 2. Many of these occur with the polymeric carbohydrates such as the starches, as they do with the simpler sugars. For example, caramelisation and pyrolysis will take place when starch itself is heated, by similar processes of condensation and C–C bond cleavage. But it is in the area of the interactions of starch with other food ingredients that the changes are most important.

First, there are the chemical changes of non-enzymic browning, typified by the Maillard reaction described in section 2.4.2. In this reaction, the reducing part of a sugar molecule reacts with suitable nitrogen compounds such as amino acids and proteins. The reaction may be inhibited by certain food additives such as sulphur dioxide, and is dependent on such factors as temperature, acidity and water activity. The reaction rate can double or treble for every 10°C rise in temperature; as pH increases, browning increases (Berry *et al.*, 1970; Wolfrom *et al.*, 1974) and the browning rate is also much influenced by water activity (McWeeny, 1973; Williams, 1976). Second, there is the chemical change brought about by interaction with lipids. Not much is known of the nature of these interactions, but it is thought (Priestley, 1973) that an amylose–lipid complex may control many of the physical changes undergone by rice starch on heating, such as gelatinisation and solubility. Third, there is the chemical change brought about by interaction with enzymes. The stability of amylases during cooking starch is important since this governs the course of dextrinisation and saccharification which occur in baking. Lastly, there is the chemical change brought about by interaction with minerals. These changes are not understood but are thought to be important in stabilising and perhaps activating the starch–enzyme complex in the digestion process (Birch, 1977).

12.4 BIOLOGICAL CHANGES ON HEATING

The most important biological change in starch brought about by heating is that of making the carbohydrate accessible to enzymes in the digestive tract. How this is achieved is not fully understood: certainly the breakdown of the starch granule and the release of the contents enables the digestive process to take place. It appears, therefore, that metabolic enzyme systems can only operate with difficulty on the surface of the native starch granules. Heat softens and disrupts these tissues, aiding mastication and the digestive processes.

The chemical changes of caramelisation and pyrolysis can give rise to potentially toxic materials in a foodstuff. This currently attracts a great deal of attention with regard to food legislation. For example, in the United States, upper limits for the level of caramel in foods and drinks have been recommended (Thompson, 1972).

Another important biological change on heating is the loss of nutritional value of the food. Vitamin supplementation of heated foodstuffs is commonly employed. The Maillard reaction has been shown to reduce nutritional value in certain cases (Miller et al., 1965). Finally, it should be mentioned that the industrial use of heat and acid to convert starches and dextrin to glucose syrups has some interesting biological possibilities, such as the possible raising of the intelligence-quotient value (Birch, 1974) and lowering of factory accident rates (Brooke et al., 1973).

12.5 BAKING

The discussion so far has described, in simple terms, the basic properties of starch-rich materials when heat is applied to them. In commercial processing of such materials, practical regard has to be given to these properties so that the end product meets the need of the consumer.

Probably the most advanced cooking techniques of this kind are employed in the baking industries, using wheat flour to produce, most importantly, bread, cakes, and biscuits.

The following is a brief outline of some aspects of modern baking practices, with particular reference to the nature and behaviour of the starch granules in the wheat flour. Obviously, in flour, the wheat starch granules are not free and exist embedded in a protein matrix in the presence of other substances such as lipids and hemicelluloses. The properties of the granule which are of importance in baking involve (1) the extent of granular disorganisation; (2) the surface properties of the granule and their modification; and (3) the interaction of the starch granules with other components in the baking system.

In summary, it would appear that the rôle of the starch granule in all forms of baked goods is very important, and is related to the stages of granular disorganisation. Table 12.1 shows the state of organisation of starch granules in various types of baked goods as revealed by optical and scanning electron microscopy. In Scottish shortbread (made only of flour, butter and sugar) the starch granules in the product retain their original characteristics and are only swollen and partly gelatinised. In biscuits, the structure ranges from a swollen to a disrupted structure depending on the type of biscuit. In cakes, disrupted and dispersed granules are present. In bread, the whole spectrum is present, whilst in wafers, there is no apparent organisational structure left.

TABLE 12.1
EXTENT OF GRANULAR DISORGANISATION IN BAKED GOODS

SWOLLEN ↓ GELATINISED ↓ DISRUPTED ↓ DISPERSED ↓ ENZYMATICALLY DEGRADED	Scottish shortbread	Biscuits	Cakes	Bread	Wafers

12.5.1 The Bread-Making Process (For a general discussion of this topic see Spicer 1975)

Flour, yeast, salt and water are the basic ingredients of all bread products to which may be added supplements (fat, yeast food or ammonium chloride, soya flour, sugar, malt flour, and also gluten), flavouring and nutritional adjuncts (milk, sugar, fat, egg, and dried fruit).

The proteins in wheat flour have the special property that, when hydrated with water and mixed into a dough, they form a three-dimensional, viscoelastic matrix, known as 'gluten'. This matrix surrounds the small air cells in the mixed dough and, after development (see below), also the gas produced by fermentation. As a result, the air cells expand and so form the basis of the characteristic loaf texture. The starch granules embedded in the protein matrix also absorb water, particularly if they have been damaged during the milling process, and contribute to the overall texture and structure. Simultaneously, they lose their organised granular characteristics during baking. Hence they become accessible to the amylolytic enzymes in the wheat flour and are degraded to other smaller carbohydrate units and sugars.

The rôle of yeast is that of an aerating agent, for the presence of the enzyme complex, zymase, will result in the formation of carbon dioxide and ethyl alcohol from simple sugars.

$$C_6H_{12}O_6 \xrightarrow{\text{zymase}} 2CO_2 + 2C_2H_5OH$$

This carbon dioxide, if produced at the right time and in sufficient quantity, will inflate the individual air cells present in the dough to increase the size of the dough piece, which contributes to the desired texture on baking. The simple sugars on which the yeast acts are not originally present in the dough but are produced as the result of the degradation of starch by α- and β-amylase into small dextrins and maltose (compare Chapter 2, section 2.4). This is followed by the action of maltase, from the yeast, which converts maltose to glucose.

Yeast also contains proteases which can facilitate interchange of sulphydryl groups with disulphide bonds, a change which improves the viscoelastic properties of the protein matrix. Salt makes a significant contribution to flavour and also stabilises the gluten structure allowing easier production of the dough. Water is used in the dough to hydrate the protein and starch, to develop the protein network, and to dissolve ingredients such as salt and sugars.

When the basic ingredients are mixed together, the immediate resultant coherent mixture is inelastic, and the derived elastic and gas-retaining properties are obtained by the process of dough development. The procedure for achieving this can involve either bulk fermentation or mechanical dough development.

In bulk fermentation, the ingredients are mixed for 20–30 min during which time some disulphide bonds are formed between the proteins. The dough is then allowed to stand for 3–4 h for enzymes present to complete the build-up of a three-dimensional, elastic, protein network. In contrast, these same changes can be accomplished in less than five minutes using the mechanical dough-development method.* Here, the ingredients are subjected to intense mechanical mixing (which involves an energy imput into the dough of 40 kJ·kg^{-1}) in the presence of an oxidising agent such as ascorbic acid (75 p.p.m.). Fermentation losses using this method are negligible; fat (0·7% based on flour weight) must be added together with extra yeast.

When dough development is complete, the dough is divided into pieces of the appropriate size and moulded into an approximate spherical shape. The dough is then allowed to rest and recover for a period of 6–16 min (first proof), remoulded, and then allowed to relax and expand, as a result of yeast fermentation, for 45–60 min (second proof), before baking into a loaf.

12.5.1.1 Bread Baking

The dough piece is baked at temperatures in the range 220–250°C, and when put in the oven, the rate of fermentation initially increases as heat is conducted through the dough. The consequent increase in gas production and the thermal expansion of gas within each cell results in a rapid expansion of the loaf volume (a phenomenon known as 'oven spring').

Steam is normally introduced into the oven during the first few minutes of baking: it is then cut off and baking continues in an essentially dry atmosphere. When the cool dough pieces enter the oven, the steam condenses, rapidly gelatinises the starch granules on the surface, and the resultant starch film produces an aesthetically pleasing glaze. At the same time, the drying and settling of the crust is retarded and full expansion of the dough piece takes place.

As the internal dough temperature rises further, yeast activity becomes reduced at about 43°C, and becomes inactive at 54°C. Other phenomena occur as the temperature increases. The starch granules begin to gelatinise at temperatures around 65°C, and so the α- and β-amylases present are enabled to attack the starch material. Amylolytic activity continues until those enzymes are inactivated at temperatures of 74–78°C.

*This method known as the Chorleywood bread-making process (Chamberlain, 1975) was developed by the Flour Milling and Baking Research Association, in 1961.

The gluten network itself begins to coagulate around 74°C and this transformation continues until the end of baking, when an internal temperature of the loaf of 93–100°C is attained.

Water and alcohol are driven off during baking (a weight loss of 6–9%), so that the internal temperature never exceeds 100°C, but the outside of the loaf reaches the full oven temperature. A greater amount of moisture is therefore driven off, and a crust is formed from coagulated protein. The final thickness of this crust is determined by the time and temperature of baking.

At the loaf surface, caramelisation of the sugars produced by the amylolytic enzymes occurs as do also Maillard-type reactions between these sugars and proteins (see Chapter 2, section 2.4.2). These series of complex reactions, which are not fully understood, principally account for the colour and flavour of the resultant loaf crust.

12.5.1.2 *Properties of the Loaf*

The crumb of the ordinary white loaf is bland in flavour, and the taste of the crumb from the central portion of such a loaf is independent of the manner in which the loaf was prepared or baked. The flavour of a white loaf resides in the crust, and depends on the diffusion of flavour constituents into the centre. Consequently, the differences in flavour between a crusty white loaf, and a sliced wrapped white loaf arise entirely from the presence of higher amounts of flavour constituents in the thicker crust.

Fermentation of the dough contributes little to the flavour of the final loaf because the fermentation products are volatile and are mostly lost during the baking process.

In the wheatmeal loaf, constituents of the bran affect the flavour, whilst in the whole-meal loaf there is the additional influence of the wheat germ.

The stickiness of the crumb is an important characteristic of bread. Stickiness can be adversely affected by incorrect baking conditions but, more commonly, by the use of flour with too high a level of α-amylase. The action of larger amounts of this enzyme causes excessive degradation of starch. In consequence, not only is the amount of water held by the starch decreased in both the dough and the bread as it is baked, but the large quantities of sugars and dextrins formed produce stickiness in the crumb which is not acceptable to the consumer. There are corresponding technical problems in slicing such a loaf, because crumb tearing can lead to loaf deformation. An investigation of crumb stickiness, and also its strength, softness and springiness, has been reported (McDermott, 1974), and these properties were related to the amount of α-amylase in the initial flour. Quite wide variations in properties occur throughout a standard-sized loaf.

12.5.1.3 The Rôle of the Starch Granule in Bread (Greenwood, 1976; Osman, 1975)

The importance of starch in determining the structure of bread is often underestimated, for although a 'loaf' can be baked from wheat starch, the product of baking wheat protein bears little—if any— resemblance to the recognised loaf structure.

One method for studying the problem of the behaviour of the starch granule in this system is to use the scanning electron microscope, and this technique is a very useful supplement to other techniques, but obviously it can never be used entirely on its own. Using this method, a section of frozen bread dough will show the starch granules, large and small, to be in a virtually unmodified state, in contrast to their lack of structural order in the bread crumb. In the latter case there are distended, disorganised starch granules, but perhaps the unusual feature is the degree of structural order which still remains in the final loaf.

Another topic which is of importance with relation to bread, is 'starch damage'. A controlled amount of starch damage in any flour is necessary because it improves loaf volume, loaf texture, and keeping quality. Unfortunately, very little is known about the nature of starch damage. This phenomenon occurs during the milling process—with hard wheats being more susceptible than soft. Damaged starch granules will imbibe water and swell more rapidly than undamaged ones, and will also stain differentially. The latter technique allows an estimation of their number to be made. The degree of structural order of the granule is also affected, and scanning electron micrographs of damaged starch granules show that these granules appear to be very disrupted and 'physically damaged'.

12.5.1.4 Staling (Osman, 1975)

Staling may be defined as the progressive firming of a loaf with time. The phenomenon occurs even if moisture loss in the loaf is eliminated, and involves complex interactions which are only partially understood. Staling, reversible to some extent as a staled loaf may be freshened by re-heating, may be related to the 'retrogradation' of starch in the bread, but any such phenomenon must involve changes in the amylopectin—the retrogradation of the amylose component is irreversible. The rate of staling depends on the temperature and can be arrested at the freezing point of bread. Thus a loaf can be stored satisfactorily by freezing at −20°C.

Another important factor influencing staling is the specific volume of the loaf, since the staling rate is lower when the specific volume increases. Specific volume is related—amongst other factors—to the protein content of the flour.

12.5.2 Flour Confectionery

Flour confectionery involves the use of a wide range of ingredients—flour, eggs, milk, fat, sugar, fruit, nuts, *etc.*—to form a large number of products. A very complex series of interactions must take place in the mixing process to form a batter. The baking process complicates the picture even further.

Most confectionery products should have a light, cellular structure and this texture is brought about by aeration. Techniques used to achieve this can involve either mechanical, chemical or fermentation methods. The mechanical process incorporates air into the batter by beating or whisking, whilst in the chemical method baking powder is used to liberate carbon dioxide during baking. In some confectionery products, particularly cakes, yeast is used to ferment the sugar present and, in these cases, as for bread, the carbon dioxide produced fills and expands the air cells. On baking, the fermentation rate accelerates to increase the cake volume before the activity of the yeast is reduced, and then stopped, by the increased temperature.

In each method of aeration, much of the gas in the bubble is retained until the whole medium sets. Cakes bake radially from the periphery to the centre and vertically from the bottom. Setting takes place when the batter temperature reaches 90–92°C, and if the batter is withdrawn from the oven prematurely, the portion of the expanded batter which has not reached this temperature will undergo complete collapse. Cake baking has been divided into three main stages (Howard *et al.*, 1968); an initial batter aeration for which soluble, foamable protein was found to be essential to retain incorporated air; the second stage required the presence of surface-active lipid to stabilise the various interfaces formed in the batter; whilst the third stage of thermal setting depended on intact starch granules with the proper gelatinisation properties.

In baking, caramelisation and Maillard-type reactions occur to give rise to the characteristic colour of the baked product.

Staling, *i.e.*, a firming of the crumb of products such as cake and sponge, occurs even in the absence of moisture loss, as is the case with bread. The factors affecting the rate of cake staling are not yet understood, but at high temperatures the rate of staling is increased.

12.5.2.1   *The Rôle of the Starch Granule in Cakes* (Greenwood, 1976; Osman, 1975)

Cakes are a most complex system, because here there is the interaction between starch and all the other ingredients—egg, proteins, sugar, fat, *etc.*—in the recipe. However, it would appear to be again the case that the rôle of the starch granule has been underestimated.

The influence of the starch is shown dramatically by baking a high-ratio yellow cake in which the wheat starch has been washed out and then replaced by various maize starches. When normal maize starch is used, the baked-cake product has good characteristics, which is perhaps not surprising as the gelation characteristics of wheat and maize starch are similar. However, when maize starch is replaced by waxy maize starch, complete collapse of the cake is evident. It rises normally in the oven and then collapses on cooling. When amylomaize, *i.e.* high amylose starch, is incorporated into the recipe, the cake never rises even in the oven. A very facile explanation of this is based on the amylograph curves for these starches shown in Fig. 12.5, as has been discussed earlier. In the amylograph, normal maize starch has a medium peak viscosity with a reasonable setback on cooling. In contrast, waxy maize starch swells to attain a very high peak viscosity which then collapses without setback. Amylomaize starch does not even swell and, therefore, produces no viscosity increase. It is not unreasonable to assume that these viscosity effects must influence the behaviour of the starch in the cake.

It is well known that chemically modified starch has pronounced beneficial effects in cake making. Very often, cakes made with normal wheat flour will collapse, whereas the problem is overcome if the cake is made from a chlorinated flour. Current evidence is that the main beneficiary of the chlorination treatment is the starch (Gough *et al.*, 1978).

Physical alteration of the surface properties of the starch granule can be shown to affect and influence the behaviour of the flour in baking; for example, by subjecting flour to the action of a pin mill, a much improved cake can be obtained.

12.5.3 Biscuits

The principal ingredients of biscuits are flour, fat and sugar. The handling properties of the dough, as well as the eating qualities of the biscuit, depend on the relative proportions of these materials in the recipe. Water is an important ingredient at the dough stage, but most of it is removed during baking, the final product having a moisture content of 1–3%.

Biscuits can be made from hard doughs which possess a gluten network (*e.g.* cream crackers), hard sweet doughs which are similar, but contain sugar (*e.g.* semi-sweet biscuits) and soft doughs which have no elasticity (*e.g.* shortbread). The dough pieces are usually baked in a travelling oven, which consists essentially of three sections, the humidity and temperature of each being carefully controlled. In the first section the dough structure is raised by either CO_2 (chemical or yeast fermentation) or by steam. The next section causes the setting of the dough structure either by coagulation of the protein network where present, or by the early stages of drying out of the dough. The last section of the oven is used to dry out the formed biscuit to the required low moisture content, whilst caramelisation and Maillard-type reactions develop the crust colour and flavour.

A different type of biscuit product are wafers, which are made from a fluid batter of flour and water, together with small amounts of other ingredients such as sodium bicarbonate. The fluid is baked in special ovens which form sheets of dehydrated biscuit.

12.5.3.1 *The Rôle of the Starch Granule in Biscuits*

Very little work concerning the rôle of starch in biscuits has been carried out, but it is apparent that the degree of disorganisation of the granule can vary enormously, depending on the type of product under investigation. In a semi-sweet biscuit, a fair number of the granules are left intact in the product, in contrast to the case of wafer biscuits, where the granules are completely gelatinised and the structure of the wafer is entirely due to the starch network. It is not surprising, therefore, that the production of wafer biscuits appears to be independent of the quantity and quality of protein present, because the starch has such a predominant rôle (Stevens, 1976).

12.6   BREAKFAST CEREALS AND OTHER PROCESSED PRODUCTS (Kent, 1975)

12.6.1   Breakfast Cereals

There is a broad range of cereal-based breakfast foods available in the developed countries. The large majority of these are 'ready to eat' in that no cooking is necessary before consumption, *i.e.* the conversion of raw to digestible starch (gelatinisation) has already taken place in manufacture. Probably the most notable exception is the traditional Scottish product, 'porridge'.

'*Porridge*' is prepared from oats: its exact preparation depends on the type of porridge which is required. The traditional type is relatively coarse in particle size and, in order to achieve this together with complete gelatinisation of the starch, involves a lengthy cooking process. The use of finer oatmeal and of partly gelatinised, rolled oats makes the domestic cooking of porridge much quicker and, therefore, more convenient. By suitable processing, even porridge can be made 'ready-cooked'. Complete gelatinisation of the starch in manufacture can be achieved by hot-rolling techniques, for example.

The 'ready-to-eat' breakfast cereals comprise a variety of forms such as puffed, flaked, shredded, and granular products. These are made from common cereals such as rice, maize, wheat, oats and barley, often enriched with sweet ingredients such as honey or sugar. The cooking processes used often give rise to dextrinisation (via 'toasting'), as well as gelatinisation (via 'cooking') of the cereal starch.

Puffed products are usually made by heating cleaned, conditioned, and de-husked cereal grains at high pressure with steam, followed by a rapid release of pressure. Sudden expansion and release of the water vapour blows up the grains to several times their original size. Pellets of cereal dough can behave similarly to the grains. The puffed products are then dried by toasting to low water content (*ca.* 3%) and packaged. The cereals most commonly used are rice, wheat and oats.

Flaked products are made by taking cleaned, conditioned grains, rolling them lightly, cooking them (sometimes at high pressure), adding flavouring and drying. The cereals are then flaked on heavy rollers, toasted, cooled and packaged. Again, rice, wheat and oats are the most widely used cereals.

Shredded products are normally prepared from wheat. The cleaned wheat grain is cooked with water until soft and rubbery, when the starch is fully gelatinised. The grain is then cooled and subsequently fed to shredder-rollers. The product is collected in matted form, cut to required size, baked, dried, cooled and packaged.

Granular products are usually made from wheat and malted barley, with salt added. A yeasted dough is formed, fermented, divided into loaves, and these are baked. The baked loaves are broken up, dried and ground.

In the manufacture of breakfast cereals, attention must be paid to two important details, the product's keeping qualities and its nutritive value. The keeping quality of the product depends very much on the content and condition of the fat present. In some countries (*e.g.* the UK) the inclusion of synthetic antioxidants in breakfast cereals is not permitted. Thus, the manufacturer has to select a suitable process since fat stability is reduced as process temperature or time is increased, or as water content at this stage of the process is reduced.

In contrast, high-temperature–short-time processes can give rise to antioxidant materials, *e.g.* via the Maillard reaction. Overall, products made from relatively fat-rich cereals, such as oats (4–11% fat) require more care in preparation from this point of view than those from less fat-rich cereals, such as wheat (1–2% fat).

The processes used in the manufacture of ready-to-eat cereals often cause significant losses in nutritive value. Vitamins of the B group, for example, are often lost in the heating stages. It is thus common practice to fortify breakfast cereals with added B vitamins. For particular products, iron and protein enrichment can also be carried out.

12.6.2 Pasta

A wide variety of pasta goods is available. These foods, such as macaroni, spaghetti, vermicelli and noodles, are prepared from semolina which is obtained from hard durum wheat by a special milling process. The semolina is made into a stiff dough, extruded at high pressure and dried. The quality of the semolina and the choice of drying process contribute greatly to the storage stability of the product with respect to good colour, low microbiological count, absence of cracking, *etc*. Pasta products are usually boiled in water before consumption: the pasta swells and softens, whilst more or less retaining the shape conferred on it at the extrusion stage of the process.

12.6.3 Cake Pre-Mixes

These are flour-based mixtures of cake ingredients, which are sold as a convenient method of cake preparation. For example, flour, fat, sugar, baking powder, milk powder, eggs, flavouring and colour are mixed together to give a powdered product, which only requires the addition of water before baking. As in the case of breakfast cereals, the content and condition of the fat used is important, and attention must be paid to the food legislation of the appropriate countries when such mixes are formulated.

The plasticity of the fat and the use of a high-ratio type of flour are also important considerations in products of this type.

12.7 MODIFIED AND DERIVATISED STARCHES

The behaviour of pastes of the common *native* starches when subjected to the effects of heat and shear used in modern food technology is often unsatisfactory, and consequently modified starches and starch derivatives with more sophisticated stability characteristics have been developed.

In this section, the characteristic properties and uses of some of these starches are outlined.

12.7.1 Acid-Modified Starch (Shildreck and Smith, 1967)

Acid-modified, or thin-boiling starches are prepared by heating starch granules with dilute hydrochloric acid at temperatures *below* that of gelatinisation. The resultant superficially unchanged granules* fragment more and appear to swell less during gelatinisation, with a consequent reduced volume and lower maximum hot paste viscosity. Solubility in hot water is increased, the extent depending on the degree of acid treatment.

Acid-degraded starch—particularly the non-waxy cereal type—is widely used in the manufacture of fruit gums on account of the strength and clarity of the resultant gel, which is much improved in comparison to an unmodified, thick-boiling starch.

---

*The extent of acid modification is described by the *fluidity number,* which is the number of millilitres of a standard alkaline paste of the starch, flowing through a special funnel, in the time required for 100 ml of water to flow through the same funnel.

The viscosity of the hot gel prepared from acid-modified starch is much lower than that prepared from the corresponding concentration of the unmodified starch. As a result, the hot gel can be easily poured into moulds. The acid treatment causes, in contrast, an increase in the resultant gel strength, probably because of the preferential degradation of amylopectin. The gel clarity is also improved.

12.7.2 Pre-Gelatinised Starches (Powell, 1967)

For many food uses, a water-holding or thickening agent is required to function *without* the application of heat, and for this purpose a pre-gelatinised starch is often used. Pre-gelatinised starch is prepared by destroying the granular structure on cooking, which simultaneously causes a considerable reduction in paste viscosity; the cooked paste is then dried on rollers or with a spray-dryer. The powdered product will easily rehydrate in cold water but, necessarily, the resultant dispersions are not equivalent to freshly prepared pastes. This is due to the starch degradation which has taken place.

The largest use of pre-gelatinised starch is in instant puddings—a packaged powder which only needs to be mixed with cold milk and allowed to stand for a few minutes, producing a simple pudding. The powders are mixtures of pre-gelatinised starch with sugar and flavourings, together with salts which produce sufficient viscosity increase in the milk to keep the starch suspended until hydration can take place.

Another widespread use is in frozen fruit-pie fillings where a pre-gelatinised starch—often a cross-bonded waxy starch—keeps the fruit suspended and helps retain the flavour without the need for heating.

12.7.3 Crosslinked and Other Derivatised Starches

A great number of esters and ethers of starch, with an infinite range of properties, can be synthesised, but only a few of these are important in the food industry.

Starch phosphates (Hamilton and Paschall, 1967), which have analogues in the amylopectin fraction of root and tuber starches, are examples of starch derivatives which are suitable as food additives. The introduction of free-acid groups in starch phosphates both increases and stabilises the paste viscosity, for the negatively charged phosphate groups expand the molecule in solution, by Coulombic repulsion, and prevent the formation of aggregates. Because of their high viscosity and paste clarity, starch phosphates are put to extensive use in foods as thickeners and texturising agents, whilst their resistance to molecular aggregation is of importance in the formulation of frozen foods.

The swelling and ultimate breakdown of starch granules during cooking can be controlled by introducing a suitable number of cross-linkages between the molecules.

Starches with low levels of phosphate crosslinking are also used in textural modifications of food. Pastes are then rendered stable under conditions of shear, high-temperature cooking or acidity, as the crosslinks stabilise the swollen granular structure. For example, crossbonded phosphate starches are used as thickeners in salad cream and fruit-pie fillings.

Crosslinked phosphate esters may be prepared commercially by esterification with trimetaphosphate. The extent of crosslinking is measured by the change in the pasting properties of the derivative.

CONCLUSIONS

From the above discussion, we can see that starch is present in foodstuffs as a natural constituent (e.g. rice), added in an unrefined (e.g. wheat flour in bread) or refined form (e.g. maize or potato starch in sauces, puddings) or as a product which has been modified physically (e.g. pre-gelatinised starch) or chemically (e.g. starch phosphate).

Our knowledge of the chemistry and properties of starch, and the reasons for the diversity of character of starch from different sources, is still far from complete. Its behaviour in complex systems such as foodstuffs is even less well understood and many of the processing parameters for starch-based goods have been derived empirically.

In order to attempt to understand its response to food processing, starch must be considered at two distinct levels (Banks et al., 1973):

(a) on a molecular level, the structure, shape and size of the component molecules must be known; and

(b) the organisation of these polymeric molecules on a macromolecular level should be determined.

Only then can the complex interactions resulting in the ultimate granular structure be elucidated, and improvements in the manufactured end-product be achieved.

REFERENCES

Anderson, R. A. (1967) In: *Starch: Chemistry & Technology*, eds. Whistler, R: L. & Paschall, E. F. Vol. II, p. 53. New York: Academic Press.

Banks, W., Greenwood, C. T. & Muir, D. D. (1973) In: *Molecular Structure and Function of Food Carbohydrate*, eds. Birch, G. G. & Green, L. F., p. 177. London: Applied Science.

Berry, R. E., Wagner, C. J., Jr. & Bissett, O. W. (1970) *Proc. Florida State Hort. Soc.*, **84**, 193.

Birch, G. G. (1974) *Biochem. Soc. Trans.*, **2**, 300.

Birch, G. G. (1977) In: *Physical, Chemical and Biological Change in Food caused by Thermal Processing*, eds. Høyen, T. & Kvåle, O., p. 152. London: Applied Science.

Brooke, J. D., Toogood, S., Green, L. F. & Bagley, R. (1973) *Proc. Nutr. Soc.*, **32**, 94a.

Chamberlain, N. (1975) In: *Bread*, ed. Spicer, A., p. 259. London: Applied Science.

Dahlberg, B. I. (1978) *Stärke*, **30**, 8.

Gough, B. M., Greenwood, C. T. & Whitehouse, M. (1978) *CRC Crit. Rev. Fd. Sci. Nutr.*, in press.

Greenwood, C. T. (1976) *Advan. Cereal Sci. & Technol.*, **1**, 119.

Hamilton, R. M. & Paschall, E. F. (1967) In: *Starch: Chemistry & Technology*, eds. Whistler, R. L. & Paschall, E. F. Vol. II, p. 351. New York: Academic Press.

Hogan, J. T. (1967) In: *Starch: Chemistry & Technology*, eds. Whistler, R. L. & Paschall, E. F. Vol. II, p. 65. New York: Academic Press.

Howard, N. B., Hughes, D. H. & Strobel, R. G. K. (1968) *Cereals Chem.*, **45**, 329.

Kent, N. L. (1975) *Technology of Cereals*, 2nd edn., London: Pergamon Press.

McDermott, E. E. (1974) *J. Fd. Technol.*, **9**, 185.

McWeeny, D. J. (1973) In: *Molecular Structure and Function of Food Carbohydrate*, eds. Birch, G. G. & Green, L. F., p. 21. London: Applied Science.

Miller, E. L., Carpenter, K. J. & Milner, C. K. (1965) *Brit. J. Nutr.*, **19**, 565.

Osman, E. M. (1975) *J. Fd. Technol.*, **29**, 30.

Powell, E. L. (1967) In: *Starch: Chemistry & Technology*, eds. Whistler, R. L. & Paschall, E. F. Vol. II, p. 538. New York: Academic Press.

Priestley, R. J. (1973) Ph.D. Thesis, Reading University.

Schoch, T. J. (1967) In: *Starch: Chemistry & Technology*, eds. Whistler, R. L. & Paschall, E. F. Vol. II, p. 79. New York: Academic Press.

Shildreck, P. & Smith, C. E. (1967) In: *Starch: Chemistry & Technology*, eds. Whistler, R. L. & Paschall, E. F. Vol. II, p. 217. New York: Academic Press.

Spicer, A. (ed.) (1975) In: *Bread*. London: Applied Science.

Stevens, D. J. (1976) *Stärke*, **28**, 25.

Thompson, J. I. (1972) *GRAS Food Ingredients—Caramel*. NTIS Rept. prepared for F.D.S.

Treadway, R. H. (1967) In: *Starch: Chemistry & Technology*, eds. Whistler, R. L. & Paschall, E. F. Vol. II, p. 87. New York: Academic Press.
Watson, S. A. (1967) In: *Starch: Chemistry & Technology*, eds. Whistler, R. L. & Paschall, E. F. Vol. II, p. 1. New York: Academic Press.
Williams, J. C. (1976) In: *Intermediate Moisture Foods*, eds. Birch, G. G. & Parker, K. J. p. 100. London: Applied Science.
Wolfrom, M. L., Kashimura, N. & Horton, D. (1974) *J. Agric. Fd. Chem.*, **22**, 796.
Yamazaki, W. T. & Kissell, L. T. (1978) *Cereal Foods World*, in press.

INDEX